# THE SEPARATI
# CHURCH & FAITH

## VOLUME ONE

# Copernicus and the Jews

# DANIEL GRUBER

*The Separation of Church & Faith, Vol.1, Copernicus and the Jews*
© Daniel Gruber, 2005
All Rights reserved under International and Pan-American Copyright Conventions
ISBN 10: 1-511-52910-5
ISBN 13: 978-1-511-52910-5


ELIJAH PUBLISHING
PO BOX 776
HANOVER, NH 03755
www.Elijahnet.net


Designed by Sandy Kent
Photo: NASA/STSci

THIS BOOK IS DEDICATED TO

*Those Who Died in the Night*

# TABLE *of* CONTENTS

CHAPTER ONE

# Copernicus and the Jews

In the time of Nicholas Copernicus, the heavens and all that was in them revolved around the earth. This was not a belief that needed to be argued, it was simply an observable fact. Every day, the sun rose in the east and set in the west. Every month, the moon circled the earth in a regular cycle. Every year, the stars moved across the earth's sky and returned to their starting place.

People could see with their own eyes that everything in the heavens revolved around the earth. Scientists, mathematicians, and philosophers affirmed it. Religious doctrine did too.

There was, however, one small problem. The known planets, in the course of their travel through the heavens, did not follow what could be called an orbit around the earth. Sometimes they went backwards in the sky instead of forwards; and they did not move at a regular speed relative to the earth. They moved in continual defiance of the science of the day, the theology that sanctified it, and the common sense that upheld it.

The planets, however, were quite insignificant in size compared to the vast heavens. The entire universe observably functioned in harmony with a cosmology that placed the earth at its center. So although the planets wandered from their proper course and did not behave according to mathematical prediction, it was not a cause for concern. The planets were too insignificant to bring the whole system into question. They only showed the need for adjusting the mathematics.

Great mathematicians produced great mathematical constructions to explain this planetary wandering. They sought to demonstrate that the planets really did revolve around the earth, even though they seemed not to. The mathematicians already knew the system, and they knew that the system was true. They simply had to find a way to secure the planets within that system. It was not easy, but, compared to the whole well established and well-documented system, how important were the planets anyway?

The mathematicians invented homocentric spheres—spheres within spheres, having a common center. They proposed epicycles and deferents—an orbit around a point on another orbit.

They designed eccentrics—orbits with a displaced center. When these proved insufficient to account for the observed motion of the planets, the mathematicians and astronomers creatively combined their devices. They produced epicycles on epicycles on deferents, and eccentrics on eccentrics on deferents.

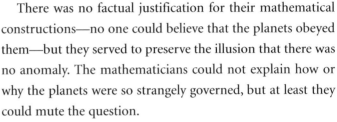

THE GREAT VALUE OF THESE MATHEMATICAL INVENTIONS WAS THAT THEY PRESERVED THE INTEGRITY OF THE ENTIRE COSMOLOGY. AND THAT, OF COURSE, WAS THEIR GREAT DISSERVICE.

There was no factual justification for their mathematical constructions—no one could believe that the planets obeyed them—but they served to preserve the illusion that there was no anomaly. The mathematicians could not explain how or why the planets were so strangely governed, but at least they could mute the question.

The great value of these mathematical inventions was that they preserved the integrity of the entire cosmology. And that, of course, was their great disservice. The mathematical accommodations gave the illusion that the anomaly did not exist, and thereby eliminated the need to question the whole system. The mathematical "solutions" preserved the false cosmology and, in so doing, hindered people from discovering what was true.

The mathematical solutions negated the little bits of data which showed the falsity of the entire system. No information, new or old, could challenge the system, because the system itself provided the means by which all information was interpreted.

"Copernicus' teachers still believed that the structure of the universe was about as described by Aristotle and Ptolemy, and their beliefs placed them in an ancient tradition. But their attitude towards those beliefs was not ancient. Conceptual schemes age with the succession of the generations that behold them. At the beginning of the sixteenth century, men still believed in the ancient description of the universe, but they evaluated it differently. Their concepts were the same, but they saw new strengths and weaknesses in those concepts."[1]

The ancients had wisdom, but there was an unsolved problem in their cosmology. Those who followed the ancients stayed within that traditional cosmology, but adjusted and modified some aspects of it. They modernized it. These changes made the system more accurate, but they never confronted the real problem. The system, the cosmology, the conceptual scheme with the earth at the center, the ancient tradition itself, was wrong, irremediably wrong. No modification or adjustment could change that.

In any age, in any field—whether astronomy, medicine, history, theology, literature, business, or sports—very few people ever see their discipline itself, their system, differently than their peers do. Some see the principles or facts better. Some understand them better, and can operate more effectively, but they do not question the system and its categories. They cannot get outside the system.

Most "experts" and "authorities" uphold the prevailing view precisely because they are "experts"—that is, they are knowledgeable in what has already been thought and what has already been done. They are "authorities" because they are recognized by others in their field who hold the same view, but cannot discern, express, and demonstrate it as well. They are experts "in" their field; they do not see their field from the outside.

Copernicus was respectful of the ancient tradition, but not enchanted by its acquired mathematical magic. He was interested instead in finding the real explanation of how the heavens and the earth related. "How are the complex and variable planetary motions to be reduced to a simple and recurrent order? Why do the planets retrogress, and how account for the irregular rate of even their normal motions?"[2]

He did not use his science and math to buttress the ancient tradition. He used it to search and examine the evidence. He used it to try to find the answers to questions that others were no longer asking. Copernicus began to reinterpret the data, in the hope of finding a consistent, coherent explanation.[3]

Strong opposition came from those who were unwilling to forsake the failed cosmology. The strongest opposition came from the theologians and Church hierarchy. *De Revolutionibus* was published in 1543, dedicated to the Pope. "Copernicus himself was the nephew of a bishop and a canon of the cathedral at Frauenburg; yet in 1616 the Church banned all books advocating the reality of the earth's motion."[4] The institution which claimed to uphold God's order in the earth set itself in direct opposition to the reality of God's order throughout the universe.

Nevertheless, the evidence in support of the theory of Copernicus began to accumulate. Better scientific tables were calculated. Kepler presented a well-argued, consistent version of the new cosmology. Galileo's telescope opened up the heavens, showing things that were inconsistent with the old cosmology but predicted by the new. Newton discovered gravity and the universal Laws of Motion.

The ancient tradition of interpretation was wrong. What everyone observed and knew was wrong. The entire universe functioned differently than the way the most knowledgeable and esteemed experts had taught. It had always functioned differently, but the experts, by the knowledge and esteem that they commanded, had been able to cover over that fact.

The history of science, like the history of many human endeavors, is filled with orthodoxy and heresy, true and false doctrines, the persecuted and the persecutors, defenders of the tradition and innovators. This is observable and verifiable. It is the way the world functions.

As Galileo wrote to Kepler: "I have for many years been a partisan of the Copernican view because it reveals to me the causes of many natural phenomena that are entirely incomprehensible in the light of the generally accepted hypotheses. To refute the latter I have collected many proofs, but I do not publish them, because I am deterred by the fate or our teacher Copernicus who, although he had won immortal fame with a few, was ridiculed and condemned by countless people (for very great is the number of the stupid)."[5]

Many fought against it, but the change in cosmology led to some very tangible changes in life on earth. Copernicus led to Newton. Newton led to Einstein. Today's technological society has come from the change in how the universe was perceived after Copernicus.

The change in cosmology brought changes greater than anyone could have imagined. The changes were not limited to technology. As Goethe explained, "Of all the discoveries and opinions, none may have exerted a greater effect on the human spirit than the doctrine of Copernicus. …No wonder his contemporaries did not wish to let all this go and offered every possible resistance to a doctrine which in its converts authorized and demanded a freedom of view and greatness of thought so far unknown, indeed not even dreamed of."[6]

THE COPERNICAN REVOLUTION BEGAN WITH A WILLINGNESS TO FACE THE ANOMALY OF PLANETARY MOTION INCONSISTENT WITH AN EARTH-CENTERED UNIVERSE.

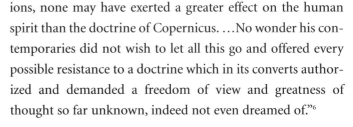

*'Very interesting, but what about Copernicus and the Jews?'*

A good question. Be patient just a little bit longer. After all, this will be an examination of the errors of the received wisdom of many centuries. That cannot be done by assertions and opinions. It can only be accomplished, step by step, by presenting more accurate data, more consistent analysis, and an interpretive cosmology that both explains and predicts the evidence rather than contradicting it.

The Copernican Revolution began with a willingness to face the anomaly of planetary motion, an anomaly that was inconsistent with an earth-centered universe. An anomaly is something whose existence is recognizable but inexplicable within the prevailing system. An anomaly presents a challenge that cannot be reconciled without departing from the system.

The planets derive their name from a Greek word meaning "wanderers." They were named "planets" because they were celestial wandering ones. To those whose minds were filled with the ancient tradition, the planets gave the appearance of wandering. Actually, the planets did not wander at all. They were simply governed by something other than what the keepers of the ancient tradition assumed to govern the rest of the universe. As it turned out, the rest of the universe also was governed differently than what everyone assumed. An accurate cosmology could only be formulated by rejecting the underlying assumption and the system built upon it.

When it comes to life on earth, there is a people who have also been labeled "wanderers". In the Septuagint, the oldest Greek translation we have of the Hebrew Scriptures, we are told that, until the time of restoration, the children of Israel will be *planetai en tois ethnesin*, i.e. wanderers among the nations/Gentiles. (cf. Hos. 9:17)

The Romans destroyed Jerusalem in 70 C.E.. In 135 C.E., they extinguished the Bar Kokhba Rebellion, the Last Revolt against Rome. That began the time of the enforced separation of the people of Israel from the land of Israel.

In the centuries that followed, the Church made the term "the Wandering Jew" a reproach. The Jews, the teaching goes, are condemned to wander forever throughout the earth for their sin of killing Christ. As John Chrysostom preached: "The Jews say that they hope to see their city restored! No, they are mistaken. The Temple will never rise again, nor the Jews return to their former polity... He whom you crucified did afterwards pull down your city, scatter your people, and disperse your nation throughout the whole world."[7]

As Luther wrote: "In brief: Because you see that after fifteen hundred years of misery (when no end is certain or will ever be so) the Jews are not disheartened nor are they even cognizant of their plight, you might with a good conscience despair of them. For it is impossible that God should let his people (if they were that) wait so long without consolation and prophecy.... And should we believe what they themselves do not and cannot believe, as long as they do not have Jerusalem and the land of Israel?"[8] Lest the point be missed, it was often delivered on the end of a sword.

Historical Christianity has theologically defined itself in opposition to, or at least in separation from, the Jewish people. As a theological system, Christianity is based upon the Divine rejection, momentary or eternal, of the Jewish people. It is a system crafted in replacement of Israel. It has produced a history that has grown from that definition.

I am well aware that there are many individuals who call themselves Christians and do not define themselves in opposition to, or in separation from, the Jewish people. Their lives, and sometimes their deaths, testify of that. But it is the system itself that is at issue here, not the behavior of a very small minority in Christendom. The behavior of that small minority is often evidence that they have not accepted the system.

Jews are the *planetoi* who demonstrate, often unwillingly and/or unwittingly, that the theological cosmology of the Church, the system itself, is not true. Perhaps everyone accepts it; perhaps common sense and all the authorities confirm it; but it still is not true. It is far from Biblical faith. It is sustained by a combination of theological invention, poor translation, and the presumed sanctity of an ancient system that nullifies the very Scriptures on which it claims to be built.

In the Christian world, there are different confessions and camps. There are the Catholic, the Orthodox, and the Protestant; the Anabaptist, the Evangelical, and the Pentecostal. There are the liberals and the conservatives, the higher critics and the fundamentalists. But they are all part of the same ancient tradition. They are warring schools of a common cosmology, each placing "the Church" in the center of God's purposes in the earth. Doing so makes it impossible to recognize the true center and build upon that knowledge. It hinders God's purposes in the earth.

The different traditions ignore or minimize the anomaly that fills the pages of Genesis to Revelation. This anomaly will not revolve around the Church, moving backwards in the Church's heavens. The Jews are that anomaly which will not go away, moving in continual defiance of the science, political and otherwise, of the day and of the theology that sanctifies it.

Like the planets, they are governed by something other than what all the authorities imagine. But what, or rather the One who, governs them, governs all the universe. The rest of the world does not operate as the authorities imagine.

Marina Tsvetaeva, a Russian poet, grasped at this in her poem, "Yevreyam/To the Jews". In Russian, the title is the same as that of the Biblical letter that is usually called "Hebrews" in English. Here are a few lines from the poem.

TO THE JEWS
In any one of you...
Christ speaks more strongly than in Mark
Matthew, John, and Luke.
...
With the last of your sons, O Israel,
In truth we will have buried Christ.

Tsvetaeva was saying that by their very existence, the Jewish people declare God's glory and His redemptive purpose in the earth. They declare who Christ is and why he is, in a way that no Christian theology can match. And if the Gentiles were to succeed in burying the last of the Jews, they would only have succeeded in burying Christ. He does not live without them.

There is no Christ without Israel. Or, more correctly, there is no such thing as a Messiah without Israel. He lived in this world as part of Israel; he gave his life as part of Israel; and he will return as part of Israel. By definition, Messiah is the King of Israel, representing, defending, and ruling over his people. His life is in his people, and the life of his people is in him.

Coming from the Russian tradition, Tsvetaeva did not seem to realize that Mark, Matthew and John are Jews. And Luke—if he was not a Jew, and it is by no means clear that he was not—received from Jews all that he wrote. They spoke through him. If these are allowed to speak as Jews, then it can be said that "Christ" speaks as loudly through them as through the rest of his brethren. But given that, and since these are not usually allowed to speak as Jews, then, as Tsvetaeva observed, one can hear Christ more strongly through the rest of his people than through a theologically distorted version of the gospels.

Great theological constructions which are the equivalent of epicycles, deferents, and eccentrics have only obscured the real problem of Christianity. For all their ingenuity, for all their manipulation of the data, the theologians have only muted the question. It is the system itself that is wrong.

No amount of theological modification and adjustment will ever change that. The system will still be wrong. And Jerusalem will still be, for the God of the Bible, the center of God's purposes in the earth, the center of His dealings with all people.

THE DIFFERENT CHRISTIAN TRADITIONS DO THEIR BEST TO IGNORE OR MINIMIZE THE ANOMALY THAT FILLS THE PAGES OF GENESIS TO REVELATION.

This book, however, is not a religious book, though it does cover topics that many understand to be religious. There will be times when this book may seem to focus on theology, but that is only an appearance. It is actually about international relations and economics. It is about education and justice. It is about Man's New World Order and God's New World Order. It just takes a little while to get there, because there is so much debris in the way.

This book presents a cosmology that will only be assimilated by those willing to embrace "a new physics, a new conception of space, and a new idea of man's relation to God." This cosmology, however, is not new. It was spoken of long ago, in a time that, admittedly, many consider primitive.

Some might say this is ethnocentric, focusing on a numerically insignificant people—only one-fourth of one percent of the world's population. It is not the Church alone that finds the chosenness of Israel abhorrent. It is equally offensive to world leaders, financial movers and shakers, sociologists, and all kinds of people who live in a world that would soon cease to exist if their own center were abandoned. Some have said that the Bible itself is ethnocentric, since it is almost all about God's relationship with this numerically insignificant people. Whatever some may say, it is neither conceit nor prejudice, it is God's peculiar way to redeem all peoples.

Will the conceptual shift to the true center make a difference in real life? It will change everything. No one in the time of Copernicus could have imagined the consequences of shifting the cosmological center of the universe. To some it was blasphemy; to others it was impudence. To most, it must have seemed that the only aberration that needed to be explained lay in the thought processes of Copernicus. And it must have seemed quite unrelated to how people lived their lives day to day. But they were wrong, all of them.

This conceptual shift will lead to a transformation of the world which will far exceed that brought by the Copernican Revolution. It will bring this world out of the brokenness, sickness, and death in which it now lies into the wholeness, freedom, and vitality of the realized kingdom of God. It will change the nature of life itself. And that is ever so much more than a succession of new technological ages.

## FOOTNOTES

1. Thomas S. Kuhn, *The Copernican Revolution: Planetary Astronomy in the Development of Western Thought*, Harvard U. Press, Cambridge, 1985, p.100

   In the thirteenth century, the Persian mathematician, Nasir al-Din al-Tusi had presented a non-Ptolemaic model of the motion of the heavenly spheres, using extra epicycles. In the fourteenth century, Ibn al-Shatir of Damascus published a theory of planetary motion that simplified some of these mathematical devices. Copernicus may well have been familiar with the work of these men.

   In earlier times, in different civilizations, some individuals had suggested other scenarios. In the 4th century B.C.E., Heraclidus of Pontus said that the earth rotated on its axis and that some of the planets revolved around the sun. In the next century, Aristarchus of Samos suggested that the earth revolved around the sun. Common sense showed such scenarios to be false.

2. Ibid., p.50

3. "Copernicus himself was a specialist, a mathematical astronomer concerned to correct the esoteric techniques used in computing tables of planetary position.... Though his *De Revolutionibus* consists principally of mathematical formulas, tables, and diagrams, it could only be assimilated by men able to create a new physics, a new conception of space, and a new idea of man's relation to God." Ibid., P. vii. It was math, the same kind of math, but it could only be assimilated by people willing to let go of a very ancient tradition, an ancient tradition which could never explain the anomaly of uncooperative planetary motion.

4. Ibid., p.106

5. Quoted in Hermann Kesten, *Copernicus and His World*, trans. by E.b. Ashton and Norbert Gutterman, NY, Roy Publishers, 1945, p.349

6. Quoted in ibid., p.viii

7. John Chrysostom, Homilies Against the Jews, c.347-407 in Williams, A. Lukyn, *Adversus Judaeos: A Bird's Eye View of Christian Apologiae until the Renaissance*, Cambridge U. Press, London, 1935, p.134;

8. Weimarer Ausgabe 50:336, 1-6; 50:323, 36-324, 8 in *The Roots of Anti-Semitism in the Age of Renaissance and Reformation*, Heiko Oberman, Fortress Press, Phila., 1983, p. 64

# PART ONE

# Finding the Center

*An Examination of Ten Systematic*

*Theological Errors*

# TEN SYSTEMATIC ERRORS

**1. THE NEW TESTAMENT IS A CHRISTIAN DOCUMENT, WRITTEN IN GREEK.**

**2. THE NEW TESTAMENT SUPERCEDES THE OLD TESTAMENT.**

**3. CHRIST IS BUILDING HIS CHURCH.**

**4. CHRIST ESTABLISHED RELIGIOUS OFFICES.**

**5. THE JEWS REJECTED AND CRUCIFIED CHRIST.**

**6. CHRISTIANS ARE THE PEOPLE OF GOD.**

**7. SUNDAY, THE LORD'S DAY, IS THE CHRISTIAN SABBATH.**

**8. CHRISTIANS WILL SPEND ETERNITY IN HEAVEN.**

**9. THE GOSPEL IS ABOUT HOW TO GET TO HEAVEN.**

**10. CHRIST ESTABLISHED CHRISTIANITY.**

CHAPTER TWO

# Parlez-vous Jewish Greek?

*The "New Testament" is a Jewish Document Written in Jewish Greek*

The contemporaries and predecessors of Copernicus used mathematical devices to maintain the traditional earth-centered cosmology. Most people couldn't understand the math the astronomers used, but math is the currency of astronomy. You can gaze at the stars. You can use them as a guide in the wilderness. You can walk along the beach, hold hands, and fall in love underneath them; but you can't do astronomy without math.

Copernicus used math to demonstrate the irrelevance of the devices which the traditionalists had invented. He used math to demonstrate that the cosmos functioned differently. He used math to demonstrate that they had the wrong center.

In this respect, theology is a lot like astronomy, only the currency is scripture—text, translation, and interpretation. In this book, we will be using scripture to demonstrate the irrelevance of theological devices. We will be using scripture to demonstrate that God has a different center in the earth than the theologians do, and that the world functions predictably around that center.

When most people talk about "the Bible," they have in mind the particular translation, or translations, with which they are familiar. Translations are necessary. If the translation is accurate, it makes the message available to people who do not know the original languages. If it is inaccurate, it distorts the original message, sometimes beyond recognition.

The translator plays a major role in determining what the audience will think the author is saying. But the translator may have a different mindset than the author, or a different mindset than the audience. He, or she, may not understand what is being said, or what is being heard. He may assign incorrect meanings to the original words, because he does not understand the context in which they were used. Additionally, the language into which he is translating may not have any equivalent way of reproducing the original.

Most translations of Matthew to Revelation contain such misrepresentations. They also contain systematic errors that come from a failure to recognize the original language and context. For the most part, this is not the result of either bad motives or lack of knowledge. It is the result of the translators' misperception of the very nature of the text. The translators translate as though they were dealing with a Greek text written in a Christian context. Neither assumption is correct.

Accurate translation requires a recognition of the original language of the text in its original context. The scriptures of Matthew to Revelation are not a Greek text, and they were not written in a Christian context. Let's start with some historical observations.

In the third century, Origen commented on the use of the word *epiousion* in the phrase "daily bread" in the Greek text of Mt. 6:11 and Lk. 11:3. "Origen informs us that the word was not employed by any Greek writer; it was neither known to the learned nor in current use among ordinary people. He suggested that it had been coined by the Evangelists themselves, in order, as his words imply, to translate 'the Hebrew'."[1]

No Greeks had ever heard of *epiousion*, a supposedly Greek word that appears in Matthew and Luke. Where did it come from? The wise men of the Greeks did not know, because the word did not come from classical Greek. The common people did not know, because it did not come from common, *koine*, Greek.

The word comes from the Septuagint [LXX], the early Jewish translation of the Hebrew (and Aramaic) Scriptures into Greek. The translation was begun in the third century B.C.E.. *Epiousa* appears in the Septuagint in Proverbs 27:1: "Do not boast about tomorrow, for you do not know what may be brought forth in the day/*epiousa*." (cf. LXX Prov. 3:28)

Though *epiousion* may have been unknown to the Greeks of the first century, it would not have been unknown to Greek-speaking Jews, or to anyone else, familiar with the Septuagint translation of the Hebrew Scriptures. The Septuagint was the bridge between the world of the Hebrew Scriptures and the Greek language.

"It is evident that the Greek in which the books of the LXX are composed contains many features that cannot be normal Greek. It is clear moreover that these features are due principally to the influence of Hebrew.... It is beyond question that the majority of the books of the LXX exhibit, to a greater or lesser extent, features that are abnormal for Greek and must be due to the influence of a Semitic language. On this there is general agreement."[2]

There are places where the Septuagint differs significantly from the Hebrew text we have. As a translation, it has its own problems. Nevertheless, it is an indispensable tool for understanding Matthew to Revelation, which I call "the Messianic Writings". (I will explain why in the next chapter.)

The Septuagint is indispensable, first, because it transforms Hebrew Biblical language and concepts for a Greek-speaking Jewish audience. Second, the Messianic Writings follow the

Septuagint in vocabulary and grammar. Third, the Messianic Writings often quote from the Septuagint.

Consequently, as with the Septuagint, the Greek of the Messianic Writings often reflects the Hebrew text rather than any standard form of Greek. "At least since the time of Dionysius, bishop of Alexandria (died A.D. 265), questions have been expressed about the un-Greek nature of the language of the Apocalypse. Dionysius drew attention to the fact (see Eusebius, Ecclesiastical History, 7,25,7ff) that the Greek of the Apocalypse contained a number of unusual constructions which cannot be explained in terms of Greek grammar and syntax."[3] That is to say, the Greek of the Apocalypse contains grammar and syntax that are not Greek.

Isidore of Pelasium, a 5th century Christian writer, commented on what ordinary and educated Greeks of his day thought of the Scriptures in Greek. He said that, "The Greeks... despise the divine Scripture as barbarous language, and composed of foreign-sounding words, abandoning necessary conjunctions, and confusing the mind with the addition of extraordinary words."[4] That is to say, through the fifth century, the Greeks found the language, vocabulary, and grammar of the Messianic Writings to be foreign, i.e. un-Greek. Not all of it, of course, but enough of it to cause ordinary Greeks to despise it. It had peculiarities which could not be found in other forms of Greek.

Christian theologians routinely claim that, "the language of the New Testament is *koine* Greek." But the Greeks who used *koine* would not have agreed with the theologians. They saw grammar, syntax, and vocabulary that were not *koine*. For them, "the language of the New Testament" was barbarous and foreign.

My oldest son has a friend from Greece named Argyrios. Argyrios grew up and was educated in Greece, but completed a Ph.D. in Russian History in the U.S. He is currently a professor of Russian History at a university in the U.S.. In my quest to know how certain passages in the Messianic Writings should be translated, I occasionally asked Argyrios for help. From the beginning, his frustration was evident, until one day he finally said, "You know, the New Testament would be a lot easier to understand if it were written in Greek, instead of in something that pretends to be Greek."

He explained that in school in Greece he, or another student, would sometimes find a particular grammatical usage in one of their papers marked wrong by a teacher. When he, or the other, protested that the usage could be found in the New Testament, the teacher would simply reply that the language of the New Testament was not Greek, but "Jewish Greek".

From a Greek grammatical point of view, Jewish Greek is "corrupt"—it is strange and somewhat unnatural. It contains sentences whose words cannot possibly be connected according to the Greek rules of grammar and syntax. Jewish men wrote Jewish thoughts with Hebrew (or some say Jewish Aramaic) grammar and syntax in what appear to be Greek words. Sometimes, however, the apparently Greek words did not previously exist in Greek, or had never been used with the same meaning.

Some linguistic scholars call this language, "translation Greek." By that, they mean that the language is often not grammatically Greek, but a very literal translation of a document, or thought, from a language with different syntax, vocabulary, and ideas. These scholars are not, however, agreed as to whether the original language is Jewish Aramaic or Hebrew. [Hebrew itself is an Aramaic language, the Aramaic language of the Hebrews.]

Whatever the case may be, whether Jewish Aramaic or Hebrew, it would be appropriate to refer to the result of translation as "Jewish Greek". "It is even highly probable that our phrase 'Hebrew or Aramaic' suggests a problem which does not exist: both languages most likely influenced an author who was so well versed in Ezekiel [in Hebrew] *and* Daniel [which has substantial passages in Aramaic], and who lived in an age when both languages were used by each other's side."[5]

In his 1551 preface to *Biblia Sacra*, S. Catellion informed his readers that, "One should know that the New Testament was written in such a way that its diction is Hebraic... [for] the Apostles were Hebrew by birth, and they hebraized when writing a foreign, that is, the Greek language."[6]

Modern scholars have recognized this same phenomenon. Matthew Black observed that, "The Gospels were written in a predominantly hellenistic environment, and they were written in Greek. But Greek was not the native language of their central Figure, nor of the earliest apostles... "[7]

David Hill pointed out that, "Not only word-meanings in the New Testament, but also the structure and syntax of New Testament language bear the impress of a special Hebraic influence channeled, *for the most part*, through the Septuagint.... The language of the New Testament is a special kind of Jewish biblical Greek (both in the syntax and in the thought-forms it expresses)..."[8]

Nigel Turner said that, "Biblical Greek... is usually so drenched in Semitic idioms and forms of syntax that it is extremely difficult to decide whether a book has been translated from Hebrew into Greek or whether it was originally composed in that language." In his study of 'The Testament of Abraham', Turner concluded simply that, "We may call this 'Jewish Greek'."[9]

To which Steven Thompson added, "The Apocalypse can accurately be described in identical terms, and with no hesitancy be categorised as 'Jewish Greek,' to the fullest extent of that term..."[10] Throughout his study of the book of Revelation, Thompson remarks on certain verses: "This is certainly not Greek, but is the literal translation of a Hebrew construction... This is not Greek, but obviously represents the Hebraic construction..."[11]

Argyrios said that the theologians in Greece claim the New Testament as Greek, because such an assessment brings honor to Greece, though it obscures the Jewish nature and mindset of its authors. However, the linguists, the grammarians, and the classicists in Greece say that the language is not Greek. They are, after all, protecting the greatness of the Greek language and its literary and philosophical contribution to human civilization.

At one time, certain Christian writers called this language "Holy Ghost Greek". They maintained that the "Holy Ghost" created this special Christian language. That view has passed away, but the assumptions behind it, which remove the text from its native context, have not. It is not incidental that the Messianic Writings were written by Jews, with the possible exception of Luke (whose material came from Paul and Mark). It is an essential aspect of the texts themselves. They were written in the same language, though centuries later, as the Septuagint.

> NOT ONLY WORD-MEANINGS IN THE NEW TESTAMENT, BUT ALSO THE STRUCTURE AND SYNTAX OF NEW TESTAMENT LANGUAGE BEAR THE IMPRESS OF A SPECIAL HEBRAIC INFLUENCE.
>
> – DAVID HILL, NT SCHOLAR.

Some scholars emphasize that there is no evidence for Jewish Greek as a distinct spoken dialect; that it exists only in the specialized writing of the Scriptures or related documents. They prefer to use the term "semitic interference" to describe the differences in word meanings, the insertion of invented words, and the departures from Greek syntax and grammar. Without arguing the extent of this "semitic interference," it is possible to note that the phrase itself sounds a little strange. It gives the impression that 'those Semites are interfering with the Greek,' when, actually, it is the Greek that is interfering with the Semitic message.

'Those Semites are always interfering with everything. Now they're even interfering with the Bible.'

The Greek text of the Messianic Writings contains proper Greek as well, and does not demonstrate that its authors suffered from a systematic failure to understand Greek grammar or syntax. The text does not indicate that the authors could not write proper Greek. It seems likely that the authors knowingly made their choices, even what appear to be their ungrammatical ones, in terms of what they wanted to communicate.

Albert Wifstrand concluded, "We cannot discover any special Greek dialect spoken by the Hellenized Jews; in phonology, accidence, syntax, word formation and many significations of words their language was ordinary koine... but in phraseology, in the formation of sentences, in preferences when equivalent expressions were at hand, in all such things .. the real foundation is, to a great extent, the Hebrew or Aramaic mode of thought."[12]

A Hebrew concept in a Jewish spiritual context had to be expressed in Greek. Sometimes the equivalent word did not exist, because of the very different historical, cultural, and spiritual Greek context. Sometimes the words could not be contextualized into Greek, because the concepts did not exist in the Greek context. So an existing Greek word was modified and used with a meaning significantly different from what it had been; or a new word was created.

Greeks, for at least the first five centuries of this era, did not consider the language of the "New Testament" to be good Greek. It was a Greek that was foreign to them. For our purposes, we can call this written language what it is, Jewish Greek. It is a form of Greek that is significantly characterized by dependence upon Hebrew Biblical language and concepts.

*'How does this affect our understanding of the Scriptures?'*

I'm glad you asked. That is exactly what I would like to discuss. The grandson of Sirach gives us some good advice. He translated the Hebrew manuscript of his grandfather into Greek in about 132 B.C.E.. He noted the difficulty he encountered in his work. "You are therefore invited to read it through, with favorable attention, and to excuse us for any failures we may seem to have made in phraseology, in what we have labored to translate. For things once expressed in Hebrew do not have the same force in them when put into another language; and not only this book, but the Law itself, and the prophecies, and the rest of the books, differ not a little in translation from the original."[13]

The challenge of such translation is to take the author's meaning, from the author's context, and accurately convey it to people who are separated from that context by both language and culture, as well as by history and perspective. Sometimes the task is almost impossible, because the reader cannot grasp the concepts unless he is brought into the original context. The actual meaning always lies in the original, not in the translation. To treat the "New Testament" as a Christian Greek document is to guarantee inaccuracy and distortion in translation, in understanding, and in the teaching that is built upon them.

## ONE VERSE

The Messiah is described and defined in Tanakh, i.e. the Law, the Writings, and the Prophets. The Messianic Writings were written to demonstrate that Yeshua fits that description and definition. The Messianic Writings begin with a genealogy in order to establish that Yeshua is qualified, in terms of his ancestry, to be the Messiah. The first verse says:

*Biblos geneseos Iesou Christou huiou Dauid huiou Abraam.*

"A written account of the origin of Yeshua the Messiah, son of David, son of Abraham." (Mt. 1:1)

The words are written in an alphabet that is Greek, but the content and concepts are not. "Not a single word in this statement, nor even the syntactic structure of the whole, is independent of the specific, preexisting cultural, literary, and spiritual heritage of Israel. By implicitly invoking that heritage, Matthew brings a particular world into the text from the very beginning and shapes its message."[14]

That particular world was the one, the only one, in which Matthew lived and breathed. That world is what informs and gives meaning to his text. It was the world in which the text itself was alive. The challenge of translation is to bring the reader into that world.

*Biblos geneseos*, "a written account of the origin," is a Hebrew phrase presented in a Greek format. The Greek words are taken from the Septuagint. The Septuagint was the primary Greek text of the Scriptures used by the disciples of Yeshua and by other Jews. The authors of the classic Bauer/Arndt-Gingrich *Greek-English Lexicon of the New Testament and Other Early Christian Literature* remind us that, "As for the influence of the Septuagint, every page of this lexicon shows that it outweighs all other influences in our literature."[15]

These particular words, *biblos geneseos*, are used in the Septuagint in Genesis 2:4 to speak of the origin of heaven and earth. They are used in Genesis 5:1 to speak of the origin of Man. The use of this phrase in Matthew is intended to point the reader back to the places in Tanakh where it appears. This was more than obvious for anyone familiar with the Scriptures. It was inescapable.

So the first two words of Matthew, if they are understood to be written in a Jewish Greek context, tell us what Matthew is writing about. This is a book about a new origin; and it is a book about a new Adam. The genealogy which follows is indispensable for determining whether or not the person spoken of physically qualifies as someone who might be the Messiah. Without that documented lineage, it would not be possible to demonstrate that Yeshua is the Messiah.

If the first two words are understood to be something other than Jewish Greek, then we will miss Matthew's meaning. We can invent our own meaning to replace his, but we then lose his meaning. We will have started on our way to the creation of a world of meaning which Matthew neither knew nor intended.

Unfortunately, this is exactly what some theologians do. They reject Matthew's Jewish world as the source and context for understanding his language, or for understanding the language of any other "New Testament" writer. They believe that the Greek letters of the text mean that God has rejected and replaced the Hebrew world and the Jewish people. Their presupposition of replacement defines their system of interpretation and justifies their theology.

From the third century B.C.E. on, most of the Jewish people were Greek speaking. Many Jewish documents were written in (Jewish) Greek. The Septuagint was. The Apocrypha was. Philo wrote in (Jewish) Greek. So did Josephus. So did many others. Jews, who understood themselves to be Jews, wrote, or were the source for, the entire text of the compiled document that these theologians call "the New Testament".

That is what provides a foundation for the text. If that foundation is removed, the text floats in the air, separated from the world. The Jewishness of the document provides content for the words that are used.

*Iesou*, is not a Greek name. It is not a Greek word. It doesn't mean anything in Greek. *Iesou*, or *Iesous*, which is the nominative case of the same word, is a Greek transliteration of the Hebrew name, "Yeshua," which is a shortened form of Yehoshua, which means "the LORD saves."

Yehoshua, or Yeshua, is generally rendered in English as "Joshua." That is the name of the man who victoriously led the people of Israel into the land of Israel. In Hebrews 4:8, *Iesous* is used to refer to Joshua.

The Greek name in Matthew 1:1 is the same as that used in the Septuagint for "Joshua" throughout the book of Joshua. It is the same as that used in the Septuagint for the name of the High Priest in the time of Zechariah. (cf. Zech. chapters 3 & 6) The use of this name in Matthew points the reader back to the texts about both Joshua/Yeshua the general and Joshua/Yeshua the High Priest. (It is also the name of the leader of the ninth priestly division in the time of David. cf. 1Chr. 24:11 The eighth division, to which Zechariah, father of John belonged, is that of Abiyah. cf. 1Chr. 24:10; Lk.1:5)

It is that content in Tanakh which makes the name more than a sound. A good translation will make it possible for the reader to find these associations and their meaning. A translation that takes the Greek transliteration and then transliterates that into English, or some other language, fails to serve the reader in this way. The Greek transliteration is only pointing to the Hebrew reality. Transliterating the Greek transliteration only removes the reader away from the Hebrew reality.

*Christou*, is an attempt to place into the Greek language a reference to, or marker for, the Hebrew Biblical concept of *Mashiakh*, i.e. the Anointed One. *Christou*, or the more familiar nominative case of *Christos*, was formed from an existing Greek word, *chrioo*, that meant to smear, as in smearing oil on a leather shield to keep it from drying out and cracking. In first-century Greek, *christos* is what we call an adjective, describing the object that was smeared, e.g. a shield that is *christos*. The Greek word referred only to a physical action and the resultant physical condition. It carried no meaning beyond that.

*Christos* did not refer to a person. *Christos* did not mean "the Anointed One". In ordinary Greek, whether classical or *koine*, *christos* simply described an object that had been rubbed with some kind of ointment.

Only in this physical meaning was it equivalent to the Hebrew forms. In the Biblical Hebrew of what Matthew is presenting, the physical action and condition are simply a symbolic representation. The King, or High Priest, was anointed with oil as a representation of his being set apart to God for a unique high position and work. The oil is "the anointing oil of the Lord." (cf. Lev.10:7) Years and years after any physical trace of the oil is gone, the individual remains "the anointed of the LORD."

"So Samuel took the horn of oil and anointed him in the presence of his brothers, and from that day on the Spirit of the LORD came upon David in power..." (1Sam. 16:13) The Hebrew here for "anointed" is *yimshakh*, which the Septuagint translates as *echrisen*. From that day on, David was "the Anointed of the LORD".

The Septuagint adopts and adapts *chrioo* for this different meaning and purpose. The word is used in many places in this way. For example, in 1Kings 19:16 (3Kgs. 19:16 in LXX), the LORD speaks to Elijah and tells him, "Anoint/*chriseis* Jehu son of Nimshi king over Israel, and anoint/*chriseis* Elisha son of Shaphat from Abel Meholah to succeed you as prophet."

*Christos* is used in Lev. 4:5 to describe the high priest. It is used in numerous places, like 1Sam. 12:3,5 (1Kgs. 12:3,5 in LXX), to describe King Saul. It is used in 2Sam. 22:51 (2Kgs. 22:51 in LXX) to describe King David. It is used in Is. 45:1 to describe the Gentile King Cyrus. It is used in Psalm 2:2 and in Daniel 9:25-26 to describe the Messiah.

Each of these was called by God for a specific high purpose. The physical anointing with oil was a symbol, and only incidental as a representation of the calling. As far as we know, Cyrus was not physically anointed with oil, and yet he is still called *christos*. In fact, the Mashiakh himself is not physically anointed at all. He is anointed with the Spirit of the Lord. (cf. Is.61:1; Mt. 3:16)

There was no comparable concept in ancient Greece. There was no "Anointed One" in ancient Greek religion or culture. There was no word that Greeks used in this way, because it would not have described anything or anyone in their world. In essence, the word was commandeered by the translators of the Septuagint for a use that is foreign to its actual Greek meaning. It was intended only to be a reference to point to the Hebrew, Biblical concept of Mashiakh. The definition of Mashiakh, i.e. what Messiah is, is to be found in the fulness of God's revelation in Tanakh. A good translation will direct the reader toward the particularity of the concept in Tanakh. A poor translation will put the reader into some other world.

In the Hindu pantheon of gods, an *avatar* is the incarnation of a deity upon the earth. To call Yeshua an avatar would be to place him in an anti-biblical context, a context of many gods with very different behavior. The content of the meaning of avatar comes from the Hindu pantheon, not from *Immanuel*. To contextualize Mashiakh as "avatar" in translations for Hindus would be an immense error. It would make correct understanding all but impossible.

In Shiite Islam, the *Mahdi* is a future leader who establishes a reign of righteousness throughout the earth. But to speak of Messiah as the Mahdi would cause hopeless confusion. The Shiite standard of righteousness is not the same as that of the Bible. The Mahdi is a Muslim, not the King of Israel. The use of "Mahdi" to translate Mashiakh would communicate the opposite of what Messiah is.

If *Christos* had been an existing word that described something in the Greek world similar to the Hebrew concept—something like "avatar" or "Mahdi"—then the word probably could not have been used. It would have been inextricably connected with the Greek pantheon of gods. What would "the Anointed One" of such gods be? It would then have been necessary to invent or commandeer another word, since whatever *christos* would have referred to in the Greek world would have been inescapably incompatible with Mashiakh, the Anointed One of the holy God of Israel.

*Christos* could be used, and was used in the Septuagint, precisely because, in the Greek world, it was devoid of content related to anyone like Mashiakh. A Greek word was used, but its content, its meaning, could only be found in the Hebrew Biblical world. It was a Jewish Greek word. To Greeks who did not know that world, this usage of *christos* was strange and incomprehensible. They did not know what the followers of Yeshua meant by Christos.

Why didn't Matthew, or whoever translated his Hebrew text into Greek, just transliterate "Mashiakh"? They transliterated "Yeshua." "Yeshua," however, is a name, but "Mashiakh" is a concept. They didn't transliterate "Mashiakh," because there were just too many such concepts that didn't exist in the Greek world. Such concepts as *kappora*, which we understand as "atonement," or *t'shuva,* which we understand as "repentance," or *tevilah*, which we understand as "baptism," were far too numerous to transliterate.

Additionally, transliteration creates a word without any meaning at all, unless the content and concept from the other world are known. Transliterated words can be used, but they seldom convey the original meaning in the original context. The goal of translation was to find, as much as possible, some way that the Biblical Hebrew concepts could be represented in Greek.

When Matthew, or whoever translated his text into Greek, used the word *Christos*, he was referring to a specific individual who is prophetically described and defined in detail in the Hebrew Scriptures. He was not presenting a Greek or universal idea or ideal. Proper translation must communicate that particularity. Transliterating the invented Jewish Greek word fails to do that.

Matthew refers to the Hebrew Biblical content of that description when he speaks of *huiou Dauid huiou Abraam*, i.e. son of David, son of Abraham. Who is David? Who is Abraham? In the Greek world, excluding the Jewish Diaspora and those who attached themselves to it, *Dauid* and *Abraam* were sounds without content or meaning. They were not names. Who their sons might be would have been census data without significance.

The syntactical form itself—"the son of..."—is a Hebrew form, not a Greek one. *Huiou*, meaning "son," was an existing Greek word, but this was not a Greek form to indicate descent. The Greek form would be more like "of David," or "David's," similar to the form that is used in Luke. The Hebrew form—the son of... the son of...—is in keeping with the Biblical delineation of God's selective choices, for His purposes, among men. This is integrally connected with the prophetic nature of the Scriptures. The Hebrew form itself carries meaning.

In the Jewish world, the reference is specific, overflowing with meaning, and powerful. "The Son of David," i.e. *ben David*, is the prophesied King and Deliverer of Israel. It means David was his ancestor, not his immediate father, but it means much more than that. In Matthew, it means God's faithfulness. It means the appointed time. It means God's ruler upon and over all the earth. That is what Matthew meant. That is what those who called Yeshua the Son of David meant. That is what would come to mind for those familiar with the Scriptures.

The same kind of expansive meaning is contained in "son of Abraham." It means Abraham was David's ancestor, not his immediate father, but it means much more than that. God called Abraham apart, that He might create through him a people who would bring the nations back to Himself. God created the Jewish people to bring the nations/goyim of the world out of their darkness into God's light. Messiah, the Son of David, the son of Abraham, is the means through which the Jewish people will fulfill this calling, a calling which brings the fulfillment of God's purpose in creating Adam and in creating the earth.

I remember showing the first chapter of Matthew in Hebrew to a Hasidic man I encountered on a nice summer day in the mountains. He never got past the first verse. "WHAT?! WHO IS THIS?! WHAT IS THIS BOOK?!" Unfortunately, when he heard the explanation, he indicated, in an equally excited manner, but in words that I do not choose to recall, that he was not interested in knowing any more. But at least he understood the first verse of Matthew. He understood its power. He understood what Matthew was saying. He didn't believe it, but he understood it.

The people and the concepts are Jewish. They are not Greek. The content comes from the Hebrew world, not the Greek. The only context in which the words can be understood, or, at least, the only context in which the words can be understood correctly, is the Divine revelation of God to Israel, i.e. the Law, the Writings, and the Prophets.

This has nothing to do with one person being better than another; or with one people being better than another. The Scriptures do not support any such illusion. Nor does a personal openness to God and to life. The issue here is the proper translation of a text, for the purpose of communicating the author's meaning.

Almost all English translations of Matthew effectively, though perhaps unintentionally, rob the text of its full meaning, by translating as though the original language were Greek, or a non-existent "Christian Greek," rather than Jewish Greek. So the verse becomes, "The book of the generation of Jesus Christ, the son of David, the son of Abraham." (KJV)

Matthew's world and meaning are obscured by such translations, rather than communicated. "Jesus" is an English transliteration of a Greek transliteration of a meaningful Hebrew name. Iesous did not mean anything in Greek, and "Jesus" doesn't mean anything in English. The name "Jesus" is not connected to Joshua, neither the military leader nor the high priest.

"Christ" is not a translation. It is an adapted English transliteration of a commandeered Greek word, a Greek word whose only purpose was to point to the Biblical Hebrew reality. Does "Christ" point English readers to the Biblical Hebrew reality of Mashiakh? Quite frankly, it does not. It points to the Greek world, where the word was all but devoid of relevant meaning. Or, highly anachronistically, it points to a "Christian" world, which did not yet even exist. It points to "Christian" history, ideology, institutions, and identity.

In common English usage, "Christ" points away from the Jewish people. That is the opposite of Matthew's intent. Good translation should convey, as much as possible, the original intent and content of the text.

Another kind of example, this time from preaching, can help illustrate the same point. In traditional Christian teaching, "*agape*" is a Greek word that means the unselfish love

ALMOST ALL ENGLISH TRANSLATIONS OF MATTHEW EFFECTIVELY, THOUGH PERHAPS UNINTENTIONALLY, ROB THE TEXT OF ITS FULL MEANING.

that comes from God, or that one has for God. That is a wonderful thing, but could there really have been such a Greek word? If so, then to which Greek god would it have been referring? Zeus? Artemis? Bacchus? Venus?

There was no such concept in the ancient Greek world as the unselfish love of God. There was no such god. The Greeks knew who knows how many gods, but they did not know God at all.

That was Paul's point in Athens. "For as I walked around and observed your objects of worship, I even found an altar with this inscription: TO AN UNKNOWN GOD. Now what you worship as something unknown I will proclaim to you." (Acts 17:23) To paraphrase, 'You Athenians know many gods, but the one you don't know, the real One, that's the One I want to tell you about.'

'*Well then, is agape just a Christian word?*'

Not at all. There were no Christian words. There was no Christian anything. The verb *agapazo*, with an apparent initial meaning of "to welcome," is an ancient word, which later acquired the meaning "to be fond of," or "to have brotherly affection." But we have no record of the existence of the noun form *agape* before the Septuagint.

The noun and the various verb forms are used in the Septuagint as equivalents for the Hebrew *ahavah*, love. It is not a specialized word, but this is the concept that is being presented. The different forms are used in that sense in the "*v'ahavta*": "you shall love/*agapeseis* the LORD your God with all your mind, and with all your soul, and with all your strength." (LXX, Dt.6:5) They are used when God says to Israel, "With an everlasting love/*agapesin*, I have loved you/*egapesa se*, therefore I have drawn you in compassion." (LXX, Jer.38:3; Masoretic, Jer.31:3)

To understand what *agape* means in relationship to God, it is necessary to understand how it is used in its Jewish Greek context, the context of a relationship with a decidedly non-Greek God. The actual meaning of *agape* in terms of a relationship between God and His Creation must be found in the Jewish world from which the original concept came.

To ignore that meaning in translation or in teaching will distort the Scriptures. A good example of this is the encounter of the risen Yeshua with Simon Peter, recorded in John 21:15-17. We are told that Jesus said, "Simon, do you *agape* me?" And Peter responded, "You know that I *phileos* you." And the exchange continues like this. The standard teaching is that Peter was only capable of brotherly love, but Yeshua was asking him if he had the love of God.

It's a nice teaching, but it does not come from the text. It does not come from the Greek words, and it does not come from the Hebrew words which they translate. It is imposed on the text by Christian theology.

In the first place, *agape* did not mean "unselfish love" or "the love of God". Luke uses the same word to translate Yeshua saying, "If you love/*agapate* those who love/*agapoontas* you, what credit is that to you? Even sinners love/*agapoontas* those who love/*agapoosin* them." (Lk. 6:32) Even sinners can have *agape*-love; it's no big deal.

The word does not have anything to do with unselfishness. Yeshua said, "No one can serve two masters. Either he will hate the one and love/*agapesei* the other, or he will be devoted to the one and despise the other. You cannot serve both God and Money." (Mt. 6:24) It is just as easy to *agape* money as it is to *agape* God. In fact, Balaam "loved/*egapesen* the reward of unrighteousness." (2Pet.2:15)

In the second place, *phileos* was not limited in meaning to "brotherly love". In the Greek text of Matthew, Yeshua says, "Anyone who loves/*philon* his father or mother more than me is not worthy of me; anyone who loves/*philon* his son or daughter more than me is not worthy of me." (Mt. 10:37) In the Greek text, Yeshua is calling for his disciples to have *phileo* love for him. This is in accordance with a standard Greek usage of the word concerning "one's nearest and dearest, such as wife and children."[16]

The word can be used to describe different types of love. Yeshua told the people, "And when you pray, do not be like the hypocrites, for they love/*philousin* to pray standing in the meeting-places and on the street corners to be seen by men. I tell you the truth, they have received their reward in full." (Mt. 6:5)

Yeshua told his disciples, "I rebuke and discipline those whom I love/*philo*. So be zealous, and repent." (Rev. 3:19) Yeshua has *phileo* love for his disciples.

In the third place, Yeshua was not speaking Greek. Nor was Peter. The standard Christian teaching may make great preaching, but it's lousy interpretation. It's a distortion of the text. Instead of reading the meaning out of the text, it reads theological conclusions into it. And it creates a false impression by removing Yeshua and Peter from their Jewish context.

In the Scriptures, the meanings of the various words do not come from Christian theology; they come from the way the words are used in their immediate and larger Biblical context. "We must stress our conviction that every word is a semantic marker for a field of meaning, a pointer to what Barr calls 'a wide area of recognised thought' (p.212), connected with it and going beyond its normal signification. Whether this be termed 'idea' or 'concept', the interpreter must be acquainted with it, if he is to assess the total meaning of the word."[17]

I was recently in Buenos Aires. Driving one day, I noticed a sign for "Avenida Corrientes". The sign was on a building on the side of the actual street. The sign identified the street, but it was not identical with the street. The sign merely signified and pointed to the reality. It would be a great mistake, and a dangerous one, to confuse the sign with the street itself. Driving in Buenos Aires is already dangerous enough.

If there were, as the urban legend envisions, 32 different words in Inupiat, or some other Eskimo language, for 32 different kinds or conditions of snow, it would be because those words were needed in that world. It would not be possible to represent these words by their Samoan equivalent, since the equivalents would not exist; there having been no need for them in the Samoan world. Nor would it be possible to contextualize the 32 Inupiat words into the Samoan culture. The best that could be done would be to first create in the Samoan world an image of the Inupiat world in which these words have specific meaning; and then to find a Samoan word or words which, though inadequate and incomplete, would give some sense of the meaning of the original Inupiat words.

It would be foolish to then turn around and treat the Samoan words as though they contained and conveyed the reality and essence of meaning. It would be foolish to think that the Samoan world provided the key to understanding the Inupiat concepts. And yet, unfortunately, that is exactly what is done by those who study, translate, and build theologies from the Messianic Writings as though these writings were in any way not Jewish.

"Because Hebraic ideas were associated with the Greek vocabulary of the New Testament writers, we must reckon with the possibility that, while these ideas communicated themselves to Jewish minds they may not have registered with Gentile hearers and readers, who would understand the words in their normal Hellenistic sense."[18] We must also reckon with the possibility that this problem has neither disappeared nor diminished with the passage of two thousand years.

In general, Gentile hearers and readers would not have encountered the Hebraic ideas, nor the Hebraic values. They would have had to learn them. That is why Yeshua commanded his Jewish ambassadors, "Therefore, as you go, make disciples of all the Gentiles..." (Mt.28:19a) Teach them who God is and what He requires, because they do not know.

"Greek thought, for instance, had no idea of the 'righteousness of God' as a divine activity bringing about salvation...

"Again, Greek thought did not operate with the notion of the 'two Ages' - this Age and the Age to come....

"The usage of the Word *pneuma*/πνευμα in Greek literature reveals nothing comparable to the Hebrew use of *ruakh*/רוח for 'human spirit' and for the powerful and active presence of God. The word pneuma/πνευμα in Greek stands essentially for a substance, fluidum, refined and ethereal, penetrating the entire cosmos, the substance of which God and the human spirit are composed..."[19]

In the Greek world, one could argue about "the substance of God," because the Greek word for "spirit" indicated a substance. From the fourth century on, in Church councils, catechisms, and websites, Christians have argued about whether the Father and the Son are of the same substance or not. In arguing about the correct understanding of the Greek, they have split hairs and heads.

In the Hebrew Biblical world, no such argument is possible. The Hebrew word for "spirit" does not indicate any substance, in any way. The God of the Bible is not composed of any preexisting substance. He simply IS.

Such differences led astray, and still lead astray, those who give Greek, or non-Jewish, content to the concepts of the Jewish Scriptures, i.e. Genesis to Revelation. That held true in the past, and still holds true today. It is equally true for interpreters, translators, and theologians. Having a different center, they imagine a different world.

Let's look at one more, very important concept as an example. Let's look at repentance. What is repentance?

If we want to know what Biblical "repentance" is, then we need to examine the concept of *t'shuva*. In Dt. 30:8, Moses speaks prophetically to Israel about a future restoration from a future diaspora. "You will return/*tashuv* and listen to the voice of the LORD and do all His commandments which I have commanded you today." Biblical repentance means turning from sin to the LORD.

The Septuagint was translated into Greek for a Jewish audience, i.e. an audience at least somewhat familiar with the God of Israel, and the context and concepts He delineates in the Scriptures. The Septuagint, therefore, gives the literal sense of *t'shuva* by *epistrepho*, i.e. "turning." In Dt. 30:8, it uses *epistraphese*, i.e. "will return."

In the Messianic Writings, there are some, but not many, passages in which this literal sense is preserved. Yeshua told his disciples, "I tell you the truth, unless you change/*straphete* and become like little children, you will never enter the kingdom of heaven." (Mt. 18:3)

In Lystra, Paul and Barnabas cried out to the Gentile crowd which was deifying them: "Men, why are you doing this? We too are only men, human like you. We are bringing you good news, telling you to turn/*epistrephein* from these worthless things to the living God, who made heaven and earth and sea and everything in them." (Acts 14:15; cf. 1Th. 1:9)

As Paul and Barnabas traveled to Jerusalem, they were "reporting the turning to God/*epistrofen* of the Gentiles." (Acts 15:3) At the council in Jerusalem, Jacob concluded, "It is my judgment, therefore, that we should not make it difficult for the Gentiles who are turning/*epistrephousin* to God." (Acts 15:19)

Paul explained to King Agrippa how Yeshua had appeared to him and sent him to proclaim the message of the kingdom. "First to those in Damascus, then to those in Jerusalem and in all Judea, and to the Gentiles also, I proclaimed that they should repent/*metanoein* and turn/*epistrephein* to God and prove their repentance/*metanoias* by their deeds." (Acts 26:20)

In general, however, the Messianic Writings use *metanoia* to represent the concept of *t'shuva*. In ordinary Greek, *metanoia* meant "a change of mind." That is part of the Biblical concept, but it is not at all the whole. If the whole of repentance is understood to be a change of mind, then the message will not be correctly understood.

Consider, for example, Rev. 2:4-5, where Yeshua speaks to the congregation in Ephesus. "But

I have this against you, that you have left your first love. Remember therefore from where you have fallen, and repent/*metanoeson*, and do the first works. And if not, I am coming to you swiftly, and will remove your lampstand out of its place, unless you repent/*metanoeses*." A change of mind would not be sufficient. There must be a change of works.

Much of the Messianic Writings, in contrast to the Septuagint, were put into Greek for a primarily Gentile audience, i.e. an audience usually not familiar with the God of Israel, nor with the context and concepts He delineates in His Scriptures. The Messianic Writings were put into Greek for an audience whose natural, cultural, and spiritual world had distorted and obscured the truths of God.

Could a contemporary Greek have understood the concept of feeling sorry for what he had done, and consciously choosing to change his behavior so that he wouldn't do it again? Of course. But he still would be missing the core of *t'shuva*—turning, returning, to God.

So it is not sufficient, and it is not correct, to say that the Greek word *metanoia* tells us what God requires as repentance. The full concept of *t'shuva* did not exist in the Greek world, because the God of the Bible, i.e. the God of Israel, was given no place in the Greek world. Therefore, the concept of returning to Him in obedience did not exist in Greek thought. *Metanoia* cannot be restricted to its standard Greek meaning, because that meaning does not contain the appropriate Biblical content. It must be understood as the Jewish authors intended, as a Jewish Greek marker for the concept of "returning to God," i.e. *t'shuva*.

Perhaps the Samoan rendering of a particular Inupiat concept could be informative, but it cannot be decisive in establishing the meaning of the concept. God's explicit plan in creating the Jewish people was to create a context in which He could be clearly seen and known. The concepts are to be found in the Hebrew Biblical world. The Greek text is a way to shine the light of the Hebrew Biblical world in another language, another culture, but an alien spiritual world.

*'But isn't the message of the Bible for everyone? Aren't the words of Jesus meant to be read and heard by more than Jews?'*

Yes, of course. That is not the issue here. The issue is, what IS the message of the Bible? What DO the words of Yeshua mean, and how can their meaning be accurately conveyed to a variety of people in a variety of cultures? The message and the meaning must first be understood in their own context, before they are accurately communicated to others who are outside that context.

Consequently, to return to our primary discussion of the meaning and world conveyed by the text, there is a crucial difference in the actual content and meaning that results from different translations. They produce differing perceptions of the background, context, and intent of the text. In English today, "Jesus Christ" is not at all equivalent to "Yeshua the Messiah," precisely because the two phrases invoke two different historical, cultural, and spiritual worlds. That of the former is entirely Christian, whereas that of the latter is entirely Jewish.

Certainly there are those who know that "Jesus Christ" was a Jew, but that is not at all the same as recognizing that he IS a Jew. There is an immeasurable theological difference between recognizing a simple historical fact and comprehending that it was the King of the Jews who suffered and died for the sins of the world. There is an immeasurable theological difference between recognizing a simple historical fact and comprehending that it is the King of the Jews who is the way, the truth, and the life.

THE WORDS "JESUS CHRIST" DO NOT DIRECT US TO MATTHEW'S WORLD. THEY DIRECT US TO A CHRISTIAN WORLD, A WORLD THAT MATTHEW DID NOT KNOW.

Though both renderings of Mt. 1:1 could be said to be literal translations of a text written in Greek letters, they are worlds apart. "Jesus Christ," which is tied to the text as though it were Greek, uses words which lack the original content of Matthew. The words "Jesus Christ" do not direct us to Matthew's world. They direct us to a Christian world, a world that Matthew did not know. They obscure the world that he did know. The concept and content to which Matthew refers can only be found in his Jewish context. "Yeshua the Messiah" treats the text as though it were Jewish Greek, and points us to Matthew's world.

The Jewishness of Yeshua is indispensable to his being the Messiah. The correct concept of Messiah only exists in the Jewish context. That is why Matthew establishes the Jewishness of Yeshua first, to point us to the content of the one whom he describes. The concept of "Christ," unfortunately, often exists both outside a Jewish context and without Jewish content.

This brings us to the end of our brief examination of one verse, the first verse of the first chapter of the first book of the Messianic Writings. If we approach the text as though it is Jewish, we are led to the Hebrew Biblical world. That is the world in which Matthew and Yeshua lived, the world in which their message is whole, the world that is central to their message. If, to the contrary, we approach the text as though it were Greek, or Christian, we will assuredly be led astray.

*'Are you saying that God made a mistake in putting these Scriptures into Greek?'*

Not at all. God called Israel to represent Him to the nations. That requires the use of many languages. Greek was the common language of the first-century world surrounding Israel. So it was necessary to put the inspired message in Greek. The question, however, is, 'How can we accurately understand that Greek?'

These Scriptures were written in a Greek that has its own peculiarities. They were written in Jewish Greek. They were written to connect the reader to the Jewish context that the God of Israel had designed for the salvation of the world. To do this, translations, teachings, and theologies must accurately communicate the authors', and Author's, meaning. The failure to approach these Scriptures in their Jewish Greek context is a great mistake.

This doesn't mean that Hebrew is better than Greek. It doesn't mean that chicken soup is better than baklava. It just means that the Scriptures should be understood in their own context.

That is why the Messianic Writings begin with a genealogy. Without the Jewish genealogy that follows this first verse, a Jesus could be many things, but he could not be the Messiah. Likewise, a Jesus who was once Jewish, but then ceased to be Jewish, would then cease to qualify as the Messiah.

And yet—and this, we might say, is where the plot begins to thicken—the "Christ" of the major creeds and statements of faith of the Christian Church is not Jewish. He is never identified in any way as a Jew: not as the son of Abraham, not as the son of David, not as the Messiah, not as the King of the Jews, not as the Lion of Judah, not as etc., etc. This amazing feat was accomplished by removing the language from its original context, and severing it from its original content.

Such a simple, fundamental distortion sheds a lot of light on a lot of Christian history. It also helps explain why the Jews cannot be fit into this system, and why the system itself is the problem.

FOOTNOTES

1. De Oratione 27, cited in *An Aramaic Approach to the Gospels and Acts*, Matthew Black, Clarendon Press, Oxford, 1967, p.203

2. J.A.L. Lee, *A Lexical Study of the Septuagint Version of the Pentateuch*, SBLSCS, Scholars Press, Chico, CA., 1983, pp.11-12

3. Steven Thompson, *The Apocalypse and Semitic Syntax*, Cambridge U. Press, NY, 1985, p.1

4. Epistle 4.28, in Migne, *Patrologia greca*, cited in *Semitic Interference in Marcan Syntax*, Elliott C. Maloney, Scholars Press, Chico, CA, 1981, p.5

5. G. Mussies, *The Morphology of Koine Greek as Used in the Apocalypse of St. John*, E. J. Brill, Leiden, 1971, pp. 352-353

6. Maloney, *Semitic Interference in Marcan Syntax*, p.5

7. Black, *An Aramaic Approach to the Gospels and Acts*, p.16

8. David Hill, *Greek Words and Hebrew Meanings: Studies in the Semantics of Soteriological Terms*, Cambridge U. Press, London, 1967, pp.14, 19-20

9. Nigel Turner, "The Testament of Abraham: Problems in Biblical Greek," NTS 1, 1955, pp.222-223, cited in *The Apocalypse and Semitic Syntax*, Thompson, p.108

10. *The Apocalypse and Semitic Syntax*, Thompson, p.108

11. Ibid., p. 14 [on Rev. 3:9] and p. 99 [on Rev. 4:1b]

12. A. Wifstrand, "Stylistic Problems in the Epistles of James and Peter," *Studia Theologica 1* (1947), pp.181-182, cited in *The LXX Version: A Guide to the Translation Technique of the Septuagint*, Staffan Olofsson, ConBOT 30, Almqvist & Wiksell, Stockholm, 1990, p.38

13. "Prologue to The Wisdom of Sirach," *The Apocrypha*, trans. by Edgar Goodspeed, Vintage, NY, 1959, p.223

14. Isaiah Gruber, "On the Practice of Literary-Semiotic History," unpublished, p.2, 4/13/01

15. Walter Bauer/Walter Arndt & F. Wilbur Gingrich, *A Greek-English Lexicon of the New Testament and Other Early Christian Literature*, Second Edition, U. of Chicago Press, Chicago, 1979, p. xxi

16. Liddell and Scott, *Greek-English Lexicon*, Oxford U. Press, Oxford, 1999, p.864

17. Hill, *Greek Words and Hebrew Meanings*, pp.12-13, referring to James Barr, *The Semantics of Biblical Language*, Oxford U. Press, Oxford, 1961

18. Hill, *Greek Words and Hebrew Meanings*, pp. 20-21

19. Ibid., pp. 294-295

CHAPTER THREE

# Dr. Frankenstein's
# Neighborhood Bible Club

*The Bible Does Not Contain a New Testament or an Old Testament*

In the last chapter we looked at the language of Matthew to Revelation, focusing on one verse. In this chapter, we will look at the way the failure of translators and theologians to approach the text as Jewish Greek has produced a misrepresentation of the Bible as a whole. This misrepresentation is the source of a tremendous amount of distortion in understanding and teaching.

That distortion obscures God's context for redemption. It obstructs God's plan for redemption. It highlights the hopeless confusion that comes from ignoring the context of the Scriptures.

The translators did not understand one word, and so they mistranslated it. Because they mistranslated that one word, they had to mistranslate another word in order to make some sense of the text. But because of these two mistranslations, the sense they made of the text was not the right sense.

Since we do not have any of the original manuscripts of the Scriptures, we must use the manuscripts and fragments that were produced by later generations, as we seek to recreate the original text. Scholars who work with these manuscripts and fragments try to closely approximate what the original text was. From this approximation, we can try to determine what the Scriptures say, keeping in mind the original language and context. Only after we determine what the Scriptures say can we then begin to talk about what they mean.

Because most of us cannot read the original languages, we rely on others to sort through all the manuscripts and fragments, and make a composite text. We rely on others to translate that derived text into a language we can read and understand. Then there are those who interpret the text. All these others are often intermediaries between us and the original text.

Throughout the centuries, many godly people have devoted their lives to these various tasks. Nevertheless, sometimes the scholars themselves produce problems. The ancient, honorable traditions of the linguists, translators, and theologians, like those of the astronomers and mathematicians, can prevent them from seeing some little, but very serious, errors in what they pass on as Truth.

Most translators and theologians do not question the system in which they operate. They know and uphold the ancient tradition, because everybody knows that the ancient tradition is true—everybody except an occasional rebel, heretic, or eccentric. Rebels, heretics, and eccentrics come and go—and they are usually dealt with as they deserve—but the ancient system remains.

All the challenges are merely little blips, flashing for a moment and then disappearing in the night sky. The observable fact that the ancient tradition has endured so long is taken as proof of its Truth. Besides, everybody who knows anything knows that all these questions were settled long ago. If there were a problem, the experts would tell us.

In this chapter, we will look at one symptom of a major problem, one the experts did not tell us about. At first it may seem to be a simple, little issue of semantics. In actuality it is

THERE IS NO SUCH THING IN THE BIBLE AS "THE OLD TESTAMENT" OR "THE NEW TESTAMENT." THE TERMS COME FROM AN ENGLISH TRANSLITERATION OF A LATIN MISTRANSLATION OF A GREEK QUOTATION OF A HEBREW TEXT.

a simple, little, fatal flaw that runs through the entire foundation of every Christian theology.

Sometimes I feel that the focus of my life is dead issues, issues that, for everyone else, have been laid to rest long ago. There are not a lot of advantages to such a focus, other than the lack of competition. There is, however, a lot of resistance to any attempt to give life to the dead.

Now just lie down, and make yourself comfortable on this hygienically clean operating table. I'm going to connect one of these high power cables to your brain, and the other to your heart. If this experiment works, you will soon have a different mind, and your heart will beat in the strange rhythm determined by the Great Physician. Your arms and legs may twitch for a while, and your tongue may start to say things that don't make sense to other people, but don't let it bother you. Anything for science. Welcome to Dr. Frankenstein's neighborhood Bible club.

*"Dearly beloved, we are gathered here today to read the last will and testament of the late..."*
Everybody knows that the Bible is composed of the Old Testament and the New Testament. But what everyone does not know is that there is no such thing in the Bible as "the Old

Testament" or "the New Testament". The terms come from an English transliteration of a Latin mistranslation of a Greek quotation of a Hebrew text.

The Vulgate translation was begun in 382 C.E., when Pope Damascus I commissioned Jerome to prepare a Latin Bible with the Apocrypha. The purpose was to replace the poorly translated Old Latin versions. The completed Vulgate text also has some poorly translated passages, and, consequently, some serious problems. Some of these problems have plagued Christianity ever since.

In the time of Jeremiah, God promised that He would "cut a new covenant/*brit*/*diatheke* with the house of Israel and with the house of Judah, not like the covenant/*brit*/*diatheke* which I cut with their fathers..." (Jer. 31:31-32/38:31-32LXX) In Hebrews 8:8-9, these verses are quoted, verbatim, from the Septuagint.

In Jer. 31:31-32, the Latin Vulgate accurately translates the Greek of the Septuagint. The Vulgate has *foedus novum non secundum pactum*, meaning "a new alliance not in accordance with the covenant..."[1] In translating these verses in Jeremiah, the Latin Vulgate is faithful to the Greek text, and is therefore faithful to the original Hebrew text, where the word *brit*, i.e. covenant, is used. It is, however, a little strange that in the first part of the verse the Vulgate translators translated *brit* as *foedus*, i.e. alliance, and four words later they translated *brit* as *pactum*, i.e. covenant, even though the text presents the same word in the same context in an obvious comparison. Either Latin word would have been correct to translate the one Hebrew word that appears twice.

In Hebrews 8:8-9, which quotes exactly the same Greek words, the Latin Vulgate significantly distorts the text. Almost every current translation adopts the Latin distortion in its text, its title, or both. So we have English (or Spanish, or French, or Russian, or pick a language) translations that reproduce the incorrect Latin translation of a Greek translation of a Hebrew original.

This mistranslation affects more than a word, a verse, or a chapter. It is the false foundation for most systems of interpretation in Christian theology. It creates the false image of the "new" Scriptures superceding the "old" Scriptures. To the contrary, however, the Scriptures do not get old. The mistranslation of the text creates a false assumption, on which the various systems of interpretation are built.

In Hebrews 8:8-9. the Latin Vulgate speaks of God making "with the house of Israel and the house of Judah a new testament not in accordance with the testament I made with their fathers—*super domum Israhel et super domum Iuda testamentum novum non secundum testamentum quod feci patribus eorum*." The verses in Hebrews 8:8-9 are a direct quotation from Jeremiah 31:31-32. For some reason, the translators of the Vulgate abandoned the two correct Latin words they had used in Jeremiah 31:31-32, *foedus* and *pactum*, and switched to an incorrect word, *testamentum*, in translating the exact same Greek words when they are quoted in Hebrews 8:8-9.

*Testamentum* is used to translate the Greek word *diatheke*, which was used to translate the Hebrew word *brit*. In the Scriptures, *brit* and *diatheke* both mean "covenant". In classical or koine Greek, *diatheke* can mean "testament," but it never carries that meaning in the Jewish Greek of the Scriptures. In the more than 300 times that *diatheke* appears in the Seputagint, it NEVER means "testament". The translators of the Vulgate understood that, because they translated *diatheke* correctly in Jer. 31:31-32, the verses which are quoted verbatim in Heb. 8:8-9.

"Testament" is a completely different concept, one that is not found in either the Hebrew or the Greek text. In Latin, as well as in English, a testament is a last will, a solitary declaration of how to dispose of one's property after one's death. The Vulgate phrase—"I will make a new testament with the house of Israel and the house of Judah"—doesn't even mean anything. There is no such thing as making a testament with someone else. A testament is a solitary declaration.

A covenant, on the other hand, is a commitment made between those who are alive as to how they will treat each other while they live. The translators had difficulty understanding the text, because they did not approach it in its Jewish Greek context. Their strange mistranslation has had monumental theological and historical repercussions.

The use of "testament" in the text hides the fact that God is making a new covenant with Israel. The mistranslation enables virtually all Christian theologians to ignore both the actual new covenant and the faithfulness of God, which is the reason for the new covenant. Calvin, for example, wrote one and a half million words in his *Institutes of the Christian Religion*, but did not see any need, or any way, to discuss God's new covenant with Israel. That is because the new covenant, being made with the Jewish people, could not be fit into his Christian religion.

That is why Christian theologians ignore the text of the new covenant which Messiah brought. The use of "testament" in translations helps legitimize the practice of ignoring the text. In a later chapter, we will examine the text of the New Covenant. Here we are examining the word "testament" as a foundational failure to read the Scriptures in their Jewish context.

The use of "testament" in the titles of the two parts of the Bible—the "New Testament" and the "Old Testament"—presents an imaginary conflict between the two parts. It fuels the illusion that Tanakh, the foundational part of the Scriptures, has passed away. And whereas the new covenant is a demonstration of God's faithfulness to Israel, the "New Testament" becomes for many a declaration that God has rejected Israel.

The terms "New Testament" and "Old Testament" convey a lot of theology. The terms are only theological ones, not Biblical ones. There is no "new testament" mentioned in the Bible.

Nor is there any "old testament" mentioned in the Bible. The Bible doesn't have anything at all to say about testaments, and the Bible is not divided into testaments.

Virtually all translators follow the error of the Vulgate. In some cases, the translators have simply not grasped the text in its Jewish Greek context. In other cases, the translators have chosen to follow tradition rather than the text. And in almost all cases, even when the translators have rejected the incorrect "testament" of the Vulgate, they still have retained this grossly incorrect designations for the two parts of the Bible. These errors feed and support some very bad theology. And since people act in response to what they actually believe, these errors have led to some very painful history.

The error in the Vulgate, and in all translations which follow it, actually comes from a misunderstanding of Hebrews 9:15-18. We will examine this passage, and the two major reasons why "testament" is completely incorrect.

1. Hebrews 9:15-18, the key passage that is misunderstood and misinterpreted, is not about testaments, but about covenants.
2. The old covenant and the new covenant are covenants, not books of the Bible.

## 1. Hebrews 9:15-18 is not about testaments, but about covenants.

Here is the King James Version, which is essentially reproduced by many other translations.

v. 15 And for this cause he [Jesus] is the mediator of the new testament, that by means of death, for the redemption of the transgressions that were under the first testament, they which are called might receive the promise of eternal inheritance.

v. 16 For where a testament is, there must also of necessity be the death of the testator.

v. 17 For a testament is of force after men are dead: otherwise it is of no strength at all while the testator liveth.

v. 18 Whereupon neither the first testament was dedicated without blood.

There are several problems with this translation. The first concerns the phrase, "the mediator of a new testament". No such thing exists. A mediator is one who serves to bring agreement or reconciliation between different parties. A testament, on the other hand, is the declaration of one individual. There is no mediator involved in the solitary issuance of a testament. There can only be a mediator when there are two or more parties involved.

The words that the author of Hebrews used in this verse, *diathekes mesites*, translated in the KJV as "the mediator of a testament," are the same words the author of Hebrews used in Heb. 8:6. In that verse, the KJV translates these same words as, "the mediator of a covenant". The statements in the two verses clearly refer to the same thing: "he is the mediator of a better covenant," and "he is the mediator of a new covenant".

The same words are used in Heb. 12:24 to speak of "Yeshua, the mediator of a new covenant." Paul uses the same word word for mediator, *mesites*, when he tells Timothy, "For there is one God and one mediator between God and men, the man Yeshua the Messiah." (1 Tim. 2:5) Yeshua is the mediator of the new covenant between God and the men with whom it is made.

The word appears in the Septuagint where Job complains of the inaccessibility of the God who has wronged him. "If only there were a mediator between us, to lay his hand upon us both." (Job 9:33) As Paul explained in Gal. 3:20, speaking of the Covenant of the Law, "A mediator, however, does not represent just one party; but God is one." There is no mediator for a testament, because there is only one individual issuing a testament.

The second problem with the translation concerns the phrase "the first testament," which appears in verses 15 and 18. Again, no such thing exists. To what does it refer? In Heb. 8:7, the KJV has "For if that first covenant had been faultless, then should no place have been sought for the second." A comparison is being made between the covenant of the Law, which God made with Israel at Sinai, i.e. the first covenant, and the new covenant, which God made with Israel in Yeshua, i.e. the second covenant. The comparison between these two covenants is made throughout the entire context that surrounds Heb. 9:15-18.

Heb. 6:20-8:6 presents a discussion of the superiority of the priesthood of Melchizedek, the priesthood in which Yeshua serves as the New Covenant High Priest, to that of Aaron, the priesthood of the Old Covenant.

Heb. 8:6-12 explains that Yeshua is the mediator of the New Covenant between God and Israel; and presents the text of that New Covenant, which God promised in Jer. 31:31-34.

Heb. 8:13-9:8 compares the covenants in terms of the sanctuary and access to it.

Heb. 9:9-14 compares the sacrifices of the Old Covenant—goats, bulls, and heifers—to the one sacrifice of the New Covenant—the voluntary death of Yeshua.

Heb. 9:19-10:22 continues this comparison of the sacrifices, focusing on the blood of the sacrifice that inaugurates each covenant, and what it has the power to accomplish.

Heb. 10:23-39 is an exhortation to stand firm in the faith, because the punishment for breaking the New Covenant will be greater than the punishment for breaking the Old Covenant.

This entire section, from Heb. 6:20 to 10:39, is a comparison between the Covenant of the Law and the New Covenant. There is no discussion of a testament. There is no "first testament" mentioned; there is no second, or new, testament mentioned. A "testament" is completely unrelated to the cleansing and purification brought by the sacrifices in the different covenants. A testament does not require a sacrifice.

To inaugurate the Covenant of the Law, Moses sacrificed animals. He then sprinkled their blood on the people of Israel, saying, "This is the blood of the covenant..." (Ex. 24:8) In Exodus 24:8, the KJV records this correctly, but in Hebrews 9:20, which quotes these very words, it changes the text to, "This is the blood of the testament..." Moses spoke about a covenant, not a testament.

Heb. 9:18 refers to this event. The KJV mistranslates the verse: "Whereupon neither the first testament was dedicated without blood." (KJV) The reference is not to any "first testament," but to a first covenant.

There is no first "testament" in the Scriptures. The covenant which God made at Sinai with Israel did not contain anyone's last will and testament. Animals were put to death to establish the covenant. They did not leave a last will and testament. The Scriptures never speak of the covenant at Sinai as a testament—neither the term nor the concept. The covenant at Sinai, made between God and Israel, was put into effect as a defining aspect of God's living relationship with Israel. It is not the testament of anyone.

This is not a matter of interpretation; it is a matter of accurate translation. "Covenant" is correct; "Testament" is not. There is no "first testament" in the Bible. There is no "old testament" in the Bible. Consequently, there cannot be a new testament. There is nothing anywhere in the Bible about a testament.

The NASV, which some consider to be the most accurate modern English translation, takes a different approach to the text.[2] The translators of the NASV recognized that the Greek word *diatheke* should be translated in Heb. 9:15-18 as "covenant," the same way it is translated in every other place it appears in the Scriptures. So that is what they did. But that led to other very serious errors in the NASV, all because of the way a related word, *diathemenou*, is translated. It is the misunderstanding of this one word that caused the problem for the translators of the KJV and almost all the others.

Here is the NASV translation:

Heb.9:15 And for this reason He is the mediator of a new covenant, in order that since a death has taken place for the redemption of the transgressions that were committed under the first covenant, those who have been called may receive the promise of the eternal inheritance.

v. 16 For where a covenant is, there must of necessity be the death of the one who made it.

v. 17 For a covenant is valid only when men are dead, for it is never in force while the one who made it lives.

v. 18 Therefore even the first covenant was not inaugurated without blood.

The errors here concern the concept of the death of "the one who made it [the covenant]." That is the way *diathemenou* is translated in the NASV in verses 16 and 17. [In the KJV, it is translated as "testator".] This error leads to another error in verse 17. *Epi nekrois*, which literally means "over dead bodies," is incorrectly translated as "when men are dead". Here are some of the reasons why this translation is still in error.

1. There is no such thing as "the one who made it." A covenant is made between different parties. It is not a solitary declaration. There must be at least two "who made it."

2. If there is only one who makes the covenant, then there cannot be a "mediator," which is what Messiah is called in verse 15. A mediator functions between two or more parties.

3. The NASV translation of Heb. 9:16 is not a true statement. "For where a covenant is, there must of necessity be the death of the one who made it." This is not true. It was not true for God's covenant with Noah. Neither God nor Noah died to establish the covenant. It was not true of God's covenant with Abraham, nor of His covenant with David, nor of His covenant with Israel. The NASV rendering is not true for any covenant. It is a false statement.

4. The NASV translation of Heb. 9:17 is not a true statement. "For a covenant is valid only when men are dead, for it is never in force while the one who made it lives." This is not true. It is the opposite of the truth. A covenant establishes a relationship between the living. If those whom the covenant binds are dead, then the covenant is of no effect.

Furthermore, since there must be at least two parties involved to make a covenant, which "one" of the parties, according to the NASV, needs to die? Or do all the parties to a covenant have to die for it to be in effect? To the contrary, however, the death of the parties would not put the covenant into effect; it would make the present and future fulfillment of the covenant impossible.

*'Are you saying that the Bible isn't true?'*

No. I'm saying that the translation isn't true; and it isn't true to the Bible either.

5. Heb. 9:15 speaks of Messiah as the mediator of the new covenant. That means that Messiah is not the maker of the covenant. He is the mediator between the parties making the covenant. The parties to the New Covenant, as presented in Jeremiah 31:31-34/Hebrews 8:8-12, are God and the house of Israel. The death of Messiah, therefore, would not satisfy the condition of the NASV translation. It would only be the death of the mediator, not "the death of the one who made it."

6. The Messianic Writings do speak of an "inheritance" for those who are faithful to God, but they always use a word, *kleronomia*, which is completely unrelated to *diatheke*. Forms of the word appear about 50 times in the Messianic Writings. (e.g. Mt.5:5; Mt.19:29; Lk.12:13; Eph. 3:6) They appear 10 times in Hebrews, including Heb. 9:15 and the related verses of 1:14, 6:12, 6:17; 11:8, and 11:9.

*Kleronomia* is also the word that is used in the Septuagint, the Greek Scriptures from which the writer of Hebrews quotes. (e.g. Num. 18:23; 2Chr. 31:1) "A good man leaves an inheritance/*kleronomesei* for his children's children, but a sinner's wealth is stored up for the righteous." (Prov. 13:22)

Yeshua told the parable about the master of the vineyard and his rebellious tenant farmers. In the parable, Yeshua presents himself as the beloved son of the master of the vineyard, sent to the rebellious tenant farmers to receive what they owe their master. "But the tenants said to one another, 'This is the heir/*kleronomos*. Come, let's kill him, and the inheritance/*kleronomia* will be ours.'" (Mk. 12:7)

So if the writer of Hebrews wanted to say "testament" rather than "covenant" in Heb. 9:16-17, he would have used *klerodotema*, not *diatheke*. If the writer of Hebrews wanted to say "testator" in Heb. 9:16-17, i.e. the one who makes a testament, he would have used *klerodotes*, not *diathemenou*.

The problem with all the standard translations stems from their mistranslation of *diathemenou*. "The one who makes the covenant" is a logical and contextual impossibility. It doesn't mean anything, since there must be at least two who make a covenant; and it doesn't relate to anything that is being discussed. "The one who makes a testament" is even worse, introducing a concept that is completely unrelated to, and inconsistent with, the discussion.

The entire argument in Hebrews is based on what is readily apparent concerning the covenant of the Law. The argument must, therefore, make sense in terms of both the covenant of the Law and the New Covenant. Otherwise, the argument would prove nothing, and would be pointless.

In the context, *diathemenou* (in vv. 16-17) is logically connected to the sacrificed Messiah (*Christou* in vv.14-15), the dead bodies (*nekrois* in v.17), and the sacrificed calves (*moschon* in v.19). These all speak of the death that confirms a covenant.

Verses 16-17 provide the reason for what is stated in v.18: "This is why even the first was not put into effect without blood." "The first" clearly refers to the first *diatheke*. According to vv.19-20, that *diatheke* involved Moses. In this passage, we are given a very simple statement: because a *diatheke* only goes into effect over dead bodies/*epi nekrois*, the calves were put to death to affirm the *diatheke* at Sinai. That *diatheke* is clearly a covenant, the first covenant, not a testament.

There is an accurate, literal way to translate *diathemenou*, a way that makes sense in terms of the argument being presented in Hebrews. It also makes sense in terms of the covenant of the Law and the New Covenant. It is both logically and contextually appropriate. The Jewish Greek word, *diathemenou*, should not be translated as "the one who makes the covenant," but rather as, "the thing that makes the covenant," or, more simply, "what establishes (or confirms) the covenant."

Here is how the text should be translated:

Heb.9:15 For this reason he is the mediator of a new covenant, since a death has occurred for the redemption of the transgressions under the first covenant, that those who have been called might receive the promise of the eternal inheritance.

v. 16 For where there is a covenant, the death of what confirms the covenant must be presented.

v. 17 For a covenant is confirmed over dead bodies, for it is never in force while what confirms the covenant lives.

v. 18 Therefore even the first covenant has not been established without blood.

This translation is literal. It makes sense, and it makes a point, a point that is true: Messiah had to die to establish the new covenant. It is compatible and consistent with the immediately preceding context, the immediately following context, and the entire Bible.

In his literal translation of the Scriptures, Robert Young, compiler of the Analytical Concordance that bears his name, translated *diathemenou* as "covenant victim." This gives the same consistent sense as that which is presented here.

This is the same consistent sense that is presented throughout Hebrews. There is a comparison between God's Old Covenant with Israel and God's New Covenant with Israel. In the section we have been looking at, the comparison is between the sacrifice which established God's Old Covenant and the sacrifice which established God's New Covenant with Israel.

This comparison is repeated at the end of the letter, in the last thing that is said about this topic. "The high priest carries the blood of animals into the Most Holy Place as a sin offering, but the bodies are burned outside the camp. And so Yeshua also suffered outside the city gate to make the people holy through his own blood." (Hebr. 13:11-12)

Why have almost all the translators throughout the centuries followed the mistranslation of the Latin Vulgate instead of the actual text in context? Why have they not grasped that "the letter to the Hebrews" must be read and understood in its Hebrew Biblical context? Why? Because they are experts within the system.

This simple mistranslation, misrepresentation, and misunderstanding is foundational to virtually every Christian theology. It creates the illusion of a conflict within the Bible itself.

## 2. The old covenant and the new covenant are covenants, not books of the Bible.

A major problem in approaching and understanding the Bible developed in the latter part of the second century. It was then that the Greek term "Old Covenant" was first used to refer to the first thirty-nine books of the Bible.[3] It was then that the term "New Covenant" was first used to refer to the last 27 books of the Bible.[4]

When the Messianic Writings refer to "the Old Covenant," "the first Covenant," or "the former Covenant," the reference is not to the first 39 books of the Bible, but to the Covenant of the Law. The "New Covenant," or "the second Covenant," is the agreement that God made with Israel through Yeshua. It is not the last 27 books of the Bible. The terms of the New Covenant are given in Jeremiah 31:31-34, and are quoted verbatim (from the Septuagint) in Heb. 8:8-12. The New Covenant declares God's faithfulness despite Israel's unfaithfulness.

**THIS SIMPLE MISTRANSLATION, MISREPRESENTATION AND MISUNDERSTANDING IS FOUNDATIONAL TO VIRTUALLY EVERY CHRISTIAN THEOLOGY. IT CREATES THE ILLUSION OF A CONFLICT WITHIN THE BIBLE ITSELF.**

The ancient Jewish custom, in effect at the time of Yeshua and still in effect today, was to divide the five books of Moses into smaller sections which were read sequentially through the year on Shabbat. In the course of a year, therefore, one reads through the five books of Moses. This practice is attested in Acts 15:21: "For Moses has been proclaimed in every city from the earliest times and is read in the meetingplaces on every Sabbath." [A corresponding portion from the Writings or the Prophets was also read. cf. Lk.4:16-20]

The Covenant of the Law was written down; and all of it is contained within the five books of Moses—actually just in the last four, since the covenant was not made until after the exodus from Egypt. Each of those four books also contains other material which is not part of the Covenant of the Law—genealogies, complaints, wanderings, battles, etc.

The Hebrew word *brit* appears about 300 times in Tanakh. It always refers to a covenant, never to a set of books or writings. In most cases, however, the covenant referred to had been written down and could be read.

The Greek word *diatheke* appears about 30 times in the Messianic Writings. There it also always refers to a covenant, never to a set of books or writings. It is used to refer to God's covenants with Abraham, the Covenant of the Law, and the New Covenant.

There is no verse in the Bible that comes remotely close to equating *brit* or *diatheke* with the books of the Bible. The equation is a theological one, not a Biblical one. There is one pair of verses that may have confused some.

Here are the verses. "But their minds were made dull, for to this day the same veil remains when the old covenant is read. It has not been removed, because only in Messiah is it taken away. Even to this day when Moses is read, a veil covers their hearts." (2Cor. 3:14-15)

Paul uses two expressions here: "when the old covenant is read," and "when Moses is read." He is referring to the common Jewish practice of reading through the five books of Moses in the course of every year.

The five books of Moses contain the history of creation and the history of Adam and his descendants. They contain God's choice of Abraham, Isaac, and Jacob/Israel. They contain the history of the descendants of Jacob, including their going down to Egypt, their affliction there, and their deliverance. They contain the history of the years in the wilderness before the conquest of Canaan.

They also contain the Covenant of the Law which God made with Israel after the deliverance from Egypt. In the course of reading the books of Moses, we read the text of the Covenant of the Law. That covenant, by virtue of God's use of "new covenant" in Jeremiah 31, becomes the "old covenant" when the new covenant is introduced.

The context of 2 Corinthians 3:14-15 makes it clear that this is Paul's subject. "He also made us competent as servants of a new covenant, not by what is written, but by spirit. For what is written condemns to death, but the spirit gives life. But if, in writing engraved in stones, what served to bring death came with glory, so that the children of Israel could not look steadfastly on the face of Moses because of the glory of his face, which was passing away, will not what brings the Spirit be with much more glory?" (2Cor. 3:6-8)

The old covenant is engraved "in letters in stones," but the new covenant is not. Moses told Israel that God "declared to you His covenant, the Ten Commandments, which He commanded you to follow and then wrote them on two stone tablets." (Dt. 4:13, cf. Ex. 31:18; 32:16)

Paul's reference to the glory of the face of Moses is specific to the descent of Moses from Mount Sinai, with the stone tablets on which the Covenant of the Law was written. "When Moses came down from Mount Sinai with the two tablets of the testimony in his hands, he was not aware that his face was radiant because he had spoken with the LORD. When Aaron and all the descendants of Israel saw Moses, his face was radiant, and they were afraid to come near him." (Ex. 34:29-30)

The first 39 books of the Bible were not engraved in stone, but the core of the Covenant of the Law was. The new covenant was written on parchment by Jeremiah, or more likely by Baruch, his scribe. It stipulates that God's law be written by God's Spirit upon the tablets of the heart. God does not use "old covenant" and "new covenant" to refer to the two parts of the Bible.

The misapplication of these terms, "old covenant" and "new covenant," to designate the books of the Bible causes people to think that the word of God passes away, even though God Himself explicitly denied that possibility. (cf. Is. 40:8) It causes people to think that Yeshua annulled the Law and the Prophets, even though Yeshua himself explicitly denied that he came to do that. (cf. Mt. 5:17-19)

It causes people to think that the good news is incompatible with the Law, the Writings, and the Prophets, even though the apostles proclaimed the good news from the Law, the Writings, and the Prophets. It causes people to ignore the Law, the Writings, and the Prophets, even though it is precisely these that Paul says are able "to give you the wisdom that leads to salvation through faith which is in Yeshua the Messiah. All Scripture is breathed by God and profitable for teaching, for reproof, for correction, for training in righteousness, that the man of God may be adequate, equipped for every good work." (2Tim.3:17) Paul was referring to the only Scriptures there were, Tanakh.

Because the Law of God is contained within the Covenant of the Law, such misuse and misapplication causes people to think that the Law of God has passed away, and that only the laws

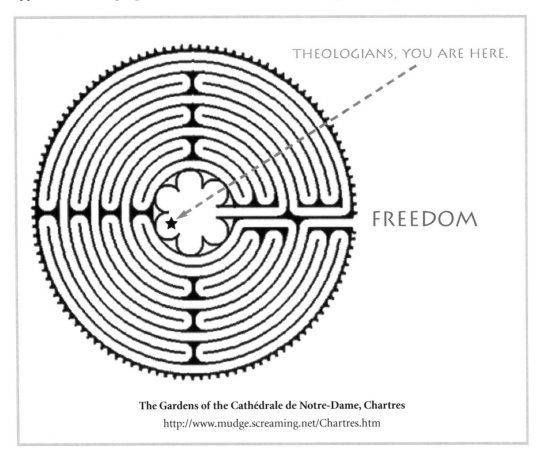

**The Gardens of the Cathédrale de Notre-Dame, Chartres**
http://www.mudge.screaming.net/Chartres.htm

of men need to be obeyed. The Law of God, both what is particular to Israel and what is universal for all people, is spiritual. (Rom. 7:14) It was given by the Spirit of God. It does not pass away.

The use of "testament" instead of "covenant" also obscures the reality that the New Covenant is between God and Israel. The astronomers created the illusion of a two-sphere universe, where different laws prevail in each sphere. This simple, little error of the theologians goes a long way towards doing the same.

It still is helpful to have names for these two parts of the Bible, though not the traditional names. The Law, the Prophets, and the Writings are adequately designated by the acronym TaNaKh, formed from the first letter of each Hebrew designation—Torah, Neviim, Ketuvim.

I have made a corresponding Hebrew acronym for the writings about Yeshua, writings which have been erroneously called the "New Testament". *BaMaShIaKh* is formed from *Besorot* (accounts of the good news), *Maasei haShalihim* (acts of those sent), *Yediot l'talmidim* (instructions for followers), and *Khazon* (vision). This is a book, therefore, of *Ketuvim BaMashiakh*, i.e. "writings in Messiah," or "Messianic Writings."

It may be that a better designation is possible, and you are certainly welcome to try, but at least this one is accurate. "Old Testament" and "New Testament" are both inaccurate and misleading. There is no "Old Testament" in the Bible. There is no "New Testament" in the Bible. They are imaginary constructs, which obscure the textual reality.

So I hope you all will come back next chapter for another meeting of our little neighborhood Bible club. If Dr. Frankenstein makes you nervous, just think of our little experiments in raising the dead as preparation for the resurrection. Be sure to invite your friends.

FOOTNOTES

1. *Foedus* is "a league, treaty, compact, or alliance." *Pactum* is an agreement, covenant, contract, stipulation, compact, or pact." http://www.perseus.tufts.edu/cgi-bin/morphindex?lang=la

2. The NIV, which may be the most widely used modern English translation, translates *diatheke* as "covenant" in verses 15 and 18, and as "will" in verses 16 and 17. In every other place, the NIV translates *diatheke* as "covenant". Consequently, though "will" is also incorrect, the word "testament" does not appear anywhere in the entire NIV Biblical text. But it was still retained as the traditional designation for the two parts of the Bible.

3. Melito of Sardis, *On Pascha and Fragments*, edited by Stuart George Hall, Oxford Clarendon Press, 1979, p. xxx

4. W.C. van Unnik, "Η καινη διαθηκη—A Problem in the Early History of the Canon," *Studia Patristica, Vol. IV*, Berlin, 1961, P.214, citing J.N.D. Kelly, Early Christian Doctrines, London, 1958, p.56

CHAPTER FOUR

# A Good Church is Hard to Find

*There is No Church in the Bible*

**I** was talking with a Jesuit priest in Krakow. I had met him ten years earlier on the recommendation of a friend who said that this man had a heart for Israel and the Jewish people. We hadn't had much time to talk on that first occasion. This time we had a very good two hour discussion.

At one point, he said to me, "What you are saying moves me very much, but I can tell that you are not speaking from within the Church. Where are you speaking from?"

I responded, "If I tell you that *ekklesia* is simply the Jewish Greek word used for *kahal*, do you understand what I mean?"

"Yes," he answered.

Very few people would have responded that way. The *ekklesia* is the center of what God is doing in the earth. In Christian theology, the Church is the *ekklesia*. This Jesuit priest was recognizing that the Biblical *ekklesia* is the *kahal* presented in Tanakh. The *ekklesia* is what contains all the redeemed, whether Jewish or Gentile.

*'What do these words mean? What are you talking about?'*

Be patient, and I'll try to explain. Maybe I also need to adjust those two high power cables.

We will start with the Hebrew words in Tanakh that are used to designate the community of Israel. Then we will examine the Greek words used in the Septuagint to translate these Hebrew words. Since the Septuagint is the main source used in the Messianic Writings for Greek quotations from Tanakh, we will then look at how these Greek words are used in the Messianic Writings.

This will bring us to a discussion of proper and improper English translation of these words as they appear in the Messianic Writings. Traditionally, these words are systematically mistranslated. Also traditionally, theologians use the classic Greek definition, rather than the normal Jewish Greek usage found in the Scriptures. It is the normal Jewish Greek usage that will bring us to the identity of the Biblical *ekklesia*.

## *EDAH* IN TANAKH

There are two Hebrew words that are used equally in Tanakh to indicate the community of Israel as a whole or an assembly or group of some kind. The words are *edah* and *kahal*. We will be more interested in *kahal*, because of the different ways in which it is translated into Greek. Both words are, however, used equally as often, and with much the same meaning. For example, in Prov. 5:14, we find both words used to designate exactly the same thing. "I was almost in utter ruin in the midst of the *kahal* and *edah*."

There is one thing worth mentioning here, whose significance we will examine later in detail. In this verse, the Septuagint translates *kahal* as *ekklesia*, and *edah* as *sunagoge* —"I was almost in utter ruin in the midst of the *ekklesia (kahal)* and *sunagoge (edah)*."

The Hebrew word *edah* is almost always translated in the Septuagint as *sunagoge*.[1] *Sunagoge* is the Greek word from which the English "synagogue" comes. In the first century, however, *sunagoge* did not mean "synagogue," i.e. a specifically Jewish, religious meetingplace. It was a common word that meant "gathering." Forms of the same root appear in the Septuagint in diverse places such as:

Gen. 1:9 "Let the waters below the heavens be gathered/*sunagogen*..."

Ex. 12:3 "Speak to all the congregation/*sunagogen* of Israel..."

Ex. 23:6 "... when you gather/*sunagoge* in your work from your field."

*Edah* is used to designate the group of 250 men who followed Korah in rebellion. (cf. Num. 26:10; 27:3) Primarily, however, it is used in numerous passages to describe all of Israel, such as when the Lord told Moses, to "gather the entire *edah* at the entrance to the Tent of Meeting." (Lev. 8:3) In this verse, the Hebrew word translated as "gather" is *ha'kahel*.

The Hebrew phrase *ha'kahel et ha'edah* meant "gather the congregation." The Septuagint translates this by the Greek phrase *sunagogen ekklesiason*. This Greek phrase uses the verb form of *ekklesia* for *ha'kahel*, and *sunagoge* for *edah*. Such phrases would be very strange combinations if the Greek words had then the meaning that they have now.

In Num. 1:18, we read, "and they assembled the whole congregation together on the first day of the second month...." The Hebrew phrase which is translated as "they assembled the whole congregation" is *kal ha'edah hik'hilu*. The Septuagint translates the Hebrew as *sunagogen sunegagon*. In this case, *edah* and the form of *kahal* are translated by essentially identical Greek terms. That is often the case in the Septuagint.

## *KAHAL* IN TANAKH

The word *kahal* is used in Tanakh to designate a community, an assembly of the community, or an association of different communities. Below are some examples of each kind of usage.

**A community:**

"Simeon and Levi are brothers—their swords are weapons of violence... let me not join their *kahal*..." (Gen. 49:5-6)

"No one is to be in the Tent of Meeting from the time Aaron goes in to make atonement in the Most Holy Place until he comes out, having made atonement for himself, his household and the whole *kahal* of Israel." (Lev. 16:17)

"But if a person who is unclean does not purify himself, he must be cut off from the *kahal*, because he has defiled the sanctuary of the LORD. The water of cleansing has not been sprinkled on him, and he is unclean." (Num. 19:20)

"...the law that Moses gave us, the possession of the *kahal* of Jacob." (Dt. 33:4)

"The enemy laid hands on all her treasures; she saw Gentiles enter her sanctuary—those You had forbidden to enter Your *kahal*." (Lam. 1:10)

**An assembly of the community:**

"The LORD wrote on these tablets what He had written before, the Ten Commandments He had proclaimed to you on the mountain, out of the midst of the fire, on the day of the *kahal*. And the LORD gave them to me." (Dt. 10:4)

Before he fought Goliath, David said to the Philistine army, "All this *kahal* will know that it is not by sword or spear that the LORD saves; for the battle is the LORD's, and He will give all of you into our hands." (1Sam. 17:47)

"I will give You thanks in the great *kahal*; among throngs of people I will praise You." (Ps. 35:18)

"I proclaimed Your righteousness in the great *kahal*. Behold, You know, O LORD, my lips did not conceal it." (Ps. 40:10/9E)

To protect Jeremiah from death, "Some of the elders of the land stepped forward and said to the entire *kahal* of people..." (Jer. 26:17)

**An association of different communities:**

Isaac said to Jacob, "May God Almighty bless you and make you fruitful and make you numerous until you become a *kahal* of peoples." (Gen. 28:3)

"And God said to him, 'I am God Almighty. Be fruitful and increase in number. A nation and a *kahal* of nations/*goyim* will come from you, and kings will come from your loins.'" (Gen. 35:11)

"And Jacob told Joseph, 'God... said to me, "Behold, I will make you fruitful and will increase your numbers. I will give you to be a *kahal* of peoples, and I will give this land to your descendants after you as an everlasting possession."'" (Gen. 48:4)

God promised judgment, "For I will stir up and bring against Babylon a *kahal* of great nations/*goyim* from the land of the north." (Jer. 50:9)

In the Septuagint, *kahal* is translated alternately by the synonymous Greek words—*sunagoge* and *ekklesia*. The words simply meant "meeting," "gathering," "community," or "assembly." Neither word in itself contained any religious meaning or connotation. Neither word was connected with any particular people group.

In standard Greek texts, *sunagoge* was used in a variety of ways to mean "a gathering". Plato used it to mean "a bringing together or uniting," or "forming an army in a column." Thucydides used the word in the sense of mustering an army for war. Polybius used *sunagoge* for "a gathering in of harvest." Aristotle used it for "a collection of writings."[2]

In standard Greek texts, *ekklesia* is simply an assembly. Herodotus and Thucydides used it this way. Thucydides and others also used *ekklesia* to designate "an assembly of the citizens regularly summoned, i.e. the legislative assembly." In Athens, there were two types of *ekklesiai*, the ordinary (*kuriai*) and the extraordinary (*sugkletoi*).[3]

It is important to understand that, in Jewish Greek texts, *ekklesia* is not used with the standard legal meaning. As William Smith observed, in his *Bible Dictionary*, "Ecclesia... originally meant an assembly called out by the magistrate, or by legitimate authority. This is the ordinary classical sense of the word. But it throws no light on the nature of the institution so designated in the New Testament. For to the writers of the N.T. the word had now lost its primary signification, and was either used generally for any meeting (Acts xix. 32), or

> IN THE SEPTUAGINT, *KAHAL* IS TRANSLATED ALTERNATELY BY THE SYNONYMOUS GREEK WORDS—*SUNAGOGE* AND *EKKLESIA*. THE WORDS SIMPLY MEANT "MEETING," "GATHERING," "COMMUNITY" OR "ASSEMBLY."

more particularly, it denoted (1) the religious assemblies of the Jews (Dt. iv. 10, xviii. 16); (2) the whole assembly or congregation of the Israelitish people (Acts vii. 38; Heb. ii. 12; Ps. xxii. 22; Dt. xxxi. 30)."[7]

Smith is basically correct in observing that for "the writers of the N.T. the word had now lost its primary signification." In Jewish Greek, however, the word had never had the primary signification that it had in standard Greek. In Jewish Greek, *ekklesia* did not signify an institution, for, unless we call the people of Israel an institution, there was no such "called-out" institution in Israel that needed to be signified.

That is why the translators of the Septuagint could appropriate the word, without its primary signification, and use it in a straightforward manner for *kahal*. The "writers of the N.T." used *ekklesia* as Jews had used it in the Septuagint and in the following centuries. Proper theology, or ecclesiology, must be built upon the usage of *ekklesia* in the Scriptures, not upon the standard Greek meaning.

Similarly, the scriptural meaning of *sunagoge* must come from the way the word is used in the Scriptures. The Septuagint translators used *sunagoge* for *kahal* in, for example, Gen. 28:3, 35:11, 48:4; Ex. 12:6; Lev. 4:13, 16:17; Num. 19:20; Dt. 33:4; and Ps. 40:10 (which is actually Ps. 39:10 in their Greek text). It did not connote or imply anything Jewish. Everywhere in the Greek world, every people had their *sunagogai*, i.e. their meetings and meeting places.

The Septuagint translators used *ekklesia* for *kahal* in, for example, Dt. 23:2-4; Ezra 10:8; Lam. 1:10; and Ps. 35:18 (which is actually Ps. 34:18 in their Greek text). *Ekklesia* is the Greek word that people today translate as "church." That was not its meaning in the first century. It was not a Christian word, nor even a religious word. It did not connote or imply anything Christian. Indeed, at the time of the Septuagint, nothing "Christian" existed. Everywhere in the Greek world, every people had their *ekklesiai*, i.e. their meetings and meeting places.

"'Vanity of vanities,' says the *kohelet*. 'Vanity of vanities, all is vanity.'" (Eccl. 1:2) The *kohelet* is one who speaks to the *kahal*. In the Jewish Greek of the Septuagint, this becomes the ekklesiastes, who speaks to the *ekklesia*. "Ecclesiastes," the common name of the Biblical book, is the Latin transliteration of the Septuagint Jewish Greek translation of *kohelet*.

In the Jewish Greek of the Scriptures, *sunagoge* and *ekklesia* were considered equivalent terms for the same thing. They were synonyms. This can be seen in the Septuagint translation of Ps. 35:18 (Ps. 34:18 in Greek) and Ps. 40:10 (Ps. 39:10 in Greek). In Hebrew, both verses use *kahal*. In the Septuagint Greek, *kahal* in Ps. 34:18 is translated as *ekklesia*. "I will give thanks to You even in a great *ekklesia*; in an abundant people I will praise You." In the Septuagint Greek, *kahal* in Ps. 39:10 is translated as *sunagoge*. "I have not hidden Your truth within my heart, and I have declared Your salvation; I have not hidden Your mercy and Your truth from the great *sunagoge*."

The original two verses refer to the same thing. In the Septuagint, the two verses still refer to the same thing, but different, synonymous words were used. "Thus the use of εκκλησια [ekklesia] for קהל [kahal] and συναγωγη [sunagoge] for עדה [edah] in LXX Psalms are not a reflection of distinctions in meaning between either the Hebrew or the Greek words but the result of a conscious stereotyping policy.... The outcome was so-called lexical Hebraisms that 'do not function as ordinary Greek words possessing Greek meanings, but rather as... mere symbols representing Hebrew words.'"[4] The Hebrew words contained the reality; the Greek words symbolized that reality. It bears repeating that, at the time of the Septuagint, neither *sunagoge* nor *ekklesia* by itself contained any religious meaning at all. There were *sunagogai* and *ekklesiai* that had no connection with anything religious at all. Neither word designated anything that was particular to any specific people or group.

## SUNAGOGE IN THE MESSIANIC WRITINGS

This same non-religious usage of *sunagoge* and *ekklesia* as equivalent to each other and as basically interchangeable Greek translations of *kahal* continues in the Messianic Writings. This is to be expected, because the authors of the Messianic Writings built upon the Law, the Writings, and the Prophets. And since, for the most part, the Messianic Writings were written in Greek, the authors often drew from the text of the Septuagint, the Greek translation of Tanakh.

In the Messianic Writings, there are many passages where forms of the root word are used in its general meaning. Here are a few from Matthew. "Gathering together/*sunagagon* all the chief priests and scribes of the people, he asked them where the Messiah was to be born." (Mt. 2:4)

"Let both grow together until the harvest. At that time I will tell the harvesters: 'First collect the weeds and tie them in bundles to be burned; then gather together/*sunagagete* the wheat into my barn.'" (Mt. 13:30)

"Once again, the kingdom of heaven is like a net that was let down into the lake and gathered/*sunagagouse* all kinds of fish." (Mt. 13:47)

The specific word, *sunagoge*, appears about 50 times in the Messianic Writings. Its meaning seems to be weighted a little more towards a meetingplace, rather than just a meeting or gathering, but not completely. For example, in Acts 13:43, Luke says that, "When the *sunagoge* broke up, many of the Jews and devout proselytes followed Paul and Barnabas, who talked with them and urged them to continue in the grace of God." Since Luke does not mention either an earthquake, a riot, or an explosion, we can assume that it was not a building that broke up. It was a meeting. That is what *sunagoge* means in this verse.

Since the word today designates something that is specifically Jewish and specifically religious, people today assume that it carried that same designation at the time of Yeshua. We have already seen that it did not carry that meaning in the Greek world. Nor does it carry that meaning in the Messianic Writings. If we impose today's meaning on a first century text, we distort the text.

Consider the following passages in Acts: "When they were at Salamis, they proclaimed the word of God in the *sunagogai* of the Jews." (Acts 13:5a)

"At Iconium Paul and Barnabas went as usual into the *sunagoge* of the Jews." (Acts 14:1a)

"When they had passed through Amphipolis and Apollonia, they came to Thessalonica, where there was a *sunagoge* of the Jews." (Acts 17:1)

"As soon as it was night, the brothers sent Paul and Silas away to Berea. On arriving there, they went to the *sunagoge* of the Jews." (Acts 17:10)

For us today, the phrase "synagogue of the Jews" is redundant. For us today, any synagogue is "of the Jews," i.e. Jewish. But the Greek phrase which Luke used was not redundant for him or for his readers. The word *sunagoge* did not denote or imply anything Jewish. It did not even denote or imply anything religious. It just meant "meeting" or "meeting place". That is why Luke had to identify what kind of *sunagogai* they were going to. They were going to *sunagogai* of the Jews.

When the *sunagogai* of the Jews happened to be buildings, these buildings were used for many different purposes. "As documented in contemporary sources, the building might have been used as a courtroom, school, or hostel, or for political meetings, social gatherings, keeping charity funds, slave manumissions, meals (sacred or otherwise), and, of course, religious-liturgical functions."[5] They functioned as centers for the community.

**THE MODERN ASSUMPTION PRODUCES A DISTORTED TRANSLATION OF THE TEXT, AND IT TENDS TO BE AN ANTI-JUDAIC DISTORTION.**

There are other verses in the gospels where, in our translations, *sunagoge* is usually assumed to mean something specifically Jewish and religious, but the reference in the Greek text is actually generic and non-religious. The modern assumption produces a distorted translation of the text, and it tends to be an anti-Judaic distortion. This distortion of the text serves to reinforce the ancient tradition that displaces and replaces the Jewish people. In the Scriptures, *sunagoge* did not mean what we think when we hear or read "synagogue".

We'll look at a few portions of scripture to see how this takes place. The first of these portions records the instructions of Yeshua to the twelve whom he sent out. It is easy to see, however, that some of his instructions went beyond the immediate situation and extended to all future disciples.

"Be on your guard against men; they will hand you over to the local councils and whip you in their *sunagogai*. On my account you will be brought before governors and kings as witnesses to them and to the Gentiles. But when they arrest you, do not worry about what to say or how to say it. At that time you will be given what to say, for it will not be you speaking, but the Spirit of your Father speaking through you." (Mt. 10:17-20)

Luke 12:11-12 is a parallel portion. "When you are brought before *sunagogai*, rulers, and authorities, do not worry about how you will defend yourselves or what you will say, for the Holy Spirit will teach you at that time what you should say."

Later, in speaking to the disciples about the last days, Yeshua said something similar. "But before all this, they will lay hands on you and persecute you. They will deliver you to *sunagogai* and prisons, and you will be brought before kings and governors, and all on account of my name." (Luke 21:12)

What is Yeshua saying in these verses? He is saying that men will deliver his disciples to councils, assemblies, government officials, governors, and kings. When that happens, it will be an occasion for Yeshua's disciples to be witnesses to the Gentiles. The disciples will be arrested and also whipped.

It is worth noting that when the 12 were sent out, none of these things happened to them. In fact, Yeshua specifically told them not to go to the Gentiles. (Mt. 10:5) So it is evident that what Yeshua said looked beyond them and that particular mission to things that would happen throughout the world in the centuries until his return.

Paul and Silas, for example, were arrested, whipped, and jailed in Philippi. They were accused and arrested by Gentiles, and the decision to strip and beat them was given by Gentile magistrates. No Jews, except Paul and Silas, were involved. In fact, the accusation against Paul and Silas was that they were Jews who were advocating that Gentiles adopt Jewish practices. That is why they were beaten. (Acts 16:16-23)

Yeshua's exhortation in these sections of the gospels is to be wary of men, not specifically Jews, but rather men in general. Human governmental institutions and their leaders will persecute the disciples of Yeshua throughout the earth and throughout the age. This is what has happened, what is happening, and what will happen.

To translate *sunagogai* as "synagogues" is to misrepresent the text. For people today, "synagogues" are Jewish places of worship, but in the text, *sunagogai* have no specific connection to Jews or to places of worship. The word is used in conjunction with different forms of government.

The word in Mt. 10:17 which is translated as "councils," or "courts," is *sunedria*, which is transliterated in English as "sanhedrins". This also was a common Greek word for a common human institution—a regional governing council. At the time of Yeshua, a time when Greek was a common language for much of the world, *sunedria* did not carry any specific Jewish connotation. It was a Greek word used for what were Greek, or Roman, institutions. The Romans established *sunedria* in Judea for their own imperial purposes.

Xenophon used the word for "a body of men assembled in council, a council-board." Polybius used it for the "council of the Roman Senate." Herodotus used it to designate "a congress of allies or confederates."[6]

There are three things to keep in mind in understanding these portions of scripture. 1. At the time Yeshua was speaking, *sunagoge* did not carry any religious connotation at all. 2. The context of what Yeshua was saying makes it clear that he was not speaking of anything specifically Jewish. And, 3. Since Yeshua wasn't speaking Greek anyway, he didn't even say *sunagoge*.

He was most likely using the equally neutral Hebrew word, *kahal*. When the authors were translating Yeshua's words into Greek, they did what the translators of the Septuagint had done. Sometimes they translated *kahal* as *sunagoge*, and sometimes they translated it as *ekklesia*.

## *EKKLESIA* IN THE MESSIANIC WRITINGS

With these things in mind, let's look at how *ekklesia* is used in the Messianic Writings. *Ekklesia* appears about 100 times in the Messianic Writings. It is used to mean a meeting or assembly. It is used without any religious connotation, neither Jewish nor Christian nor any other. It is simply used as the most equivalent Greek word for *kahal*. That, of course, is what the authors were trying to do, bring the Biblical Hebrew world into the Greek language.

We can see this specific usage clearly in Hebrews 2:12. Hebrews 2:12 quotes what is Psalm 22:23 in Hebrew, Psalm 21:22 in the Septuagint, and Psalm 22:22 in Christian English versions. It is quoted, from the Septuagint, as a prophetic declaration of Yeshua: "He says, 'I will declare Your Name to my brothers; in the presence of the congregation, I will sing Your praises.'" In the Hebrew text, the word translated as "congregation" is *kahal*. In the Greek text, it is *ekklesia*. *Ekklesia* is used to translate *kahal*.

The identity of this *kahal* in Ps. 22 is inescapable. The following verse says: "You who fear the LORD, praise Him! All you descendants of Jacob, glorify Him! Be in awe of Him, all you descendants of Israel!" (Ps. 22:24H) *Ekklesia* is used to refer to the congregation of Israel.

Let's look at some other examples which should be equally clear. Stephen was brought before the council/*sunedrion*. In his defense, he maintained that his faith was consistent with and mandated by God's dealings with Israel as recorded in Tanakh. Luke records that Stephen said, "He [Moses] was in the *ekklesia* in the desert, with the angel who spoke to him on Mount

Sinai, and with our fathers; and he received living words to pass on to us." (Acts 7:38)

What is the meaning of *ekklesia* here? To what does it refer? Keep in mind that Stephen was not speaking Greek, and so he actually did not use the word *ekklesia*. That is simply Luke's Greek translation of what Stephen actually did say. Speaking to a Jewish audience in Jerusalem, Stephen was speaking in first-century Hebrew or Jewish Aramaic. Beyond all question, he used the word *kahal* to indicate the assembly/congregation/community of Israel. Even more specifically, he used it as Moses did in Dt. 9:10, 10:4, and 18:16 to indicate the specific gathering where Israel received the Ten Commandments. (In Dt. 9:10, and 18:16, the Septuagint translates *kahal* as *ekklesia*. In 10:4, it does not contain the phrase in which *kahal* appears.)

"The LORD gave me two stone tablets inscribed by the finger of God. On them were all the commandments the LORD proclaimed to you on the mountain out of the fire, on the day of the *kahal*/assembly/*ekklesia*." (Dt. 9:10)

"The LORD wrote on these tablets what He had written before, the Ten Commandments He had proclaimed to you on the mountain, out of the midst of the fire, on the day of the *kahal*/assembly. And the LORD gave them to me." (Dt. 10:4)

"For this is what you asked of the LORD your God at Horeb on the day of the *kahal*/assembly/*ekklesia* when you said, "Let us not hear the voice of the LORD our God nor see this great fire anymore, or we will die." (Dt. 18:16; cf. Ex. 20:19) In Dt. 4:10, the Septuagint also refers to this occasion as "the day of the *ekklesia*".

In translating Stephen's remarks into Greek, Luke used *ekklesia* for *kahal*, just as it had been used throughout at least the three centuries from the beginning of the Septuagint to his day. Stephen was specifically speaking of the assembly of the congregation of Israel. To then translate Luke's use of *ekklesia* into English as "church," as the KJV does, is almost inexcusable. It presents a gross distortion and misrepresentation of what Stephen was saying, rather than a translation. Stephen knew nothing at all of "church," and Moses knew less.

Let's look at another example. Yeshua asked the disciples who they thought he was, and "Shimon Kefa answered, 'You are the Messiah, the Son of the living God.'

"Yeshua replied, 'Blessed are you, Shimon son of Jonah, for this was not revealed to you by man, but by my Father in heaven. And I tell you that you are Kefa, and on this rock I will build my *ekklesia*, and the gates of Sheol will not overcome it.'" (Mt. 16:16-18) [*Petros* is the Greek translation of Kefa.]

How should *ekklesia* be translated here? Keep in mind, again, that Yeshua was not speaking in Greek, and Matthew, as far as we know, was not writing in Greek. Yeshua did not say "*ekklesia*," and Matthew did not write "*ekklesia*." *Ekklesia* in our Greek text is already translated from the original Hebrew word.

What Hebrew word did Yeshua say? What Hebrew word did Matthew write? There are really only two possibilities, *kahal* or *edah*. It is possible that Yeshua used edah, because the homonym *edah* also has the sense of "a witness," and Yeshua's congregation, or community, will be witnesses for him. It is possible that he had that sense in mind. But if Yeshua had used *edah*, then it almost assuredly would have been translated into Greek as *sunagoge*, not *ekklesia*—consistent with the practice established by the translators of the Septuagint, and followed by their successors. Therefore, almost certainly, Yeshua used *kahal*.

## THE BIBLICAL *EKKLESIA* IS THE *KAHAL* OF ISRAEL.

Whether Yeshua used *edah* or *kahal*, however, one thing is clear. Both the meaning of what he said and the entity to which he was referring are to be found in the Hebrew Scriptures. God's *edah* and God's *kahal* are both explicitly Israel. The foundation stone is laid in Zion; and it is the fallen royal house of Israel which Messiah raises up. [The chapter "Zion & Sons Building Co." covers this in greater detail.]

If Yeshua had been proclaiming that he was going to build a community that could not be found in the Biblical Hebrew context, then he would have been putting himself outside the God-given, Biblical definition of the Messiah. God had promised long before to make Israel a community of nations. Messiah comes to fulfill what God promised, not to annul or abandon it.

God had promised to make Israel His community/*kahal*/*ekklesia* of nations. Through Messiah, God was fulfilling His promise, not creating some other redeemed community which He had never mentioned before. The apostles understood this. They knew what God had already said about the *ekklesia* of the LORD.

Moses instructed Israel that,"No Ammonite or Moabite or any of his descendants may enter the assembly of the LORD/*kahal YHVH*, even down to the tenth generation." (Dt. 23:4; 23:3 in Christian English translations) As for Edomites and Egyptians, "The third generation of children born to them may enter the assembly of the LORD/*kahal YHVH*." (Dt. 23:9; 23:8 in Christian English translations) The nations are to be brought into the *kahal YHVH*, which is Israel.

The Septuagint translates *kahal YHVH* (in Dt. 23:2,3,4,9) as *ekklesian kuriou*. In English, this means, "the community/congregation/assembly of the LORD." These verses do not refer to the Church. They refer, as do other verses, to Israel as the "*ekklesia* of the Lord." (cf. 1Ch. 28:8; 29:20; Mic. 2:5) There is no textual reason to insert any other meaning, especially not a contrary meaning. The Biblical *ekklesia* is the *kahal* of Israel.

Let's look at one more example. Yeshua spoke to his disciples about the sequence of steps to take with an offending brother. First, speak privately to the one who has sinned against you. If he is not responsive to that, then take two or three other believers and speak to him. "If he refuses to listen to them, tell it to the *ekklesia*; and if he refuses to listen even to the *ekklesia*, treat him as you would a Gentile or a tax collector." (Mt. 18:17)

Many translations—e.g. KJV, NASV, NIV—use the word "church" in this verse for *ekklesia*. Once again, that is a very strange choice. Yeshua used a Hebrew word, most likely *kahal*, and that is what Matthew recorded. Yeshua wasn't speaking Greek, and, as far as we know, Matthew wasn't writing in Greek. *Ekklesia* was simply used by whoever translated Matthew's Hebrew text into Jewish Greek.

Neither Yeshua nor Matthew used a Hebrew word that signified a Christian institution. Not only was there no such institution, there was no such word that signified it. There was no word that Yeshua could have said that meant "church". And if there had been such a word, there would have been no one who could have understood it.

Nor was there any Greek word for "church," because there was no such thing as "church" in the Greek world. The Greeks did not have a word hanging around for centuries that meant "church". What would "church" have meant in the Greek world? Nothing. What would "church" have meant to the Jewish disciples of Yeshua? Nothing. The Greek word *ekklesia* had meaning, but it didn't mean "church".

Additionally, distorting the Biblical text by imposing the word "church" upon it makes Yeshua's statement very strange. What would it mean to say that the Church should treat such an unrepentant brother as the Church would treat a Gentile or a tax collector? In Israel, tax collectors served Rome and made themselves rich by extorting the people. Consequently, tax collectors were outcasts from Israel.

But for centuries, the Church had its own tax collectors. Most of the rest of the time, because the Church was allied with the State, the State supported the Church with tax revenues. Not only did tax collectors enrich themselves, they also greatly enriched the Church—Protestant, Catholic, and Orthodox alike. Tax collectors were not outcasts from the historical Church; in many cases, they were its lifeblood. The way that the Church treats tax collectors has nothing to do with what Yeshua was saying.

What about treating the unrepentant brother as though he were a Gentile? Gentiles have no natural standing in Israel. They are, by nature, outcasts from the community of Israel.

But how does the Church treat Gentiles? Gentiles are not outcasts from the Church. 99.99% of the Church is Gentile. What would it mean to tell the Church, "treat him as you would a Gentile"? The Church embraces Gentiles. It makes them pastors, teachers, theologians, bishops, popes, etc..[8] The way that the Church treats Gentiles has nothing to do with what Yeshua was saying.

Yeshua's statement only makes sense if the word translated as *ekklesia* is the *kahal* of Israel. It makes no sense if the word translated as *ekklesia* is then translated as "church". Yeshua was saying, 'If the brother will not listen, then treat him as an outcast from the community of Israel.'

Fortunately, by God's grace, that is not the end of God's plan for the Gentiles. Contrary to nature, God is able to graft Gentiles, as wild branches, into Israel's cultivated olive tree. God is able to make them fellow-citizens, as Gentiles, in the *kahal/ekklesia* of Israel. It depends, even for a Jesuit priest in Krakow, upon the condition of the heart and its submission to the King of the Jews. We will examine this in more detail in a later chapter.

*'But couldn't Jesus and his apostles have intended something that God was going to bring into existence?*

Certainly, but there would have to be a word and a reason for it. There is no textual reason to think that God was going to bring into existence something He had never mentioned before. Yeshua and his Jewish ambassadors knew what God meant by *kahal*, and they knew that *ekklesia* was used to translate *kahal* into Greek. There was no need for some new religious institution that neither existed nor was anticipated in either the Biblical Hebrew world or the Greek world. God had promised many centuries before that Gentiles were going to be restored to Him by inclusion in the commonwealth/*ekklesia* of Israel.

It is important to remember that in the Messianic Writings, as in classical Greek texts and as in the Septuagint, *ekklesia* has no specific religious meaning. On one occasion when Paul was in Ephesus, the idol makers started a riot to try to stop him from proclaiming Yeshua, a proclamation which they considered a threat to their commercial interests. The tumultuous mob rushed into the theater, where they shouted for hours, "Great is Diana of the Ephesians."

The Greek word used to describe this riotous mob in the city theater is *ekklesia*. "The *ekklesia* was in confusion. Some were shouting one thing, some another. Most of the people did not even know why they were there." (Acts 19:32) Whether or not that accurately describes some church to which you have been, Luke simply used *ekklesia* to refer to an assembly of people.

As the town clerk said in quieting the mob, "'If there is anything further you want to bring up, it must be settled in a legal *ekklesia*. As it is, we are in danger of being charged with rioting because of today's events. In that case we would not be able to account for this commotion, since there is no reason for it.' After he had said this, he dismissed the *ekklesia*." (Acts 19:39-41)

One more point that merits repeating: *Ekklesia* and *sunagoge* are used as synonyms in the Septuagint, primarily to translate *kahal*. In the Messianic Writings, they are almost synonyms, with *sunagoge* tending to signify the place or act of meeting, and *ekklesia* tending to signify the people in the meeting or the meeting itself.

We see this clearly in the book of Jacob. (For some reason, Christian English translators choose not to follow the text in giving the name of the different Jacobs in the Messianic Writings. The Greek is *Iakobou* for the Hebrew *Yaakov*. Instead of "Jacob," Christian English translators insert "James". That is not a translation; it is a distortion. It obscures Jacob's identity. "James" is no more accurate than "Rumpelstiltskin," "Omar," or "Betsy".)

Jacob wrote to "the twelve tribes in diaspora." (Ja. 1:1) In the beginning of the letter, he warns them against the sin of valuing people differently because of their outward appearance. "Suppose a man comes into your *sunagoge* wearing a gold ring and fine clothes, and a poor man in shabby clothes also comes in." (Ja. 2:2) At the end of the letter, Jacob encourages people to pray with faith. "Is any one of you sick? He should call the elders of the *ekklesia* to pray over him and anoint him with oil in the name of the Lord." (Ja. 5:14)

Jacob uses *sunagoge* and *ekklesia* to refer to different aspects of the same thing, a meeting, a community. For him, *sunagoge* is not Jewish; *ekklesia* is not Christian. In traditional and popular theology, the two words are opposites. In the Scriptures, they are synonyms.

Any proper understanding of the Scriptures must also take into account that these words are not used as religious terms. Here, as everywhere else in the Messianic Writings, to translate *ekklesia* as "church" is to impose a meaning on the word which it did not have until centuries after the Messianic Writings were written. The same holds true of "synogogue", though the transition came sooner.

## EKKLESIA IN THE TRANSLATIONS

The goal of William Tyndale's life was to produce an accurate translation of the Scriptures for the people of England. His New Testament was published in 1525. In it, he translates *ekklesia* as "community". There is no "church" in Tyndale's translation.

For Tyndale's efforts, the Church had him burned at the stake as a heretic. It is not without significance that, throughout history, the greatest, most enduring opposition to the Scriptures has come from the Church. As Tyndale faced death, he said, "I call God to record, that I have never altered, against the voice of my conscience, one syllable of his Word. Nor would do this day, if all the pleasures, honors, and riches of the earth might be given me."[9]

Some say that 90% of the King James Version is taken from Tyndale's translation. Whatever the exact percentage may be, the KJV translators chose to take most of their translation from Tyndale. They did not choose, however, to use his translation of *ekklesia*. They were commanded not to.

The translators of the KJV had rules that governed how they were to translate the text. The third rule said, "The old Ecclesiastical Words to be kept, viz. the Word Church not to be translated Congregation, & c." The Church of England and the King of England, who was the head of the Church, needed the word "Church" in the Bible, even though it wasn't there. So a rule was established to prevent the translators from correctly translating *ekklesia*. They therefore rejected the "community" of Tyndale's translation and the "congregation" of Puritan translations. King James, who was an ardent advocate of the divine and unchallengeable right of kings to rule over all, had an important stake in the translation of the text.

When the KJV first came out, its Church of England translators were under great attack for some decisions they had made. In order to justify these translation decisions, they tried to respond to all these attacks in a very lengthy preface. One of their justifications, a derogatory one, is of interest to us here. "Lastly, we have on the one side avoided the scrupulosity of the Puritans, who leave the old Ecclesiastical words, and betake them to other, as when they put... CONGREGATION instead of CHURCH."

"Scrupulosity" is often a very positive commendation of someone's efforts. After all, it means the quality of being careful, being precise and exact, being conscientious about details. Why did the translators of the KJV choose to avoid, or denigrate, "the scrupulosity of the Puritans"?

According to these Church of England scholars, the Puritans did not use some traditional "Ecclesiastical" words, i.e. "Church" words. That is true. In seeking to make accurate translations of the Scriptures, the Puritans sought to choose words which were precise and exact, rather than those which were traditional. They were not trying to support a tradition or a particular power, but rather to be as faithful to the original as they could.

In seeking to make accurate translations of the Scriptures, the Puritans, just like Tyndale, did not use the word "CHURCH." They did not use the word because there was no Greek word in the text that could and should be accurately translated that way. Instead of using this "Ecclesiastical" word, the Puritans accurately translated *ekklesia* as "CONGREGATION." They did that because, according to their Church of England opponents, they wanted to scrupulously give the meaning and intent of the Biblical text. The Puritans were persecuted by the Church of England because they would not submit to its authority.

Luther published his German Bible in 1535. He did not use the word "*kirche*," the German equivalent of "church," for *ekklesia*. Instead, he appropriately translated *ekklesia* as "*gemeinde*," i.e. community.[9]

It appears that the Geneva Bible of 1560 was the first English Bible to use the word "church." In 1395, Wycliffe, who translated from the Latin Vulgate, had come close with "chirche." The

Vulgate had simply transliterated to *ecclesia*, and Latin based languages followed the Vulgate in doing the same, e.g. *église* in French, and *iglesia* in Spanish.

The Dutch Staten Vertaling uses *gemeente*. The standard Danish (*menighed*), Norwegian (*menighet*), and Swedish (*församling*) translations use "congregation" for *ekklesia*.

In his different versions, J. N. Darby translated *ekklesia* as "assembly." Robert Young, compiler of the Analytical Concordance that bears his name, also used "assembly" in his literal translation of the Scriptures. In his *Interlinear Greek-English New Testament*, George Ricker Berry also translated *ekklesia* as "assembly." There is no "church" in these translations.

There is no "church" in these translations, because there is no "church" in the Biblical text. The "Church" is not the Biblical *ekklesia*. Every time you see the word "church" in a Bible, you are seeing a place where the translators did not translate the text, but distorted it instead, for the sake of tradition. Often it is done without thinking about it, simply because the hold of Christian tradition is so strong.

It may give you a headache, but say to yourself, "There is no 'Church' in the Bible." Say it to yourself as many thousands of times as you have read or heard the word. Say it to yourself every time you read or hear the word from now on. That will help you to understand what is in the Bible, though it may also make you difficult to get along with at the annual Church picnic.

'Maybe "Church" is the wrong word, but it is still the assembly of Christ, or however you want to say it.'

If you are still having difficulty understanding how significant the distortion is, try substituting the word "mosque" for "church" every place it appears in the translation you read. Does it introduce an alien concept? Does it introduce a hostile concept? "Mosque" may seem strange to you at first, but it won't be too long before you begin to think "that is what the Bible says." "Church" is no more a translation of *ekklesia* than "mosque" is, or "umma," the guiding community of Islam.

In passing, it is worth mentioning that since there is no "Church" in the Bible, there can hardly be a "Church Age". The "Church Age" is not mentioned in the Scriptures. It is a theological device, designed solely for the purpose of casting aside the Jewish people, if not forever, then at least for the present, the only time in which we live. Other theological devices revolve around this invention of a "Church Age" as though they were homocentric spheres.

In passing, it is also worth noting that all the wars fought in defense of "the true Church" were fought in vain. There is no true Church. If we are true to the Scriptures, we do not find any Church at all, much less a true one. There is an *ekklesia* in the Bible, but it is not the Church.

What would it mean to acknowledge that? What would it mean to acknowledge that Yeshua is building the commonwealth/*ekklesia* of Israel, which God had promised to Abraham, Isaac, and Jacob? It would be disorienting, but people who are committed to the faith and life presented in the Scriptures will be able to cope. Those who are primarily committed to a particular tradition, whether or not it nullifies the Scriptures, will stick with that tradition. In any event, when one understands the *ekklesia* to be the kahal of Israel, it make a great difference in understanding who God is and what He is doing in the earth.

The word "church," and the different forms of it that appear in other languages, are said to be a transliteration of the invented Greek word *kuriakon*, meaning "house of the Lord." It is not a word that appears in the Scriptures. As Liddell and Scott remark, in their *Greek-English Lexicon*, regarding *kuriakos*: "Assumed to be original of the Teutonic *kirk, kirche, church*; but how this Greek name came to be adopted by the Northern nations, rather than the Roman name *ecclesia*, has not been satisfactorily explained."[10]

Others suggest that church/kirk comes from the Latin root that gives us "circle," "circus," and related words. The reasoning here is that the word was chosen because the worshippers formed a circle in their meetings. "The derivation of the word Church is uncertain. It is generally said to be derived from the Greek kuriakon (κυριακον), 'belonging to the Lord.' But the derivation has been too hastily assumed. It is probably connected with kirk, the Latin circus, circulus, the Greek kuklos (κυκλος)."[11]

AT THE TIME THAT YESHUA WAS SPEAKING TO JOHN, *SUNAGOGE* DID NOT MEAN, NOR DID IT IMPLY, SOMETHING SPECIFICALLY JEWISH.

Whatever the case may be, "assembly," "congregation," and "community" are adequate translations of *ekklesia* in the Biblical context. "Church" is not a translation. It is an invention that replaces proper translation. It gives a meaning which is not contained in *ekklesia*. It conveys a concept that is not in the Scriptures.

*'But what about my local church? Are you saying that I shouldn't go there? Are you saying that they're not saved?'*

I am not saying anything even remotely like that. I have never been to your local church, or at least I don't remember having been there. I'm sure it's a very nice place, or at least I hope it's a very nice place.

What I am saying is that the Scriptures speak of the body of Messiah, and they speak of the commonwealth of Israel. They do not speak of "church," and they do not speak of a body of believers that is unconnected to the Jewish people. Those who are saved are connected to the King of the Jews and his people.

## *"SUNAGOGE* OF SATAN"

Before closing this chapter, I think it would be helpful to scrupulously look at two additional verses which use *sunagoge*. In these prophetic verses, Yeshua is speaking to John, one of his Jewish ambassadors, about groups of people who claim to be Jews, but who are not.

"I know your afflictions and your poverty—yet you are rich! I know the slander of those who say they are Jews and are not, but are a sunagoge of Satan." (Rev. 2:9) "I will make those who are of the *sunagoge* of Satan—who claim to be Jews though they are not, but are liars—I will make them come and bow down at your feet and acknowledge that I have loved you." (Rev. 3:9)

*'Isn't it obvious who is intended? Yeshua must be referring to unbelieving Jews, because he says that this group is a synagogue.'*

That would mean that the ones "who claim to be Jews though they are not" are the Jews. That would mean that the Jews are the ones who are not Jews. This is the standard view of Christian theology. Some of the Church fathers pointedly used these verses to refer to all Jews and incite hatred against them. They believed that all Jews are not Jews, and should therefore be hated because they are Jews.

Is that what Yeshua is saying? Is that the group to which he is referring? At the time that Yeshua was speaking to John, *sunagoge* did not mean, nor did it in any way imply, something specifically Jewish. It was simply a generic Greek word which meant "meeting" or "meeting-place". *Sunagoge* did not mean "synagogue". A synagogue, as everyone knows, is a religious Jewish meetingplace. That is not what *sunagoge* meant in the first century. That is not what Yeshua said.

For that matter, we don't know in what language Yeshua was speaking to John. When they grew up together, they spoke in Jewish Aramaic or Hebrew. Could Yeshua have been speaking to John in Greek on the isle of Patmos? Possibly, but not likely. It was not their native language.

In Acts 26:14, Paul said that the risen Yeshua spoke to him in Hebrew. Luke tells us that when Paul was speaking to the crowd in Jerusalem, he spoke in Hebrew. (cf. Acts 21:40; 22:2) Hebrew speaking Jews spoke to each other in Hebrew.

In Rev. 9:11 and 16:16, John refers to the original Hebrew for Abaddon and Har Megiddo. He also refers to the original Hebrew for other words in John 5:2; 19:13, 17; and 20:16. In Jn. 1:42, John gives us the original Hebrew name which Yeshua gave to Simon, and then explains that the more familiar Greek name is simply a translation. "And he (Andrew) brought him to Yeshua. Yeshua looked at him and said, 'You are Simon son of John. You will be called Kefa,' (which, when translated, is Peter)."

Hebrew was John's native language. It was also Yeshua's native language. It was the language in which they had spoken to each other for years. Almost certainly, Yeshua continued to speak to John in Hebrew. In that case, Yeshua would not even have used the word *sunagoge.*

In whatever language Yeshua did speak to John, it is possible that he was referring to a Jewish group. He could have had the same thing in mind that Paul points out in Romans 2:28-29: God's covenant of circumcision with Abraham is not just an external sign. It is intended as an external sign of the internal circumcision of the heart. That is what being Jewish is truly about.

It is possible that Yeshua had that sense in mind. If that is the case, then Yeshua was saying that there are some Jews who have set themselves in opposition to God's purpose for themselves, and who therefore are not fully Jews in terms of what God created and called them to be. But clearly, Yeshua, the King of the Jews, was speaking to John, one of his tens of thousands of Jewish followers at the time. In other words, Yeshua may have been speaking of some Jews, but he could not have been speaking of all Jews.

However, this is a prophetic message, speaking of things that are to come. John was alone in Patmos, exiled there by non-Jews. Yeshua could just as easily have been referring to a group of Christians, or any number of cults which have appeared, which claim to be Jews, but are not. At least, such groups claim to be Jews as far as the promised blessings are concerned. They do not seem to make such claims concerning the promised judgments. Apparently, they only consider themselves half-Jews, the blessing half. Nor do they seem to make such claims when the persecution comes.

All the Catholic churches claim to be Israel. So do the Orthodox churches and the Reformed churches. So do a multitude of a variety of other churches. They all think they have replaced the Jews.

A few months after I turned to the Lord, I was introduced to a traveling evangelical speaker. He asked me, "So you're Jewish?" "Yes," I said. In a challenging tone, he replied, "I'm just as Jewish as you are." At the time, I didn't know what he was talking about. He obviously wasn't Jewish. All I understood from his attitude and his statement was his hostility towards the Jewish people.

In the more than thirty years since, I have found that his view is quite common. I often encounter Christians who say that they are Jews. Their thinking goes like this: 'When it comes to the Jews, being Jewish is a bad thing, and they are cast off from God because of it. But there are a lot of good promises to the Jews. So if the Jews aren't Jews, then the Christians must be Jews.' Last month, I was supposed to meet with a theologian who claims that Christians are more Jewish than Jews are. This is just a normal bizarre teaching. Unfortunately, we couldn't work out a time to meet.

But back to Revelation. Let's look at the text. The book of Revelation describes the events on earth and in the heavens which lead up to the return of Yeshua to destroy the enemies of Israel, followed by his rule in Jerusalem in the Messianic Age. That is then followed by his rule in the new Jerusalem on the new earth. What will happen following Yeshua's triumphant return to Jerusalem to deliver Israel? He will gather the non-Jews/*ethnos*/*goyim* and judge them on the basis of one thing: "whatever you did for one of the least of these brothers of mine, you did for me." (Mt. 25:40) It will be done as God promised Abraham, Isaac, Jacob, and all Israel it would be. "I will bless those who bless you, and I will curse those who curse you."

It brings to mind what the LORD said to Israel in the time of Jeremiah. Israel had become unclean by turning away from the LORD, bringing the judgment of exile. Jeremiah was persecuted by some of his brethren, but God promised restoration for Israel, and proclaimed the promise of judgment on the nations according to what they do to Israel. "But all who devour you will be devoured; all your enemies will go into exile. Those who plunder you will be plundered; all who make spoil of you I will despoil." (Jer. 30:16)

In this same section, the Lord then said to Israel, "I have loved you with an everlasting love." (Jer.31:3a) In this verse, the Septuagint has *egapesa se* for "I have loved you." (LXX Jer.38:3) That is the exact Greek phrase that John chose to use in Rev. 3:9: "I will make them come and bow down at your feet and acknowledge that I have loved you/*egapesa se*."

The Greek phrase that John uses for "they will bow down at your feet"—*proskunesousin enopion ton podon sou*—comes from Isaiah 49:23, another section about the redemption of Zion and the descendants of Jacob. "Kings will be your foster fathers, and their queens your nursing mothers. They will bow down before you with their faces to the ground; they will lick the dust at your feet. Then you will know that I am the LORD. Those who hope in Me will not be disappointed." (Is. 49:23)

It is quite similar to the promise of the Mighty One of Jacob to Jerusalem: "The sons of your oppressors will come bowing before you. All who despise you will bow down at your feet and will call you the City of the LORD, Zion of the Holy One of Israel." (Is. 60:14)

There are two more things that we should scrupulously notice. The first concerns the context in which Yeshua repeats the false claim. A common translation of the key phrase in Rev. 2:9 is, "I know the slander of those who say they are Jews and are not." A more literal translation of the phrase is, "I know the slander of those who declare themselves to be Jews and are not." In the same chapter, both before and after this message to the community in Smyrna, Yeshua uses the same kind of language to address similar situations in two other communities.

In Rev. 2:2, Yeshua says to the community in Ephesus, "you cannot tolerate evil men, and have tested those who declare themselves to be apostles, and they are not, and found them false." In that community of believers, there were those who called themselves apostles, but they were not.

In Rev. 2:20, Yeshua says to the community in Thyatira, "I have this against you, that you tolerate the woman Jezebel, she who calls herself a prophetess." Among the believers, there was a woman who called herself a prophet, but she was not. These false claims, before and after the false claim cited in v.9, were being made by individuals within the community of believers.

The second thing we should note is that the word *Ioudaioi*, translated as "Jews," appears about 60 times in the Gospel of John. John, by the inspiration of the Holy Spirit, calls the Jews "Jews". He records that the other disciples called the Jews "Jews". The Samaritan woman called the Jews "Jews". Pilate called the Jews "Jews". The Roman soldiers called the Jews "Jews". And Jesus called the Jews "Jews".

This is not a case of someone calling himself, or herself, something that he, or she, is not. This is a case of everybody calling the Jews "Jews". Was John wrong in calling them "Jews"? Was the Holy Spirit wrong? Was Jesus wrong?

If the Jews are no longer Jews, then what have they become? Chinese? Martians? Avocados? And why has the Church slandered and persecuted them for 1700 years for being Jews, if they are not Jews?

Listen again to what Yeshua said to his Jewish ambassador from Israel. It sounds different to Jewish ears than it does to traditional Christian ones. "I will make those who are of the congregation of the Adversary—who claim to be Jews though they are not, but are liars—I will make them come and fall down at your feet and acknowledge that I have loved you." (Rev. 3:9) It sounds like the everlasting love of the God of Israel for His people Israel.

Within Israel at that time, there were many Jews, like John, who believed in Yeshua. There were also many who did not believe, and many who hadn't heard anything about Yeshua, or at least not enough to make a decision. The issue we are discussing concerns a particular text in its context. What is the proper translation of *sunagoge* in Rev. 2:9 and Rev. 3:9? It did not mean "synagogue," so it should not be translated as "synagogue," especially if such translation communicates the opposite of what Yeshua said.

To read the Messianic Writings and treat *sunagoge* as though it designated something exclusively Jewish, and treat *ekklesia* as though it designated something specifically Christian is to read meaning out of the text that the authors of the text never put into the text. It was not their intent. It was not their meaning. Such treatment of the text distorts rather than conveys its meaning. It creates an illusion that hides the anomaly and preserves the system.

## FOOTNOTES

1. Here are some exceptions: Num. 17:5 in the Hebrew and the Septuagint, which is Num.16:40 in Christian English translations, where it is translated as *episustasis*, meaning "a gathering together against"; Ps. 1:5 in Hebrew, which is Ps. 1:3 in Christian English translations and in the Septuagint, where it is translated as *boule*, meaning "a council"; Job 15:34, where it is translated as *marturion*, meaning "testimony"; and other verses such as Num. 27:20, Josh. 22:12,18, and 1Kings 8:5 where it is not directly translated.

   There is another word *edah* that has the meaning of "witness" or "testimony." "As the LORD commanded Moses, Aaron put the manna in front of the Testimony/*ha'edah*, that it might be kept." (Ex. 16:34) On another occasion, Joshua said to all the people, "This stone will be a witness/*edah* against us. It has heard all the words the LORD has said to us. It will be a witness/*edah* against you if you are untrue to your God." (Josh. 24:27) The Septuagint translates edah in such passages as marturia, i.e. a witness.

   The Tabernacle itself is described as the "Tent of Meeting," "Tent of Testimony," or "Tent of Witness." The word translated as "Meeting," or "Testimony," or "Witness" is mo'ed, from the same root as *ed*.

2. *An Intermediate Greek-English Lexicon* [founded upon the Seventh Edition of Liddell and Scott's Greek-English Lexicon], Oxford Univ. Press, Clarendon, 1999, sunagoge—p. 766

3. ibid, ekklesia—p. 239

4. Staffan Olofsson, *The LXX Version: A Guide to the Translation Technique of the Septuagint*, ConBOT 30, Almqvist & Wiksell, Stockholm, 1990, p.19-20, citing Emanuel Tov, "Three Dimensions of LXX Words,' Revue Biblique 83, 1976, pp. 529-544

5. Lee I. Levine, *The Ancient Synagogue—The First Thousand Years*, Yale U. Press, New Haven, 2000, p.27

6. *An Intermediate Greek-English Lexicon*, op. cit., sunedrion—p. 771

7. "Church," *Smith's Bible Dictionary*, William Smith, Revell, Old Tappan, NJ, 1980, pp. 108-109

8. My appreciation to Casey Villard for this observation.

9. My thanks to Willis J. Hartman, Jr. for pointing out to me this information about Luther's Bible.

10. *An Intermediate Greek-English Lexicon*, op. cit., kuriakos—p.458

11. "Church," *Smith's Bible Dictionary*, op. cit., pp. 108-109

CHAPTER FIVE

# Office Directory

*Transliteration Creates the Illusion of Christian Religious Offices*

**B**ut isn't there an entirely new structure of authority and responsibility in the Church?'

No. In the Messianic Writings, there are some particular words which describe functions, but these were just common Greek words which described the same functions in all spheres of life. The Church turned them into ecclesiastical titles by transliterating them instead of translating them. Transliteration keeps the words foreign and outside of normal understanding. It helps create a special religious world. Translating the words would have enabled people to understand them.

Besides that, all of these functions already existed in Biblical Israel. Exodus 18:21-22 is a simple, key text for understanding the organization of authority in the *kahal*, the community and congregation of Israel. Jethro, the father-in-law of Moses, told Moses to, "select capable men from all the people—men who fear God, trustworthy men who hate dishonest gain—and appoint them as officials over thousands, hundreds, fifties and tens. Have them serve as judges for the people at all times, but have them bring every difficult case to you. The simple cases they can decide themselves. That will make your load lighter, because they will share it with you." (cf. Dt.1:15-17; 1Tim. 3:1-12)

It's a simple plan. Give men of godly character responsibility for small groups of the people. Give some of these men responsibility over groups of these groups.

*'What about the five offices of Ephesians 4?'*

Let's take a look. Messiah gave "some to be apostles, some to be prophets, some to be evangelists, and some to be shepherds and teachers." (Eph.4:11) Which of these hadn't been appointed in Israel in earlier times? Certainly there were prophets, shepherds, and teachers in Israel. What about apostles, i.e. "sent ones," and evangelists, i.e. "those who bring good news"?

The Greek word *apostello*, to send, is a very common word. Forms of it appear hundreds and hundreds of times in the Messianic Writing. Here is how it is used.

Yeshua applied Malachi 3:1 to John, his forerunner. The Greek text says, "I will *apostello* My messenger ahead of you, who will prepare your way before you." (Mt. 11:10)

Yeshua told a crowd of Pharisees and scribes, "I *apostello* you prophets and wise men and teachers." (Mt. 23:34)

"As soon as the grain is ripe, he *apostellei* the sickle to it, because the harvest has come." (Mk. 4:29)

"If anyone asks you, 'Why are you doing this?' tell him, 'The Lord needs it and will *apostellei* it back here shortly.'" (Mk. 11:3)

"I am going to *apostello* you what my Father has promised; but stay in the city until you have been clothed with power from on high." (Lk. 24:49)

"The Pharisees *apostellousin* their disciples to Yeshua to trap him." (Mt.22:16; Mk. 12:13)

"The angels are *apostellomena* to serve those who will inherit salvation." (Hebr. 1:14)

The word is equally common in the Septuagint. Here are two examples from the Septuagint:

"Jacob sent messengers [*apesteile de Iakob aggelous*] ahead of him to his brother Esau in the land of Seir, the country of Edom." (Gen. 32:3)

"The elders of Jabesh said to him, 'Give us seven days so we can send messengers [*aposteloumen aggelous*] throughout Israel. If no one comes to rescue us, we will surrender to you.'" (1Sam. 11:3)

An "apostle" is, literally, "one who is sent," i.e. an envoy or ambassador. *Shaliakh*, the Hebrew word for "one who is sent," also comes from a very common word. Here are some relevant examples of its usage in Tanakh.

Artaxerxes gave Ezra a letter of commendation and authorization. He told Ezra, "You are sent [*shaliakh*] by the king and his seven advisers to inquire about Judah and Jerusalem with regard to the Law of your God, which is in your hand." (Ezra 7:14)

It was common for kings to send emissaries, envoys, or ambassadors to represent them before their own people or to represent them in other lands. Such ambassadors carried the message and authority of their sovereign. It was, and is, just a normal function of government, whatever words or language are used. Isaiah 18:2 mentions a land which sends [*hasholayakh*] envoys by sea in papyrus boats over the water...." 1Kings 5:14 [1Kgs. 4:34 in English Christian versions] records that, "Men of all nations came to listen to Solomon's wisdom, sent by all the kings of the world, who had heard of his wisdom."

God continually sent men to carry His message and authority. Sometimes, as with the prophet Ahijah, it wasn't good news that they brought. "So when Ahijah heard the sound of her footsteps at the door, he said, "Come in, wife of Jeroboam. Why this pretense? I have been sent [*shaluakh*] to you with bad news." (1Kgs. 14:6)

Yeshua did what had been done before. "He appointed twelve—designating them *apostolous* —that they might be with him and that he might *apostelle* them to preach and to have authority to drive out demons." (Mark 3:14-15)

Paul wrote to the community in Philippi: "But I think it is necessary to send back to you Epaphroditus, my brother, fellow worker and fellow soldier. He is also your *apostolon*, whom you sent to take care of my needs." (Phil. 2:25) Epaphroditus was the apostle of the community in Philippi to Paul.

Congregations had "apostles". God had "apostles". Kings had "apostles". Even businessmen had "apostles". The Church, by using transliteration instead of translation, appropriated the word for itself by removing it from the context of life, and sequestering it in religion. "For what she had lost of religion as faith, she replaced with religion as magic."[1]

Did the role of one who brings good news, i.e. what is called "an evangelist," already exist in Israel? Or more precisely, did the role already exist in the context of Israel, or did it require a new context?

Both the Hebrew word *besorah* and the Greek *euaggelion*, which is translated as "good news," were used especially to refer to news of a military victory or deliverance from one's enemies. Here are some verses which refer to the end of Absalom's rebellion against David. In the brackets, I have placed the Hebrew word first, followed by the Greek of the Septuagint.

"Now Ahimaaz son of Zadok said, 'Let me run and take the news [*avasrah/euaggelio*] to the king that the LORD has delivered him from the hand of his enemies.'" (2Sam. 18:19)

"'You are not the one to take the news [*eesh besorah/aner euaggelias*] today,' Joab told him. 'You may take the news [*besorta/euaggelie*] another time, but you must not do so today, because the king's son is dead.'" (2Sam. 18:20)

"The watchman called out to the king and reported it. The king said, 'If he is alone, he must have good news [*besorah/euaggelia*].' And the man came closer and closer." (2Sam. 18:25)

"Then the watchman saw another man running, and he called down to the gatekeeper, 'Look, another man running alone!' The king said, 'He must be bringing good news [*mevaser/euaggelian*], too.'" (2Sam. 18:26)

In the days of Elisha the prophet, the army of Aram surrounded and besieged Samaria. Four lepers, thinking they might find mercy from the army, and knowing that they would die in the city, went out to the besieging army. They found that the army of Aram had fled in terror and had left everything in their camp, including an abundance of food and drink. At first, they ate and drank, and took silver, gold, and clothing for themselves.

"Then they said to each other, 'We are not doing right. This is a day of good news [*besorah/euaggelias*] and we are keeping it to ourselves. If we wait until daylight, punishment will overtake us. Let's go at once and report this to the royal palace.'" (2Kgs. 7:9)

It was a day of deliverance from death. It was a day of the LORD putting the enemy to flight. It was a day to share the good news with others.

Even more particular than that, the "good news" of Yeshua's victory includes the essential proclamation that it is the God of Israel who reigns over all. "How beautiful on the mountains are the feet of those who bring good news [*mevaser/euaggelizomenou*], who proclaim peace, who bring good tidings [*mevaser tov/euaggelizomenos*], who proclaim salvation [yeshuah/soterian], who say to Zion, 'Your God reigns!'" (Is. 52:7)

That is the context for the proclamation and the one who proclaims it. "You who bring good tidings [*mevaseret/euaggelizomenos*] to Zion, go up on a high mountain. You who bring good tidings to Jerusalem, lift up your voice with a shout, lift it up, do not be afraid; say to the cities of Judah, 'Behold your God!'" (Is. 40:9)

"Behold on the mountains, the feet of him who brings good news [*mevaser/euaggelizome-nou*], who proclaims peace! Celebrate your festivals, O Judah, and fulfill your vows. No more will the wicked invade you; they will be completely destroyed." (Nah. 1:15)

### 'What about elders? bishops? deacons?'

These also appear in the context of Israel. The Church has made these words into ecclesiastical terms and offices, but, in the Scriptures, they are simply ordinary descriptive words.

Elders are mentioned more than one hundred times in Tanakh. A town, a tribe, or a people had elders. The elders were those whose views carried a certain amount of weight, formally or informally, because of their experience and judgment.

The English "bishop" is derived from the Latin form of the Greek word *episkopos*. *Episkopos* means "one who watches over," i.e. an overseer, supervisor, or guardian. It carried no particular religious meaning or identification. It simply designated a responsibility. For example, Peter warns believers against being *allotri-episkopos*, i.e. self-appointed overseers of the affairs of others. (1Pet. 4:15)

Paul instructed Titus to "appoint elders in every city, as I directed you, if anyone is blameless, the husband of one wife, having children who believe, who are not accused of loose or unruly behavior. For the overseer must be blameless, as God's steward, not self-willed, not easily angered, not given to wine, not violent, not greedy for dishonest gain" (Titus 1:5b-7) The elders whom Titus appoints will be overseers. The Greek word that is translated literally as "overseer" is *episkopos*. The KJV translates it here as "bishop". The "elders in every city" are "bishops". They are overseers, supervisors, superintendents.

*Episkopos* appears in the Septuagint, often as the translation of the Hebrew word *pakid*. It is used this way in Num. 4:16 for Eleazer the son of Aaron. *Episkopos* is used this way in Judges 9:28 for Zebul, the leader of Shekhem. It is used for pakid in Neh. 11:9, 14, 22 to describe those who were over a group of people, over a portion of the army, or over the Levites. *Pakid* is translated as "overseer," "officer," "deputy," "chief officer," and "official."

The sons of Merari had oversight [*episkepsis*] of certain responsibilities in the Tabernacle. (Num. 3:36) Certain men in Hebron were responsible for oversight [*episkepseus*] in Israel west of the Jordan for all the work of the LORD and for the king's service. (1Chr.26:30)

In describing the position Judas had had before he betrayed Yeshua, Peter quotes from Ps. 109:8. (Acts 1:20) In the Greek text of Acts, *episkopen* is used for *pekudat. Pekudat* appears in Num. 3:32 for Eliezer's responsibility of oversight of those who served in the holy place.

The Hebrew text of Is. 60:17 contains this promise for Zion: "I will make peace your *pakid* and righteousness your ruler." In the Septuagint, it is, "I will make your princes peaceable and your *episkopous* righteous."

"Deacon" is simply an English transliteration of the Greek *diakonos.* The word means "servant." It is from a common root, appearing in many verses in the Messianic Writings. Here are some examples to give a broad sense of how it is used:

"Not so with you. Instead, whoever wants to become great among you must be your *diakonos*." (Mt. 20:26)

"But Martha was distracted by all the *diakonian* that had to be made. She came to him and asked, 'Lord, don't you care that my sister has left me to do the work by myself? Tell her to help me!'" (Luke 10:40)

"And the master of the banquet tasted the water that had been turned into wine. He did not realize where it had come from, though the *diakonoi* who had drawn the water knew. Then he called the bridegroom aside." (John 2:9)

"They urgently pleaded with us for the privilege of sharing in this *diakonias* to those set apart." (2Cor. 8:4)

"to prepare God's people for works of *diakonias*, so that the body of Messiah may be built up." (Eph. 4:12)

"*Diakonous*, likewise, are to be men worthy of respect, sincere, not indulging in much wine, and not pursuing dishonest gain." (1Tim. 3:8)

"Each one should use whatever gift he has received to *diakonountes* others, faithfully administering God's grace in its various forms." (1Pet. 4:10)

It is primarily service, not title, position, or authority that is in view. There were, of course, many kinds of servants in Israel. The patriarchs had them, kings had them, sometimes even prophets had them. When the word is translated instead of transliterated, the title disappears, but the function becomes clear. The transliteration serves to create an aura of a religious realm that is separate from common life. In the religious realm, there are deacons who do not serve.

All of the forms of service that are mentioned in the Messianic Writings are also mentioned in Tanakh. They all existed in the Biblical context of Israel. None of these forms of service required a new context. In Tanakh, God describes Messiah as functioning in Israel, the context He created.

**ALL OF THE FORMS OF SERVICE THAT ARE MENTIONED IN THE MESSIANIC WRITINGS EXISTED IN THE BIBLICAL CONTEXT OF ISRAEL.**

The "apostles" were very careful to demonstrate that all they believed and all they practiced came from Tanakh. It could not be otherwise, because that is the only place that legitimacy, both in the eyes of God and in the eyes of the people of God, could be found. As Paul expressed it in identifying himself in Rom. 1:1-3: "Paul, a servant of Yeshua the Messiah, called to be an ambassador and set apart for the good news of God—the good news He promised beforehand through His prophets in the Holy Scriptures regarding His Son, who came physically as a descendant of David."

God promised the good news to Israel through the prophets. Yeshua came to fulfill that promise, not to abolish it. The creation of an "ecclesiastical" vocabulary obscures this reality, and creates an alternate, anti-biblical context.

Christian doctrine in opposition to the Jewish people misidentifies and mischaracterizes the *ekklesia* which God established. It creates the illusion of a God separating from Israel, but the New Covenant, which brings redemption, is made with Israel. It is not made with a "new Israel." It is made with the same old Israel whose fathers broke the covenant that God made with them at Sinai after He brought them out of Egypt.

Part of God's promise to that old Israel was to make the nation a means for the redemption of all peoples. Part of God's promise to that old Israel was to make it the context, the commonwealth, for the redemption of the nations. When Yeshua said, "Salvation is from the Jews," he meant the Jews who are Jews, not Gentiles who are Gentiles.

Church ecclesiology is not Biblical ecclesiology. The Biblical *ekklesia* is the *kahal*/congregation/commonwealth of Israel. The concept of a separate "Church" was invented and imposed upon the text, in defiance of the text. It was imposed upon the text in defiance of God's faithfulness to the Jewish people.

FOOTNOTE

1. *The Bridge of San Luis Rey*, Thornton Wilder, Washington Square Press, NY, 1960, p.30

CHAPTER SIX

# The People Came to Him

*The Jews Responded Positively to Yeshua*

*Maybe some of the things you have said are true. Maybe. But that doesn't change the fact that the Jews rejected Christ.'*

If "Christ" refers to Messiah, then this statement, though generally believed, is far from being a fact. It is, in fact, false. It was Jews who told the Gentiles about him. It was Jews who turned the idolatrous first-century world upside down. It was Jews who gave the writings of Matthew through Revelation to the world. These were Jews who acted in obedience to the command of their King to, "Make disciples of all the Gentiles." (Mt. 28:19)

The claim that "the Jews rejected Christ" is made in order to justify the theological casting off the Jews and selecting a new people for God. The claim is false, and it demeans God's grace, faithfulness, and power. In the next four chapters, we will examine different aspects of this claim.

Luke tells us about the tens of thousands of Jews in Jerusalem alone who accepted Yeshua. (cf. Acts 21:20) The Greek word, *myriades*, means tens of thousands. It is translated that way in Acts 19:19, Rev. 5:11, and Rev. 9:16. That is also its meaning in numerous passages in the Septuagint, such as Dt. 33:17 and Ezra 2:64/1Esd. 5:41. There is a different word, *chiliades*, that is used to indicate thousands.

For some reason, when it comes to the number of Jewish believers, the translators usually translate *myriades* as "thousands" instead of "tens of thousands". That is not what it means. The mistranslation feeds the false belief that the response of the Jewish people to Yeshua was overwhelmingly negative.

The Scriptural text gives a very different picture. All of his disciples were Jews. All the believers in the early years following the resurrection were Jews.

The "apostles" were Jews, not in the sense that they ONCE were Jews and then became Christians, but in the sense that all they ever were was Jews. They were faithful Jews serving the

King of the Jews. There was nothing else they were supposed to be. There was nothing greater that they could be. Everything that they did, they did as Jews.

It is difficult to gauge first century numbers or percentages, but it seems clear that most Jews in the first century did not believe in Yeshua. It is not clear, however, that most Jews in the first century even heard of Yeshua. Of those who heard, many believed. Those who believed brought life to a dead world, light to a dark world.

Of those who heard and did not believe, there were those who chose to strongly oppose the message. Some, like Saul of Tarsus, violently opposed the message. Because Saul was zealous for God, he strongly opposed the spread of what he believed to be a false message. The claims of Yeshua do not invite a lukewarm response. A lukewarm response indicates a lack of understanding.

Of those Jews who opposed the message, some, like Saul of Tarsus and Sosthenes of Corinth (cf. Acts 18:17 and 1Cor. 1:1), later came to believe that the message was true. Consequently, in their zeal for God, they sought to spread the message. Jews like these brought Messiah to the world, to the Gentile world. They were fulfilling their calling to be "a light to the Gentiles".

For the time before the resurrection, we also lack comprehensive statistics, percentages, and polls. We can, however, with great certainty, characterize the view presented by the writers of the gospels. That is the focus of this chapter.

According to the gospels, when Yeshua walked in Israel, the Jewish people received him with an overwhelming openness. There were a few exceptions to this positive reception, but only a few. After we look at these exceptions, we will look at the rest of the record.

The first exception is the reception in his own home town of Nazareth. At first, the people responded positively. "All spoke well of him and were amazed at the gracious words that came from his lips. 'Isn't this Joseph's son?' they asked." (Luke 4:22) But they were unwilling to accept his teaching about God's equal concern for the Gentiles. "All the people in the meetingplace were furious when they heard this." (Luke 4:28)

Related to this was the way he was received in Korazin and Beit Tzaida. These two cities witnessed more of his miracles than any others, but they were unwilling to repent. (cf. Mt. 11:20) As Yeshua explained, a prophet has no honor in his own hometown or his own house. (cf. Mt. 13:57) Those who were the members of his own family did not receive him. (cf. Mk. 3:21; Jn. 7:3, et al.)

The second exception is the response of the people in the area where the man possessed by a legion of evil spirits was delivered. "Then all the people of the region of the Gerasenes asked Yeshua to leave them, because they were overcome with fear...." (Luke 8:37; cf. Mt. 8:34) What they witnessed of the conflict between Yeshua and the evil spirits was too much for them.

The third exception is the debate recorded in the gospel of John. Some of the people were speaking in favor of Yeshua, some were doubting, and some were speaking in opposition. (cf. John 7:12,40-44) That is the response we would expect anywhere.

Jn. 12:34-42 is related to this. Many in the crowd did not believe, but "many, even among the leaders, did believe in him." In these verses, John also maintains that, in fulfillment of prophecy, God blinded the eyes and hardened the hearts of those who did not believe.

There is only one more exception, the most significant one. The gospels tell us that the theopolitical rulers in Israel responded quite hostilely to Yeshua. We will look at their response in the next chapter.

## THE RESPONSE OF INDIVIDUALS

In general, Matthew, Mark, Luke, and John indicate that the response of the Jewish people to Yeshua was overwhelmingly positive. We can see this first in the response of particular individuals.

"As Yeshua went on from there, he saw a man named Matthew sitting at the tax collector's booth. 'Follow me,' he told him, and Matthew got up and followed him." (Mt. 9:9) Matthew had a lucrative, though despised, government position. He left it to follow Yeshua. Matthew was a Jew.

"While Yeshua was having dinner at Levi's house, many tax collectors and sinners were eating with him and his disciples, for there were many who followed him." (Mark 2:15) People who were brazen sinners, living in rejection of God's ways, sought out Yeshua and followed him. These were Jews.

Zaccheus, a chief tax collector, "wanted to see who Yeshua was, but being a short man he could not, because of the crowd." (Luke 19:3) Yeshua came to him, and Zaccheus responded, "... Here and now I give half of my possessions to the poor, and if I have cheated anybody out of anything, I will pay back four times the amount." (Luke 19:8) Zaccheus had found greater riches. Zacchaeus was a Jew.

Two blind men had heard about Yeshua, and called out to him, "Have mercy on us, Son of David!" What they had heard from others convinced them that he was the Messiah. He healed them, and "they went out and spread the news about him all over that region." (Mt. 9:31) They were Jews.

By Jericho, Bartimaeus, another blind man, also cried out "Yeshua, Son of David, have mercy on me!" From what he had heard from others, he knew that Yeshua could heal him. Yeshua did heal him. (Mark 10:47) Bartimaeus was a Jew.

Everywhere, people believed that Yeshua could heal them. "The blind and the lame came to him at the Temple, and he healed them." (Mt. 21:14) They came to him everywhere, with faith and hope. "A woman who had been subject to bleeding for twelve years came up behind him and touched the edge of his cloak." (Mt. 9:20) These people he healed were Jews.

In Cana of Galilee, there was a royal official whose son was dying. He went to Yeshua and begged him to come and heal his son. Yeshua told him to return home, and his son would live. As he returned home, some of his servants came to tell him that his son had recovered. "Then the father realized that this was the exact time at which Yeshua had said to him, 'Your son will live.' So he and all his household believed." (John 4:53) These were Jews.

"A man named Jairus, a ruler of the congregation, came and fell at Yeshua's feet, pleading with him to come to his house because his only daughter, a girl of about twelve, was dying. As Yeshua was on his way, the crowds almost crushed him." (Luke 8:41-2) Jairus, his daughter, and the crowds were Jews.

Nicodemus "came to Jesus at night and said, 'Rabbi, we know you are a teacher who has come from God. For no one could perform the miraculous signs you are doing if God were not with him.'" (John 3:2) Nicodemus said, "WE know," i.e. he came representing other leaders who also believed that

THESE WERE PEOPLE WHO DID NOT KNOW WHAT LEISURE TIME WAS. THEY LEFT WHATEVER THEY WERE DOING TO COME TO YESHUA, MULTITUDES OF PEOPLE... THESE WERE CROWDS OF JEWS.

Yeshua was a teacher sent from God. There were many of them. (cf. Jn.12:42) These leaders were Jews.

## THE RESPONSE OF THE CROWDS

The above are just a few examples, but there were so many individuals like these that large crowds followed Yeshua and gathered to him wherever he went. These were people who did not know what leisure time was. They left whatever they were doing to come to Yeshua, multitudes of people. That is the big picture. Occasionally we read of a Gentile in a particular crowd, but these were crowds of Jews.

The best way, the only way, to know what the gospels say about the response of the Jewish people to Yeshua is to examine the gospels themselves. They tell an important story. I have tried to provide you with every relevant verse.

## MATTHEW

7:28-8:1 When Yeshua had finished saying these things, the crowds were amazed at his teaching, because he taught as one who had authority, and not as their teachers of the law. When he came down from the mountainside, large crowds followed him.

8:16 When evening came, many who were demon-possessed were brought to him, and he drove out the spirits with a word and healed all the sick.

8:18 When Yeshua saw the crowd around him, he gave orders to cross to the other side of the lake.

9:33 And when the demon was driven out, the man who had been mute spoke. The crowd was amazed and said, "Nothing like this has ever been seen in Israel."

9:36-38 When he saw the crowds, he had compassion on them, because they were harassed and helpless, like sheep without a shepherd. Then he said to his disciples, "The harvest is plentiful but the workers are few. Ask the Lord of the harvest, therefore, to send out workers into his harvest field."

13:2 Such large crowds gathered around him that he got into a boat and sat in it, while all the people stood on the shore.

14:13 When Yeshua heard what had happened, he withdrew by boat privately to a solitary place. Hearing of this, the crowds followed him on foot from the towns.

14:35 And when the men of that place recognized Yeshua, they sent word to all the surrounding country. People brought all their sick to him

15:30 Great crowds came to him, bringing the lame, the blind, the crippled, the mute and many others, and laid them at his feet; and he healed them.

16:13-14 When Yeshua came to the region of Caesarea Philippi, he asked his disciples, "Who do people say the Son of Man is?" They replied, "Some say John the Immerser [whom the people believed to be a prophet]; others say Elijah; and still others, Jeremiah or one of the prophets."

19:2 Large crowds followed him, and he healed them there.

20:29 As Yeshua and his disciples were leaving Jericho, a large crowd followed him.

21:8-11 "A very great multitude spread their garments on the road. Others cut branches from the trees, and spread them on the road. The multitudes who went before him and who followed kept shouting, 'Hoshana to the Son of David! Blessed is he who comes in the name of the LORD! [Ps. 118:26] Hoshana in the highest!'"

   When he had come into Yerushalayim, all the city was stirred up, saying, "Who is this?" The multitudes said, "This is the prophet, Yeshua, from Natzeret of the Galil."

21:46 They looked for a way to arrest him, but they were afraid of the crowd because the people held that he was a prophet.

22:33 When the crowds heard this, they were astonished at his teaching.

23:1 Then Yeshua said to the crowds and to his disciples...

26:4-5 and they plotted to arrest Yeshua in some sly way and kill him. "But not during the Feast," they said, "or there may be a riot among the people."

I know that you may be tempted to think that you have gotten the point after having read just these verses in Matthew. You may be tempted to think that you should skip the rest of this chapter, because you strongly suspect that the other gospels will show exactly the same thing, and you don't like to read lists of scriptures. It is true that the other gospels do show exactly the same thing, but that is the very reason why you should continue to read this chapter. You don't yet know for yourself what the other gospels show. You are only guessing. I am trying to help you, but you can't take my word for it. When you have finished reading the chapter, then you will know for yourself.

## MARK

1:5 The whole Judean countryside and all the people of Jerusalem went out to him [Yohanan, the forerunner of the Lord]. Confessing their sins, they were immersed by him in the Jordan River.

1:21-22 They went to Kfar Nahum, and when the Sabbath came, Yeshua went into the meetingplace and began to teach. The people were amazed at his teaching, because he taught them as one who had authority, not as the teachers of the law.

1:27-28 The people were all so amazed that they asked each other, "What is this? A new teaching —and with authority! He even gives orders to evil spirits and they obey him." News about him spread quickly over the whole region of Galilee.

1:33 The whole town gathered at the door,

1:37 and when they found him, they exclaimed: "Everyone is looking for you!"

1:45 Instead he went out and began to talk freely, spreading the news. As a result, Yeshua could no longer enter a town openly but stayed outside in lonely places. Yet the people still came to him from everywhere.

2:1-2 A few days later, when Yeshua again entered Kfar Nahum, the people heard that he had come home. So many gathered that there was no room left, not even outside the door, and he preached the word to them.

2:13 Once again Yeshua went out beside the lake. A large crowd came to him, and he began to teach them.

3:7-8 Yeshua withdrew with his disciples to the lake, and a large crowd from Galilee followed. When they heard all he was doing, many people came to him from Judea, Jerusalem, Idumea, and the regions across the Jordan and around Tyre and Sidon.

3:32 A crowd was sitting around him, and they told him, "Your mother and brothers are outside looking for you."

4:1 Again Yeshua began to teach by the lake. The crowd that gathered around him was so large that he got into a boat and sat in it out on the lake, while all the people were along the shore at the water's edge.

5:20-21 So the man went away and began to tell in the Decapolis how much Yeshua had done for him. And all the people were amazed. When Yeshua had again crossed over by boat to the other side of the lake, a large crowd gathered around him while he was by the lake.

5:24 So Yeshua went with him. A large crowd followed and pressed around him.

6:31 Then, because so many people were coming and going that they did not even have a chance to eat, he said to them, "Come with me by yourselves to a quiet place and get some rest."

6:54-56 As soon as they got out of the boat, people recognized Yeshua. They ran throughout that whole region and carried the sick on mats to wherever they heard he was. And wherever he went —into villages, towns or countryside —they placed the sick in the marketplaces. They begged him to let them touch even the edge of his cloak, and all who touched him were healed.

7:24 Yeshua left that place and went to the vicinity of Tyre. He entered a house and did not want anyone to know it; yet he could not keep his presence secret.

8:1 During those days another large crowd gathered. Since they had nothing to eat, Yeshua...

9:14-15 When they came to the other disciples, they saw a large crowd around them and the teachers of the law arguing with them. As soon as all the people saw Yeshua, they were overwhelmed with wonder and ran to greet him.

10:1 Yeshua then left that place and went into the region of Judea and across the Jordan. Again crowds of people came to him, and as was his custom, he taught them.

11:8-9 Many people spread their cloaks on the road, while others spread branches they had cut in the fields. Those who went ahead and those who followed shouted, Hosanna! " "Blessed is he who comes in the name of the Lord!"

11:18 The chief priests and the teachers of the law heard this and began looking for a way to kill him, for they feared him, because the whole crowd was amazed at his teaching.

12:12 Then they looked for a way to arrest him because they knew he had spoken the parable against them. But they were afraid of the crowd; so they left him and went away.

12:37 David himself calls him 'Lord.' How then can he be his son?" The large crowd listened to him with delight.

14:1-2 Now the Passover and the Feast of Unleavened Bread were only two days away, and the chief priests and the teachers of the law were looking for some sly way to arrest Yeshua and kill him. "But not during the Feast," they said, "or the people may riot."

*'OK, I get the point. I think I'll skip the rest of the chapter.'*

There were a lot of these verses in Mark; it's true. Perhaps you should stand up and stretch. I'm sure you are starting to get the point, but these are just verses from the Bible. You do want to know what the Bible teaches, don't you?

## LUKE

4:14-15 Yeshua returned to Galilee in the power of the Spirit, and news about him spread through the whole countryside. He taught in their meetingplaces, and everyone praised him.

4:32 They were amazed at his teaching, because his message had authority.

4:37 And the news about him spread throughout the surrounding area.

4:42 At daybreak Yeshua went out to a solitary place. The people were looking for him and when they came to where he was, they tried to keep him from leaving them.

5:1 One day as Yeshua was standing by the Lake of Gennesaret, with the people crowding around him and listening to the word of God,

5:15 Yet the news about him spread all the more, so that crowds of people came to hear him and to be healed of their sicknesses.

5:19 When they could not find a way to do this because of the crowd, they went up on the roof and lowered him on his mat through the tiles into the middle of the crowd, right in front of Yeshua.

6:17 He went down with them and stood on a level place. A large crowd of his disciples was there and a great number of people from all over Judea, from Jerusalem, and from the coast of Tyre and Sidon,

7:11 Soon afterward, Yeshua went to a town called Naim, and his disciples and a large crowd went along with him.

7:16 They were all filled with awe and praised God. "A great prophet has appeared among us," they said. "God has come to help His people."

7:29 All the people, even the tax collectors, when they heard Yeshua' words, acknowledged that God's way was right, because they had been immersed by John.

8:4 While a large crowd was gathering and people were coming to Yeshua from town after town, he told this parable:

8:40 Now when Yeshua returned, a crowd welcomed him, for they were all expecting him.

9:11 but the crowds learned about it and followed him. He welcomed them and spoke to them about the kingdom of God, and healed those who needed healing.

9:37 The next day, when they came down from the mountain, a large crowd met him.

14:25 Large crowds were traveling with Yeshua, and turning to them he said:

19:36-39 As he went along, people spread their cloaks on the road. When he came near the place where the road goes down the Mount of Olives, the whole crowd of disciples began joyfully to praise God in loud voices for all the miracles they had seen: "Blessed is the king who comes in the name of the Lord!" "Peace in heaven and glory in the highest!"

Some of the Pharisees in the crowd said to Yeshua, "Teacher, rebuke your disciples!"

19:47-48 Every day he was teaching at the Temple. But the chief priests, the teachers of the law and the leaders among the people were trying to kill him. Yet they could not find any way to do it, because all the people hung on his words.

20:19 The teachers of the law and the chief priests looked for a way to arrest him immediately, because they knew he had spoken this parable against them. But they were afraid of the people.

21:37-38 Each day Yeshua was teaching at the Temple, and each evening he went out to spend the night on the hill called the Mount of Olives, and all the people came early in the morning to hear him at the Temple.

22:2 and the chief priests and the teachers of the law were looking for some way to get rid of Yeshua, for they were afraid of the people.

23:27 A large multitude of the people followed him, including women who also mourned and lamented him.

23:48 All the multitudes that came together to see this, when they saw the things that were done, returned home beating their breasts.

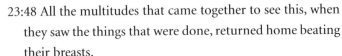

"A LARGE CROWD WAS GATHERING AND PEOPLE WERE COMING TO YESHUA FROM TOWN AFTER TOWN..."

You may stop reading this chapter if you like. You are a free moral agent, unless, of course, you are a Calvinist. If you are a Calvinist, you don't have any choice, so stop complaining and just read the rest of the chapter. You know, with all the time you've spent complaining, you could have been finished by now.

**JOHN**

2:23 Now while he was in Jerusalem at the Passover Feast, many people saw the miraculous signs he was doing and believed in his name.

4:45 When he arrived in Galilee, the Galileans welcomed him. They had seen all that he had done in Jerusalem at the Passover Feast, for they also had been there.

6:2 and a great crowd of people followed him because they saw the miraculous signs he had performed on the sick.

6:5 When Yeshua looked up and saw a great crowd coming toward him, he said to Philip, "Where shall we buy bread for these people to eat?"

6:24 Once the crowd realized that neither Yeshua nor his disciples were there, they got into the boats and went to Capernaum in search of Yeshua.

7:31-32 Still, many in the crowd put their faith in him. They said, "When the Messiah comes, will he do more miraculous signs than this man?" The Pharisees heard the crowd whispering such things about him. Then the chief priests and the Pharisees sent Temple guards to arrest him.

7:48-49 "You mean he has deceived you also?" the Pharisees retorted. "Has any of the rulers or of the Pharisees believed in him? No! But this multitude that knows nothing of the law are accursed."

8:29-30 "The One who sent me is with me; He has not left me alone, for I always do what pleases him." Even as he spoke, many put their faith in him.

10:41 and many people came to him. They said, "Though John never performed a miraculous sign, all that John said about this man was true."

12:9 Meanwhile a large crowd of Jews found out that Yeshua was there and came, not only because of him but also to see Lazarus, whom he had raised from the dead.

11:45-46 Therefore many of the Jews who had come to visit Mary, and had seen what Yeshua did, put their faith in him. But some of them went to the Pharisees and told them what Yeshua had done.

12:10-12 So the chief priests made plans to kill Lazarus as well, for on account of him many of the Jews were going over to Yeshua and putting their faith in him. The next day the great crowd that had come for the Feast heard that Yeshua was on his way to Jerusalem.

12:17-19 Now the crowd that was with him when he called Lazarus from the tomb and raised him from the dead continued to spread the word. Many people, because they had heard that he had given this miraculous sign, went out to meet him. So the Pharisees said to one another, "See, this is getting us nowhere. Look how the whole world has gone after him!"

12:42 Yet at the same time many even among the leaders believed in him. But because of the Pharisees they would not confess their faith for fear they would be put out of the congregation;

## AFTER THE RESURRECTION

After the resurrection, the positive response continued.

Acts 2:37-41 "Then those who gladly received his word were immersed. There were added that day about three thousand souls." These were Jews.

Acts 4:4,21 "Many of those who heard the word believed, and the number of the men became about five thousand." These were Jews too.

Acts 5:14 "More and more men and women believed in the Lord and were added to their number." These also were Jews.

The people as a whole were very favorable towards the Jewish apostles of Yeshua. It was the high priest and all those with him who wanted to get rid of the apostles. So they sent the captain of the Temple guard with his officers to arrest them. "Then the captain went with the officers, and brought them without violence, for they were afraid that the people might stone them." (Acts 5:26) The captain of the Temple guard and his officers were afraid to mistreat the apostles, because they feared that the Jewish people would revolt against them and stone them to death.

Acts 6:7 So the word of God spread. The number of disciples in Jerusalem increased rapidly, and a large number of priests became obedient to the faith.

Acts 21:20 "... Then they said to Paul: 'You see, brother, how many tens of thousands of Jews have believed...'"

I would like to congratulate you for having read through this entire chapter; that is, if you actually did read through this entire chapter. If you only skimmed it and skipped to the end, then what can I tell you? Should I congratulate you for a half-hearted effort? Should I encourage you to continue in your practice of avoiding anything in life you find difficult? Far be it from me to condemn anyone, but whom do you think you're kidding?

In any case, you can always look at these scriptures again if you are in doubt. They do not seem to be difficult to understand. The view that "the Jews rejected Christ" is so contrary to the view in the Scriptures, that one must wonder where it came from. The tragic history of this ancient, but false, tradition is written in blood.

The next chapter examines the opposition from the theopolitical rulers. The chief priests and Pharisees testified of the overwhelming response to Yeshua among the Jewish people. They said to the Sanhedrin, the ruling council established by Rome: "If we let him go on like this, everyone will believe in him, and then the Romans will come and take away both our place and our nation." (John 11:48) They said to each other, "... Look how the whole world has gone after him!" (John 12:19)

Yeshua was a threat to what they had grabbed for themselves.

〜

I am indebted to my son Isaiah for the concept of this chapter and for the compilation of most of these scriptures.

CHAPTER SEVEN

# Theopolitical Rulers

*The Rulers Had Him Killed*

As a whole, the Jewish people responded quite positively to the message and actions of Yeshua. The theopolitical rulers did not. I have coined the term "theopolitical" to convey the nature of their identity and their conflict with Yeshua. These men were politicians who manipulated the national levers of power under the pretense of serving God.

The battle between the Pharisees and the Sadducees, for example, was not just one of scriptural interpretation, but one for control of the nation. Torah is primarily national law, not religious law. Whoever determined the Law controlled the nation, subject to Rome, of course.

Understanding this makes it possible to understand the nature of the conflict that took place between Yeshua and these rulers. It makes it possible to understand the nature and purpose of the change that took place with the resurrection. It makes it possible to understand why Yeshua will return.

The Roman Empire was not a benign bystander in the crucifixion of Yeshua. All the land was in subjection to Rome. All "authority" in the land existed subject to Rome. If we alter Paul's statement in Rom. 13:1, we can express the code by which Rome ruled: 'Everyone must submit himself to the governing authorities, for there is no authority except that which Rome has established. The authorities that exist have been established by Rome.' The conflict that led to Yeshua's execution can only be properly understood in light of this political dynamic.

Caesar had become master in Israel. Hanukkah commemorates the rededication of the Temple in 135 BCE, after the successful Jewish revolt against the dominion and values of Antiochus Epiphanes and his Seleucid Empire. Much of the battle, however, was internal between those Jews who wanted to remain true to God, His values, and His laws versus those who wanted to be like all the other nations, embracing their gods, their values, and their laws.

The Maccabees, also called Hasmoneans, led the successful revolt. Their descendants ruled for about one hundred years, but that rule degenerated into warring factions. Two brothers who each wanted to rule appealed to Rome to resolve the conflict between them. That appeal quickly led instead to Roman control in 63 BCE.

Six years later, in 57 B.C.E., Gabinius "divided the country into five districts and put them under the governorship of five *synhedria* (councils), instead of a central one in Jerusalem."[1] Later, the central *synhedrion* in Jerusalem became pre-eminent. Rome ruled the land through its own governor and the rulers it appointed to this indigenous council. This was similar to Roman practice throughout the empire.

As an institution, the Sanhedrin was not religious in nature, except insofar as it served the religion of power. Rome gave these appointed rulers power to maintain the obedience, or subservience, of the people. These appointed rulers were power brokers who knew how to manipulate and control their competitors.

Rome also appointed the high priesthood, something Antiochus had previously done, because the priesthood had natural, native authority. "The high priesthood, which had been abused for a long time, was frequently held by people who were thieves such as Jason and Menelaus, and was not given to the legitimate Zadokite house already from Hasmonean times. The position was granted to people as a reward for certain deeds by Herod, his successors, and the Romans.... When Gratus arrived to become governor of Judea in 15 C.E., he was given the authority to appoint high priests, as were the Roman governors following him (18.33-35)."[2]

Such position brought power and the wealth that power can bring. It brought privilege, and upward accountability. "[T]he High Priests were supposedly responsible for the guidance and protection of the interests of Jewish society as a whole. But as the leaders of the Jewish aristocracy in particular, they were expected by Rome to control Jewish society in the interest of the imperial order, and they were dependent on Roman power for the maintenance of their own position of power."[3]

They were not chosen by the people; they were not chosen by God. They were not chosen to serve or represent the people. Nor were they chosen to serve or represent God. They were chosen by Rome to serve and represent Rome.

"The provincial upper classes were by and large loyal to the imperial regime that guaranteed their own position. The aristocracies apparently preferred to enjoy their wealth and power rather than to risk the drastic penalties they knew would result from any unsuccessful revolt for independence."[4]

The gospels present a very negative picture of the High Priestly family that was put in power in the time of Yeshua. The Talmud and Josephus give us exactly the same picture. The Talmud says that these men were violent, greedy men who robbed both the common people and the common priests, and disregarded all appeals to restrain themselves.[5]

This High Priestly family enriched themselves through their commerce in the Temple: "This (Temple) market was what in Rabbinic writings is styled 'the bazaars of the sons of Annas' (Chanuyoth beney Chanan), the sons of that High-Priest Annas, who is so infamous in New Testament history... From the unrighteousness of the traffic carried on in these Bazaars, and the greed of the owners, the 'Temple-market' was at the time most unpopular. This appears, not only from the conduct and words of the patriarch Simeon [the grandson of Hillel, cf. Ker. i.7] and of Baba ben Buta... [Jerus. Chag. 78a], but from the fact that popular indignation, three years before the destruction of Jerusalem, swept away the Bazaars of the family of Annas, and this, as expressly stated, on account of the sinful greed which characterized their dealings."[6]

Josephus remarks, "As for the high priest Ananias... [he] was a great hoarder up of money... He also had servants who were very wicked, who joined themselves to the boldest sort of the people, and went to the thrashing-floors, and took away the tithes that belonged to the priests by violence, and did not refrain from beating such as would not give these tithes to them. So the other high priests acted in the like manner, as did those his servants, without any one being able to prohibit them; so that (some of the) priests, that of old were wont to be supported with those tithes, died for want of food..."[7]

**THE GOSPELS PRESENT A VERY NEGATIVE PICTURE OF THE HIGH PRIESTLY FAMILY THAT WAS PUT IN POWER IN THE TIME OF YESHUA. THE TALMUD AND JOSEPHUS GIVE US EXACTLY THE SAME PICTURE.**

Josephus says that, "A sedition arose between the high priests, with regard to one another; for they got together bodies of the people, and frequently came, from reproaches, to throwing of stones at each other; but Ananias was too hard for the rest, by his riches,—which enabled him to gain those that were the most ready to receive. Costabarus, also, and Saulus, did themselves get together a multitude of wicked wretches... but still they used violence with the people, weaker than themselves. And from that time it principally came to pass, that our city was greatly disordered, and that all things grew worse and worse among us."[8]

The particular Annas, or Ananias, to whom Josephus refers is not the same as the one depicted in the gospels. He is of the same family, only a generation later. He may well be the same Ananias referred to in the confrontation recorded in Acts 23 between Paul and the Sanhedrin. These theopolitical rulers, with few exceptions, were violent, lawless men.

In that confrontation, Ananias ordered Paul to be struck. Realizing that he would not be given a hearing, and "knowing that some of them were Sadducees and the others Pharisees,

Paul then called out in the Sanhedrin, 'My brothers, I am a Pharisee, the son of a Pharisee. I stand on trial because of my hope in the resurrection of the dead.'

"When he said this, a dispute broke out between the Pharisees and the Sadducees, and the assembly was divided. (The Sadducees say that there is no resurrection, and that there are neither angels nor spirits, but the Pharisees acknowledge them all.)

"There was a great uproar, and some of the teachers of the law who were Pharisees stood up and argued vigorously. The dispute became so violent that the commander was afraid Paul would be torn to pieces by them. He ordered the troops to go down and take him away from them by force and bring him into the barracks." (Acts 23:6-10) These theopolitical rulers, with few exceptions, were violent, lawless men.

The High Priests had position, wealth, power, and no scruples about using what they had to get what they wanted. Plus, though they lived in defiance of the core of the Scriptures, their position itself carried and conveyed Biblical legitimacy. They were the natural ruling aristocracy in Israel.

All of this is what brought them into conflict with Yeshua. He had no position, but he acted like he owned the place. "Yeshua entered the Temple courts, and, while he was teaching, the chief priests and the elders of the people came to him. 'By what authority are you doing these things?' they asked. 'And who gave you this authority?'" (Mt. 21:23)

They thought his claim to forgive sins was blasphemy. He responded, "'So that you may know that the Son of Man has authority on earth to forgive sins'—then he said to the paralytic— 'Get up, take your mat and go home.' And the man got up and went home. When the crowd saw this, they were filled with awe; and they praised God, who had given such authority to men." (Mt. 9:6-8)

"On reaching Jerusalem, Yeshua entered the Temple area and began driving out those who were buying and selling there. He overturned the tables of the moneychangers and the benches of those selling doves, and would not allow anyone to carry merchandise through the temple courts. And as he taught them, he said, 'Is it not written: *My house will be called a house of prayer for all nations*? But you have made it *a den of robbers*.' The chief priests and the teachers of the law heard this and began looking for a way to kill him, for they feared him, because the whole crowd was amazed at his teaching." (Mark 11:15-18)

He had no wealth, but he warned each one who did: "God said to him, 'You fool! This very night your life will be demanded from you. Then who will get what you have prepared for yourself?' This is how it will be with anyone who stores up things for himself but is not rich toward God." (Luke 12:20-21) He had no wealth, but he warned those who thought they were rich. "So if you have not been trustworthy in handling worldly wealth, who will trust you with true riches?" (Luke 16:11)

He had no political power, but he claimed to be an insider with the ultimate Powerbroker. He told Pilate, "You would have no power over me if it were not given to you from above...." (John 19:11) He was not intimidated by those who arrested him. "Do you think I cannot call on my Father, and He will at once put at my disposal more than twelve legions of angels?" (Mt. 26:53)

Yeshua submitted to the positional authority which belonged to the High Priests, but defied their exercise of power. He did not seek their presence and favors, but instead served the common people and the outcasts. He taught and acted with authority, an authority that did not come from the High Priests, nor from Rome.

He rejected the claim of the religious rulers to authority over Shabbat. He healed a man, "But they were furious and began to discuss with one another what they might do to Yeshua." (Luke 6:11) He rejected their claim, and asserted his own. "For the Son of Man is Lord of Shabbat." (Mt. 12:8)

Yeshua warned his disciples not to tell anyone that he was the Messiah, the legitimate and righteous king and ruler of Israel. He came to deliver his people Israel from those who oppressed them. (e.g. Luke 1:67-79) He knew what the response of the unrighteous rulers would be. "From that time on Yeshua began to explain to his disciples that he must go to Jerusalem and suffer many things at the hands of the elders, chief priests and teachers of the law, and that he must be killed and on the third day be raised to life." (Mt. 16:21; cf. Mark 8:31; Luke 9:22)

> THEY CAME AT NIGHT, BECAUSE THEY FEARED THE PEOPLE. THEY ARRESTED YESHUA, AND HE "DISAPPEARED" IN THE MIDDLE OF THE NIGHT, A COMMON PRACTICE OF CORRUPT POLITICAL RULERS EVERYWHERE.

When that time came, these theopolitical rulers sent a crowd of their own people to arrest Yeshua. "Just as he was speaking, Judas, one of the Twelve, appeared. With him was a crowd armed with swords and clubs, sent from the chief priests, the teachers of the law, and the elders." (Mark 14:43)

They came at night, because they feared the people. They arrested Yeshua, and he "disappeared" in the middle of the night, a common practice of corrupt political rulers everywhere.

His illegal trial before the Roman-appointed Sanhedrin was held in the early morning, before anyone even knew that he had been arrested. Only those who could be depended upon were invited. Nicodemus, for example, was not. "Early in the morning, all the chief priests and the elders of the people came to the decision to put Yeshua to death. They bound him, led him away and handed him over to Pilate, the governor." (Mt. 27:1-2)

It was taken care of before the city was awake. "Very early in the morning, the chief priests, with the elders, the teachers of the law and the whole Sanhedrin, reached a decision. They bound Yeshua, led him away and handed him over to Pilate." (Mark 15:1) Hardly anyone among the people knew anything at all about what was going on.

The chief priests, the elders, the teachers of the law and the Sanhedrin brought Yeshua to Pilate, and they brought their crowd with them. They had decided to put Yeshua to death. "And they began to accuse him, saying, 'We have found this man subverting our nation. He opposes payment of taxes to Caesar and claims to be Messiah, a king.'" (Luke 23:2)

Notice the three charges. 1. He is causing sedition. 2. He is preaching tax rebellion 3. He claims to be a self-appointed king.

Pilate wanted to set Yeshua free. He had the power to do it. He could have done it. But these were very serious charges coming from the Roman-established Synhedria. Pilate knew that the charges were false, "for he knew it was out of envy that they had handed Yeshua over to him." (Mt. 27:18)

On the basis of the charges they had brought against Yeshua, the theopolitical rulers threatened Pilate: "'If you let this man go, you are no friend of Caesar. Anyone who claims to be a king opposes Caesar.' When Pilate heard this, he…" changed his mind. (John 19:12b-13a)

The theopolitical rulers were Roman-appointed officials. "[T]he imperial government held the provincial aristocrats accountable not simply for the steady flow of tax revenues but also (under the authority and supervision of the Roman governor) for maintenance of order in their society. This apparently included accountability for breaches of public order by those supposedly under their control—just as a Roman governor was held responsible for outbreaks of disorder in the territory subject to his authority."[9]

The rulers carefully selected the charges they brought against Yeshua. If Pilate did not act according to the seriousness of these crimes, they could bring charges to Rome against him. "The Roman system also made provision for dealing with unjustified exploitation and brutality by its governors. In many cases of unsatisfactory behavior the governor was simply recalled. But it was also possible for the provincial authorities to bring accusations before the Senate or the Emperor. Of course, it was extremely difficult for the provincials to mount the necessary expedition of accusers to Rome, and the Senate was inclined to treat members of its own order somewhat leniently. Nevertheless, in the large majority of known cases the accused governors were convicted—or committed suicide before the trial."[10]

Pilate wanted to release Yeshua, but not at the cost of his own career, or his own life. So he seized the opportunity to send him to Herod, hoping that Herod would take the responsibility, since Yeshua was from Herod's jurisdiction in Galilee. The chief priests and the teachers of the law followed Yeshua to Herod, accusing him vehemently. They wanted him dead.

Herod was a brutal man, but he had neither reason nor inclination to bring the wrath of the theopolitical rulers down upon himself. Besides that, some of the Pharisees had already plotted with the followers of Herod to kill Yeshua. (cf. Mark 3:6) For that purpose, the chief priests, the teachers of the law and the elders "later sent some of the Pharisees and Herodians to Yeshua to catch him in his words." (Mark 12:13) It was a convenient political alliance.

But Herod did not want the responsibility of putting Yeshua to death, for it would have increased popular resentment against him, without benefiting him in any way. "Then Herod and his soldiers ridiculed and mocked Yeshua. Dressing him in an elegant robe, they sent him back to Pilate." (cf. Luke 23:7-11) This is the same Herod who later had Jacob, the brother of John, arrested and killed. He then arrested Peter and was about to kill him, too, but Peter was supernaturally delivered. (cf. Acts 12:1-10)

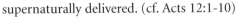

THE PEOPLE EAGERLY LISTENED TO YESHUA. THE PEOPLE DID NOT SUPPORT THE BRUTAL ROMAN RULE, NOR THE CORRUPT SANHEDRIN WHICH ENFORCED IT.

Pilate tried again to release Yeshua, but the high priests persuaded the crowd, which was filled with the people they had brought, to call out for the death of Yeshua. Knowing Yeshua was innocent, but "wanting to satisfy the crowd, Pilate released Barabbas to them. He had Yeshua flogged, and handed him over to be crucified." (Mark 15:15)

Before we leave this subject, we need to look at two historically important verses. "When Pilate saw that he was getting nowhere, but that instead an uproar was starting, he took water and washed his hands in front of the crowd. 'I am innocent of this man's blood,' he said. 'It is your responsibility!'

"All the people answered, 'Let his blood be on us and on our children!'" (Mt. 27:24-25)

There is no need to elaborate on the murderous use to which these verses have been put, but we should remember four things. First, only Pilate had the legal authority to condemn Yeshua to death. No one else did. Pilate's act of washing his hands in front of the crowd was political theater. It did not change the legal reality that it was Pilate alone who sentenced Yeshua to death. Pilate knew that Yeshua was innocent, but he had him flogged, and he had him crucified.

Second, "All the people" means all the people who were there—not all the people in the world, not all the people who are Jews, and not even all the people who were then in Jerusalem—just all the people who were at that place at that time. Third, we know that the followers of the theopolitical rulers formed the major component of all these people, the most vocal component. That is the way big city bosses operate. Fourth, the blood of Yeshua atones for sin.

As for the response of the Jewish people as a whole to Yeshua: "Every day he was teaching at the Temple. But the chief priests, the teachers of the law and the rulers among the people were trying to kill him. Yet they could not find any way to do it, because all the people hung on his words." (Lk. 19:47-48)

The people eagerly listened to Yeshua. The people did not support the brutal Roman rule nor the corrupt Sanhedrin which enforced it. When Yeshua was led through the city, "A large number of people followed him, including women who mourned and wailed for him. (Luke 23:27) These were Jewish people.

How did the disciples of Yeshua view the crucifixion? As they explained to a risen Yeshua whom they did not recognize, "The chief priests and our rulers handed him over to be sentenced to death, and they crucified him." (Luke 24:20) That is the simple Biblical view.

These were Jewish disciples, the only kind there were at the time. These were part of the faithful remnant in Israel that God always kept for Himself. The rulers had to be replaced, not the people.

Now let's take a look at what is the single most anti-semitic mistranslation of the Scriptures, the mistranslation of *Ioudaioi* in the gospel of John.


FOOTNOTES

1. Doron Mendels, *The Rise and Fall of Jewish Nationalism, Jewish and Christian Ethnicity in Ancient Palestine*, Doubleday, NY, 1992, p.247

2. Ibid., pp.317, 295

3. Richard A. Horsley, "High Priests and the Politics of Roman Palestine," *JSJ, 17*, 1986, p.24

4. Ibid., p.29

5. For example, the skins of the animals sacrificed at the Temple were traditionally divided among all the priests who served. These particular high priests violently took all the skins for themselves, depriving the common priests of a significant part of their livelihood.

   They were entreated to consider the needs of others, "Yet the chief priests still seized (them) by force...Abba Saul b. Bothnith said in the Name of Abba Joseph b. Hanin: 'Woe is me because of the house of Boethus; woe is me because of their staves! [with which they beat the people.] Woe is me because of the house of Kathros; woe is me because of their pens! [with which they wrote their evil decrees.] Woe is me because of the house of Ishmael the son of Phabi; woe is me because of their fists! For they are High Priests and their sons are Temple treasurers and their sons-in-law are trustees and their servants beat the people with staves!

   "Our Rabbis taught: Four cries did the Temple Court cry out. The first: 'Depart hence, ye children of Eli,' for they defiled the Temple of the Lord…" Pes.57a The bracketed comments are in the Soncino footnotes.

Eli was the High Priest when Samuel, who later anointed Saul and then David as Israel's kings, was a boy. In this first cry of the Temple Court the Rabbis called the High Priestly families, "children [sons] of Eli." What they meant is clear from the Scriptures. "Now the sons of Eli were worthless men; they did not know the Lord." (1 Sam. 2:12) They robbed the people of their sacrifices, and "they lay with the women who served at the doorway of the tent of meeting." (1 Sam. 2:22)

6. Alfred Edersheim, *The Life and Times of Jesus the Messiah*, Anson D.F. Randolph and Company, New York, 1883, Vol. I, pp.371-2, citing Siphre on Dt. sec.105, end, ed. Friedmann, P.95a; Jer. Peah i.6

7. Josephus, *Ant., XX, 9, 2-4*

8. Ibid.

9. Horsley, op. cit. p.28

10. Ibid.

CHAPTER EIGHT

# John's Ιουδαιοι

*Bad Translation Distorts Reality*

We read in the gospels of Matthew, Mark, and Luke that though there were a few times of conflict between some of the common people and Yeshua, in general they gladly listened to him. With his own disciples Yeshua also had times of conflict. These conflicts are never presented as something Yeshua sought to avoid. On the contrary, such conflict was an inevitable part of the process of challenging and enlightening his listeners.

With certain theopolitical authorities, the nature of the conflict was quite different. These bitter disputes were the result of the unwillingness of these authorities to hear and acknowledge Yeshua and his message as coming from God. On his part, Yeshua did not acknowledge their conception of their authority, so they determined to destroy him. They conspired against him, arrested and tried him, and demanded that he be put to death.

All of this is quite clear, but many translations make it appear that the gospel of John describes a very different situation, i.e. that ALL the Jewish people were opposed to Yeshua. The key to this difference is to be found in the words and actions which John attributes to the *Ioudaioi*, and how this Greek word is translated. Many translations always translate *Ioudaioi* as "the Jews," even though that was not its only, nor even its primary meaning. That is definitely not its primary meaning in the gospel of John. This error in translation supports errors in theology, and disaster in history.

The word *Ioudaioi* appears more than 50 times in John, about four times as often as in all the other gospels combined. If we subtract the references using the phrase "King of the Jews," which was on the cross, *Ioudaioi* appears only four times in the first three gospels, but still some 50 times in John. The usages in John are significant not only numerically, but also historically. For centuries, they have been used to legitimize anti-Jewish feeling, doctrine, and policy in the Church. In furtherance of this purpose, *Ioudaioi* is always understood to mean "the Jews," that is, all Jews. That is not, however, the primary way that the gospel of John uses the term. In a further flight of malevolent fantasy, theologians and preachers make it refer to all Jews of all time.

The gospel of John uses the term with three different meanings, depending upon the context. 1. A general term for the descendants of Abraham, Isaac, and Jacob; 2. The inhabitants of Judea, in distinction from the inhabitants of Galilee or some other part of the land of Israel; and 3. The Jewish authorities as a whole, or sectarian Jews, specifically the Pharisees and their leaders.

The third meaning is the primary one used by John. That will become apparent as we look at every verse where John uses the word. For the sake of simplification, the different Greek declensions of *Ioudaioi* will also be rendered as *Ioudaioi*. Comments within brackets [ ] connected to the verses are mine.

THE MISTRANSLATION OF THIS ONE WORD HAS CONTRIBUTED SIGNIFICANTLY TO THE MURDER OF MILLIONS OF JEWS THROUGHOUT CHRISTIAN HISTORY.

It is not unusual for a word to have different meanings depending upon the context in which it appears. Many words have significantly different meanings in different contexts. The word "Yankee" provides a good parallel English example.

In the course of a few centuries of usage, the word has developed widely different meanings. Initially, it referred to Dutch settlers. In the American Civil War, Southerners used it to designate all Northerners. In the turbulent 1960s, it was used in Latin America to designate all citizens of the United States.

And, as every Boston Red Sox fan knows, "Yankees" is a very negatively charged term that refers to a specific baseball team from New York. In December 2002, the President of the Boston Red Sox referred to the Yankees as "the evil empire". [This is our year.[1]]

The word has different meanings, depending upon the context in which it is used. On the other hand, some languages have more than one word to designate what, in English, is simply "Jews." In Russian, there are two words, *iudei* and *evrei*. *Evrei* does not have any religious connotation; it designates a people group. *Iudei* does have religious connotation. There are *evrei* who are not *iudei*.

This same dichotomy exists in Israel today. There are nonreligious Jewish Israelis who say, "I'm not a Jew, I'm an Israeli. A 'Jew' is a follower of Judaism." In saying this, they distinguish themselves from the religious orthodox. But they do not mean that they are Gentiles. Whether or not they consider themselves "Jews" depends upon the context in which the word is used.

(There are ultra-orthodox Jews who strongly agree that such nonreligious Jews are not really Jews. For them, a Jew must believe as they do in order to really be a Jew.)

Because of the historical and theological consequences, it is important to know how *Ioudaioi* should be translated in the gospel of John. What did John mean when he used this Greek word? Usually the context makes the meaning sufficiently clear. Words should always be translated according to their intended meaning.

By examining every verse where *Ioudaioi* appears, we can establish the way in which John used it. This may seem tedious to you, but the mistranslation of this one word has contributed significantly to the murder of millions of Jews throughout Christian history. This is more than an academic exercise.

### 1. *Ioudaioi* as a general term for the descendants of Abraham, Isaac, and Jacob.

The word is often used this way throughout the Messianic Writings. In this sense, it is the equivalent of "the people of Israel". For example, Luke tells us, "Now there were staying in Jerusalem God-fearing *Ioudaioi* from every nation under heaven.... Parthians, Medes and Elamites; residents of Mesopotamia, Judea and Cappadocia, Pontus and Asia, Phrygia and Pamphylia, Egypt and the parts of Libya near Cyrene; visitors from Rome (both *Ioudaioi* and proselytes); Cretans and Arabs..." (Acts 2:5,9-11a)

Luke tells us in Greek that when Peter spoke to these *Ioudaioi*, he said, "Men *Ioudaioi* and all of you who live in Jerusalem, let me explain this to you; listen carefully to what I say." (Acts 2:14b) To the same crowd of *Ioudaioi*, he also said, "Men of Israel, listen to this..." (Acts 2:22) Clearly, Peter used "Men *Ioudaioi*" and "Men of Israel" as equivalent terms.

In his Greek text, John sometimes uses *Ioudaioi* in this general way. The text of the gospel of John indicates that it was written primarily for a non-Hebrew speaking audience. Some people believe that John wrote for a Jewish audience, but that may not be the case. John often explains Hebrew words to his readers. Or, at least, he is careful to designate the Greek word which represents the original Hebrew.

"They said, 'Rabbi' (which means Teacher)..." John 1:38

"... 'We have found the Messiah' (that is, the Christos)." John 1:41

"... 'You will be called Kefa' (which, when translated, is Peter )." John 1:42

"...the Sea of Galilee (that is, the Sea of Tiberias)." John 6:1

"... 'wash in the Pool of Siloam.' (this word means Sent)...." John 9:7

"Then Toma (called Didymus)..." John 11:16 [*T'om* is the Hebrew word for "twin." *Didymus* is the Greek equivalent.]

"... a place known as the Stone Pavement (which in Hebrew is *Gabbata*)." John 19:13

"... the place of the Skull (which in Hebrew is called *Golgota*)." John 19:17

"... 'Rabboni!' (which means Teacher)." John 20:16

John occasionally identifies the feasts of Israel in a similar way, a way which would seem to be superfluous for a Jewish audience.

"...Yeshua went up to Jerusalem for a feast of the *Ioudaioi*." Jn. 5:1

"The Passover Feast of the *Ioudaioi* was near." Jn. 6:4

"Now the feast of the *Ioudaioi*, Tabernacles, was near," Jn. 7:2

"When it was almost time for the Passover of the *Ioudaioi*..." Jn. 11:55

"Because it was the day of Preparation of the *Ioudaioi*..." Jn. 19:42

It is possible that there was a time difference between the Judean observance of the feasts and the Galilean observance, but it is not likely that, if there were such a difference, it would be worth noting for John's audience. The most likely meaning of *Ioudaioi* in these verses is Jews in general. Accordingly, that is how it should be translated in these verses.

There are other passages where that also seems to be the case. These occasionally involve non-Jews, who would be more likely to use a general designation. "The Samaritan woman said to him, "You are a *Ioudaios* [a singular form of *Ioudaioi*] and I am a Samaritan woman. How can you ask me for a drink, since *Ioudaioi* do not associate with Samaritans?" Jn. 4:9

Yeshua's later response to her uses the same general sense. "You Samaritans bow down to what you do not know; we bow down to what we do know, for salvation is from the *Ioudaioi*." Jn. 4:22

There are several uses of the word with this general sense in connection with Pilate and the crucifixion. "But it is your custom for me to release to you one prisoner at the time of the Passover. Do you want me to release 'the king of the *Ioudaioi*'?" Jn. 18:39

The Roman soldiers "went up to him again and again, saying, 'Hail, king of the *Ioudaioi*!' And they struck him in the face." Jn. 19:3

"Pilate then went back inside the palace, summoned Yeshua and asked him, 'Are you the king of the *Ioudaioi*?'" Jn. 18:33

"Pilate had a notice prepared and fastened to the cross. It read: YESHUA OF NAZARETH, THE KING OF THE *IOUDAIOI*." Jn. 19:19

There are passages where an otherwise unidentified multitude of the Jewish people are present. The Greek word *ochlos*, which means "crowd" or "multitude" is generally used by John to signify the common people, in contrast to the Jewish authorities. "John, in the Gospel, distinguishes between the multitude (*ho ochlos*) and the Jews (*Ioudaioi*). By the former he means... the *mass* of the people, chiefly Galileans; by the latter, more particularly Judeans, the leaders of Judaism in opposition to Jesus."[2]

There may be a few exceptions, cases where *Ioudaioi* is used, instead of *ochlos*, to refer to the people as a whole. In the sixth chapter of John, there is a crowd/*ochlos* that follows Yeshua across the Sea of Galilee. (cf. Jn. 6:24) Some from the crowd ask him questions, and he responds. In describing the reaction of the crowd, John uses *Ioudaioi* rather than *ochlos*. Either John meant the entire crowd, or he meant the *Ioudaioi* who were in the crowd.

"At this the *Ioudaioi* began to grumble about him because he said, 'I am the bread that came down from heaven.'" Jn. 6:41

"Then the *Ioudaioi* began to argue sharply among themselves, 'How can this man give us his flesh to eat?'" Jn. 6:52

"'I have spoken openly to the world,' Yeshua replied. 'I always taught in synagogues or at the Temple, where all the *Ioudaioi* come together. I said nothing in secret.'" Jn. 18:20

"Many of the *Ioudaioi* read this sign, for the place where Yeshua was crucified was near the city, and the sign was written in Hebrew, Latin and Greek. The chief priests of the *Ioudaioi* protested to Pilate, 'Do not write *The King of the Ioudaioi*, but that this man claimed to be king of the *Ioudaioi*.'" Jn. 19:19-21

"Taking Yeshua's body, the two of them wrapped it, with the spices, in strips of linen. This was in accordance with burial customs of the *Ioudaioi*." Jn. 19:40 It is possible that the reference here is to Pharisaic burial practices, since Nicodemus and Joseph of Arimathea were Pharisees, rather than to the burial customs common to all the people. However, if that were the case, John would most likely have used the word *paradosin*, i.e. tradition. That is the word used in Mt. 15:2,3,6 and in Mk.7:3,5,13.

"Yanqui" del ingles yankee es el apelativo con el que se conoce a los estadounidenses de los estados norteños. Me cuenta Carlos de Vicente que tiene su origen en las grandes inmigraciones de holandeses, en el s. XVII y XVIII, con destino a esa zona; eran colonos de procedencia humilde que llevaban, como alimento para la larga travesía, el producto nacional holandés: un queso. Como el nombre de varón más frecuente entre los holandeses era Jan Kaas, rápidamente recibieron un mote: Jan Cheese (Juan Queso). A partir de ahí, se mantuvo la fonética con la correspondiente simplificación ortográfica.[3]

["Yanqui," from the English "Yankee," is the name by which the people of the nothern states of the United States are known. Carlos de Vicente has told me that the name has its origin in the great migrations from Holland to that area in the 17th and 18th centuries. They were pilgrims from humble backgrounds, who carried cheese, the national product of Holland, for the long journey. Since the most popular name among them was Jan Kass, they quickly received the name of Jan Cheese (Juan Queso). Ever since then, the phonetic has remained with its corresponding simplified spelling.]

## 2. *Ioudaioi* meaning the inhabitants of Judea, in distinction from the inhabitants of Galilee or some other part of the land of Israel.

Originally, the Hebrew *Yehudim* signified members of the tribe of Judah/*Yehudah*. In the days of the divided kingdoms, it served to designate all the inhabitants of the southern kingdom of Judah, as opposed to the northern kingdom of Israel. In the time of the exile, it was used to designate all the descendants of Abraham, Isaac, and Jacob.

The Septuagint routinely uses *Ioudaioi* to translate *Yehudim* in the approximately 60 places where it appears. Most of the occurrences are in Jeremiah, Esther, and Nehemiah. In Jeremiah, leading up to the exile of the southern kingdom of Judah/Judea, the meaning is "Judeans". In Esther and Nehemiah, which took place in the time of the exile and the return, the meaning is "the Jewish people".

In translation, "Jews" and "Judea" don't even look related, but in the first century Mediterranean world, the connection between the people and the land is both obvious and necessary. People are identifiable by their (ancestral) land. By definition, *Ioudaioi*/"Jews" are the people from *Ioudaia*/"Judea". The word *Ioudaioi* contained geographic content.

In the land of Israel, Judea was a particular geographic area. The geographic distinction between Judea and the other parts of Israel appears in all of the gospels, as well as elsewhere in the Messianic Writings.

"Joseph also went up from the town of Nazareth in Galilee to Judea/*Ioudaia*, to Bethlehem the town of David, because he belonged to the house and line of David." Luke 2:4 Joseph was living in Galilee, but his ancestral hometown was in Judea.

"Yeshua withdrew with his disciples to the lake, and a large crowd from Galilee followed. When they heard all he was doing, many people came to him from Judea, Jerusalem, Idumea, and the regions across the Jordan and around Tyre and Sidon." Mark 3:7-8

Yeshua and his earliest disciples, including John, were from Galilee. John knew, and notes, the difference between being in Galilee and being in Judea. For example, "When the Lord learned of this, he left Judea and went back once more to Galilee." Jn. 4:3

Since the most powerful theopolitical authorities lived in Judea, there are times when the theopolitical and the geographical designations overlap. In Jn.7:1, *Ioudaioi* has a geographic sense, but the primary designation is the theopolitical authorities. "After this, Yeshua went around in Galilee, purposely staying away from Judea/*Ioudaia* because the *Ioudaioi* were waiting to take his life." This records the beginning of the occasion when the chief priests and Pharisees sent the Temple guard to try to arrest Yeshua. Galilee was filled with Jews, but it was the theopolitical leaders in Judea who were seeking to kill Yeshua.

The death and resurrection of Lazarus took place in Judea. The account begins when Yeshua "said to his disciples, 'Let us go back to Judea.'

" 'But Rabbi,' they said, 'a short while ago the *Ioudaioi* tried to stone you, and yet you are going back there?'" Jn. 11:7-8 In this case, the disciples were referring to the incident recorded in Jn. 10:31. That was an encounter with some Pharisees. So the *Ioudaioi* who tried to stone Yeshua, to whom the disciples referred, were Pharisees.

In the rest of the account in chapter 11, John uses *Ioudaioi* to designate the Judeans.

"And many of the *Ioudaioi* had come to Marta and Miriam to comfort them in the loss of their brother." Jn. 11:19

"When the *Ioudaioi* who had been with Miriam in the house, comforting her, noticed how quickly she got up and went out, they followed her, supposing she was going to the tomb to mourn there." Jn. 11:31

"When Yeshua saw her weeping, and the *Ioudaioi* who had come along with her also weeping, he was deeply moved in spirit and troubled." Jn. 11:33

"Then the *Ioudaioi* said, 'See how he loved him!'" Jn. 11:36

"Therefore many of the *Ioudaioi* who had come to visit Miriam, and had seen what Yeshua did, put their faith in him." Jn. 11:45

*Ioudaioi* here refers to the Judeans and not to the Pharisees. This is borne out by what immediately follows, where the *Ioudaioi* are treated as distinct from the Pharisees. "But some of them [*the Ioudaioi*] went to the Pharisees and told them what Yeshua had done. Then the chief priests and the Pharisees called a meeting of the Sanhedrin. 'What are we accomplishing?' they asked. 'Here is this man performing many miraculous signs.'

"... So from that day on they [these members of the Sanhedrin] plotted to take his life. Therefore Yeshua no longer moved about publicly among the *Ioudaioi*. Instead he withdrew to a region near the desert, to a village called Ephraim, where he stayed with his disciples." Jn. 11:46-47,53-54

Why does John use the same word so differently? Those are the different meanings of the same word. The context provides the necessary clarification. We also use words like this, words that have associated but different meanings, depending upon the context in which they appear. When Yeshua later returned to visit Lazarus and his sisters, *Ioudaioi* is again used to designate the Judeans, because the event described takes place in Judea.

"Meanwhile a large crowd of *Ioudaioi* found out that Yeshua was there and came, not only because of him but also to see Lazarus, whom he had raised from the dead. So the chief priests made plans to kill Lazarus as well, for on account of him many of the *Ioudaioi* were going over to Yeshua and putting their faith in him." Jn. 12:9-11

The intended meaning of *Ioudaioi* in these verses is "Judeans". So that is how it should be translated in these verses.

> Near Chattahoochee
> Fulton Co.
> July 15th, 1864
>
> Dear Sister,
>
> We go down to the edge of the river on our side and the Yankees come down on their side and talk to each other. ...The Yankees are very much in want of tobacco, and our Government gives it to us, and we used to trade tobacco with them for knives and canteens. There is a rock near the middle of the river to which they would swim and trade. After a while they got so well acquainted that some of our men would swim clear across and land among the Yankess. The Yankees were not so bold for a long time, but a few days ago they got to coming across also. That has been broken up now and if any trading is carried on, it is done contrary to orders....
>
> Write to me soon.
>
> Yours truly,
> (s)O.D. Chester[4]

### 3. *Ioudaioi* meaning the Jewish authorities as a whole, or sectarian Jews, specifically the Pharisees and their leaders.

In the vast majority of cases, John uses *Ioudaioi* in this sense. "The Pharisees," as opposed to "some Pharisees," generally designates the leaders of the Pharisees. The leaders of the Pharisees were also members of the Sanhedrin.

"Now this was John's testimony when the *Ioudaioi* of Jerusalem sent priests and Levites from Jerusalem to ask him 'Who are you?'" Jn. 1:19 Who were the *Ioudaioi* who had sent these priests and Levites? The answer is given in a following verse, Jn. 1:24: "And they had been sent out from the Pharisees."

Verse 1:19 is John's first use of *Ioudaioi*. In 1:24, he explicitly says whom he means by the term. That should inform us as we read all of John's gospel.

In commenting on the use of *Ioudaioi* in this verse, and elsewhere in John, *The Expositor's Greek Testament* says, "In this Gospel it is used with a hostile implication as the designation of the 'entire theocratic community as summed up in its official heads... Here 'the Jews' probably indicates the Sanhedrim, composed of priests, presbyters, and scribes...".[5]

In this context, the Greek word *Ioudaioi* does refer to the "priests, presbyters, and scribes," and so it should be translated in such a way that it communicates that meaning. The purpose of translation is to give the correct meaning. To the contrary though, when translators put "the Jews," they are communicating something different from what is in the text.

In some cases, the political or sectarian content of what is at issue indicates who is meant. For example, Jn. 2:6: "Nearby stood six stone water jars, the kind used by the *Ioudaioi* for ceremonial washing, each holding from twenty to thirty gallons." Ceremonial washing was pre-scribed by the Pharisees. This is explained in Mark 7:3: "The Pharisees and all the *Ioudaioi* do not eat unless they give their hands a ceremonial washing, holding to the tradition/para-dosin of the elders."

How do we know who is intended by *Ioudaioi* in this verse? Most Jews of the time did not follow the tradition of the elders. [This is amply demonstrated by repeated Talmudic condemnations of "the people of the land," who did not follow these traditions.] The Pharisees did. This particular confrontation recorded in Mark came about because, "The Pharisees and some of the Scribes who had come from Jerusalem gathered around Yeshua and saw some of his disciples eating food with hands that were 'unclean,' that is, unwashed." (Mark 7:1-2) These disciples of Yeshua were, of

> WHEN TRANSLATORS [OF JOHN] PUT "THE JEWS" HERE, THEY ARE COMMUNICATING SOMETHING DIFFERENT FROM WHAT IS IN THE TEXT.

course, Jews—Jews who did not follow the tradition of the elders. Mark, therefore, and John also, are using *Ioudaioi* in this context to denote the sectarian Jews.

It is important to keep in mind that these theopolitical rulers were, in effect, officials of the Roman Empire. The High Priests were directly appointed by the Roman governor. The Sanhedrin was used by the Romans as a ruling council. Its members functioned under, and for, Roman authority. This was a very significant factor when the *Ioudaioi* questioned Yeshua's authority.

"Then the *Ioudaioi* demanded of him, 'What miraculous sign can you show us to prove your authority to do all this?'

"Yeshua answered them, 'Destroy this temple, and I will raise it again in three days.'

"The *Ioudaioi* replied, "It has taken forty-six years to build this Temple, and you are going to raise it in three days?" Jn. 2:18-20

The issue was the authority that Yeshua was exercising. For whom was that an issue? It was a primary issue for the ones who claimed to have that authority themselves. "Yeshua entered the Temple courts, and, while he was teaching, the chief priests and the elders of the people came to him. 'By what authority are you doing these things?' they asked. 'And who gave you this authority?' " Mt. 21:23

Scholars understand that John uses *Ioudaioi* to designate the Jewish authorities. "οι Ιουδαιοι, as frequent in John, means 'the Jewish authorities'..."; " 'the Jews',...as usual in John, the authorities...".[6] Since John uses the word in these passages to indicate "the Jewish authorities," that is how *Ioudaioi* should be translated. It is a mistake to translate *Ioudaioi* as "the Jews," when that is not what it means.

If we understand the context, we know who is being designated. In Jn. 3:25: "An argument developed between some of John's disciples and a certain *Ioudaiou* [a singular form of *Ioudaioi*] over the matter of ceremonial purification." And again, in Jn. 18:28 "Then the *Ioudaioi* led Yeshua from Caiaphas to the palace of the Roman governor. By now it was early morning, and to avoid ceremonial uncleanness the *Ioudaioi* did not enter the palace; they wanted to be able to eat the Passover." Ceremonial purity was a very important issue for the Pharisees and the theopolitical authorities who led Yeshua to Pilate.

In John 5 there is a similar confrontation about Shabbat. Yeshua healed a lame man on Shabbat. The man picked up the mat on which he had been lying and walked on his way.

"And so the *Ioudaioi* said to the man who had been healed, 'It is Shabbat; the law forbids you to carry your mat.'... The man went away and told the *Ioudaioi* that it was Yeshua who had made him well. So, because Yeshua was doing these things on the Sabbath, the *Ioudaioi* persecuted him.... For this reason the *Ioudaioi* tried all the harder to kill him; not only was he breaking Shabbat, but he was even calling God his own Father, making himself equal with God." Jn. 5:10,15-16,18

The basic law for Shabbat is given in Ex. 23:12: "Six days do your work, but on the seventh day do not work, so that your ox and your donkey may rest and the slave born in your household, and the alien as well, may be refreshed." In Jer. 17:21-22, there is this exhortation: "This is what the LORD says: 'Be careful not to carry a load on the Sabbath day or bring it through the gates of Jerusalem. Do not bring a load out of your houses or do any work on the Sabbath, but keep the Sabbath day holy, as I commanded your forefathers.'" (cf. Neh.13:15) The prohibition against carrying a load was directed towards work.

According to Pharisaic interpretation of the Law, the man was prohibited from carrying his mat on Shabbat. The Pharisees recognized that certain loads could be carried within one's house, but they prohibited the carrying of a load from a public to a private place, or from a private to a public place (cf. the discussions on *eruv* in the Talmudic tractate" Shabbat"). Carrying a bed outside would not be permitted.

The *Ioudaioi* who were admonishing the man, and who sought to kill Yeshua for breaking their laws for Shabbat, were Pharisees. The Pharisees were a small, but powerful minority in Israel. Some were zealous for God. Some were violent, some were not. Saul of Tarsus was a Pharisee. So was Nicodemus.

The events of chapter 6 take place in Galilee. A large crowd has followed Yeshua. Within that crowd, there are those who are designated as *Ioudaioi*. These *Ioudaioi* are from Galilee, they are not Judeans. We can tell that because they say, "Isn't this Yeshua, the son of Yosef, whose father and mother we have known?..." Jn. 6:42 So John's meaning in this section is probably the sectarian Jews, i.e. the Pharisees.

"At this the *Ioudaioi* began to grumble about him because he said, 'I am the bread that came down from heaven.'" Jn. 6:41

"Then the *Ioudaioi* began to argue sharply among themselves, 'How can this man give us his flesh to eat?'" Jn. 6:52

In John 7, Yeshua has another confrontation in the Temple. There are two groups who are mentioned, the *Ioudaioi* and the multitudes. "Now at the Feast the *Ioudaioi* were watching for him and asking, 'Where is that man?'

"Among the multitudes there was widespread whispering about him. Some said, 'He is a good man.' Others replied, 'No, he deceives the people.' But no one would say anything publicly about him for fear of the *Ioudaioi*. Not until halfway through the Feast did Yeshua go up to the Temple courts and begin to teach.

"The *Ioudaioi* were amazed and asked, 'How did this man get such learning without having studied?'" Jn. 7:11-15

Everyone involved was Jewish—Yeshua, the multitudes, and the *Ioudaioi*. Whom did John mean when he used the word *Ioudaioi*? That is answered later in the account. "Still, many in the multitude/*ochlou* put their faith in him. They said, 'When the Messiah comes, will he do more miraculous signs than this man?' The Pharisees heard the multitude/*ochlou* whispering such things about him. Then the chief priests and the Pharisees sent Temple guards to arrest him." Jn. 7:31-32 The *Ioudaioi*, the group of whom the Jewish people were afraid, were the Pharisees and the chief priests.

Their question—"How did this man get such learning without having studied?"—also affirms this. The Pharisees saw their particular type of study and tradition as the only way to approach God. There was a prevailing attitude among them towards the people who did not accept their teaching—"This multitude/*ochlos* that does not know the law is accursed." Jn. 7:49

"Rabbinic interpretations of normative Jewish religious behaviour carried little inherent authority immediately after the Destruction [of the Second Temple in 70 CE.]. Attached though most Jews may have been to the ancient rites of the Sabbath and circumcision, and steadfast though the majority were in the observance of the Biblical commandments affecting their diet and sexual relations, few were immediately predisposed to perform such practices in accordance with the rigid dictates of Pharisaic halakhah."[7]

The incident in John 7 is followed by another confrontation between Yeshua and the Pharisees, recorded in John 8:1-11. "The teachers of the law and the Pharisees brought in a woman caught in adultery...." Jn. 8:3

Because some manuscripts do not contain Jn.7:53-8:11, some scholars believe that Jn.8:12 follows directly after Jn.7:52. If that is so, it would not affect our understanding of the use of *Ioudaioi* in context, since Jn.8:12-59 presents yet another confrontation between Yeshua and the Pharisees. This one also took place "in the Temple area". Jn.8:20

"The Pharisees challenged him, 'Here you are, appearing as your own witness; your testimony is not valid.'" Jn. 8:13

He responded, " 'In your own Law it is written that the testimony of two men is valid. I am one who testifies for myself; my other witness is the Father, who sent me.'... Once more Yeshua said to them, 'I am going away, and you will look for me, and you will die in your sin. Where I go, you cannot come.'

"This made the *Ioudaioi* ask, 'Will he kill himself? Is that why he says, Where I go, you cannot come?' " John 8:17,21-22

The meaning here of *Ioudaioi* is clear in its context, a confrontation in the Temple area between Yeshua and the Pharisees. The confrontation in Jn.7 between Yeshua and the Pharisees, which also took place in the Temple area, helps to clarify its meaning. On that occasion, "the chief priests and the Pharisees sent Temple guards to arrest him." John 7:32

Yeshua then responded, " 'You will look for me, but you will not find me; and where I am, you cannot come.'

"The *Ioudaioi* said to one another, 'Where does this man intend to go that we cannot find him? Will he go where our people live scattered among the Greeks, and teach the Greeks?'" John 7:34-35

That is why Jn.8:21 says, "Once more Yeshua said to them, 'I am going away, and you will look for me, and you will die in your sin. Where I go, you cannot come.'"

John uses *Ioudaioi* several times more in this passage in describing the continuing confrontation. The consistent meaning for *Ioudaioi* is the Pharisees, or specifically the leaders of the Pharisees.

" 'To the *Ioudaioi* who had believed him, Yeshua said, "If you hold to my teaching, you are really my disciples.' " Jn. 8:31

"The *Ioudaioi* answered him, 'Aren't we right in saying that you are a Samaritan and demon-possessed?' " Jn. 8:48

"At this the *Ioudaioi* exclaimed, 'Now we know that you are demon-possessed! Abraham died and so did the prophets, yet you say that if anyone keeps your word, he will never taste death.' " Jn. 8:52

" 'You are not yet fifty years old,' the *Ioudaioi* said to him, 'and you have seen Abraham?!' " Jn. 8:57

Were there Pharisees who believed in Yeshua? The leaders of the Pharisees had said, "Has any of the rulers/*arcontes* or of the Pharisees believed in him?!" John 7:48 They thought the answer was an unequivocal, "No." They were mistaken. On that very occasion, right in their midst was Nicodemus. The rulers and Pharisees were divided. Some believed in Yeshua. Some did not. cf. Jn. 9:16; 12:42

In John 9, Yeshua healed a man on Shabbat who had been blind from birth. "They brought to the Pharisees the man who had been blind.... Therefore the Pharisees also asked him how he had received his sight..."

"Some of the Pharisees said, 'This man is not from God, for he does not keep the Sabbath.' But others asked, 'How can a sinner do such miraculous signs?' So they were divided. Finally they turned again to the blind man, 'What have you to say about him? It was your eyes he opened.'

"The man replied, 'He is a prophet.' The *Ioudaioi* still did not believe that he had been blind and had received his sight until they sent for the man's parents." Jn. 9:13,15,16-18

Whom does John mean when he says, "The *Ioudaioi* still did not believe"? The answer is made clear in the context. John uses *Ioudaioi* to designate the leaders of the Pharisees.

Then the *Ioudaioi* asked his parents how their son was healed. " 'how he can see now, or who opened his eyes, we don't know. Ask him. He is of age; he will speak for himself.' His parents said this because they were afraid of the *Ioudaioi*, for already the *Ioudaioi* had decided that anyone who acknowledged that Yeshua was the Messiah would be put out of the congregation." Jn. 9:21-22

Yeshua is a Jew, and so were his followers. The man's parents were also Jews. Of whom were they afraid? Who were these *Ioudaioi* who "had decided that anyone who acknowledged that Yeshua was the Messiah would be put out of the congregation"? They were the ones who had the power to put someone out of the congregation. The congregations were a Pharisaic power base.

In this case, John is using *Ioudaioi* to designate the leaders of the Pharisees. Jn. 12:42 is explicit: "Yet at the same time many even among the leaders believed in him. But because of the Pharisees they would not confess their faith for fear they would be put out of the congregation."

That is, in fact, what the Pharisees did to the man who was healed. "To this they replied, 'You were steeped in sin at birth; how dare you lecture us!' And they threw him out." John 9:34

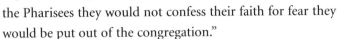

IN THIS CASE, JOHN IS USING *IOUDAIOI*, TO DESIGNATE THE LEADERS OF THE PHARISEES.

The Talmud says, "Greater is the hatred wherewith the 'amme ha-arez [the people of the land], hate the scholar than the hatred wherewith the goyim hate Israel..." (Pesachim 49b)

In John 10:1-21, Yeshua is responding to the question of "Some Pharisees who were with him". John 9:40

"At these words the *Ioudaioi* were again divided. Many of them said, 'He is demon-possessed and raving mad. Why listen to him?'

"But others said, "'These are not the sayings of a man possessed by a demon. Can a demon open the eyes of the blind?'" Jn. 10:19-21 The *Ioudaioi* who were divided were Pharisees. Some believed in him, some did not.

John 10:22-39 records another confrontation in the Temple area that took place at Hanukkah. Here it is not quite as clear who the *Ioudaioi* are, but again they seem to be the Jewish authorities. The Temple was their precinct. That indicates the priests.

"The *Ioudaioi* gathered around him, saying, 'How long will you keep us in suspense? If you are the Messiah, tell us plainly.' " Jn. 10:24

"... 'I and the Father are one.' Again the *Ioudaioi* picked up stones to stone him, but Yeshua said to them, 'I have shown you many great miracles from the Father. For which of these do you stone me?'

" 'We are not stoning you for any of these,' replied the *Ioudaioi*, 'but for blasphemy, because you, a mere man, claim to be God.'

"Yeshua answered them, 'Is it not written in your law, I have said you are gods?' " Jn. 10:31-34

In this confrontation, Yeshua again presents himself as the Good Shepherd, as he had in responding to the Pharisees in the earlier incident in this same chapter. It takes place in the Temple area, where many of the confrontations between Yeshua and the Pharisees took place. Many Jews who were not Pharisees also frequented the Temple area, and Yeshua often responded to the people with scripture. This time Yeshua responds from the Scriptures, calling it "your law," which was his characteristic way of challenging the Pharisees. Who were the ones who felt free to stone someone, i.e. to execute someone without being afraid of the Roman authorities, for what they considered blasphemy? With Stephen, it was the theopolitical authorities.

John 10:39 says, "Again they tried to seize him, but he escaped their grasp."

Who was it that had tried to seize Yeshua before? In John 5:18 and 8:20, it was the theopolitical rulers; but in John 7:30, and possibly 7:44 as well, it was some of the people. It seems most likely that this incident was part of Yeshua's ongoing confrontation with the theopolitical authorities. It is grouped that way in the text. It seems likely that here also *Ioudaioi* indicates the theopolitical authorities, as it usually does in John.

Yeshua spoke to his disciples at Passover, after Judas had gone out. He said, "My children, I will be with you only a little longer. You will look for me, and just as I told the *Ioudaioi*, so I tell you now: Where I am going, you cannot come." Jn. 13:33

His disciples were Jews, but they were not included in this use of *Ioudaioi*. Whom did Yeshua tell "Where I am going, you cannot come"? He said this to the *Ioudaioi* in Jn.7:34 and 8:21-22. In both those cases, the *Ioudaioi* were the theopolitical authorities.

Chapters 14, 15, and 16 contain Yeshua's final admonition to the disciples. Chapter 17 contains his prayer. None of these chapters contain the word *Ioudaioi*. Chapters 18 and 19 describe his arrest and crucifixion. There is a verse in Luke that summarizes the immediate view that the disciples had of these events.

As two disciples walked to Emmaus after the crucifixion, the risen Yeshua joined them. Not recognizing him, they explained to him what had happened to Yeshua of Nazareth. "He was a prophet, powerful in word and deed before God and all the people. So the chief priests and our rulers handed him over to be sentenced to death, and they crucified him." Luke 24:20

These two disciples explained what all the gospel writers, including John, document: the people recognized Yeshua as a powerful prophet, but the authorities saw him as a threat to their position and power. "So the chief priests and our rulers handed him over to be sentenced to death, and they crucified him." Let's look at John's account.

"So Judas came to the grove, guiding a detachment of soldiers and some officials from the chief priests and Pharisees...."

"Then the detachment of soldiers with its commander and the officials of the *Ioudaioi* arrested Yeshua. They bound him and brought him first to Annas, who was the father-in-law of Caiaphas, the high priest that year." Jn. 18:3,12-13

Whose officials were these? They were the officials of the chief priests and Pharisees. It is the chief priests and Pharisees who are designated by this use of *Ioudaioi*.

"Caiaphas was the one who had advised the *Ioudaioi* that it would be good if one man died for the people." Jn. 18:14 Whom was Caiaphas advising? That is, whom did John mean when he used *Ioudaioi*?

The occasion when Caiaphas gave that advice is recorded in John 11:47-53. "Then the chief priests and the Pharisees called a meeting of the Sanhedrin....Then one of them, named Caiaphas, who was high priest that year, spoke up, 'You know nothing at all! You do not realize that it is better for you that one man die for the people than that the whole nation perish.'" John 11:49-50 So, John uses *Ioudaioi* in 18:14 to designate the chief priests and the Pharisees, the members of the Sanhedrin.

The account in chapter 18 continues. "When Yeshua said this, one of the officials nearby struck him in the face. 'Is this the way you answer the high priest?' he demanded.... Then Annas sent him, still bound, to Caiaphas the high priest.

"...Then they led Yeshua from Caiaphas to the palace of the Roman governor. By now it was early morning, and to avoid ceremonial uncleanness they did not enter the palace; they wanted to be able to eat the Passover." Jn. 18:22,24,28

Yeshua had been interrogated by Caiaphas before a very select group of Caiaphas' own supporters. It was a secret meeting, held at night, because they were afraid of the people. The members of this group were part of the plot to kill Yeshua.

In Matthew, we read this description of their prior intent: "Then the chief priests and the elders of the people assembled in the palace of the high priest, whose name was Caiaphas, and they plotted to arrest Yeshua in some sly way and kill him. 'But not during the Feast,' they said, 'or there may be a riot among the people.'" Mt. 26:3-5

It was members of this group from the chief priests and the Pharisees who brought Yeshua to Pilate. They are the ones who were more concerned with ritual cleanness than with the cleanness of their hearts. Throughout the encounter with Pilate, up to the crucifixion, these are the *Ioudaioi*.

"Pilate said, 'Take him yourselves and judge him by your own law.'

" 'But we have no right to execute anyone,' the *Ioudaioi* objected." Jn. 18:31

Under Roman jurisdiction, the Sanhedrin had the right to try and punish alleged criminals, except in cases that required capital punishment. The ordinary people didn't have the right to try or impose sentence on anyone. Only the theopolitical authorities who sat on the Sanhedrin had that Rome-given right. Pilate was speaking to them. The theopolitical authorities responded that, under Roman jurisdiction, they could not legally execute anyone. That is why they have brought Yeshua to Pilate, so that he will execute him.

Pilate interrogated Yeshua. "... Yeshua said, 'My kingdom is not of this world. If it were, my servants would fight to prevent my arrest by the *Ioudaioi*. But now my kingdom is from another place.... Everyone on the side of truth listens to me.'

"... 'What is truth?' Pilate asked. With this he went out again to the *Ioudaioi* and said, 'I find no basis for a charge against him.'" Jn. 18:36-38 Yeshua's "servants" were his Jewish disciples, but they are contrasted with the Ioudaioi, the ones who arrested Yeshua. Again, it is the theopolitical authorities who had Yeshua arrested. For John, they are the *Ioudaioi*. Pilate disputes their arrest of Yeshua by saying that he himself finds no guilt in him.

"Once more Pilate came out and said to the *Ioudaioi*, 'Look, I am bringing him out to you to let you know that I find no basis for a charge against him.'" Jn. 19:4

"The *Ioudaioi* insisted, 'We have a law, and according to that law he must die, because he claimed to be the Son of God.' " Jn. 19:7

"From then on, Pilate tried to set Yeshua free, but the *Ioudaioi* kept shouting, 'If you let this man go, you are no friend of Caesar. Anyone who claims to be a king opposes Caesar.'" Jn. 19:12

The High Priests and the rest of the *Ioudaioi*, as members of the Sanhedrin, were Roman officials in their own right. Ultimately, that provided them with the leverage they needed to force Pilate to comply with their judgment. Common people did not have that right or power.

The High Priests had position, wealth, and power. They had no scruples about using what they had to get what they wanted. Rather than put his own life or career in jeopardy, Pilate chose to order the execution of an innocent man.

"It was the day of Preparation of Passover Week, about the sixth hour. 'Here is your king,' Pilate said to the *Ioudaioi*.

"But they shouted, 'Take him away! Take him away! Crucify him!'

" 'Shall I crucify your king?' Pilate asked.

" 'We have no king but Caesar,' the chief priests answered." Jn. 19:14-15

"Now it was the day of Preparation, and the next day was to be a special Sabbath. Because the *Ioudaioi* did not want the bodies left on the crosses during Shabbat, they asked Pilate to have the legs broken and the bodies taken down." Jn. 19:31 Which *Ioudaioi* had the authority to ask Pilate to do that? The chief priests and the leaders of the Pharisees. Which *Ioudaioi* were concerned with the details of Shabbat, but not with the execution of an innocent man? The chief priests and the leaders of the Pharisees.

"Later, Joseph of Arimathea asked Pilate for the body of Yeshua. Now Joseph was a disciple of Yeshua, but secretly because he feared the *Ioudaioi*. With Pilate's permission, he came and took the body away." Jn. 19:38

Joseph. like Nicodemus, was a member of the full Sanhedrin. He was a Jew. Probably, like Nicodemus, he was a Pharisee. Joseph of Arimatea and Nicodemus were Jews. Of whom were they afraid? The Jewish people? No. The Judeans? No. Of whom were they afraid? They were afraid of the same men who had killed Yeshua. They were afraid of the hostile theopolitical authorities.

It was the same later for the disciples. "On the evening of that first day of the week, when the disciples were together, with the doors locked for fear of the *Ioudaioi*, Yeshua came and stood among them and said, 'Peace be with you!' " Jn. 20:19 The disciples were all Jews. Of what *Ioudaioi* were they afraid? The people? No. The Judeans? No. They were afraid of the same men who had killed Yeshua. The hostile, Roman-appointed, Jewish authorities.

The meaning of *Ioudaioi* in these verses is the theopolitical authorities. That is how it should be translated. John describes these confrontations in the same way the other gospel writers do. Luke 23:35 serves to characterize what took place at the crucifixion. "The people stood watching, and the rulers were sneering at him saying, 'He saved others; let him save himself if he is the Messiah of God, the Chosen One.' "

As a final note here, many modern critics say that the conflict between "the Jews" and "the disciples" in the gospel of John is evidence that it was written later when the conflict between Jews and Christians, between the Church and the Synagogue, had more fully developed. But neither John nor any other Biblical author even mentions "Christians". Neither John nor any other Biblical author mentions "the Church". In history and theology, there is a conflict between Jews and Christians, a conflict between the Church and the Synagogue, but that conflict does not exist in the Scriptures.

THE TEXT OF JOHN DOES NOT CONTAIN WHAT THE MODERN CRITICS IMAGINE. JOHN'S PRIMARY USAGE OF *IOUDAIOI* IS TO TRANSPARENTLY SIGNIFY THE THEOPOLITICAL JEWISH AUTHORITIES.

The Biblical authors speak of Jews who believe and Jews who don't believe. They speak of Gentiles who believe and Gentiles who don't believe. They speak of Gentiles who, because of their submission to the King of the Jews, are brought into the commonwealth, the *ekklesia/kahal*, of Israel.

Even if someone believes that the gospel of John was written yesterday, or tomorrow, it is still a Jewish document, written by a Jew who believes that Yeshua is the one about whom Moses and the prophets prophesied. The text still presents a Yeshua who claims that salvation is of the Jews, and who dies as the King of the Jews. His followers think of themselves as part of Israel, and not as members of some other non-Jewish or anti-Jewish community. The text still presents Israel as God's chosen context of salvation, the only context of salvation.

The text of John does not contain what the modern critics imagine. John's primary usage of *Ioudaioi* is to transparently signify the theopolitical Jewish authorities. The conflict in history and theology arises, to a great degree, from the failure to read the original text in context. The resulting failure to accurately translate the text produces a landslide of inaccurate and deadly interpretation.

The purpose of translation is to make the words and thoughts of one language understandable in another. Translation that communicates something different than the original is not good translation. In the case of *Ioudaioi* in the gospel of John, good translation means faithfully rendering the word according to the different meanings it has in context.

Bad translation means tragedy. It has provided centuries of fuel for the fires of anti-semitism. It has distorted the Biblical message, and made it inaccessible to multitudes of people.

## FOOTNOTES

1. This year, 2004, proved to be, in fact, our year. The Red Sox defeated the Yankees and the St. Louis Cardinals, another longtime nemesis, to win the World Series.

2. cf. *Word Studies in the New Testament*, M.R. Vincent, AP&A, Wilmington, DE, 1972, p.398

3. http://etimologias.dechile.net/?Y My thanks to Peter Citelli for the translation.

4. http://ngeorgia.com/history/cwletter.html

5. *The Expositor's Greek Testament*, Vol.I, p.692

6. Ibid., Pp.709, 763

7. S.A. Cohen, *The Three Crowns: Structure of Communal Politics in Early Rabbinic Jewry*, Cambridge, 1990, p.148

CHAPTER NINE

# Das Herrenvolk und Des Herrn Volk

*In the Bible "The People of God" Are The Jews*

I have an old military belt buckle that says, "Gott mit uns". I don't know exactly where it is right now—I just looked for it and couldn't find it—but I know I have it somewhere. I would like to find it, but I don't want to take the time to search through my boxes.

The buckle which I have, somewhere, comes from the First World War. It was a German soldier's expression of his faith. They all wore these belt buckles into battle. Wars often produce fervent expressions of faith.

The Germans and the French, the Russians and the English have all made their battlefield claims. But so have the Incas, the Emperors of China, and the tribal chiefs of Africa. The Muslims constitute a special case. In the next volume, we'll look at that special case.

Some Nazi concentration camp guards wore the same kind of belt buckle in the Second World War, while they carried out the slaughter of millions of Jews. Sometimes their buckles had an added *Hakenkreuz*, the crooked cross of the Nazi party. In English, we call it a swastika. "Gott mit uns" expressed their confidence that they were not performing their work of extermination alone, but "God with us".

We should not automatically assume that such people are mistaken when they make these claims. There are many gods in this world. Each god has his or her own people. It may well be that some god was with them. It is likely.

Hitler thought so. He said so, though he was mistaken about the identity of the god he served. "Hence today I believe that I am acting in accordance with the will of the Almighty Creator: by defending myself against the Jew, I am fighting for the work of the Lord."[1] Though the claim was false, most German Christians did not dispute it.

In Nazi theology, their god approved what they were doing. The German people themselves were *das Herrenvolk*—the people who are lords—made lords by their god. They were the Master race, the ultimate authority in the earth. They did what they pleased, they killed whom they pleased. They saw themselves as Nebuchadnezzar saw himself. "Those the king wanted to put to death, he put to death; those he wanted to spare, he spared. Those he wanted to exalt, he exalted; and those he wanted to humble, he humbled." (Dan. 5:19b)

The Nazis were especially pleased to kill the Jews. For you see, in this theology, the Jews are the inferior people, the people rejected by god and man. They are replaced by the superior, triumphant new people. The *Herrenvolk* are the new people of god, or, more correctly, the people of a new god.

Who are "the people of God"? This is a simple enough question, once we determine which god we mean. Yet it is a question over which men have slaughtered each other for thousands of years. Establishing the identity of the God of der Bibel also establishes the identity of the people of the God of der Bibel.

The God of the Bible, as we have seen, is the LORD, the God of Israel. This is not a declaration of the superiority of His people, but rather a declaration of His own power and faithfulness. It does not guarantee Israel victory in battle or in any international arena. It does not guarantee success of any kind. It only guarantees accountability and ultimate restoration.

Many people turn rabid at the mention of the Jews as God's Chosen People. Like Korah, they reject God's choice of Moses and Aaron, and choose themselves instead. They don't seem to realize that God chose Moses and Aaron for the benefit of Korah and the rest of Israel. They don't seem to realize that being chosen by God makes life a lot harder.

In Martin Luther's German Bible, the Jews are called *des HERRN Volk*, "the LORD's people". (e.g. Num. 17:6/16:41E; Jdg. 5:11; 1Sam. 2:24) Luther's Bible declares that the people of Israel are *das Volk des HERRN*, "the people of the LORD". (e.g. 2Sam. 6:21; 2Kings 9:6) ) Luther's Bible tells us that the Jews are *die Gemeinde des HERRN*, the community of the LORD. (e.g. Num. 27:17)

In one of the most degraded times in Israel's history, the people as a whole had to go into battle against one of their own tribes. It was a tragedy with tremendous loss and suffering on both sides. There was no rejoicing.

"The leaders of all the people of the tribes of Israel took their places in the assembly of the people of God, four hundred thousand soldiers armed with swords." (Jdg. 20:2) For "the assembly of the people of God," the Septuagint has *ekklesia tou laou tou theou*. In the Septuagint, the tribes of Israel, even in this degraded condition, are the *ekklesia* of God.

For "the assembly of the people of God," Luther has *der Versammlung des Volkes Gottes*. In Luther's translation, the tribes of Israel, even in this degraded condition, are still the people of God.

A week ago, I spoke in a church where I have spoken many times before. I asked them, "Who are the people of God?" One man replied, "All those who love the Lord Yeshua." I said, "That's a very nice answer, but it is a theological answer. In the Bible, who are 'the people of God'?" Someone else answered, "The Jews."

In the Bible, "God with us," or "Gott mit uns," is not a battle cry of Israel. It is simply a translation of the Hebrew name "Emmanuel," a name for the Messiah which comes from Is. 7:14. It is a promise of God to Israel, not a declaration of Israel to God. The name indicates that Messiah will demonstrate God's faithfulness to Israel. Messiah is the King of Israel whom God raises up to restore His people, Israel. "For the LORD's portion is His people, Jacob His allotted inheritance." (Dt. 32:9)

As all Israel prepared to commit themselves anew to the Covenant of the Law, Moses and the priests said to the people, "Be silent, O Israel, and listen! You have now become the people of the LORD your God.'" (Dt. 27:9. LXX: *laon kuriou tou theou sou*; Luther: *Volk des HERRN*; Vulgate: *populus Domini Dei tui*) Israel is the people of God, because the LORD is the God of Israel.

Hebrews 11:25 tells us that Moses "chose to be mistreated along with the people of God rather than to enjoy the pleasures of sin for a short time." (Luther has *dem Volk Gottes*. The Greek has *to lao tou theou*. The Vulgate has *populo Dei*.) Who are "the people of God" with whom Moses chose to be mistreated? The answer is both obvious and inescapable: the twelve tribes of Israel, who were enslaved in Egypt.

"The LORD said, 'I have indeed seen the misery of My people in Egypt. I have heard them crying out because of their slave drivers, and I have known their suffering.'" (Ex. 3:7)

When the God of the Bible speaks of His people, He means the people of Israel. Unfortunately, there are reasons, many reasons, why people want to escape from this clear answer. Some Jews want to escape because the cost of belonging to God is very high, and often beyond comprehension. Much is required of those who have been given much. Much more is required than most people know or understand. It is a calling and responsibility, not a free ride.

Some Gentiles want to escape from the reality of God's choice of Israel because they think it makes them second-class. They do not understand that God created the Jews so that He could bring the Gentiles back to Himself. Accepting God's right to choose takes honesty, humility, and half an ounce of sanity. God is not impressed by anyone. No one deserves His grace, and no one can overturn His choice.

So if you want to do as Moses did and tie your identity and destiny to this persecuted and despised people, then welcome aboard. If you want to say with Ruth, "Your people will be my people; your God will be my God," then, please, sit next to me. If, on the other hand, you refuse to be identified with the Jewish people, then you might want to look closely at your ticket. I think we're on different flights.

The chosen people with whom Moses chose to be mistreated were not noted for their faith, nor for their righteousness. They were noted for their unbelief and their complaining. It was not because of their goodness or faithfulness that God made them His people, it was because of His goodness and His faithfulness.

"The LORD did not set His affection on you and choose you because you were more numerous than other peoples, for you were the fewest of all peoples. But it was because the LORD loved you and kept the oath He swore to your fathers that He brought you out with a mighty hand and redeemed you from the land of slavery, from the hand of Pharaoh king of Egypt." (Dt. 7:7-8)

THOSE WHO THINK THAT GOD HAS REJECTED ISRAEL FOR UNFAITHFULNESS, AND HAS CHOSEN THEM INSTEAD, ARE ONLY DELUDING THEMSELVES.

The chosenness of Israel does not depend upon Israel's merit or worthiness to be chosen. It depends upon God's love and His promises to Abraham, Isaac, and Jacob. No one is chosen because he, she, or they deserve to be chosen. "So then it is not from the one who desires, nor from the one who runs, but from God who shows mercy." (Rom. 9:16)

The chosenness of Israel is demanded by the failure of the Gentiles. At the time that God chose Abram, none of the nations were winning any awards from God. No trophies, no certificates. Nor have they accumulated many awards since. God chose the smallest, least powerful, most despised people, so that He could show His love and His power, and bring down the big, mighty, and esteemed.

Those who think that God has rejected Israel for unfaithfulness, and has chosen them instead, are only deluding themselves. If they think they themselves are faithful, if they think they themselves have shown themselves worthy, then they do not see themselves clearly. Nor have they begun to understand the necessity of Messiah's atoning death.

Bad translation also plays a part in this tragedy. Both the Hebrew word *goyim* and the Greek *ethne* signify the peoples who are not Jewish. The words communicate physical ancestry, not a condition of unbelief. But many translators, in many languages, incorrectly translate the word as "heathen" or "pagan." (cf. Rom. 15:8-18) That makes it almost impossible for Gentile believers to understand that they are Gentile believers, wild branches grafted into Israel's olive tree. Instead, they think of themselves as a new people who replace the Jews.

"God, I thank you that I am not like other men—extortioners, unjust, adulterers, or even as this tax collector." (Lk. 18:11b) '*God, I thank you that I am not like the Jews.*' A man may justify himself in his own eyes or in the eyes of other men, but he cannot justify himself in the eyes of God. When you condemn Israel, you condemn yourself. When you cast off Israel, you cast off yourself. Not a wise choice.

Paul had some good advice for Gentile believers. "Do not boast over those branches. If you do, consider this: You do not support the root, but the root supports you.... Do not be arrogant, but be afraid." (Rom. 11:18,20b) Your theology won't get you in, but it could keep you out.

Christian theology makes Christians the people of God. Every Christian theology is defined by the ways in which it claims that Christians replace the Jews as the people of God. Islamic theology makes Muslims the people of God. Neither claim is Biblical. Both are blatant forms of identity theft.

The Bible is explicit. "With Your mighty arm You redeemed Your people, the descendants of Jacob and Joseph. Selah." (Ps. 77:15)

Gentiles who bow down to the God of Israel and choose to serve the King of the Jews are grafted into Israel's olive tree. In this way, they become connected to the people of God, the people He had already chosen. They cannot replace Israel, but by entering into Israel's commonwealth, they become part of this people.

As Paul explained in Antioch, "Men of Israel and you Gentiles who fear God, listen to me! The God of the people of Israel chose our fathers..." (Acts 13:16b-17a) The God of the people of Israel chose Abraham, Isaac, and Jacob to make a people for His own possession.

It is "the God of the people of Israel whom the Gentiles (and the Jews) should fear. He is the One to whom they should bow down. For Paul, Israel, even in unbelief, is the people of the God of Israel.

Was Paul saying this because he was ethnocentric or because he despised non-Jews? Not at all, quite the contrary. Was he saying this because he had a very narrow, parochial view of God? No. He was simply saying this because that is the way that the God of the Bible presents Himself. There was no reason for Paul to hide what God had said about Himself. It is the Truth that sets people free.

There is no new people of God in the Bible, only in theology. There is no "new Israel," or "spiritual Israel," in the Bible, also only in theology.

*'But what about this scripture? What about that scripture?'*

The Scriptures can be understood correctly when seen in their own context, not when seen in the imposed context of an external theology. When an external theology becomes the context for viewing the Scriptures, a foreign meaning is imposed upon the text.

Certainly there are some places in the Scriptures that are hard to understand, perhaps obscure, or even ambiguous. Why should a man think that he can understand everything that

God says? But that is no excuse for reading doctrines into the text, nor for rejecting what is explicit in the text. Nor is it a hindrance to those who want to build on what is both clear and explicit.

It is not possible to examine every claim that someone makes for one verse or another. There are just too many claims, often yielding certainty for their proponents and bewilderment for everybody else. Sometimes the problem is that the explicit meaning of the text is rejected in favor of an imagined implication, an implication demanded by the theological tradition. When looking through a theologically distorted, anti-Judaic lens, people often see what is not there.

I cannot count the number of discussions I have had where I vainly pleaded, "Don't tell me what the text means; tell me what it says." Many people are simply unable to do that. They cannot see the text. Their tradition tells them what the text means, and that's all they can see. In a certain sense, they really do not care what the text says; they see no need to see anything from outside their tradition. Everyone, everyone in their particular circle, knows that their particular tradition is true.

It is not possible to examine every text that someone might interpret as declaring the replacement of the Jewish people as the people of God, but let's take the time to examine an important passage from Hosea the prophet. Peter quotes from this passage. So does Paul. In general, Christian theologies understand the text to indicate a rejection of the Jews as God's people and their replacement by Christians. The text does not say anything even close to that. Only the assumptions that are brought to the text do.

First we'll look at the passage in Hosea. That will help us to find the meaning in its original context. Then we will look at how Peter uses the passage, followed by a look at how Paul uses the passage.

Hosea the prophet lived in the time when Israel was divided into two kingdoms (or houses), the southern kingdom of Judea and the northern kingdom of Israel. God used Hosea's life to illustrate His own faithful love despite the unfaithfulness of the northern kingdom of the house of Israel. That is the continual theme throughout the book of Hosea, God's faithfulness to Israel despite Israel's unfaithfulness to God.

The LORD spoke to Hosea about his second child. "Call her 'No Compassion,' for I will no longer show compassion to the house of Israel, that I should at all forgive them. Yet I will show compassion to the house of Judah, and I will save them—not by bow, sword or battle, or by horses and horsemen, but by the LORD their God." (Hosea 1:6-7) At the same time that God declared judgment on the house of Israel, the northern kingdom, He also declared His compassion on the house of Judah, the southern kingdom. The text tells us that the savior of Judea is "the LORD their God."

The LORD spoke to Hosea about his third child. "Call him *Lo-ammi*, for you are not My people, and I am not your God. Yet the children of Israel will be like the sand on the seashore, which cannot be measured or counted. In the place where it was said to them, 'You are not My people,' they will be called 'sons of the living God.' The people of Judah and the people of Israel will be reunited, and they will appoint one leader and will come up out of the land, for great will be the day of Jezreel." (Hos. 1:9-11/1:9-2:2H)

In context, God is saying that He will turn away from the northern tribes, the house of Israel, for a time, but He will later regather them back to Himself. He promises to join them again to the tribes in Judea, the house of Judah, and give them one leader. The northern kingdom of Israel had rejected the LORD and chosen other gods. Even though they had chosen not to be His people, the LORD promised to bring them back and make them His people. He will bring them back to the same place where they turned away from Him, but this time they will turn to Him.

God promised, "I will plant her for Myself in the land; I will have compassion on 'No Compassion.' I will say to 'Not My people, ' 'You are My people'; and he will say, 'You are my God.' " (Hos. 2:23/2:25H) All of this discussion concerns the northern kingdom, the house of Israel. It is God's promise to restore the very tribes from whom He turned away in bringing judgment. God said to call the northern kingdom of Israel, "Not My people," at that time. And He promised that in the same place, to the same people, He would again say, "You are My people."

All of the text speaks of God's undeserved faithfulness to Israel. That is what the book of Hosea is about. The text does not refer to any other people.

In his first letter, Peter quotes from these verses in Hosea. To understand Peter's use of these verses, we need to first know who his primary audience is. That will give us the proper context for understanding what Peter wrote.

Peter was sent by Messiah as a Jewish ambassador to the Jewish people. (cf. Gal. 2:7) His first letter is written to "those chosen who are living as strangers in the Diaspora in Pontus, Galatia..." (1Pet. 1:1) This is a clear reference to Jews living in Diaspora. Nothing in the text indicates in any way that it refers to anyone else.

Gentile believers could be said to be strangers and sojourners wherever they lived, but they could not be said to be living in Diaspora. For the most part, Gentile believers in Pontus, Galatia, etc. were not scattered from their homelands. They were living in their homelands, among their own Gentile people. As an ambassador of the King of the Jews to the Jewish people, Peter could be expected to write to Jews living in Diaspora. Who Peter is, what his calling is, and how he identifies his audience, all indicate that the letter is written to Jews.

Next we need to see what Peter is saying, and how he is saying it. The arguments he presents, and the evidence he uses to support them, help to indicate who the audience is. All of this forms the actual context for understanding what he says.

In the letter, Kefa uses one quotation from Tanakh after another, about a dozen quotations in all. Only twice does he introduce the quotations in any way. The rest of the time, he simply presents the specific quotations as though he expects his readers to recognize them. If they do not recognize the verses, there is very little in what Peter says that will tell his readers that these are quotations. So Peter expects his audience to be familiar with Tanakh.

It was probably reasonable for Peter to make such an assumption concerning an audience of Jewish believers. Simple literacy was widespread among Jews; and those who lived in Diaspora had long had the Septuagint. Simple literacy was not widespread among Gentiles. Perhaps a well-discipled group of Gentile believers, one which had for years been listening to the weekly reading of the Torah and the Prophets, would also be able to recognize the quotations, but it would have been less likely. But even that would not have been the situation of all Gentile believers in Pontus, Galatia, etc..

In contrast, Peter's second letter is addressed generally "to those who have obtained like precious faith." That would seem to apply equally to Gentiles as to Jews. Peter writes this letter differently than he did his first. In this letter, Kefa quotes only one scripture, which he introduces as a proverb. (cf. 2 Pet. 2:22) Moreover, it is a proverb that could easily be found or known outside of the Scriptures. He mentions various people in Tanakh, as he did in the first letter, with whom he expects his readers to be familiar. But he does not presume that his audience knows the Scriptures well enough to recognize unintroduced quotations.

The content of the first letter is another indication that its audience is Jewish. One of the major issues addressed is the challenge of living clean lives in the Greco-Roman world. Both Jewish and Gentile believers faced this challenge, but notice how Kefa presents it. "Beloved, I urge you, as foreigners and sojourners, to abstain from fleshly lusts, which war against the soul; having your behavior among the Gentiles virtuous, so that in that which they speak against you as evil-doers, they may, having witnessed your good works, glorify God in the day of visitation." (1 Pet. 2:11-12; cf. 3:15-17; 4:3-4)

It makes a lot of sense to caution Jews about their "behavior among the Gentiles," but it does not make any sense to caution Gentiles about their "behavior among the Gentiles". If Peter were writing to Gentile believers about their behavior among Gentile unbelievers, then it would make sense to emphasize the contrast between believers and unbelievers. In other words, he would have said, 'Beloved, I urge you, as foreigners and sojourners, to abstain from fleshly lusts, which war against the soul; having your behavior among the unbelievers virtuous...'

That is not what he says. He writes to those who are foreigners and sojourners among the Gentiles. That can only refer to Jews.

In the same way, Kefa writes, "For the past time is sufficient to have worked out the will of the Gentiles... They think it strange that you do not plunge with them into the same flood of dissipation, and they heap abuse on you." (1 Pet. 4:3-4) If he were writing to Gentile believers, then he should have said, "For the past time is sufficient to have worked out the will of the unbelievers." He did not say that.

In 1:20, Peter says that the recipients of his letter "believe in God" through Yeshua. So if he had wanted to speak in 2:11-12 and 4:3-4 about everyone, whether Jew or Gentile who does not "believe in God" through Yeshua, he certainly could have done that. Instead, he spoke about the difficulty of living among the Gentiles. That makes sense when addressing Jewish believers living in Diaspora.

Some translators change the text. In 2:12, the NIV has, "Live such good lives among the pagans that..." In 4:3, the NIV has, "For you have spent enough time in the past doing what pagans choose to do..." The word *ethnos/ethnesin* did not mean "pagans". It did not refer in any way to whether someone believed in the one true God or not. The Greek word meant "nations". In Jewish Greek, it was simply used to translate the Hebrew word *goyim*, i.e. the Gentiles/ nations/non-Jewish peoples of the world. To translate it otherwise distorts the text.

Kefa encouraged those to whom he writes that, "it is written, "You shall be holy; for I am holy." (1Pet.1:16; cf. Lev. 11:44, 19:2, 20:7) What he quotes was first said when God command- ed Israel not to eat unclean animals. (cf. Lev. 11:44) Then God said it to "all the assembly of Israel" in reviewing the Ten Commandments. (cf. Lev. 19:2) Then God said it again when He commanded Israel not to walk after the idolatrous and immoral ways of the Gentiles in Canaan, whom God was about to destroy. (cf. Lev. 20:7, 23) In these passages, the verse is a commandment to Israel not to be like the Gentiles.

Yes, Gentiles need to be holy, too, but there are other verses which would have demonstrat- ed that in a much more direct way. What Peter quotes had been specifically addressed to Israel, in distinction from the Gentiles. The point of his using the quotation is to remind his audience that what God said to Israel in the time of Moses still applies to Israel, whether in the land or not, at the time that Peter was writing.

In 1:18, Kefa says, "you were redeemed from the empty/*mataias* way of life/*anastrophes* of your fathers' traditions/*patroparadotou*." There are two other places in the Messianic Writings where there is parallel language. These can help us to understand what Peter had in mind.

In Mk. 7:8-9, Yeshua rebukes some Pharisees and teachers of the law for holding to their "vain traditions/*matev paradosin*" instead of to the commandments of God. Paul was a

Pharisee. In Gal. 1:13-14, he says that, "in my previous way of life/*anastrophen*, I was extremely zealous for the traditions of my fathers/*patrikon mou paradoseon*."

"Josephus not only characterizes the Pharisaic ordinances as 'unwritten', but as 'handed down by the fathers' (*ex pateron diadoche*)."2 The communities to which Kefa was writing understood this language and this claim. 1 Peter 1:18 can be, and should be, understood in its Jewish context.

Peter then reminds these Jewish believers in Diaspora that they have purified themselves and therefore need to live accordingly. "For 'All flesh is like grass, and all of man's glory like the flower of the grass. The grass withers, and its flower falls, but the word of the LORD endures forever.' Now this is the word of the good news which was proclaimed to you. " (1Pet.1:24-25; cf. Is. 40:6, 8)

Peter is quoting from a chapter in Isaiah. The beginning of this chapter in Isaiah is a command from the LORD, "Comfort, comfort My people.... Speak to the heart of Jerusalem, and call out to her that her warfare has ended. Her iniquity has been remove, she has received double for all her sins from the hand of the LORD." (Is. 40:1-2) The verse in Isaiah that follows Peter's quotation says, "Get yourself up on a high mountain, O Zion, bearer of good news. Lift up your voice mightily. O Jerusalem, bearer of good news, lift it up, do not fear. Say to the cities of Judah, 'Here is your God!'" (Is. 40:9) The context of the quotation is God's faithfulness to Israel.

Kefa, a Jew, was quoting from the Jewish Scriptures to remind his Jewish audience of what the God of Israel had already said to them about how to live. What God said to Israel in the time of Isaiah still applies to Israel in the time of Kefa. A lot of theological error is avoided when the Scriptures are read in context.

Kefa then quotes the Messianic promise which declares that what God is building has its foundation in Jerusalem. "Because it is contained in Scripture, 'Behold, I lay in Zion a chief cornerstone, chosen, precious. He who believes in him will not be disappointed.'" (1Pet.2:6; cf. Is. 28:16) Though the Jews to whom Peter writes are in Diaspora, they are still "being built like living stones into a spiritual house to be a holy priesthood..." (1 Pet.2:5) That is God's calling for all Israel.

To these quotations from the Law and the Prophets, Peter then adds one quotation from the Writings and another one from the prophets. "Therefore, to you who believe, he is precious, but to those who are disobedient: 'The stone which the builders rejected, has become the head of the corner,' and, 'a stone of stumbling, and a rock of offense.'" (1Pet.2:7-8a; cf. Ps. 118:22 & Is. 8:14)

"The builders," i.e. the rulers, rejected the foundation which God laid in Zion. They were disobedient. As the disciples said, "The chief priests and our rulers handed him over to be sentenced to death, and they put him to death on the tree." (Luke 24:20) These disciples, Peter, and multitudes of the Jewish people believed and were built, like living stones, upon that Rock.

Kefa reminds his audience of what God has already said in the Law, the Writings, and the Prophets. God said these things to Israel. What—in the context of the letter, not in the context of someone's theological tradition—would be the point of quoting these verses to Gentiles who do not know the Scriptures and to whom these verses were not addressed?

Kefa then returns to the Torah to remind the Jews in Diaspora of how God had described Israel's calling when He brought all Israel out of Egypt. "But you are a chosen seed, a royal priesthood, a holy nation, a people for God's own possession, that you may show forth the virtues of Him who called you out of darkness into His marvelous light." (1 Pet.2:9; cf. Ex. 19:6; Is. 43:20) Again, this is something that the God of Israel said specifically to the people of Israel. To Jewish believers in Diaspora, it is an encouraging reminder. (Gentiles who are grafted in can share in these responsibilities.)

Then Peter refers to God's promise from Hosea to restore the tribes of the northern kingdom of Israel. Peter does it to emphasize both the consequences of disobedience and also the mercy of God as motivations for obedience to holiness.

"'You once were not a people, but now are God's people—who had not obtained mercy, but now have obtained mercy.' Beloved, I beg you, as foreigners and sojourners, to abstain from fleshly lusts, which war against the soul; having your behavior among the Gentiles virtuous, so in that which they speak against you as evil-doers, they may, having witnessed your good works, glorify God in the day of visitation." (1 Pet. 2:10-12; cf. Hos. 1:10, 2:23)

Can Jews, who are a people, be called "not a people"? The original reference in Hosea does exactly that. It is addressed to Jews. Long before, when the tribes of Israel were enslaved in Egypt, God had told Pharaoh, "Let My people go!" Even so, there are many places where God puts the fulfillment of that identity as His people in the future. Here are some examples.

Jer. 30:22 "So you will be My people, and I will be your God."

Jer. 31:1 "At that time," declares the LORD, "I will be the God of all the families of Israel, and they will be My people."

Ezek. 37:27 My dwelling place will be with them; I will be their God, and they will be My people."

Zech. 8:8 "I will bring them back to live in Jerusalem; they will be My people, and I will be faithful and righteous to them as their God."

These Jews in Diaspora, to whom Peter writes, were foreigners and sojourners among the Gentiles. Gentiles are mentioned twice in the letter, both times as the hostile environment in which these Jewish believers lived. Everything in the letter—its opening designation, its content, its appeal to the calling of Israel and the promises to Israel presented from Tanakh—is consistent with Kefa's own calling as an ambassador of God to the Jewish people. Nothing in it indicates otherwise.

In 2:24-25, Kefa refers to what God had said to Israel about Messiah's death bringing atonement and restoration. "He himself bore our sins in his body on the tree, so that we might die to sins and live for righteousness; by his wounds you have been healed. For you were like sheep going astray, but now you have returned to the Shepherd and Overseer of your souls."

**KEFA WAS WRITING TO OTHER FAITHFUL JEWS TO REMIND THEM OF THE PROMISES OF THE GOD OF ISRAEL.**

This is a clear reference to Is. 53:4-6. "Surely he took up our infirmities and carried our sorrows, yet we considered him stricken by God, smitten by Him, and afflicted. But he was pierced for our transgressions, he was crushed for our iniquities; the punishment that brought us peace was upon him, and by his wounds we are healed. We all, like sheep, have gone astray, each of us has turned to his own way; and the LORD has laid on him the iniquity of us all."

This was spoken directly to Israel, the people who went astray. It is a call to return to the Shepherd of Israel. To say "you have returned," Peter uses the Jewish Greek word from the Septuagint, *epistraphete*, that indicates repentance, i.e. returning to God. As a rule, the word was not used when Gentiles were addressed, because they did not know the identity of the God to whom they needed to return.

One faithful Jew, Kefa, was writing to other faithful Jews to remind them of the promise of the God of Israel to restore the people of Israel to Himself. He used the Jewish Scriptures and the promises of the God of Israel to do that. Along come the theologians of the ancient tradition to claim that what this Jew really meant was that God had rejected the Jews and made the Christians His people. How perverse is that?

## PAUL'S QUOTATION OF HOSEA

Paul also quotes from these verses in Hosea. In Rom. 9, he begins by explaining that he himself is willing to be anathema, cut off from Messiah and damned for eternity, if it would bring the rest of Israel to God. Then he gives a short list of what belongs to the Jewish people—"the children of Israel: theirs is the right as sons, the glory, the covenants, the giving of the Law, the service, and the promises, whose are the fathers, and from whom is the Messiah as concerning the flesh, who is over all God blessed forever. Amen." (Rom. 9:4-5) This is what God has given to Israel, even to those in Israel who have not received these things. These things do not belong to any other people. Paul does not put Israel's inheritance in the past tense. In his day, these were the things that still belonged to the Jewish people.

In the following verses, Rom. 9:6-15, Paul explains how God's faithfulness to Israel has continued in the same way that He dealt with Abraham, Isaac, and Jacob, the fathers of the Jewish people. Abraham had two physical sons, but only one of them, Isaac, was chosen to inherit the promise. Rebekah and Isaac had two sons, but only one of them, Jacob, was chosen for God's redemptive purpose.

Paul does not have any discussion here of God disinheriting Abraham, Isaac, Jacob, and their descendants to choose another people. The discussion is about choosing some, but not all, of their physical descendants to inherit what was promised to them. What God said to Moses—"I will have mercy on whom I have mercy, and I will have compassion on whom I have compassion" (Ex. 33:19)—is further evidence that this is the way God has always dealt with the physical descendants of Abraham, Isaac, and Jacob. Some of Israel is Israel indeed, being what God created and called them to be. Some of Israel falls short. Except for God's grace, all fall short.

Then Paul shows how the sovereignty of God in choosing some, but rejecting others, is the way He deals with all people. (cf. Rom. 9:16-24) It is at this point that he cites what God said to Israel through Hosea, as an illustration of God's faithfulness to Israel, an illustration that can be applied to all believers.

"Even us, whom He also called, not only from the Jews but also from the Gentiles. As He says in Hosea: *I will call those who are 'Not My people' 'My people'; and I will call her who is 'Not My loved one' 'My loved one,' and, It will happen that in the very place where it was said to them, 'You are not My people,' they will be called 'sons of the living God.'*" (Rom. 9:24-26)

"In the place where it was said to them, 'You are not My people,' they will be called 'sons of the living God.'" To whom was this said? It was said to the tribes of Israel which had turned away from following both the LORD and the royal house of David. In what place was it said to them? It was said to them in the land of Israel.

What does the text say? It says that God once said to some people in a particular place, "You are not My people." The text says that, in the same place, this same people will yet be called "sons of the living God". Now that we know what the text says, we can begin to talk about what it means.

Context is always important in understanding any communication. The context of the verses in Hosea communicates God's faithfulness to Israel. Paul uses these verses to make exactly the same point that Hosea made. He applies the verses to himself and all other Jewish believers. Paul includes Gentile believers in his application—"not only from the Jews"—because what God did for the Jewish believers He also did for the Gentile believers. The fact that God did it for the Jewish believers shows that He can also do it for the Gentile believers.

Paul does not indicate in any way that the inclusion of Gentile believers means a rejection of Israel. How could he? That would mean that he himself was rejected. Paul says that those God has called are "not only from the Jews, but also from the Gentiles." It is similar to what he says in Rom. 1:16. "For I am not ashamed of the good news of Messiah, for it is the power of God unto salvation for everyone who is believing, both to the Jew first and to the Greek."

The original meaning of the verses in Hosea—God's faithfulness despite Israel's infidelity—is what Paul appeals to. If that original meaning were cancelled, if God's faithfulness were cancelled, then there would be no point in applying the verses to other people. If God did not mean what He said to the rebellious tribes of Israel, what would be the point of applying His words to the rebellious tribes of Gentiles?

Paul is explicit about this in the very next verse. *"Isaiah cries out concerning Israel: Though the number of the people of Israel be like the sand by the sea, only the remnant will be saved."* (Rom. 9:27) God's faithfulness to all Israel is demonstrated by His keeping a remnant of Israel faithful to Himself. That is Paul's point.

He develops it at length in Romans 11. "So too, at the present time there is a remnant chosen by grace." (Rom. 11:5) He explicitly rejects the teaching that God has rejected Israel for any length of time. "I ask then: Did God reject His people? By no means! I am a son of Israel myself, a descendant of Abraham, from the tribe of Benjamin." (Rom. 11:1) Paul points to his own physical descent to demonstrate God's unbroken faithfulness to Israel.

Then Paul continues, "God did not reject His people whom He knew before. Or do you not know what the Scripture says about Elijah?..." (Rom. 11:2) The Greek word translated here as "knew before" is the same word that appears in Rom. 8:29 "Because those whom He knew before, He also appointed before to be conformed to the image of His Son, that he might be the firstborn among many brethren." Israel is the people whom God knew before, the people whom He appointed before to be conformed to the image of His Son, the Messianic King of Israel. Israel has an appointment with God.

"The LORD will call you back as if you were a wife deserted and distressed in spirit—a wife who married young, only to be rejected,' says your God. 'For a brief moment I abandoned you, but with deep compassion I will bring you back. In a surge of anger I hid my face from you for a moment, but with everlasting kindness I will have compassion on you,' says the LORD your Redeemer." (Is. 54:6-8)

The LORD told Moses, "I have indeed seen the misery of My people in Egypt. I have heard them crying out because of their slave drivers, and I am concerned about their suffering. So I have come down to deliver them..." (Ex. 3:7-8) He said, tell Pharaoh, "Let My people go..." (Ex. 5:1; 7:16; 8:1,20; 9:1,13; 10:3)

Even in the decadent time of the Judges, Deborah called Israel "the people of the LORD." (Jdg. 5:11,13) God never stopped being the God of Israel. Israel never stopped being the people of God.

Through the prophets, God warned the Gentiles against mocking Israel or taking their land. "'Therefore, as surely as I live,' declares the LORD Almighty, the God of Israel, 'surely Moab will become like Sodom, the Ammonites like Gomorrah—a place of weeds and salt pits, a wasteland forever. The remnant of My people will plunder them; the survivors of My nation will inherit their land. This is what they will get in return for their pride, for insulting and mocking the people of the LORD Almighty.'" (Zeph. 2:9-10)

God promises to bring His people Israel back to their land of Israel. "The days are coming,' declares the LORD, 'when I will bring My people Israel and Judah back from captivity and restore them to the land I gave their forefathers to possess,' says the LORD." (Jer. 30:3) " 'And you, O mountains of Israel, will produce branches and fruit for My people Israel, for they will soon come home." (Ezek. 36:8) Those removed from the land will be returned to the land.

WHO ARE "THE PEOPLE OF THE LORD?" ISRAEL. THE BIBLE IS QUITE CLEAR, EVEN IN LUTHER'S TRANSLATION.

The nations who refuse to submit to the LORD God of Israel will fight against this restoration. That is not a wise choice. "I will gather all nations and bring them down to the Valley of Jehoshaphat. There I will enter into judgment against them concerning My inheritance, My people Israel, for they scattered My people among the nations and divided up My land." (Joel 3:2)

The Herrenvolk, who think they can get rid of the Jews and replace Israel as a new people of god, will not fare well. It will be seen that what they really have done is to replace the God of Israel with a new god. The HERRN Volk will be protected, restored, and delivered by their HERR, the LORD God of Israel. The conflict will be resolved.

Who are "the people of the LORD"? Israel. The Bible is quite clear, even in Luther's translation. Neither the phrase nor any equivalent phrase is ever used for anyone else, with one and a half exceptions.

The one exception is when the LORD speaks of a future day in which Egypt and Assyria will turn to Him. "The LORD Almighty will bless them, saying, 'Blessed be Egypt My people, Assyria My handiwork, and Israel My inheritance.'" (Is. 19:25) May your eyes see that blessed day when Egypt and Assyria turn to the LORD and are joined with Israel. When God has Israel as His inheritance, then Assyria will be His handiwork, and Egypt will be His people.

The half exception also involves future repentance among the nations. God promises Israel that there will be repentance among the nations. "'Shout and be glad, O Daughter of Zion. For I am coming, and I will live among you,' declares the LORD. 'Many nations will be joined with the LORD in that day and will be to Me for a people. I will live among you and you will know that the LORD Almighty has sent Me to you. The LORD will inherit Judah as His portion in the holy land and will again choose Jerusalem.'" (Zech. 2:14-16/10-12E)

When Israel is restored, the LORD will live in the midst of Zion. Many nations will then be joined to Him and become part of His people. The LORD will have Judah as His own portion, and His promise to make Israel a community of nations will be fulfilled.

Messiah came to make this possible. He came to God's people. "But you, Bethlehem, in the land of Judah, are by no means least among the rulers of Judah. For out of you will come a ruler who will be the shepherd of My people Israel." (Mt. 2:6; Mic. 5:2)

Gentiles can be joined to Israel, because God planned from the beginning for Israel to serve as a commonwealth of nations. Gentiles can humble themselves and be joined to Israel, and thereby become part of the people of God. But nowhere does the Bible speak of replacing Israel with a new people of God. Nowhere does the Bible speak of an "Israel" that is *judenrein*, i.e. free of Jews or free of its Jewish identity.

Yet most Christian theologies imagine the creation of a new people of God in place of the Jews. But if God does not keep His promises to the Jewish people, why would He keep the same promises for some other people, some other people to whom the promises were never made?

As we have seen, God never speaks of "Christians" as His new people. In fact, as we will see, God never speaks of "Christians" at all.

FOOTNOTES

1. Adolf Hitler, *Mein Kampf*, ed. by Ralph Mannheim, Mariner Books, NY, 1999, p. 65
2. Joseph Baumgarten, "The Unwritten Law in the Pre-Rabbinic Period," JSJ, Vol.III, No.1, 10/72, p.13

# CHAPTER TEN

# A Little Case of Mistaken Identity

*There Are No Christians in the Bible*

"WHAT'S IN A NAME? THAT WHICH WE CALL A ROSE BY ANY OTHER NAME WOULD SMELL AS SWEET." *Juliet, Romeo and Juliet, William Shakespeare*

Juliet was not quite right. She thought that Romeo would be the same, no matter what his last name was. But his last name indicated his history and identity. His last name indicated that he was from a family of enemies. If he had had a different last name, their life together might have worked out, though it would have been decidedly less romantic.

Juliet was an emotional person. There is nothing wrong with that. She had good feelings about Romeo. That's okay, too. But she let her emotional attachment to Romeo blind her to reality. Juliet's good feelings led her to some bad decisions.

She also was not thinking in marketing terms. A rose [or a Montague] under the name of "oobleck" or "poison," or some other less than appealing name will not be properly represented. The "oobleck" would still smell sweet, but people would not know that, because they would not be interested in smelling it. Or this particular "poison" would still smell sweet, and would cause no ill effects, but it would be difficult to convince people to come and sniff, because they know something else by exactly the same name, something that causes death.

"Juliet insists the thing she knows would remain the same, at least in terms of our sensory perception of the thing, even if it were called something else. In the last few decades, philosophers have questioned the arbitrary and 'clean' nature of this relationship. Experience shapes language, and language shapes experience. A rose/thing simply may not smell as sweet when called by another name; on the other hand, the rose/name and its various material and symbolic accompaniments might not exist if not for the sweet-smelling experience of the rose/thing. Signifier and signified exist intertwined in the complex life of the sign."[1]

History, i.e. experience, gives meaning to a name. That meaning may be different from what the name originally signified. That meaning may be different from what one thinks the name *should* signify, or different from what one wants the name to signify. It is very difficult to undo history.

Juliet loved Romeo, but she was mistaken in how she identified him. She thought that it made no difference what he was called. She was tragically wrong. Juliet is not the only one who has made such a mistake.

Everyone knows what "Christians" are, don't they? No, not really. It depends upon whom you ask. Orthodox Christians have their definition; Catholics have theirs; Evangelicals have theirs. To Jews or Muslims, the meaning of "Christian" is different from all of these.

Because of history, what one group of people *knows* that "Christians" are is not at all the same as what another group *knows*. Some Christian groups argue with each other over what a "real" Christian is. Millions have been killed in these arguments.

The name signifies different things, depending upon how one reads history. It doesn't really depend upon how one reads the Bible, because the Bible does not speak of Christians.

*'My Bible does!'*

Your translation does, but the Bible doesn't. It's just a little case of mistaken identity—a double mistake, one which has been going on for more than nineteen hundred years. It has caused immense confusion and tragedy.

The word "Christian" appears three times in most English translations—Acts 11:26, Acts 26:28, and 1Pet. 4:16. Readers take it to be a new name for the followers of "Christ". As a new name, it is theologically understood to indicate a new people of God, replacing the Jews, or replacing "the old Israel."

There are, however, three things that should be noted. First, in each of the three passages, it is evident that this was not something which the disciples called themselves, nor something which God called them, but rather a term which Gentile unbelievers used to designate the disciples. Second, the term is a transliteration, not a translation. Third, English translations are almost assuredly not correct in giving the word as "Christian."

As for the first point, here are the three verses where Christian translations have the word "Christian."

The first verse is: "... The disciples were called *Christians* first at Antioch." (Acts 11:26) The disciples in Antioch did not call themselves that. God did not call them that. They were called that by other people in Antioch.

The second verse is: "Then Agrippa said to Paul, 'Do you think that in such a short time you can persuade me to be a *Christian*?" (Acts 26:28) Paul did not call himself or anyone else by that name. Agrippa did.

The third verse is: "Let none of you suffer as a murderer, or thief, or evil-doer,... but if as a *Christian*, let him not be ashamed; and let him glorify God in this respect." (1 Pet. 4:16) The followers of Yeshua were being made to suffer under a particular name. They were being arrested and imprisoned under this particular name. They were put to death under this particular name. This name is not given as a name by which they were calling themselves, but as a name under which they were forced to suffer. This will become clearer as we examine the history of the text and the historical events to which it points.

Christian translations render this name as "Christian," but this is not a translation; it is a transliteration. A transliteration has no meaning, unless one knows the word in its original context. In its context, the word would mean "a follower of Christos". "Christos," in its original Jewish Greek context, is an invented word, unfamiliar to Greeks, that points to the Hebrew Biblical concept of Messiah, the Son of David.

As for the third point, the translations are almost assuredly not correct even in their transliteration. The International Standard Bible Encyclopedia, a standard reference work for the last 90 years, points out that, "In all three NT passages the uncorrected Codex Aleph reads 'Christian.' We know from many sources that this variant was widely current in the 2d century.... On the whole it seems probable that this designation, though bestowed in error, was the original one....

"The name, then, did not originate with the Christians themselves. ... The word must have been coined by the heathen population of Antioch....1Pe simply takes it over from the anti-Christian judicial procedure of the law courts, without in any way implying that the Christians used it among themselves.

"The Christians originally called themselves 'Disciples'..."[2]

The ISBE article makes four points.

1. Unchanged manuscripts have *Chrestian*, not *Christian*.

2. Second century historical sources have *Chrestian*.

3. *Chrestian*, though it was an erroneous designation, was probably the original designation.

4. The "Christians" did not call themselves "Christians"; they called themselves "Disciples".

Let's look at the supporting evidence for these points.

## 1. Unchanged manuscripts have *Chrestian*, not *Christian*.

Codex ℵ [Alef] contains all three passages, and has *Chrestian* in each one. Codex Alef is one of the major Alexandrian texts, which are "usually considered to be the best text and the most faithful in preserving the original."[3] In addition, the Codex Bezae, one of the most important sources of the Western text, also has *Chrestian*. The fragment called Text 81 contains Acts 11:26, and has Chrestian.

Though there is support in many Greek manuscripts for *Christianou*, the many manuscripts are probably not correct. The minority of manuscripts, which give *Chrestianou*, are most likely correct. It is not rare for the reading of the minority to be considered correct, and for the reading of the majority to be considered incorrect.

GOD DOES NOT PREVENT SCRIBES OR TRANSLATORS FROM MAKING ERRORS. HE DOES NOT PREVENT THEOLOGIANS OR PREACHERS FROM DISTORTING THE TEXT.

The issue centers on one simple Greek letter, an *eta* (H, η), rather than an iota (I, ι). This is, to be sure, a small item, but one of great significance. The correct determination of this name is critically important to the existence of the whole Christian system. After all, it would make a significant difference if the Bible does not refer to Christians at all.

'*Couldn't the scribes who copied the Codex Alef, the Codex Bezae, and the others in which Chrestian appears just have made a mistake?*'

It is possible, but not at all likely. These scribes certainly knew that *Christos* was correct, and they never mistakenly copied it as *Chrestos*. In the five hundred times that *Christos* appears in the Messianic Writings, those who produced these manuscripts never mistakenly render it as *Chrestos*. But *Chrestos* is the name, albeit incorrect, that appears in contemporary historical sources.

In giving the name which unbelieving Gentiles used for the disciples, these faithful scribes copied *Chrestianou*. This is, in fact, the incorrect name that appears in other historical sources.[4] In other words, Luke, in Acts, and Peter, in 1 Peter, accurately recorded the incorrect name which unbelieving Gentiles used to designate the disciples. Early scribes faithfully copied what Luke and Peter had written.

Sometime much later, most likely in the fourth century, the *Chrestianou* used by the first and second century Greek and Roman population no longer made sense to Christian scribes. They understood themselves to be followers of *ho Christos*, not some unknown *Chrestos*, and they did not know the historical and linguistic reasons for the appearance of the incorrect designation. So they "corrected" the Biblical text from *Chrestianou* to *Christianou*, which they found meaningful. That is why the ISBE refers to *Chrestian* as the "uncorrected" designation.

They probably meant no harm, but were simply seeking to "correct" the text to make it say what they thought it should say, and to make it intelligible to themselves. That may sound to some like a wild accusation, but it is not. It was not an unusual practice. It is one of the major reasons why there are so many small differences between the multitude of Greek manuscripts that we have. (Similarly, it is a common practice among translators to add words or phrases to make the original meaning, or what they think is the original meaning, clear.)

For the twenty-eight chapters of Matthew, Bruce Metzger, in his *A Textual Commentary on the Greek New Testament*, notes about 200 places where different manuscripts have differences in the text. For the twenty-eight chapters of Acts, Metzger notes about 600. Sometimes the differences are only a single letter, sometimes a single word.

Somewhere, at some point in time, there was an original text, but we do not have any of the original texts. We have various manuscript copies. There are thousands of places in the different Greek manuscripts where one community or another, one scribe or another, presented a variation. In some cases, copyists consciously changed the text they received in order to make it more understandable.

Metzger points out that, "The text of the book of the Acts of the Apostles circulated in the early church in two quite distinct forms, commonly called the Alexandrian and the Western."[5] That is why there are so many places where the manuscripts differ. Yet, some of the best copies of both the Alexandrian and the Western text preserve *Chrestian* as the correct reading. They have "quite distinct forms," but they agree on *Chrestian* as the original designation. Scribal error is not a plausible explanation for the appearance of *Chrestian* in these Greek manuscripts.

*'But wouldn't God have protected the text?'*

We have different texts. Did God protect what appears in most texts or did He protect what appears in some texts? We have to determine which reading is most likely faithful to the original. God does not prevent scribes or translators from making errors. He does not prevent theologians or preachers from distorting the text. He does not prevent individuals or groups from misrepresenting Him and His Word.

## 2. Second century historical sources use Chrestian.

We have textual, linguistic, and extra-biblical historical support for "Chrestian" being the actual reading of the Biblical text. This is a reading that appears in some of the most important manuscripts. It is linguistically consistent with what was contemporary practice. And all the historical evidence indicates that this is the correct reading, reporting the common error.

The Roman historian Suetonius referred to the edict of the Emperor Claudius in the year 49, saying, "Since the Jews constantly made disturbance at the instigation of *Chrestus*, he expelled them from Rome."[6] The edict is cited in other sources. We know, for example, that Aquila and Priscilla left Rome, "because Claudius had ordered all the Jews to leave Rome." (Acts 18:2)

There is an interesting scholarly debate over whether Suetonius was referring to *Christos* or not. Some scholars say he was; others say that he was referring instead to either an unknown

Jewish rebel by the name of Chrestus, or, reading the text differently, a Greek or Roman by that name who influenced Claudius to expel the Jews.[7]

If Suetonius was using the name *Chrestus* to refer to *Christos*, then this would be direct support for the reading in the minority of manuscripts. On the other hand, in terms of our discussion here, it doesn't really matter whether Suetonius was referring to *Christos* or not. What does matter here is that Paulus Orosius, a fifth century Christian historian, a protégé of Augustine, changed the text when he quoted Suetonius. "Orosius wrote as follows... 'Claudius expelled from Rome the Jews constantly rioting at the instigation of Christus.' Orosius did make a single significant change. Suetonius wrote 'Chrestus,' and Orosius edited with 'Christus,' so applying a Christian twist by the change of an 'e' to an 'i.'... The same twist occurs in Orosius' account (Historiarum 7.6.12) of the conversion of Helena of Adiabene to Christianity rather than to Judaism."[8]

The original text said *Chrestus*, but Orosius changed it to *Christus*. Orosius made the same change, albeit in Latin, that, according to the ISBE editors, was made in the majority of the Greek manuscripts for Acts 11:26, Acts 26:28, and 1Pet. 4:16. Orosius was trained by Augustine. Throughout the Middle Ages, the work of Orosius was the standard Christian textbook for world history. The original text said Chrestus, but Orosius changed the text, and put Christus, because he believed that the original text should have said that. People read and believed Orosius, even though he had changed the original text.

The Latin text of Book 15:44 of the *Annals* of Tacitus, a Roman historian who wrote at the beginning of the second century, also shows this same change. Most of the Latin texts speak of "a class of men, loathed for their vices, whom the crowd called Christianos... Christus, the founder of the name had undergone the death penalty in the reign of Tiberius, by sentence of the procurator Pontius Pilatus." That is what most of the surviving texts have, but some of the Latin manuscripts of the *Annals* have, "whom the crowd called Chrestianos [*vulgus Chrestianos appellabat*]... Christus, the founder of the name..." Many of the scholars who have prepared Latin editions of Tacitus's *Annales* believe that *Chrestianos* is the correct, original text, and *Christianos* appears only in later manuscripts that were changed. Many of the scholars who have prepared Latin editions of Tacitus's Annales believe that Chrestianos is the correct, original text, and Christianos appears only in later manuscripts that were changed. So did the ISBE editors and other historians.[9]

The "uncorrected" manuscripts show that Tacitus knew the correct name *Christus*, and he also knew that the common people incorrectly called his followers *Chrestianos*. Later scribes changed the text of Tacitus from *Chrestianos* to *Christianos*, because they "knew" that *Christianos* was correct.

The Christian writers Tertullian and Lactantius confirm this same thing in their defense of the faith. Tertullian wrote: "'But Christian, so far as the meaning of the word is concerned, is derived from anointing. Yes, and even when it is wrongly pronounced by you 'Chrestianus' for you do not even know accurately the name you hate, it comes from sweetness and benignity.' Lactantius, The Divine Institutes IV, VII, 5, similarly says: 'But the meaning of this name must be set forth, on account of the error of the ignorant, who by the change of a letter are accustomed to call him Chrestus.'"[10] Tertullian's writing is dated 197, and that of Lactantius 304.

In the second half of the second century, Justin, in his First Apology, used the plural form, *chrestianoi*, to indicate the name under which the disciples were then being accused. "For we are accused of being *Chrestianoi*, and to hate what is *chreston* [good, useful] is unjust."[11] Justin himself knew that the disciples followed *Christos*, not *Chrestos*. He used *Chrestianoi* because it was the actual name by which the disciples were accused. He used it to make a linguistic appeal for a cessation of the trials, since the disciples were in actuality followers of what is good and useful, i.e. *chreston*, not what is evil.

Paul wrote to Philemon about Onesimus. "Formerly he was useless/*a-chreston* to you, but now he has become of good use/*eu-chreston* both to you and to me." (Phlm. 11) Paul told Timothy that believers should depart from unrighteousness, to be "sanctified and of good use/*eu-chreston* to the master." (2Tim. 2:21)

In the "Wisdom of Solomon" 4:5, this same word is used, and the verse may have suggested to Paul some of his illustration in Romans [11]. "The imperfect branches shall be broken off, their fruit useless/*a-chrestos*, not ripe to eat, good for nothing."

What do the early "Christian" sources say? Justin said that the common people called the followers of Christ *Chrestianoi*. Tertullian said the same thing, explaining that the people mistakenly thought that *Chrestus* was the right name. Lactantius said exactly the same thing. That is because ordinary Greeks, from the lowest to the highest, were unfamiliar with the Jewish Greek word, *Christos*, which the translators of the Septuagint had commandeered. For Greeks who used *koine* or classical Greek, *Christos* had no recognizable meaning when applied to a person.

What do the early non-Christian sources say? The Roman historian Suetonius wrote *Chrestus*, and the Christian historian Orosius changed it to *Christus*. The Roman historian Tacitus wrote *Chrestianos*, and later Christian scribes changed it to *Christianos*. The Christian scribes were just trying to correct what they thought was an error that the previous copyist had made. There were other cases where Christian scribes went a little further to make their point. "A Byzantine forger even fabricated the Apostolic decree ordering the name of the followers of Christ to be changed from 'Galileans' to 'Christians.'"[12] Perhaps "Galileans" seemed too Jewish to the Christian forger, too tied to the land of Israel. Or perhaps it just didn't mean anything to him; it was unconnected to what he thought faith in Christ should be. So even though Yeshua and his original disciples were Galileans, the forger saw a need to override the Biblical text and create the false impression that the apostles had decreed the change.

The conservative theologians and editors of the *International Standard Bible Encyclopedia* concluded that "Chrestian" was probably the actual designation, as it appears in the "uncorrected" manuscripts. Later manuscripts were "corrected," i.e. changed, to read "Christian". The editors do not even suggest that there were two different manuscript traditions. The reason is that the historical and linguistic evidence for "Chrestian" is compelling.

### 3. *Chrestian*, though it was an erroneous designation, was probably the original designation.

The historical evidence shows that the Gentile unbelievers did not call the disciples "Christians"; they called them "Chrestians/*Chrestianou*." They did not call the disciples followers of *christos*, because they did not know what a *christos* was. In order to sensibly designate the disciples, the unbelieving Gentiles identified them as the followers of some "Chrestos," a fairly common name.

To the Greek name Chrestos, the Latin suffix -*ianus* was added. "In Greek it became a fashion, under the Empire, to form proper names with this Latin suffix, such as *Diogenianos*," added to a name."[13] In this way, a follower of "Chrestos" was designated as a *Chrestianus*. The plural form is *Chrestianoi*, or *Chrestianou* in a different case. *Chrestus* is the Latin form of the Greek *Chrestos*.

When speaking in Greek, the disciples used the *ho Christos* of the Septuagint translation of the Hebrew scriptures to refer to Messiah. They understood the term, because they knew the Biblical content. But the term made no sense to the general Greek and Roman population, who knew neither the word nor the Biblical content. It was nonsensical to them.

So the general population "corrected" the term to *Chrestos*, which was an actual name, and therefore meaningful to them. The three passages in the Messianic Writings merely record the incorrect designation used by the general population. That is, in fact, the actual designation by which the disciples were then legally accused.

Later scribes thought they were correcting an error in the text when they changed it. They did exactly the same thing that those who "corrected" the texts of Tacitus and Suetonius did.

Luke accurately recorded the origin of the incorrect designation (Acts 11:26). He also recorded its use by Agrippa (Acts 26:28). Peter correctly cited the incorrect designation as the name by which the disciples were legally persecuted (1Pet. 4:16).

## 4. The "Christians" did not call themselves "Christians," they called themselves "Disciples".

"Disciple(s)" appears almost three hundred times from Matthew through Revelation. [The Hebrew is *talmid*. The Greek is *mathetes*. "Disciple" comes from the Latin *discipulis*.] It is what all the authors of the Messianic writings call the followers of Yeshua. They did not call them "Christians".

*'Well what difference does it make if they were called disciples, or Chrestians, or Christians? We know what they meant. We know today what a Christian is.'*

My dear Juliet, it makes a world of difference. In the first place, "Chrestian" is what Biblically ignorant people called the disciples. It is not what the disciples called themselves, nor how they identified themselves, nor how God identified them. "Christian" is what historically ignorant scribes then changed the text to be.

The word "disciple(s)" appears about three hundred times in the Messianic Writings. "Chrestian" appears three times. The word "Christian" does not appear in the Bible at all. These disciples were NOT what the word "Christian" means today.

Secondly, there is no fixed definition of what a Christian is.[14] You may think you know what the word means, but the family across the street, across the border, or across the ocean doesn't agree with your definition. And we cannot talk about "the Biblical definition" if the word isn't even in the Bible.

I have an Italian-American friend who is a Pentecostal preacher. A number of years ago, Joe went on a preaching tour of Italy. The amount of Italian he had learned in his childhood was insufficient for him to preach in Italian, but it was enough for him to understand much of what the translator said.

As he preached, he began to get upset with the translator. Every time that Joe said "Christian," the translator would say "believer" instead. Finally, Joe pulled the translator aside and said, "Why are you doing that? Why don't you just say 'cristiano' when I say 'Christian'?"

"Because everyone here is a Christian," the translator responded. "That's not what you mean. I'm saying what you mean."

"Christian" didn't mean what Joe thought it meant. It didn't mean what he wanted it to mean. He was saying the wrong word for what he thought was a Biblical concept.

Why is this important? "Christian" doesn't mean what you want it to mean. It is defined by theology, culture, and history. It is not defined by the Bible. It is not a Biblical term for "followers of Christ". Most "Christians" do not follow "Christ". They do not follow Messiah.

"Christians" does not mean "Messianics". If it did, then no one would think that the followers of Messiah are disconnected from the Jewish people. The Jewish people are the only people to whom God defined and sent a Messiah. "Messiah" is the King of the Jews.

As a new name for the followers of Yeshua, "Christian" is used theologically to indicate a break from the Jewish past. No such break took place in the Bible. It took places centuries later in history. The name by itself, because of seventeen hundred years of history, communicates a false cosmology, and obscures the Biblical reality.

For Muslims, the heroic figures that appear in the Bible are Muslims. From their point of view, it makes perfect sense. For them, by definition, a Muslim is one who is submitted to God. All the great figures of the Bible were submitted to God. Consequently, they were Muslims, even if they lived many centuries or thousands of years before Muhammed.

So in the Islamic view, Adam was a Muslim. So were Abraham, Moses, David, Solomon, and Elijah. Jesus was a Muslim, too. The problem is that, though these Biblical figures were submitted to God, they were not Muslims. They were not followers of Muhammed, and calling them Muslims creates a very different impression of who they were, a false impression. So does it matter if we call the apostles "Muslims"?

Yeshua was not a Muslim; he was not a Christian. He was a Jew. Paul was not a Muslim; he was not a Christian. He was a Jew. Peter was neither a Muslim nor a Christian. He was a Jew. The same is true for John, Matthew, Mark, and the rest. Why not speak and think of them as what they were? There are disciples of the Messiah in the Bible, but there are no Christians in the Bible.

*'OK, maybe the word doesn't appear in the Bible, but they were what we today mean when we say "Christian".*

No they were not. That is precisely the point. They could not even have imagined Christianity, much less the multitude of definitions that are given for the word "Christian". They didn't think to call themselves Christians, and God didn't either. It was not their category, concept, or identity.

"Christian" is not a later word that faithfully describes what they were. It is a later word that describes something that they were not. It does not accurately describe the Jewish followers of Yeshua in the first century. It does not accurately describe the Gentile followers of Yeshua in the first century. It creates a false impression.

Times past are filled with many godly followers of Yeshua who called themselves, or were called, "Christians". The same is true today. But today and the past centuries are also filled with many, many more people who called themselves "Christians" and followed evil—Christians, for example, who burned the Bible, and Christians, for example, who tortured and burned people. The name "Christian" does not indicate what the person who is called that believes; nor does it indicate whom the person is following. It does not indicate how the person will behave or what he will do.

We cannot control what others call us, but the word "Christian" communicates an indistinct faith system, and an indistinct behavioral system. It communicates a system that is often anti-Jewish, and almost always centered outside of God's relationship with Israel. In that sense, it is anti-Biblical, and does not smell like a rose. It communicates a large historical package that is rather unpleasant. It often invokes a *Christos* who is not the Messiah.

That may not be what it communicates to you, but there are 6 billion people in this world. There is the historical record of more than eighteen hundred years. There is the behavior and faith of one billion people who call themselves "Christians" today.

The Scriptures do not give any particular name for the followers of Messiah. His followers cannot be identified by a particular name; they can be identified by a particular way of living. You may be emotionally attached to the name "Christian," but it is not a name that God gave. It is more important that you be attached to Messiah himself. And in that, it is more important that you be attached to the Jewish people.

## FOOTNOTES

1. http://www.public.iastate.edu/~arch690/Pages/first%20level/dilemma.html The site gives the source of the internal quotation as Richard Scott Hirsch, "Moving Forward into the Past: Restoration and Re-use on Printers' Row, Chicago" (MS thesis, University of Wisconsin-Madison, 1996): 106

2. "Christian," *ISBE, Vol. 1*, The Howard-Severance Company, Chicago, 1915, p.622

3. Bruce M. Metzger, *A Textual Commentary on the Greek New Testament*, United Bible Societies, London, 1971, p. xvii

4. If, as seems likely, Acts was written for Paul's legal defense in Rome, then the phrase in Acts 11:26—"The disciples were first called Chrestians in Antioch"—is simply an account of how the commonly used, but erroneous term first appeared. Those who are interested in this view of the Book of Acts should read the book by John Mauck, *Paul on Trial*, Thomas Nelson, Nashville, 2001

   Mauck concludes that the opponents of Paul were charging him with starting a new religion, but that his defense against this charge is summed up in Acts 24:14. "But I admit that I worship the God of our fathers as a follower of the Way, which they call a sect. I believe everything that agrees with the Law and that is written in the Prophets."

5. Metzger, *A Textual Commentary on the Greek New Testament*, op. cit., p.259

6. C. Suetoni Tranquili, *De Vita Caesarum, Bk. 8*, B.G. Teubneri, 1907, p.218

7. Others say that, since Christ wasn't in Rome at the time, he couldn't have been instigating any trouble there. They conclude that it must, therefore, refer to some unknown Chrestus who was in Rome at that time.

   This was a significant edict—all Jews were expelled from Rome, all because of some Chrestus. It doesn't seem likely that someone too insignificant to leave any historical record other than his name could have been the cause of such a major decree.

Some scholars say that "all" must be understood in terms of the historical context. That is true, of course. They say that the sentence in Suetonius may also be read as: "He expelled from Rome the Jews constantly making disturbances at the instigation of Chrestus." In that case, only the Jews who were "constantly making disturbances at the instigation of Chrestus," Aquila and Priscilla among them, were expelled. As for the phrase in Acts 18:2, "all the Jews/παντας τους Ιουδαιους," "παντα" [all] in the predicate position need not imply 'every'; it may be translated indefinitely as 'Jews', that is 'some Jews'." [e.g. The Mystery of Romans, Mark D. Nanos, Fortress Press, Minneapolis, 1996, P. 376. See Nanos's complete discussion of this issue in his Appendix 2, Pp.372-387.] That may be so, however, in any case, the expulsion was significant enough to be mentioned both by Suetonius, writing about sixty years after the event, and by Luke.

As for the identity of *Chrestus*, which is the Latin form of *Chrestos*, the Book of Acts documents the "disturbances" which Christos caused throughout the Roman Empire in different Jewish communities, when he wasn't there, but Paul proclaimed him. Paul and Barnabas were expelled from Pisidian Antioch by Jews who rejected his message. (Acts 13:50) In Iconium, "The Jews who didn't believe stirred up the Gentiles and poisoned their minds against the brothers." (Acts 14:2) The whole city was divided. (Acts 14:4)

Some of these Jews from Antioch and Iconium who didn't believe came to Lystra and stirred up the city. (Acts 14:19) In Philippi, Paul cast a spirit out of a slave girl who earned money for her owners by prophesying. Her owners brought Paul and Silas before the magistrates and said, "These men are Jews, and are throwing our city into an uproar." (Acts 16:20) There were no other Jews involved, but the magistrates had these two Jews, Paul and Silas, stripped, severely beaten, and thrown into prison because of the disturbance they had caused by their *Christos*. (cf. Acts 16:18)

Such disturbances were not unusual when they proclaimed *Christos*. They were the norm. In Ephesus, the whole city "was in an uproar," and they screamed out of control for two solid hours. (cf. Acts 19:29,34) Could this same *Christos* have caused enough disturbance in Rome for all the Jews to be expelled? Definitely yes. Could someone totally unknown to us in history have caused enough of a disturbance? It is possible, but not likely.

Whoever this *Chrestus* was, Aquila and Priscilla were expelled from Rome because of him. We know that they were connected with a particular *Chrestus*, i.e. Yeshua, who caused disturbances throughout the Roman world at the time of the expulsion by Claudius. We have a likely fit. In Thessalonica, some Jews who were offended by the message of Yeshua, "... rounded up some bad characters from the marketplace, formed a mob and started a riot in the city.... they dragged Jason and some other brothers before the city officials, shouting: 'These men who have caused trouble all over the world have now come here... They are all defying Caesar's decrees, saying that there is another king, one called Jesus.' When they heard this, the crowd and the city officials were thrown into turmoil." (Acts 17:5-8)

*'But Jesus was dead, and the report of Suetonius indicates that Chrestus was alive.'*

Jesus had died many years before the riot that took place in Jerusalem, when Paul was arrested in the Temple. As Festus explained to Agrippa: "they had some points of dispute with him about their own religion and about a dead man named Jesus who Paul claimed was alive." (Acts 25:19)

*'But why Chrestos, or the Latin form Chrestus, instead of Christos?'*

Christos was not a name. It made no sense to those who knew neither Yeshua nor the Septuagint. It is a Jewish Greek word used by the translators of the Septuagint to signify *Mashiakh*. Christos was only familiar and meaningful to those who knew the Septuagint. "Now, 'Christus is, of course, a literal, and for this reason, unintelligible, rendering of the Hebrew *Mashiah*..." [Bickermann, "The Name of Christians," op. cit., p. 119] Chrestus, on the other hand, was familiar to everyone, and it therefore had meaning, though the meaning was not to be found in the Scriptures.

8. H. Dixon Slingerland, *Claudian Policymaking and the Early Imperial Repression of Judaism at Rome*, Scholars Press, Atlanta, 1997, p.205

9. cf. the different editions of Tacitus' *Annales* by Erich Koestermann, Franz Romer, and Henricus Heubner.

   Karl Nipperdey's note in his edition of Tacitus is interesting. He recognized that the manuscript initially had *Chrestianos*, and it was later changed to *Christianos*. "This form of the name [*Christianos*] was created through correction in the manuscript; previously, the manuscript had *Chrestianos*."—"Diese Namensform ist in der Hdschr. erst durch Korrektur geschaffen; vorher hatte sie Chrestianos."

   But then Nipperdey argues that, since Tacitus correctly knew the name Christos, it is not believable that he would give *Chrestiani* instead of *Christiani*, even though the common people used the incorrect form. P. Cornelius Tacitus, erklaert von Karl Nipperdey, Berlin, Weidmann, 1908-15, p.264 note on *Christianos*: It is not clear why Nipperdey could not believe that Tacitus would correctly give the incorrect designation used by the common people. (My thanks to Ginny Boutin for her help in translating the German.)

   The ISBE points out that, "The Tacitus manuscript has since been published in facsimile. This has shown, according to Harnack (Mission and Expansion (English translation), I, 413, 414), that "Chrestian" actually was the original reading, though the name "Christ" is correctly given. Harnack accordingly thinks that the Latin historian intended to correct the popular appellation of circa 64 AD, in the light of his own more accurate knowledge. "The common people used to call them 'Chrestians,' but the real name of their founder was Christ." p.622

10. Stephen Benko, "The Edict of Claudius of A.D. 49 and the Instigator Chrestus," Theologische Zeitschrift, Vol. 25, #6, 1969, P.409, citing Apologeticum 3, Corpus Christianorum 1

11. Iustini Martyris, *Apologiae pro Christianis*, ed. by Misorslav Marcovich, Walter de Gruyter, NY, 1994, p.12, 4:25

12. Elias Bickermann, "The Name of Christians," *Harvard Theological Review, Vol. 42*, Jan. 1949, p. 114

13. Ibid., pp. 116-117

14. We could take a minimal definition of "'a follower of Christ," but that would not be acceptable to the many Christian churches that claim that only they are truly following Christ. And then there is the question, "Which Christ?" The one who, as the Son of David, will return to restore the kingdom to Israel by establishing his throne in Jerusalem? Or the one who is opposed to the existence of Israel?

    There is the triumphant Christ of Constantine, the Christ of the Crusades and the Inquisition and the pogroms. There is the Christ of the Church of the Third Reich, and the Christ of all the other Churches that sought to destroy the people of the King of the Jews. Historically, the followers of this Christ are called "Christians". That is what they called themselves.

    There are other Christs, too. There is Luther's Christ who "has abolished every law of Moses that ever was." That Christ is opposed to the Christ who comes to establish God's Law in the earth.

    Back in "the dawning of the age of Aquarius," a young man told me that Christ was an hallucinogenic mushroom. Perhaps his Christ was, but the Messiah in the Bible is not. Hundreds of millions of people who call themselves Christians, although they do not march to the beat of that young man's drummer, still do not follow the Messiah presented in the Scriptures.

CHAPTER ELEVEN

# What Are You Doing on Sunday?

*Sunday is Neither the Lord's Day nor a New Sabbath*

ot long ago, a nice couple from Scotland came into my office. They wanted to get acquainted and find out something about Messianic faith. The wife was particularly interested in the nature of our weekly meetings, so I described our erev Shabbat/Friday evening meetings. Then she asked, "Why don't you meet on the Lord's Day since Jesus commanded it and that's what the early Church did?"

That is a fair enough question, one that is often in the minds of Christians. The answer to the question is very straightforward. This is what I said.

1) Yeshua never commanded the observance of Sunday as a day of meeting. Yeshua himself observed Shabbat, as, at Sinai, God had commanded all the descendants of Israel to do. Yeshua never spoke about meeting on the first day of the week. The first day of the week is mentioned eight times in the Messianic Writings, none of them by Yeshua. He never said anything about meeting on any particular day.

As for "Sunday," the Gentiles generally named the days of the week after their gods. So the English "Sunday" is named for the Sun god. The name means that the day belongs to the Sun god. The name itself is a rejection of the LORD God of Israel. God never abdicated any part of His Lordship over time. He never consecrated any day of the week to the gods of the Gentiles.

Does that mean that we shouldn't say the names of the normal days of the week? I don't think so. In the "enlightened" time in which we live, the words don't evoke a meaning connected to the different gods of mythology. But in the first century they did.

God commanded Israel, "Be careful to do everything I have said to you. Do not invoke the names of other gods; do not let them be heard on your lips." (Ex. 23:13) Often, we do not think about what we say. Yeshua always did. He never broke a commandment. He never attributed any day to the gods of the nations.

More than that, Sunday does not correspond to any day which God created. In Biblical terms, it is part of the first day joined to part of the second day. The first day begins with the sundown before Sunday. We have no reason to believe that God ever switched calendars. His days still begin at sundown.

2) It was not the practice of the early "Church". To begin with, of course, there is no "Church" in the Bible—no early Church and no late Church, no high Church and no low Church, no Church at all. The Scottish woman asked her question that way because that's what she believed to be true. She did not know that mistranslation played such an important part in sustaining, through illusion, the ancient tradition in which she believed.

We can rephrase the question to be, "Did the early followers of Yeshua meet on Sunday?" There is one verse that speaks of believers meeting every day. "Every day they continued to meet together in the Temple courts. They broke bread in their homes and ate together with glad and sincere hearts." (Acts 2:46) So at that particular time in Jerusalem, they met in the courts of the Temple at a time which the Romans called Sunday—though they themselves did not recognize "Sunday" as a day—as well as on every other day of the week.

There is one other occasion mentioned when the early believers gathered to meet on the first day of the week, but it was not Sunday, it was Saturday night. "On the first day of the week we came together to break bread. Paul spoke to the people and, because he intended to leave the next day, kept on talking until midnight." (Acts 20:7)

The Biblical day begins at sundown. The first day of the week begins at what most people today would call sundown on Saturday. The believers gathered together at the end of Shabbat and shared a communal meal. Then Paul spoke to them until midnight. He continued to talk until sunrise Sunday morning. (cf. Acts 20:11) It was a twelve hour meeting. That, however, is not presented as the norm then, nor the pattern for anyone now. Other than this, there is not a single verse in the Bible that speaks of the early believers gathering to meet on the first day of the week.

Paul's custom was to meet on Shabbat. (Acts 17:2; cf. Acts 13:14, 42, 44; 16:13; 18:4) He never spoke of establishing a new practice. Nor did he ever speak about the creation of some new "Christian Sabbath". God set aside the seventh day as Shabbat, a day of rest, as part of His perfect work in creating this world.

There is one verse where Paul writes to believers about the first day of the week. He encouraged the believers in Corinth to give for humanitarian relief in Jerusalem. "On the first day of every week, each one of you should set aside a sum of money in keeping with his income, saving it up, so that when I come no collections will have to be made." (1Cor. 16:2) The verse says nothing about meeting on Sunday. It says nothing at all about meeting. It talks about setting aside money to help with the humanitarian needs in Israel. Set that money aside first, as you would do with a tithe.

3) The Biblical phrase, "the Lord's Day," does not mean Sunday. The phrase appears only once in the Bible, in the book of Revelation. The book of Revelation is a series of visions that John received from the Lord. He tells us, "I was in the Spirit on the Lord's day, and I heard behind me a great voice, as of a trumpet." (Rev. 1:10) This is the only time the phrase appears in the Bible. There is nothing in the text that identifies it with a particular day of the week.

Traditional Christian teaching says that "the Lord's day" is Sunday, the day of the week on which Yeshua was raised from the dead, the day when the Church should meet. But John was not in a meeting when Yeshua spoke to him. Most likely, he was completely alone. He was, after all, in exile on Patmos. So whatever "the Lord's day" is, in the one time it is mentioned in the Scriptures, it is not related in any way to church meetings.

The first day of the week is mentioned eight times in the Messianic Writings. Five of these times speak of the exact day on which Yeshua was raised from the dead. (Mt. 28:1; Mk. 16:2,9; Luke 24:1; Jn. 20:1) One time is an occasion when Yeshua appears to his disciples after the resurrection. (Jn. 20:19) One time is when Paul spoke in Troas from Saturday night to Sunday morning. (Acts 20:7) The other time is when Paul told the believers in Corinth to set aside money to help the believers in Jerusalem. (1Cor. 16:2) None of these verses call the first day of the week "the Lord's day."

THE BIBLICAL PHRASE, "THE LORD'S DAY," DOES NOT MEAN SUNDAY. THE PHRASE APPEARS ONLY ONCE IN THE BIBLE, IN THE BOOK OF REVELATION.

In John's gospel, he mentions "the first day of the week" twice. (Jn. 20:1,19) If he wrote his gospel before his exile, then apparently he did not know at the time he wrote it that the first day of the week had become "the Lord's day," since he does not call it that. If he wrote his gospel after he returned from exile in Patmos, and if he had learned in Patmos that Sunday was "the Lord's day," then it is strange that he did not call the first day of the week that in his gospel. That designation and any consequent command to meet on that day would have had monumental significance, yet John never speaks of Sunday as "the Lord's day"; and he never speaks of meeting on Sunday. He never speaks of Sunday.

Some say that John didn't refer to Sunday as "the Lord's day" because everyone already knew that was its designation. But if everyone already knew that Sunday was "the Lord's day," how do we know that everyone already knew? We have no record of anyone ever referring to it that way. How is it possible to know that everyone already knew something when there is no record of anyone even mentioning it? We have no record of anyone in the first century referring to it that way. We have no record of anyone in the second century referring to "the Lord's day" that way either.[1]

The history of how Sunday became the Christian day of worship is interesting, but it is not Biblical. Our concern here is with the meaning of "the Lord's day" in the book of Revelation.

What does the Biblical phrase mean? "The Lord's day" (*kuriake emera*) and "the day of the Lord" (*emera tou kuriou*) are in the same grammatical case and have the same meaning. What do they mean?

Paul wrote to the believers in Corinth: "Therefore you do not lack any spiritual gift as you eagerly wait for our Lord Yeshua the Messiah to be revealed. He will keep you strong to the end, so that you will be blameless on the day of our Lord Yeshua." (1Cor. 1:7-8)

It is apparent here that for Paul, "the day of the Lord Yeshua" is a reference to the time when "our Lord Yeshua the Messiah ... [will be] revealed." This is consistent with the meaning of "the day of the Lord" throughout the Scriptures. The phrase refers to a specific time of divine visitation and judgment. It is used this way in Isaiah, Ezekiel, Joel, Amos, Obadiah, Zephaniah, and Malachi.

In addition to 1Cor. 1:7-8, "the day of the Lord" is also used this way in 1Cor. 5:5; 2Cor. 1:14, 1Th. 5:2, 2Th. 2:2, and 2Pet. 3:10. It points to a future revelation of the glory of God and His judgment upon evil. That, in fact, is what the book of Revelation is, a description of the final time of divine judgment. It makes no connection between "the Lord's day" and the resurrection of Yeshua. And it is not about church meetings.

After I explained these things, the Scottish woman turned to her husband and asked if these things were true. "Yes," he said. "Meeting on Sunday is just a tradition."

4) God has given Israel Shabbat. This is another reason why Jews meet on Shabbat. On the seventh day of the week of Creation, God rested from His labors. He made Shabbat holy. The holiness of Shabbat itself does not come from the Ten Commandments, nor from any commandments given at Sinai. It comes from God's decree in Creation.

The observance of Shabbat as a day of rest is given to Israel as an eternal covenant to commemorate God's creation of the world and His ownership of all that is. "The descendants of Israel are to keep the Sabbath, to do the Sabbath, for their generations. It is an everlasting covenant. It will be a sign between Me and the descendants of Israel forever, for in six days the LORD made the heavens and the earth, and on the seventh day He ceased His labor and was rested.'" (Ex.31:16-17)

So we keep and observe Shabbat. It has nothing to do with "getting saved". It is an everlasting covenant which God has made with us. It is a way to honor God and testify that He created all things.

It is a sanctuary in time. The LORD told Israel, "There are six days when you may work, but the seventh day is a Sabbath of rest, a day of holy assembly. You are not to do any work; wherever you live, it is a Sabbath to the LORD." (Lev. 23:3)

Observing Shabbat is also a way to be grateful. "Remember that you were slaves in Egypt and that the LORD your God brought you out of there with a mighty hand and an outstretched arm. Therefore the LORD your God has commanded you to observe the Sabbath day." (Dt.5:12-15) The observance of Shabbat is for Israel a way to remember that God delivered us from Egypt.

It is a way to be obedient. It is a way to be blessed with a taste of the fullness of God's rest, which we will enjoy in the age to come. By observing Shabbat we demonstrate our faith that God will provide for us. It is like a tithe of our time.

The observance of Shabbat will continue in the Messianic age. (e.g. Ezek. 45:17, 46:1-4) The observance of Shabbat will continue in the ages to come, even in the time of the new heavens and earth. In that time, all the nations will join with Israel in celebrating Shabbat.

God promised Israel that "'As the new heavens and the new earth that I make will endure before Me,' declares the LORD, 'so will your name and descendants endure. From one New Moon to another and from one Sabbath to another, all mankind will come and bow down before Me,' says the LORD." (Is. 66:22-23).

It has long been said that, "More than Israel has kept Shabbat, Shabbat has kept Israel." Shabbat contains within itself something important about the God who ordained it. Shabbat contains within itself something important about the calling of Israel, the people whom God created to represent Himself in the earth.

Gentiles are not commanded, but they are invited to receive the blessing and joy of Shabbat now. (cf. Is. 56:1-7) God did not create Shabbat for Himself. As Yeshua said, "Shabbat was made for Adam, and not Adam for Shabbat." (Mk.2:27) Adam needed Shabbat. That is why God made it for him.

Sunday is a fine day for meeting, worshipping God, resting, or commemorating the resurrection of Messiah; but the Bible says nothing, pro or con, about using it for those purposes. It is not the first day, and it is not the seventh day. The seventh day is the one which God made holy, and made a day of "holy assembly". It is the only day of the week which God has given as Shabbat. Shabbat commemorates the completion of God's creative work.

If one can imagine the first day being decreed to be a new seventh day, then what would the original seventh day become? the 13th day of the week? Or would the original seventh day be eliminated altogether from the week, since God's purpose for it would have been taken over by the first day?

Centuries after the resurrection, Sunday began to be called "the Lord's Day" as part of the general Church rejection and replacement of everything Jewish. It has been called "the Christian Sabbath" to distinguish it from the Jewish Sabbath, i.e. God's Sabbath. Biblically, there is no replacement.

As long as this Creation exists, God wants the Jewish people to commemorate the seventh day of Creation, the day on which He Himself rested. When this Creation is replaced by the new heavens and the new earth, then all the descendants of Adam will keep the seventh day as Shabbat. That is why God created Shabbat, for Man.

## FOOTNOTE

1. "Clement, of Alexandria, A.D. 194, uses this title with reference to 'the eighth day.' If he speaks of a natural day, he no doubt means Sunday. It is not certain, however, that he speaks of a natural day, for his explanation gives to the term an entirely different sense. Here are his words: 'And the Lord's day Plato prophetically speaks of in the tenth book of the Republic, in these words: And when seven days have passed to each of them in the meadow, on the eighth they are to set out and arrive in four days. By the meadow is to be understood the fixed sphere, as being a mild and genial spot, and the locality of the pious; and by the seven days, each motion of the seven planets, and the whole practical art which speeds to the end of rest. But after the wandering orbs, the journey leads to Heaven, that is, to the eighth motion and day. And he says that souls are gone on the fourth day, pointing out the passage through the four elements. But the seventh day is recognized as sacred, not by the Hebrews only, but also by the Greeks; according to which the whole world of all animals and plants revolve.'" *The Miscellanies of Clement*, Book v. Chap. xiv, cited in *Sabbath and Sunday in Early Christianity*, by Robert L. Odom, *The Review and Herald Publishing Association*, pp. 247-248

    Plato was giving a mystical chronology and cosmology. Clement cites Plato as the prophetic source for calling the eighth day "the Lord's day," though Plato never even used the term. Not only did Plato never use the term, the reference which Clement cites does not seem at all to be referring to a particular day of the week. Furthermore, it is not clear that Clement himself was referring to a particular day of the week. If Clement meant the eighth day to be Sunday, he could have said so. He didn't. If that is what he meant, even though he didn't say it, he still would have been attributing that designation to Plato. That would not tell us what the Biblical phrase "the Lord's day" means. John was not a disciple of Plato.

    In Biblical chronology, there is no day of the week that is the eighth day. God created heaven and earth in six days, and rested on the seventh. The seventh day, the rest of God, was made for Adam.

CHAPTER TWELVE

# Those Pearly Gates

*The Followers of Messiah Will Rule Upon the Earth*

"WE TRAVELED FOR MILES IN LIBERIA. I TALKED TO HUNDREDS OF PEOPLE AND ANSWERED THOUSANDS OF QUESTIONS ABOUT ISRAEL, MANY OF THEM ABOUT ISRAEL AS THE LAND OF THE BIBLE. A VERY NICE YOUNG WOMAN FROM THE LIBERIAN FOREIGN OFFICE ACCOMPANIED US, AND I REMEMBER THAT ON THE LAST DAY OF MY VISIT SHE SAID VERY BASHFULLY TO ME, 'I HAVE AN OLD MOTHER TO WHOM I EXPLAINED THAT I WOULD BE BUSY ALL WEEK WITH A VISITOR FROM JERUSALEM. MY MOTHER JUST STARED AT ME. DON'T YOU KNOW, SHE SAID, THAT THERE IS NO SUCH PLACE AS JERUSALEM? JERUSALEM IS IN HEAVEN. DO YOU THINK, MRS. MEIR, THAT YOU COULD POSSIBLY SEE HER FOR A MINUTE AND TELL HER ABOUT JERUSALEM?'

"OF COURSE, I WENT TO MEET HER MOTHER THAT DAY AND TOOK WITH ME A LIT-TLE BOTTLE OF WATER FROM THE JORDAN RIVER. THE OLD WOMAN JUST WALKED AROUND AND AROUND ME, THOUGH SHE NEVER ACTUALLY TOUCHED ME. 'YOU COME FROM JERUSALEM,' SHE KEPT ON SAYING. 'YOU MEAN, THERE'S A REAL CITY, WITH STREETS AND HOUSES WHERE REAL PEOPLE LIVE?'

"'YES, I LIVE THERE,' I ANSWERED, BUT I DON'T THINK SHE BELIEVED ME FOR A MOMENT. IT WAS A QUESTION THAT I WAS ASKED ALL OVER AFRICA, AND I USED TO TELL THE AFRICANS THAT THE ONLY THING THAT WAS HEAVENLY ABOUT JERUSALEM WAS THAT IT STILL EXISTED!"

Golda Meir, *My Life*, G.P. Putnam's Sons, NY, 1975, pp. 322-323

Someone taught these people in Africa about Jerusalem. Whatever they taught made the people incapable of comprehending the reality that Jerusalem and Israel are real upon the earth. Whatever they taught was very different from, and in conflict with, what is in the Scriptures.

How could these teachers have taught that Yeshua is the Messiah, without mentioning that he came to Jerusalem as the prophesied Son of David? How could these teachers have failed to mention that he taught in God's Temple in Jerusalem, wept over the city and promised to return to it? How could these teachers have failed to mention that Jesus, the King of the Jews, was crucified outside Jerusalem? How could these teachers have taught about bringing good news to the world without mentioning that Yeshua commanded his followers to begin in Jerusalem?

I think I know how they did it. They taught about a Christ who isn't Jewish. They taught about a god who isn't interested in this world. They taught a gospel of escape rather than one of overcoming this world. They taught about harps and crowns in heaven rather than the establishment of God's righteous kingdom upon the earth. They taught without context or content.

Those teachers in Africa were not unusual. In much of the Church, heaven has been substituted for the kingdom of God. Consequently, the Christians who feed on this teaching long for heaven rather than for justice upon the earth. They leave the earth to its present rulers, the very rulers who will be destroyed when the earth's rightful Ruler returns.

They suffer under one of the same conceptual errors that prevailed in the time of Copernicus. People then believed in a two-sphere universe, the earthly sphere and the heavenly sphere. They imagined that the earth was governed differently than the heavens. They were wrong. There is one universe where the same laws prevail throughout.

In much of traditional theology, there is no understanding of the universality of God's rule. People are taught that they will spend their time on the earth, and then spend their eternity in the heavens. They do not comprehend the coming reality of God's kingdom upon the earth. There are some basic reasons for this error. We will look at them one by one.

1. Confusion as to where Yeshua will reign.

2. The improper identification of the new Jerusalem as heaven.

3. The cutting off of the Church from Israel's olive tree.

4. A Neo-platonic understanding of the relationship of the material and the spiritual realms.

## 1. Confusion as to where Yeshua will reign.

Yeshua did not come to earth so that he could reign in heaven. He was already reigning in heaven. He came to earth to become a son of Adam. He became a son of Adam in order to redeem the children of Adam and to redeem the earth that had been entrusted to Adam.

Yeshua became a son of Abraham because the promise of inheriting the earth had been given to Abraham. (cf. Rom. 4:13) He became a son of David that he might become the

Messiah, the King of Israel, and rule from David's throne in Jerusalem over all the earth. Jerusalem is the city of the Great King. (cf. Ps. 48:2; Mt. 5:35)

The message Yeshua proclaimed is that the Kingdom of God is coming to earth. "The Kingdom of God" and "the Kingdom of Heaven" were synonymous terms used to indicate the time when God would dwell upon, and rule over the earth.[1] The ancient Rabbis understood that, "the goal of Creation is that the Kingdom of God… shall be established on earth, as it is in heaven."[2]

That was and is God's intention. That is why Yeshua taught his disciples to pray, "Your kingdom come;" which will be the day that, "Your will be done—as it is in heaven, so also upon the earth." God now rules in heaven, but one day He will also rule upon the earth. Heaven and earth are different realms of Creation, but God is One. God is over all, and the Creator of all. His will should be done in both heaven and earth. Yeshua did not tell his disciples to pray, "Take us to Your Kingdom." He taught them to pray, "Bring Your Kingdom here."

YESHUA DID NOT TELL HIS DISCIPLES TO PRAY, "TAKE US TO YOUR KINGDOM." HE TAUGHT THEM TO PRAY, "BRING YOUR KINGDOM HERE."

He said to those disciples, "Truly I say to you, that in the time of restoration, when the Son of Adam will sit on his glorious throne, you who have followed Me, you also will sit upon twelve thrones, judging the twelve tribes of Israel." (Mt.19:28; cf. Mt.12:27; Luke 22:28-30)

The sense of "judging" here is that of a continuing administration for God, as in the ministry of Samuel and the other "judges". The tribes of Israel will be upon the earth. Those who judge them, those who exercise God's rule over them, will do so upon the earth. The twelve tribes, the thrones, the disciples, and Yeshua the King Messiah will be upon the earth.

Yeshua said, "I am the living bread that came down out from heaven [*ek tou ouranou*]… For the bread of God is that which comes down out from heaven [*ek tou ouranou*], and gives life to the world." (Jn.6:51,33) He was in heaven, but He came down to the earth. He came into the world to give life to the world, not to abandon it to its corrupt condition.

"For I have come down from heaven [*apo tou ouranou*], not to do my own will, but the will of Him who sent me." (Jn.6:38) Yeshua came to earth to do the will of his Father upon the earth. He did not need to be in heaven to do God's will. Nor do we.

Yeshua told Pilate, "My kingdom is not from this world [*ek tou kosmou*]. If my kingdom were from this world [*ek tou kosmou*], then my servants would be fighting, that I might not be delivered up to the Jewish rulers. But as it is, my kingdom is not from here." (Jn.18:36) That Yeshua's kingdom is "not from this world" does not mean that it is "not in this world." He him-

self was not from this world, but he came into it.

What did Yeshua mean when he said his kingdom was not "from this world"? He meant that his kingdom was made of different stuff than the kingdoms of this world. It is not about eating, drinking, profit, and power. It is about justice, peace, and joy. (cf. Rom.14:17)

YESHUA WILL RECEIVE THE KINGDOM FROM HIS FATHER. THAT KINGDOM IS NOT FROM THIS WORLD, BUT IT WILL BE IN THIS WORLD.

Did he mean that his kingdom was not located upon the earth, but in heaven? No, not at all. He meant that if his kingdom were made of the same stuff as the kingdoms of this world, then it would have to be established by worldly means. Yeshua's Jewish disciples would then have had to physically fight against the Jewish rulers and the Roman rulers in order to establish it, because that is the way the kingdoms of this world are established.

Since his kingdom is not a worldly kingdom, it cannot be established by worldly means—not then, and not now. That does not mean that it cannot be established upon the earth. It can be, and it will be, but not by worldly means, and not for worldly purposes.

The Accuser showed Yeshua all the kingdoms of the world. And he said to him, "'I will give you all their authority and splendor, for it has been given to me, and I can give it to anyone I want to. So if you bow down to me, it will all be yours.'"

"Yeshua answered, 'It is written: 'Bow down to the LORD your God and serve Him only.'" (Lk. 4:6-8) Politicians continually bow down to the Accuser in the hope of gaining power. Yeshua refused the offer. He will receive the Kingdom from his Father. That Kingdom is not from this world, but it will be in this world.

We can see this same relationship in other passages. Yeshua told a group of Pharisees that they were from this world [*ek tou kosmou*], but he was not. (Jn. 8:23-24) Yeshua was living and serving God and Man upon the earth, but the world was not the source of how he lived. It was not the source of his identity.

Yeshua prayed to his Father, "I manifested Your name to the men whom You gave me from the world [*ek tou kosmou*]. They were Yours, and You gave them to me, and they have kept Your word. ... I have given them Your word, and the world has hated them, because they are not from the world [*ek tou kosmou*], even as I am not from the world [*ek tou kosmou*]. I do not ask You to take them from the world [*ek tou kosmou*], but to keep them from the evil one." (Jn.17:6,14-15)

His disciples were given to Yeshua by the Father "from the world." Though the disciples were living in the world, they were no longer from it. The source and substance of their lives had been composed of worldly things, but that changed. Having been redeemed, the source and substance of their lives came from God. Their life is from above, but they live it on the earth.

Their lives became like that of the one they followed. Even as Yeshua himself was in the world, but not from it, so they also are now to be in the world, but not from it. That is why Yeshua prayed that they should not be removed from the world, but rather that they should be enabled to serve God in it. Since the world is hostile to God, that is not easy to do, but it is what sets his disciples apart.

John saw that only the Lion of Judah, the root of David, could "overcome so as to open the book and its seven seals.... And they sang a new song, saying, 'You are worthy to take the book, and to break its seals, because you were slain, and purchased for God with your blood men from every tribe and tongue and people and nation. And you have made them to be a kingdom and priests to our God; and they will reign upon the earth.' " (Rev. 5:9-10)

The identity of those who have been purchased for God by the blood of the Lion of Judah, the Lamb that was slain, is clear. They are those who have been redeemed "from every tribe and tongue and people and nation." They have been redeemed so that they can serve God.

"And You have made them to be a kingdom and priests to our God; and they will reign upon the earth." They are destined to exercise rule for God upon the earth. They were made from the earth; they were designed for it.

*'But don't they go to heaven?'*

Yes, they do, for a short time. The marriage supper of the Lamb takes place in heaven. But from there, Messiah returns to the earth with his bride to establish his kingdom and reign over all the earth. Yeshua remains in heaven until the time which the Father has fixed by His own authority, the time for the restoration of the kingdom to Israel. (cf. Acts 1:7; 3:21) The army that follows him is identifiable because it is clothed in the same fine linen, bright and pure, as the bride. (cf. Rev. 19:8,14)

God gave John a brief view of the time following the triumphant return of Messiah to Jerusalem. "And I saw thrones, and they sat upon them, and judgment was given to them. And I saw the souls of those who had been beheaded because of the testimony of Yeshua and because of the word of God, and those who had not received the mark upon their forehead and upon their hand; and they came to life and reigned with Messiah for a thousand years." (Rev.20:4)

Where do they reign with Messiah? For a thousand years, they will reign with Messiah upon the earth. During that time, the Gentiles will come again to Jerusalem, but it will be to bow down to the King. "In the end of days, the mountain of the house of the LORD will be established as the chief of the mountains, and will be raised above the hills; and all the Gentiles will stream to it. And many peoples will come and say, 'Come, let us go up to the mountain of the LORD , to the house of the God of Jacob; that He may teach us concerning His ways, and that we may walk in His paths. For the law will go forth from Zion, and the word of the LORD from Jerusalem.'" (Is. 2:2-3)

Yeshua told the congregation in Thyatira, "Nevertheless what you have, hold fast until I come. And the one who overcomes, and the one who keeps My deeds until the end, to him I will give authority over the Gentiles; and he shall rule them with a rod of iron..." (Rev.2:26-27a) Those who overcome will be given authority to rule over the Gentiles. The Gentiles will be upon the earth. Those who rule over them will do so upon the earth.

"And it will be that whichever of the families of the earth does not go up to Jerusalem to worship the King, the LORD of hosts, there will be no rain on them." (Zech.14:17) The families of the earth will come to Jerusalem to worship the King, the LORD of hosts, because that is where he will be. They will not be going up to heaven to worship him, they will be going up to the capital of Israel upon the earth.

In the following age, the time of the new heaven, new earth, and new Jerusalem, Yeshua will continue to reign upon the earth. "I did not see a temple in the city, because the LORD God Almighty and the Lamb are its temple. The city does not need the sun or the moon to shine on it, for the glory of God gives it light, and the Lamb is its lamp. The nations will walk by its light, and the kings of the earth will bring their splendor into it." (Rev. 21:22-24)

The nations will be upon the earth. The kings of the earth will be upon the earth. The new Jerusalem, with the Lamb enthroned, will be upon the earth also.

## 2. The improper identification of the new Jerusalem as heaven.

"By faith Abraham, when he was called, obeyed by going out to a place which he was to receive for an inheritance; and he went out, not knowing where he was going. By faith he lived as a foreigner in the land of promise, as in a foreign land, dwelling in tents with Isaac and Jacob, fellow-heirs of the same promise; for he was looking for the city which has foundations, whose architect and builder is God." (Heb.11:8-10)

Abraham went to the "place which he was [one day] to receive for an inheritance." Abraham did not go to heaven, he went to the land that was then called Canaan. That, not heaven, is the land Abraham will receive as an inheritance.

"He lived as a foreigner in the land/*ge* of promise." Isaac and Jacob lived with him as "fellow-heirs of the same promise," and as "foreigners in the land of promise." They did not live as foreigners in heaven. Heaven is not the land of promise. The land of promise was the land of Canaan, soon to be called by God the land of Israel. (cf. Gen.13:14-17; 15:7-21; 17:8)

Heb.11:13 repeats that they "lived as foreigners and strangers on the land/*ge.*"

The context shows that *ge* should be translated as "land," as it is in v. 9, not as "earth". That is also consistent with what we are told in Tanakh. "Jacob lived in the land [*ge* in LXX] where his father had stayed, the land [*ge* in LXX] of Canaan." (Gen. 37:1)

The patriarchs had the promise of God concerning the land of Canaan, but there was more to the promise than the land they saw. God intended to make them a holy people in a holy land. They were not looking for something that existed upon the earth at that time, but "for the city which has foundations, whose architect and builder is God." What city is that? The new Jerusalem. A city designed and prepared by God for His purposes in the earth.

"But as it is, they desire a better one, that is a heavenly one. Therefore God is not ashamed to be called their God; for He has prepared a city for them." (Heb.11:16)

*'If their city is a "heavenly" one, isn't it in heaven?'*

No. That is simply its origin and character.

Yeshua was a heavenly man, i.e. a man from heaven. (cf. 1Co.15:47-49) But he was a heavenly man upon the earth. His followers are being remade into his image. They share in "the heavenly calling." (Heb. 3:1) "The heavenly calling" is not a calling **to** heaven, but a calling **from** heaven to serve upon the earth.

The earth itself is eagerly waiting for Yeshua to return, and groaning for his kingdom to be established. That should also be true of all believers. "For our commonwealth/*politeuma* has its beginning/*huparchei* in the heavens, from which we are also awaiting a savior, the Lord Yeshua the Messiah." (Phil.3:20) The Savior will come from heaven to the earth. So will the commonwealth. Believers are awaiting both.

The city, the capital of the commonwealth, will also come from heaven. "For we do not have here an enduring city, but we are seeking **the one that is coming.**" (Heb. 13:14) Even as the Savior did not and will not stay in heaven, neither will the city. Yeshua spoke of, "... the city of my God, the new Jerusalem, which is **coming down out of heaven** [*ek tou ouranou*] from my God..." (Rev. 3:12) The new Jerusalem will come down out of heaven, where it was prepared, to the earth.

In a vision, John saw that event take place. "And I saw a new heaven and a new earth; for the first heaven and the first earth passed away, and there is no longer any sea. And I saw the holy city, new Jerusalem, **coming down out of heaven** [*ek tou ouranou*] from God, made ready as a bride adorned for her husband. And I heard a loud voice from the throne, saying, 'Behold, the tabernacle of God is among men, and He shall dwell among them, and they shall be His peoples, and God Himself shall be among them.' " (Rev. 21:1-3)

John saw a new heaven and a new earth. The new Jerusalem comes down out of heaven.

Where does it come to? There is only one other place in existence, the new earth. The new Jerusalem comes down out of heaven to the new earth.

It is the city that Abraham, Isaac, Jacob, and their faithful descendants have been seeking all along. They lived "as foreigners in the land of promise." In the ultimate fulfillment of God's promise and purpose for the land, the new Jerusalem comes down out of heaven to the "place which he [Abraham] was to receive for an inheritance." And God will dwell among men.

John saw more. "And he carried me away in the Spirit to a great and high mountain, and showed me the holy city, Jerusalem, **coming down out of heaven** [*ek tou ouranou*] from God, having the glory of God.... It had a great and high wall, with twelve gates ... and names were written on them which are those of the twelve tribes of the sons of Israel.... And the wall of the city had twelve foundation stones and on them were the twelve names of the twelve ambassadors of the Lamb." (Rev. 21:10-12,14)

All of Jerusalem's children, those who have been redeemed, will walk through the gates under the names of the twelve tribes of Israel. The very gates of the new Jerusalem declare that God is faithful to the Jewish people, faithful to fully restore Jerusalem, as He promised. The foundation stones of her walls carry the names of the twelve Jewish men whom the LORD graciously used to bring the Gentiles back to Himself. (cf. Is. 60:18)

John tells us that, "The Gentiles/nations will walk by its light and the kings of the earth will bring their splendor into it. Its gates will never be shut by day—for there will be no night there—and they shall bring the glory and the honor of the Gentiles/nations into it so that they may enter." (Rev. 21:24-26)

He saw and described what Isaiah had seen and described concerning "the City of the LORD, Zion of the Holy One of Israel" (Is. 60:14b): " Gentiles/nations will come to your light, and kings to the brightness of your dawn. ... Your gates will always stand open, they will never be shut, day or night, so that men may bring you the wealth of the Gentiles/nations—their kings led in triumphal procession. For the nation or kingdom that will not serve you will perish; it will be utterly ruined." (Is. 60:3,11-12)

John tells us that, "There will be no more night. They will not need the light of a lamp or the light of the sun, for the Lord God will give them light. And they will reign for ever and ever. (Rev. 22:5) Again, he was seeing and describing the same city about which Isaiah had prophesied. "The sun will no more be your light by day, nor will the brightness of the moon shine on you, for the LORD will be your everlasting light, and your God will be your glory." (Is. 60:19)

Jerusalem will finally have peace. "No longer will violence be heard in your land, nor ruin or destruction within your borders, but you will call your walls Salvation and your gates Praise." (Is. 60:18) It is a city on earth with a King from heaven, but a King who is one of the sons of the city.

The tower of Babel shows us what is in the minds of men. God wanted man to increase, fill the earth, and rule it for Him. (Gen. 9:1) Instead, Man wanted to build a city with a tower that would get them to heaven. (Gen. 11:4) The new Jerusalem is not a city that men enter by going up to heaven. It is a city that God brings down from heaven to earth.

The Lord showed John what He had already proclaimed to Isaiah. "For behold, I create [*bara*] new heavens and a new earth; and the former things shall not be remembered or come to mind. But be glad and rejoice forever [*adey ad*] in what I create [*bara*]; for behold, I create [*bara*] Jerusalem for rejoicing, and her people for gladness. I will also rejoice in Jerusalem, and be glad in My people; and there will no longer be heard in her the voice of weeping and the sound of crying." (Is. 65:17-19) The new Jerusalem is a new creation, not made of the things of this world or this age, just like the new earth on which it is situated.

It reads much the same whether we read it in Isaiah or in Revelation. "And He who sits on the throne said, 'Behold, I am making all things new.' And He said, 'Write, for these words are faithful and true.'" (Rev.21:5) God is not making all new things, He is making all things new. There is an important difference. Heaven is made new. The earth is made new. Jerusalem is made new.

It is similar to the change that takes place when someone becomes a new creature. (cf. 2Co.5:17) God gives a new spirit and a new heart. (e.g. Ezek.11:19) He does this so that "we too might walk in newness of life." (Rom.6:4b)

A man dead in the sins of the world is transformed into a new creature alive to God. He is the same man, but he is not the same man at all. He has been made new. The totality of the difference has not yet appeared.

When the totality of that difference appears, those who overcome will receive "a new name." (Rev.2:17) Jerusalem will receive "a new name." (Is.62:2) Still, it is Jerusalem. Yeshua will have a new name. (cf. Rev. 3:12) Still, he will be Yeshua.

*'But what about all the scriptures that talk about storing up treasure in heaven? Yeshua told his listeners to* "store up for yourselves treasures in heaven, where moth and rust do not destroy, and where thieves do not break in and steal. For where your treasure is, there your heart will be also." (Mt. 6:20-21; cf. Mt. 19:21; Luke 12:33) *'Doesn't that mean that we will enjoy our treasure in heaven?'*

No. It means that whatever treasures you accumulate on earth can be taken from you, while those which you accumulate in heaven cannot be taken from you. You will enjoy them upon the earth when Yeshua returns.

There are also scriptures that talk about storing up wrath in heaven. Men are warned, "because of your stubbornness and your unrepentant heart, you are storing up wrath against yourself for the day of God's wrath, when His righteous judgment will be revealed." (Rom. 2:5) God's wrath is stored up in heaven until the day when it is poured out upon the earth.

Yeshua brings his reward and his wrath from heaven to the earth. "The LORD has made proclamation to the ends of the earth: Say to the Daughter of Zion, 'See, your Savior comes! See, his reward is with him, and his recompense accompanies him.' " (Is. 62:11) The treasure, i.e. the reward for serving the Lord, is kept secure in heaven, but it will be given upon the earth. The judgments, i.e. the plagues, disasters, wars, and wrath are prepared in heaven, but poured out upon the earth. (e.g. Rev.9:15)

Yeshua says the same thing in the last chapter of the Bible. "Behold, I am coming soon! My reward is with me, and I will give to everyone according to what he has done." (Rev. 22:12) God had said it earlier. "You who bring good tidings to Zion, go up on a high mountain. You who bring good tidings to Jerusalem, lift up your voice with a shout. Lift it up, do not be afraid, say to the cities of Judah, 'Behold your God! See, the LORD God comes with power, and His arm rules for Him. See, His reward is with Him, and His recompense accompanies Him.'" (Is. 40:9-10) He brings his reward and recompense to the earth.

The heavens are not big enough to contain God, but He dwells there. The earth is not big enough to contain God, but He will dwell here, too. (cf. 2Chr. 6:18) As He promised Israel, He will dwell in the midst of His people, in the new Jerusalem.

### 3. The Church cutting itself off from Israel's olive tree.

The Scriptures teach that, "Salvation is of the Jews." (Jn.4:22) Individual Gentiles who believe in Messiah, the King of the Jews, are grafted into Israel's olive tree. (cf. Rom. 11:16-27) All believers receive their life in Messiah through Israel's olive tree. To be cut off from that cultivated olive tree is to be cut off from the life God gives. Gentiles who have not been brought into the commonwealth of Israel are still "foreigners to the covenants of the promise, without hope and without God." (Eph.2:12b)

Nevertheless, the bulk of historical and contemporary theology presents a Church that is separate from the Jewish people. One of the consequences of this theological severing of the Church from Israel's olive tree is that the Church then considers itself too "spiritual" for any part in the restored kingdom of David. That restored kingdom is rejected as being carnal or ethnocentric. Even those who believe in the restoration of Israel believe that they themselves will be in heaven instead.

Israel then becomes, at best, the earthly seed of Abraham, and the Church becomes the heavenly seed. There is no support for such a concept in the Scriptures. There are a few scriptures that compare the children of Abraham, Isaac, and Jacob to the stars of the heavens, the sands by the sea, and the dust of the earth. A review of all these scriptures makes it clear what God actually intends the comparison to signify.

When Abraham questioned whether he would ever have a natural descendant to be his heir, the LORD told him, "'one who shall come forth from your own inward parts, he shall be your heir.' And He took him outside and said, 'Now look toward the heavens, and count the stars, if you are able to count them.' And He said to him, 'So shall your seed be.'" (Gen.15:4-5) In this instance, God pointed to the stars to indicate to Abraham how numerous the people descended from him would be.

Abraham's question concerned his lack of physical descendants. God's answer was a promise of physical descendants—from your own inward parts.

Later, after the offering of Isaac, the LORD told Abraham, "because you have done this thing, and have not withheld your son, your only son, indeed I will greatly bless you, and I will greatly multiply your seed as the stars of the heavens, and as the sand which is on the seashore. And your seed shall possess the gate of his enemies. And in your seed all the Gentiles of the earth will be blessed, because you have obeyed My voice." (Gen.22:17-18)

No distinction is made here between two different seeds of Abraham, one that is earthly and one that is heavenly. Only one seed is mentioned. The LORD is again promising to Abraham a great multitude—as the stars of the heavens and as the sand of the sea—which will be descended from him. It is this multitude that will be a blessing to the Gentiles of the earth.

After Abraham had died, the LORD appeared to Isaac and promised him, "I will multiply your seed as the stars of heaven, and will give your seed all these lands. And by your seed all the Gentiles of the earth will be blessed, because Abraham obeyed Me and kept My charge, My commandments, My statutes and My laws." (Gen.26:4-5) Here again, the LORD is speaking of multitude, not location. The same seed that will be as numerous as the stars of the heaven will receive "all these lands" upon the earth. In this same seed, "all the Gentiles of the earth will be blessed."

The LORD then appeared to Jacob when he was fleeing from Esau, and said, "I am the LORD, the God of your father Abraham and the God of Isaac; the land on which you lie, I will give it to you and to your seed. Your seed shall also be like the dust of the earth, and you shall break through to the west and to the east and to the north and to the south. And in you and in your seed shall all the families of the earth be blessed." (Gen.28:14)

Jacob's seed, multiplied as the dust of the earth, will receive the land of Canaan, and will spread abroad in the earthly directions of west, east, north, and south. In that seed, all the families of the earth will be blessed.

When Moses was on Mt. Sinai with God, and the people of Israel were worshipping the golden calf, the LORD told Moses, " '...let Me alone... that I may destroy them...' Then Moses entreated the LORD his God, and said, '...Remember Abraham, Isaac, and Israel, Thy servants to whom Thou didst swear by Thyself, and didst say to them, "I will multiply your seed as the stars of the heavens, and all this land of which I have spoken I will give to your seed, and they shall inherit it forever."' So the LORD changed His mind about the harm which He said He would do to His people." (Ex.32:9-14)

Moses understood God's promise to Abraham, Isaac, and Jacob—the promise of a seed multiplied as the stars of the heavens—to refer to their physical descendants, those whom God was threatening to destroy. The LORD understood His promise the same way, since He accepted the intercession of Moses for the people on earth to be multiplied as the stars of the heavens.

When Moses spoke to the next generation of the children of Israel in the wilderness, he said, "The LORD your God has multiplied you, and behold, you are this day as the stars of heaven for multitude. May the LORD, the God of your fathers, increase you a thousand-fold more than you are, and bless you, just as He has promised you." (Dt.1:10-11) He reminded them, "Your fathers went down to Egypt seventy persons in all, and now the LORD your God has made you as numerous as the stars of heaven." (Dt.10:22) When he warned them of the consequences of disobedience to the LORD, he said, "Then you shall be left few in number, whereas you were as the stars of heaven for multitude, because you did not obey the LORD your God." (Dt.28:62) The only purpose of the comparison to the stars of heaven is for multitude, not for location.

King David commanded that a census be taken of the sons of Israel. "But David did not count those twenty years of age and under, because the LORD had said He would multiply Israel as the stars of the heaven." (1Ch.27:23) David understood the promise and comparison of the LORD to refer to the number of the physical descendants of Abraham, Isaac, and Jacob.

After God brought destruction and exile upon the children of Israel for their disobedience, the LORD brought back a remnant of the captive ones of Zion. Then the Levites and the priests prayed, reviewing God's dealings with Israel, "...And You made their sons numerous as the stars of heaven, and You brought them into the land which You had told their fathers to enter and possess..." (Neh.9:23) "The stars of the heaven" are used to indicate number, nothing more.

By faith, a barren Sarah received power to conceive Isaac, in fulfillment of God's promise. "Therefore, also, there was born of one man, and him as good as dead in these things, as many descendants as the stars of heaven in number, and innumerable as the sand which is by the seashore." (Heb.11:12) The Messianic Writings specifically interpret the comparison to the stars of the heavens as relating to the birth of Isaac and the number of his descendants.

In every case, the Bible explains the promise to Abraham that his seed would be as the stars of the heavens as referring to the numerical multitude of his descendants through Isaac and Jacob. It is never interpreted as referring to the difference between Israel and "the Church". The comparisons of their seed to the sand of the sea and the dust of the earth also refer to the promised numerical multitude of that seed, not to its nature or destiny.

God has only one chosen people, Israel. Some theologians recognize the restoration of the kingdom to the Jews, but create a more "spiritual" destination for the Church. There is nothing, however, more spiritual than the Messianic kingdom.

Some have created theological devices that would be the envy of the pre-Copernicus mathematicians. They find themselves unable to keep the new Jerusalem in heaven, because John said, "I saw the Holy City, the new Jerusalem, coming down out of heaven from God, prepared as a bride beautifully dressed for her husband." (Rev. 21:2) But they are unwilling to let it come to the earth, because that would mean that the kingdom of God will be upon the earth. And such a kingdom would have an inescapable Jewish dimension to it. So they explain that the new Jerusalem hovers a short distance above the earth.

But its entrance gates are engraved with the names of the twelve tribes of Israel. Its foundation stones are engraved with the names of the twelve ambassadors of the King of the Jews. It is the root and offspring of David who will establish the city. Besides that, God only created two places, heaven and earth; and two places to replace them, the new heaven and the new earth.

Some theologians deny completely that the kingdom will be restored. They do not understand that in doing so, they are denying that Jesus is the Messiah. The one thing that prophetically defines Messiah, more than anything and everything else, is that he restores the Davidic kingdom. So if there is a Jesus who does not do that, then that Jesus is not the Messiah.

## 4. A Neo-platonic understanding of the relationship of the physical and the spiritual realms.

Greek philosophy permeates much of Church theology. From Justin Martyr to Thomas Aquinas, and down to their heirs today, many theologians have presented Platonic/Aristotelian philosophy as being compatible with the Biblical revelation. They see the writings of Plato as the Gentile equivalent of the Law, the Writings, and the Prophets—i.e. a divine revelation leading to Messiah. Sometimes even more than that, they maintain that the Scriptures must be interpreted through this Greek philosophy.

The mind of Man is a wonderful thing. The ability to reason is a precious gift. But neither is sufficient. Each must have a starting place, and rules of the road for proceeding on. If Man himself is the starting place, if Man himself is the legislator, then his thoughts will be hopelessly circular, ever learning, but never able to come to the knowledge of the Truth.

In Platonic, or Neo-platonic, philosophy, the physical and spiritual realms may touch, but they do not mix. The physical is seen as only the shadow or corruption of the spiritual, which is the ideal or good. The person who is spiritual seeks to disengage from and escape from the physical world.

The Scriptures present a very different reality. God created a material world for specific good purposes—purposes which will yet be realized. The Creation itself was "very good". God exists before, and distinct from, His Creation, but He freely enters into it. The Spirit of God hovered over the waters of this created world, in this created world, before God created the different material forms.

According to the Scriptures, it is the spiritual that not only gives form, but also gives life to the material in this world. God breathed into a lifeless mass of matter, and it became a living being, Adam. Adam was formed from the ground (*adamah*), but the breath of life came directly from God. Adam, a physical man, was created in the image and likeness of God, who is spirit.

Adam was created to have dominion over the earth and its creatures. But Adam rebelled, and he and his descendants corrupted their way on the earth. Adam was created to do what was good and right upon the earth, but he choose to do what was evil and wrong. Adam chose to depart from the image and likeness of God.

That made it necessary for God to send a second Adam, to fulfill His original purpose for man and the earth. "The Word became flesh and planted his tent among us." (Jn. 1:14a) Again, the Spirit of God gave life in this physical world. The message of the incarnation is that the spiritual can inhabit and direct the physical. That is God's intention. To a neo-platonist, the incarnation is impossible and nonsensical.

Those who are born of the Spirit are to live in this world the way Adam should have lived. Biblically, the person who is spiritual seeks to serve God upon the earth, even as Yeshua did. That is the reason for the promise of the New Covenant, "I will put My Spirit within you." It is why man needs the Spirit of God: "And I will put My Spirit within you and cause you to walk in My statutes and My judgments that you may observe and do them." (Ezek. 36:27) "So I say, walk in the Spirit, and you will not gratify the desires of the sinful nature." (Gal. 5:16)

Closeness to God does not mean that we seek to disengage from and escape from the physical world. To the contrary, it means that we seek to serve Him here and now, while we live in physical bodies. Part of that service is that we seek the establishment of His kingdom upon the earth. And if we die before the Lord returns to do that, we will be resurrected and will return to the earth with him. He returns to establish his kingdom on the earth.

Belief in the resurrection of the body is indispensable to Biblical faith. (cf. 1Co.15:13-20) It is a foolish absurdity to Greek philosophy. (cf. Acts 17:18,32) "Tertullian was right in proclaiming that Athens can never agree with Jerusalem—even though for two thousand years the foremost thinkers of the Western world have firmly believed that a reconciliation is possible and have bent their strongest and most determined efforts toward effecting it."[3] "What for Athens is wisdom is for Jerusalem foolishness: Tertullian said nothing else."[4]

Paul explained bodily resurrection to the believers in Corinth: "It is sown a natural body, it is raised a spiritual body. There is a natural body, and there is a spiritual body. So it is written: 'The first man Adam became a living being'; the last Adam, a life-giving spirit." (1Cor. 15:44-45)

What is a "spiritual body"? I don't know, but Yeshua had one. Such a thing is impossible in a Neo-platonic world. There cannot be a "spiritual body." The spirit and the flesh do not mix.

In the Bible, however, physical Man was created in the image and likeness of a spiritual God, to inhabit and manage a physical earth. From the beginning, God, who is spirit, walked in the garden of Eden. He also walked with Enokh. Man was made with both flesh and spirit, to serve God in a material world.

When Yeshua rose from the dead, he had a spiritual body. The disciples could see him, hear him, and touch him. (cf. John 20:27) He could cook fish and bread, and eat physical food. (cf. Lk. 24:39-43; Jn. 21:9)

Even in normal physical bodies, those who are born of the Spirit are called to walk in the Spirit—i.e., to live for God upon the earth. The fact that they are spiritual does not in any way mean that they cannot inhabit the earth. It does not in any way imply that they must live in heaven.

Those who have a Neo-platonic view of reality cannot understand or accept the Biblical revelation. For them, those who are spiritual must have their life in the spirit realm, not upon the earth. For them, those who are spiritual can inhabit heaven for eternity, but not the earth. They do not understand that heaven is just as much a created place as the earth is—"In the beginning, God created the heavens and the earth ..." They do not understand that God made Man from the earth, for the earth.

God has never abandoned His purposes for Man and the earth. Some people may not like these purposes, and may not submit to them, but God has good, yet to be fulfilled, spiritual purposes for Man upon the earth. All of creation awaits that fulfillment.

"For the anxious longing of the creation waits eagerly for the revealing of the sons of God. For the creation was subjected to futility, not of its own will, but because of Him who subjected it, in hope that the creation itself also will be set free from its slavery to corruption into the freedom of the glory of the children of God.

"For we know that the whole creation groans and suffers the pains of childbirth together until now. And not only this, but also we ourselves, having the first fruits of the Spirit, even we ourselves groan within ourselves, waiting eagerly for our adoption as sons, the redemption of our body." (Rom.8:19-23)

Beyond dispute, heaven is more glorious than we can imagine. It is not, however, our destination. God placed Man upon the earth and directed him to exercise God's dominion over the earth. Man rejected God's purpose, and sought to ascend to heaven. They said, "Come, let us build ourselves a city, with a tower that reaches to the heavens, so that we may make a name for ourselves and not be scattered over the face of the whole earth." (Gen. 11:4) There is no need to rebel against God's purpose for Man upon the earth.

The fullness of the kingdom of God upon the earth is also more glorious than we can imagine. The earth is the place that God made for Man. We are being made new. The earth will be made new. Heaven can function alright without us.

## ALL'S WELL THAT ENDS WELL

The last chapter in the Bible brings us back to a restored beginning. In the beginning, God placed Adam in the Garden of Eden. "In the middle of the Garden were the tree of life and the tree of the knowledge of good and evil." (Gen. 2:9b) God told Adam that he could eat from any tree in the Garden, except the tree of the knowledge of good and evil. The rest is history, all of history.

The LORD banished Man from the Garden, saying, "He must not be allowed to reach out his hand and take also from the tree of life and eat, and live forever." (Gen. 3:22b, cf. 3:24) Everlasting life upon the earth had been available to Man in the beginning, but he had been fascinated instead by what God had not given to him. That had been his downfall. That had removed everlasting life from his reach, and had opened his world to sickness, death, and all the fruit of life in defiance of God.

In the time of the new heavens and new earth, however, in the time of the restoration, that will all be changed. John saw a new Jerusalem, a restored Jerusalem, upon the new earth. "Then the angel showed me the river of the water of life, as clear as crystal, flowing from the throne of God and of the Lamb down the middle of the great street of the city. On each side of the river stood the tree of life, bearing twelve crops of fruit, yielding its fruit every month. And the leaves of the tree are for the healing of the nations." (Rev. 22:1-2)

It will be the time of a new beginning. There, in the new Jerusalem, upon the new earth, Man will have free access to the tree of life. Every month it will bear fruit, and its leaves will bring healing.

Centuries earlier, God had shown Ezekiel a similar vision of a restored Jerusalem. "The man brought me back to the entrance of the house, and I saw water coming out from under the threshold of the house toward the east (for the house faced east). The water was coming down from under the south side of the house, south of the altar. ...Fruit trees of all kinds will grow on both banks of the river. Their leaves will not wither, nor will their fruit fail. Every month they will bear, because the water from the sanctuary flows to them. Their fruit will serve for food and their leaves for healing." (Ezek. 47:1,12)

There is no doubt about whether this river is in heaven or upon the earth. "This water flows toward the eastern region and goes down into the Arabah, where it enters the Sea. When it empties into the Sea, the water there becomes fresh. Swarms of living creatures will live wherever the river flows. There will be large numbers of fish, because this water flows there and makes the salt water fresh; so where the river flows everything will live. Fishermen will stand along the shore; from En Gedi to En Eglaim there will be places for spreading nets. The fish will be of many kinds —like the fish of the Great Sea. But the swamps and marshes will not become fresh; they will be left for salt. Fruit trees of all kinds will grow..." (Ezek. 47:8-11)

God does not give up on the descendants of Adam. He does not give up on the descendants of Jacob. He does not withdraw from the earth, in defeat, into heaven. He is able to accomplish His purpose in the earth.

"The highest heavens belong to the LORD, but the earth He has given to the children of Adam." (Ps. 115:16) Is there something wrong with that?


FOOTNOTES
1. E.g. Berakhot II.1
2. Pesakhim 54a, Soncino n.31
3. Bernard Martin in his introduction to Lev Shestov, *Athens and Jerusalem*, translated by Bernard Martin, Ohio U. Press, Athens, OH, 1966, p.31
4. Ibid., Lev Shestov, p.287

CHAPTER THIRTEEN

# A Dispatch From the Front

*The Good News is that the Kingdom of God is Coming to this Planet*

There is a war in heaven over who will reign upon the earth. (Rev. 12) Michael, the great prince who stands to defend the Jewish people (cf. Dan. 12:1), is fighting against Satan, the great dragon who comes against the Jewish people. Michael and his angels will be victorious. The Serpent will be cast down, and the Kingdom of God will be established upon the earth.

Long ago, in a vision God gave to Zechariah, "The LORD said to Satan, 'The LORD rebuke you, Satan! The LORD, who has chosen Jerusalem, rebuke you!" (Zech. 3:2a) The war in heaven is about who rules over Jerusalem.

In ancient Greece, the word *euangelion* signified the reward given to the messenger who brought a good report from the battlefield.[1] Communication was much slower then, and much more dangerous. Military commanders and units, as well as civilian populations, all depended upon the men who risked their lives to deliver a message from the midst of a battle.

A bad report might dictate flight or surrender. A good report was cause for rejoicing. Sometimes it was a privilege or an honor to be chosen to be the messenger. Those who brought a good report merited a reward.

In the Jewish Greek of the Septuagint, *euangelion* was used with a slightly modified meaning. The Septuagint consistently uses forms of *euangelia* to translate *besorah* or *mevasser*, i.e. the good report itself, or to proclaim the good report. Forms of *euangelia* appear in the Septuagint in 2Sam. 4:10 (2Kings 4:10 in LXX), in 2Sam. 18:25-27,31 (2Kings 18:25-27,31 in LXX), and in 1Kgs. 1:42 (3Kgs. 1:42 in LXX), and in Is. 52:1-10. These are passages which speak of good reports from the battlefield.

One of the interesting places where *besorah/euangelia* appears is in 2Kgs. 7. The army of Aram had surrounded Samaria, the capital of the northern kingdom of Israel, and was starving it into submission. God had supernaturally put the army to flight, but no one in the city knew it.

"Now there were four men with leprosy at the entrance of the city gate. They said to each other, 'Why are we sitting here until we die? If we say, *We'll go into the city*—the famine is in the city, and we will die there. And if we sit here, we will die. So now let's go and surrender to the camp of the Arameans. If they keep us alive, we live; if they kill us, then we die." (2Kgs. 7:3-4)

Because their disease excluded them from the community, these men depended upon the gifts of others to keep them alive. But people in the city were starving; a pair of mothers had agreed to eat their own children. There was no help or hope for the lepers in the city. Nor was there any point in sitting or living outside the gate until they died. So they went to the camp of the besieging army.

"The men who had leprosy reached the edge of the camp and entered one of the tents. They ate and drank, carried away silver, gold and clothes, and then went off and hid them. They returned and entered another tent and took things from there and hid them also. Then they said to each other, 'We are not doing right. This is a day of good news/*besorah*/*euangelia* and we are keeping it to ourselves. If we wait until daylight, punishment will overtake us. Let's go at once and report this to the house of the king." (2Kgs. 7:8-9)

When the king heard, he suspected that it was a trap. That was the only thing that made sense. But he finally agreed to send a small group from the city to check out the report. The group confirmed the report, the king and the inhabitants of the city went out to retrieve the abundant food in the camp, and they all survived.

*Besorah* had come to them, and they received it. The Hebrew word contains the sense of victory, deliverance, and salvation. That is the meaning assigned to *euangelion* in the Jewish Greek of the Septuagint and the Messianic Writings.

Yeshua and his followers proclaimed "the good news of the kingdom," the news of the Davidic restoration. They proclaimed a good report from the battlefield between God and the Adversary, a battlefield where the eternal destiny of men is determined. Yeshua's atoning death and resurrection assure final and complete victory over all spiritual and human adversaries, but the war is still raging.

The Scriptures say that one day evil spirits will come forth to lead the human rulers of men. "They are spirits of demons performing miraculous signs, and they go out to the kings of the whole world, to gather them for the battle on the great day of God Almighty." (Rev. 16:14)

In the Scriptures, the "good news" is that Messiah will reign over all the earth. It is "the good news of the kingdom," an announcement that the God of Israel is going to restore the kingdom of David to Israel through Messiah. It is an announcement that God will expand that kingdom over all the earth, thereby blessing the Gentiles through Abraham. It is an announcement that the King of the Jews gave himself to be put to death by the power elites of this world, that he might atone for the sins of all, and set free those who believe in him, freeing them from the oppressive and destructive power of the Adversary. It is an announcement that God is going to do all that He promised through the prophets of Israel.

This good report from the battlefield, this *euangelia* is usually translated into English as "gospel." The word "gospel" comes from the Old English "godspell," which is formed from *God* and *spellian*, to talk or announce. It is a usable word, but it unfortunately does not usually communicate the nature and context of the Biblical message that is supposed to be transmitted.

## THE POWER OF GOD

When Yeshua sent out the twelve he had chosen as his ambassadors, he told them, "Do not go among the Gentiles or enter any town of the Samaritans. Go rather to the lost sheep of Israel. As you go, proclaim this message: 'Heaven's kingdom is near.'" (Mt. 10:5-7)

As far as we know, the twelve did not ask him why they were not to go to the Gentiles. They hadn't been thinking of going to the Gentiles. For the twelve, the message was for Jews only. This was not because they were exclusive or because they looked down on others. It was because the message itself, by its very nature, was for Jews. Everything about it was for Jews. It was not clear to them how it could be applied to Gentiles.

During the years after the resurrection, thousands and tens of thousands of Jews, both in the land and in Diaspora, believed in Yeshua. No one thought about bringing the message to the Gentiles. God had begun the restoration of Israel.

Then God sent an angel to Cornelius to tell him to send men to Shimon. God sent a vision to Simon, and commanded him to go with the men Cornelius had sent. (cf. Acts 10:19-20) But after this encounter with Cornelius and his household, Shimon, who was also called Peter, made no effort to bring the message to any other Gentiles. Neither did Shaul, who was also called Paul. Nor did anyone else.

Then God supernaturally spoke to the leaders of the congregation in Antioch, and commanded that Shaul and Barnabas be sent off to bring the message to the Diaspora. So they went to the Jews of Salamis in Cyprus. Then they went to the Jews of Antioch in Pisidia. They did not think about bringing the message to Gentiles. They did not think about it even though God had called Shaul to be His "chosen instrument to carry My Name before the Gentiles and their kings and before the people of Israel." (Acts 9:15)

In Antioch of Pisidia, many of the Gentiles gathered on Shabbat to hear the message along with the Jews. They asked if they also could hear. It was not something that Shaul or Barnabas had planned or sought. Yet it led to the good news actively being brought to Gentiles. From that point on, Shaul continued to bring the message to the Jews first, but he began also to bring the message to the Gentiles. The message could be adapted for the Gentiles.

Many Gentiles accepted the message, but that in itself was very perplexing. What was the relationship of these Gentiles to the God of Israel, the house of Israel, and the King of Israel? Eventually, a council was called in Jerusalem, Messiah's capital, to answer these questions. Did the Gentiles who believed in Messiah have to become Jews, or could they remain Gentiles?

It seemed to most of the disciples that the Gentiles needed to become Jews. After all, Messiah is the King of the Jews, and he brings the New Covenant, which is made between God and Israel. Nevertheless, God began to show, by the Scriptures and by His Spirit, that He had planned for the Gentiles to come to the Son of David, but still remain Gentiles.

Shaul was specifically called to be Messiah's ambassador to the Gentiles, and the leaders in Jerusalem recognized and sanctioned this. "They saw that I had been entrusted with the good news of the uncircumcision, just as Peter had been with that of the circumcision." (Gal. 2:7) It was in that capacity that Paul wrote to the congregation at Rome, to explain their relationship to Israel, to explain that they were wild branches grafted into Israel's olive tree among the faithful natural branches, etc.. (cf. Rom. 11)

In the beginning of Paul's letter to the believers in Rome, he presented a working definition of the good news itself: "For I am not ashamed of the good news of Messiah, for it is the power of God unto salvation for everyone who is believing, both to the Jew first and to the Greek." (Rom.1:16) This is the only verse in the Bible that says, "the good news is ...," though elsewhere we are told, "the good news is not ..." (cf. Gal. 1:11)

An indispensable part of this definition that Paul presents is the fact that the good news is "to the Jew first." None of the apostles ever had any difficulty understanding that. There was nothing about it that was difficult to understand. After all, it is "the good news of Messiah," and Messiah is the King of the Jews. It is the "good news of the kingdom," and Israel is God's kingdom. For the apostles, the difficulty lay in understanding the "and to the Greek" part.

In the Christian tradition, the situation is more than reversed. Most of "the Church" does not believe that the good news is to the Jew first. Much of "the Church" does not believe that the good news is to the Jew at all. But the Biblical good news remains, by its nature, "to the Jew first."

What does that mean? Some say the verse refers to the historical manner in which the message was communicated. In other words, *'the good news was brought to the Jew first.'* That is an historically accurate description of what happened throughout the Book of Acts, but it is not an accurate understanding of the verse.

The verse says, "the good news IS," not "the good news WAS." There is only one verb in the main clause, *estin*, i.e. IS. If we change it to past tense, then we have, 'For I am not ashamed of the good news of Messiah, for it WAS the power of God unto salvation for everyone who believes, both to the Jew first, and to the Greek.' That is clearly not what Paul was saying.

Some say the verse refers to an ongoing priority in evangelism. In other words, '*the good news is always to be brought to the Jew first.*' This accurately describes what happened throughout the Book of Acts, and presents that as a continuing priority. As Shaul and Barnabas said to a Jewish crowd in Pisidian Antioch, "It was necessary that God's word should be spoken to you first." (Acts 13:46b)

Nevertheless, this still does not give us an accurate understanding of Rom. 1:16, because the verse does not speak of bringing anything to anyone, nor even of going anywhere. It simply says, "the good news IS ..." The verse does not address what one does or does not do with the message. The verse addresses the nature of the message itself.

The NATURE of the good news is "to the Jew first." It is "the good news of Messiah," the King of the Jews. As Paul promises the believers in Rome: "I know that, when I come to you, I will come in the fullness of the blessing of the good news of Messiah."(Rom.15:29) That is what the Biblical good news IS.

How should we understand the word "first"? We should understand it in terms of priority and applicability, in the same way that it appears in "Seek first the kingdom of God and His justice." Yeshua did not mean that the first thing we should do each day is to seek God's kingdom and His justice, and after that do whatever we want to do. He meant that the priority in all that we do, all the time, must be God's kingdom and His justice.

That is the nature of our quest. In the same way, the good news, by its very nature, IS to the Jew first. Only by changing the message can one make it other than "to the Jew first." Let's look at twelve simple reasons why that is so.

### 1. The good news is a call to turn to the God of Israel and serve Him.

The peoples of this world have many gods. The Bible speaks of "gods of silver or gods of gold", and "gods of wood and stone". The Bible speaks of those whose "god is their stomach, and their glory is in their shame. Their mind is on earthly things." (Phil. 3:19) The Bible speaks of the different gods of all the Gentiles.

The God of the Bible, the one true God, calls Himself the God of Israel. Every other god is a false god. "O LORD, my strength and my fortress, my refuge in time of distress, to You the Gentiles will come from the ends of the earth and say, 'Our fathers possessed nothing but false gods, worthless idols that did them no good.'" (Jer. 16:19) There is no salvation in any god who is not the God of Israel. There is no good news that does not call people to turn to the God of

Israel. The God of the Bible is specific, not generic.

That is why the good news includes the proclamation to Zion, "Your God reigns!" "How beautiful on the mountains are the feet of those who bring good news/*mevaser*/*euaggelizome-nou*, who proclaim peace, who bring good tidings/*mevaser*/*euaggelizomenou*, who proclaim salvation, who say to Zion, 'Your God reigns!'" (Is. 52:7; cf. Rom. 10:15) There is a Biblical equivalence between "proclaiming salvation," which in Hebrew is *yeshuah*, and in LXX is *soter-ian*, and saying to Zion, "Your God reigns!" Each requires the other.

Naaman learned that lesson. "Then Naaman and all his attendants went back to the man of God. He stood before him and said, 'Now I know that there is no God in all the world except in Israel. Please accept now a gift from your servant.'" (2Kgs. 5:15) As long as the God of Israel is God, the good news is to the Jew first.

## 2. The good news is the means of fulfilling God's oath to Abraham to make him a great nation.

In anticipation of the birth of Messiah, the Ruakh haKodesh said through Zekharyah, "Praise be to the Lord, the God of Israel, because He has come and has redeemed His people. He has raised up a horn of salvation for us in the house of His servant David (as He said through His holy prophets of long ago), salvation from our enemies and from the hand of all who hate us— to show mercy to our fathers and to remember His holy covenant, the oath He swore to our father Abraham." (Lk. 1:68-73)

God promised Abraham that He would make his descendants through Isaac and Jacob, i.e. Israel, a great nation. As Kefa said to a Jewish audience in Jerusalem, "The promise is for you and your children and for all who are far off —for all whom the Lord our God will call." (Acts 2:39) The good news is God's means of making that happen. So as long as God is faithful to His promise to Abraham, the good news is to the Jew first.

## 3. The good news is the means of fulfilling God's promise to Abraham to make him the context of blessing for all the nations.

"The Scripture, foreseeing that God would make the Gentiles righteous from faith, proclaimed the good news beforehand to Abraham, saying, 'In you all the Gentiles will be blessed.'" (Gal.3:8; Gen. 12:3) In Abraham, the Gentiles can be blessed. Outside of the promises to Abraham, there is no good news for the Gentiles.

As Peter said to a responsive Jewish crowd in Jerusalem, "And you are sons of the prophets and of the covenant God made with your fathers, saying to Abraham, 'Through your offspring all peoples on earth will be blessed.'" (Acts 3:25; cf. Acts 4:4) From Abraham, God created Israel as the means of bringing the blessing of Abraham to the Gentiles. Without the Jewish people, there is no good news to bring to the Gentiles. So as long as God intends to bless the Gentiles, the good news is to the Jew first.

### 4. Israel is God's first-born son.

"Then say to Pharaoh, 'This is what the LORD says: *Israel is My firstborn son, and I told you, "Let My son go, so he may worship Me." But you refused to let him go; so I will kill your firstborn son.'"* (Ex. 4:22-23)

The position of the first-born son is one of pre-eminence. God is a Father to Israel first. Israel is the means and context for bringing the nations into God's family.

I have a friend named Mehran, who grew up in Iran as a Muslim. He hated Jews because he was taught to hate Jews. Whenever he passed the Jewish area of his city, he would fill his pockets with stones and then throw the stones at the Jewish inhabitants. He and his friends would grab Jews and take them to the river, forcing their heads under the water until they confessed that Allah is great.

GOD IS A FATHER TO ISRAEL FIRST. ISRAEL IS THE MEANS AND CONTEXT FOR BRINGING THE NATIONS INTO GOD'S FAMILY.

When Mehran came to faith in Jesus, his hatred for Jews did not change, at least not at first. Then God began to deal with him. We spent a weekend together and he asked many questions. At one point, he said, "I understand what you are saying, but what is this about the good news being to the Jew first?"

I started to explain, "God told Moses to tell Pharaoh that Israel is God's first-born son, and ..." Mehran stopped me and said, "You don't have to say anymore. I understand. I have two sons. I give the older one more because I expect more from him. I love them both, but I don't treat them the same. That is the way it is in my culture. It's not like in America."

Mehran now goes to Christian pastors he knows and asks them questions. "Why aren't you praying for Israel? Why don't you preach about the Jews? ... ?" He understands that the good news IS to the Jew first.

### 5. Israel is God's portion.

"When the Most High gave the nations their inheritance, when He divided all mankind, He set up boundaries for the peoples according to the number of the sons of Israel. For the LORD's portion is His people, Jacob His allotted inheritance." (Dt. 32:8-9)

God is not selfish, but He always says, "Me first." God's portion and God's inheritance come first.

## 6. The good news is the means of fulfilling God's promises to Israel.

Israel, the nation God created from Abraham, Isaac, and Jacob, is God's chosen heir to Abraham. As Miriam, with Messiah growing within her, explained: "He has helped His servant Israel, remembering to be merciful to Abraham and his descendants forever, even as He said to our fathers." (Lk. 1:54-55)

Paul was "consecrated for the good news of God, which He promised before through His prophets in the holy Scriptures, concerning His Son, who came from the seed of David according to the flesh." (Rom. 1:1b-3) God promised the good news through the prophets. Through His prophets, God promised to send Israel a king, descended from David, who would redeem them from all their enemies.

That's why Shaul proclaimed to Jews in the Diaspora, "We tell you the good news: What God promised our fathers He has fulfilled for us, their children, by raising up Yeshua. As it is written in the second Psalm: 'You are My Son; today I have become your Father.'" (Acts 13:32-33)

What is this good news? All that God promised to Israel in Tanakh will be fulfilled, because He raised up Yeshua, as He had promised. There is no good news outside of the promises to Israel.

## 7. The center of the good news is "Messiah, i.e. the King of the Jews, crucified."

Paul said, "we proclaim Messiah crucified." (1Cor. 1:23) Messiah is prophetically defined. That is the only way to know whether or not someone is the Messiah. If an individual fulfills what God said through the prophets the Messiah would be and do, then he is the Messiah. If an individual does not fulfill the Messianic prophecies, then he is not the Messiah.

The primary identification of Messiah is the King of the Jews, the Son of David. Most of the prophecies speak of his rule over Israel from David's throne in Jerusalem. Some of the prophecies speak of his atoning death.

Being King of the Jews is the crime for which Yeshua was hung on the tree. It is an essential part of the good news. The content and meaning of his death come from the sacrifices and atonement, the covenants, holy days, and deliverances that God gave to Israel. Someone who is not the King of the Jews is not the Messiah.

A lot of Christian preaching proclaims "Christ crucified," but very little of it proclaims "Messiah crucified". Unfortunately, the Christ of the Church is often not the same as the Messiah of the Scriptures. In the preaching, and in the different forms of what is called "the gospel," this Christ is not identified as the Messiah. He does not do what God says Messiah will do.

Paul explained, "For what I received I passed on to you as of first importance : that Messiah died for our sins according to the Scriptures, that he was buried, that he was raised on the third day according to the Scriptures." (1Co. 15:3-4) Paul is talking about Messiah, an individual who is prophetically defined, primarily as the King of the Jews. Paul speaks of what happened to Messiah "according to the Scriptures. In other words, he is not simply stating what happened, he is proclaiming that the God of Israel told of these things in advance in the Law, the Writings, and the Prophets.

This is an important way in which the God of Israel declares His sovereignty: "Remember

**UNFORTUNATELY, THE CHRIST OF THE CHURCH IS OFTEN NOT THE SAME AS THE MESSIAH OF THE SCRIPTURES.**

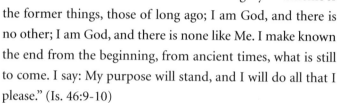

the former things, those of long ago; I am God, and there is no other; I am God, and there is none like Me. I make known the end from the beginning, from ancient times, what is still to come. I say: My purpose will stand, and I will do all that I please." (Is. 46:9-10)

This is how we can know and can demonstrate that Yeshua is the Messiah. God defined Messiah through the prophets; Yeshua is the one the prophets defined. This is the only way to demonstrate that he is the Messiah, "... For the testimony of Yeshua is the spirit of prophecy." (Rev. 19:10)

There were tens of thousands of others who were crucified by the brutality of the Roman Empire. Many of them were also identified by a sign stating their name and their crime. But there are no others whose death was foretold to be God's way to bring atonement to those who submit to him. There is no good news without the prophesied King of the Jews.

## 8. The good news is the good news of the kingdom, and the coming Kingdom of God is the restored Davidic kingdom.

David said, "Of all my sons —and the LORD has given me many—He has chosen my son Solomon to sit on the throne of the kingdom of the LORD over Israel." (1Chr. 28:5) If Solomon and his descendants were faithful, the LORD promised David, "you will never fail to have a man on the throne of Israel." (1K. 2:4b) Solomon was to sit, as his father David had done, on the throne of Israel, the throne of God's kingdom.

As Gabriel said of Yeshua, "He will be great and will be called the Son of the Most High. The Lord God will give him the throne of David, his father, and he will reign over the house of Jacob forever; his kingdom will never end." (Lk. 1:32-33) Upon the throne of David, the throne of Israel, Yeshua will rule over all the earth.

Those who bring good news are to say to Zion, 'Your God reigns!'" (Is. 52:7) But this is not an abstract announcement, it is the prophetic anticipation of an imminent event, an event which follows the proclamation of the good news to Zion. That is why the text continues: "The voice of your watchmen is lifted up; they shout for joy together, because eye to eye they will see it, when the LORD returns to Zion." (Is. 52:8) Those who are watching for the deliverance of Jerusalem rejoice with the proclamation, because they see what it brings. The good news is a declaration of the coming return of the Lord to Zion.

The good news is a declaration that the holy kingdom of God will be established upon the earth through Messiah, the king of the Jews; and that there is both a need and a way to be prepared for it. "And this good news of the kingdom will be proclaimed in the whole world as a testimony to all nations, and then the end will come." (Mt. 24:14; cf. Mt. 4:23, 9:35; Lk. 4:43, 8:1, 16:16; Acts 8:12; et al.)

What is the end that is coming? All the nations will come against Jerusalem to destroy the city of the great King. The great King will then descend and destroy those nations. (Zech. 14:1-15)

Before that happens, there will be those from the nations who choose to submit to Israel's King. "Shimon has described to us how God at first showed his concern by taking from the Gentiles a people for Himself. The words of the prophets are in agreement with this, as it is written: "'After this I will return and rebuild David's fallen hut. Its ruins I will rebuild, and I will restore it, that the remnant of men may seek the LORD, and all the Gentiles who bear My Name, says the LORD, who does these things'" (Acts 15:14-17) It is the fallen hut, the house, of David that is raised up and restored in Yeshua, so that Gentiles too can be saved.

Philip went to Samaria to proclaim the message of Messiah. "And when they believed Philip as he proclaimed the good news of the kingdom of God and the name of Yeshua the Messiah, they were immersed, both men and women." (Acts 8:12) There is no good news without the proclamation of the coming kingdom of Messiah, King of the Jews.

### 9. Israel is God's means for bringing the good news to all the earth.

Yeshua directed his Jewish followers to make disciples of the Gentiles. "As you go then, make disciples of all the Gentiles, immersing them in the name of the Father and of the Son and of the Ruakh haKodesh, teaching them to observe all things which I have commanded you." (Mt. 28:19-20)

This commandment is an extension of the instruction that God had commanded the children of Israel concerning their own families: "Teach them diligently to your children; speaking about them when you sit at home and when you walk along the road, when you lie down and when you get up." (Dt. 6:6-7)

The LORD declared to Israel: "I have revealed and saved and proclaimed—I, and not some foreign god among you. You are My witnesses that I am God." (Is. 43:12; cf. Is. 44:8) Israel is called to testify that only the LORD God of Israel is God; and that He saves. Yeshua, the specific means of that salvation, said the same thing to his disciples: "You will receive power when the Holy Spirit comes on you; and you will be my witnesses in Jerusalem, and in all Judea and Samaria, and to the ends of the earth." (Acts 1:8)

In bringing the good news to the Gentiles, Paul was fulfilling the calling of a Jew to bring the nations to God. "For so the Lord has commanded us, saying, 'I have set you for a light to the goyim, that you should bring salvation to the uttermost parts of the earth.'" (Acts 13:47; quoting Is. 42:6, 49:6)

God had told Israel, "Although the whole earth is Mine, you will be for Me a kingdom of priests and a holy nation." (Ex. 19:5b-6a) In bringing the good news to the Gentiles, Paul was fulfilling the calling of a Jew to be a priest unto God. As he said, "that I should be a servant of Messiah Yeshua to the Gentiles, ministering as a priest the good news of God—that the offering up of the Gentiles might be made acceptable, sanctified by the Ruakh haKodesh." (Rom. 15:16)

Yes, Gentiles who believe can be used by God to bring the good news, but that is because they have become part of Israel's promised *kahal goyim*/commonwealth of nations. Otherwise, they would have no good news to proclaim.

## 10. The good news is fulfilled through God's New Covenant relationship with the Jewish people.

"'The time is coming when I will make a new covenant with the house of Israel and with the house of Judah. It will not be like the covenant I made with their forefathers when I took them by the hand to lead them out of Egypt, because they broke My covenant, though I was a husband to them,' declares the LORD. 'This is the covenant I will make with the house of Israel after that time, I will put My law in their minds and write it on their hearts. I will be their God, and they will be My people. ... I will forgive their wickedness and will remember their sins no more.'" (Jer. 31:31, 33-34)

God makes the New Covenant with the same people who broke the covenant He made with them at Sinai. Without the Jewish people, there is no New Covenant.

At Pesakh, the feast of redemption, Yeshua sat and ate with his Jewish ambassadors. He announced the New Covenant and the sacrifice which puts it into effect. "In the same way, after the supper he took the cup, saying, 'This cup is the new covenant in my blood, which is poured out for you.'" (Lk. 22:20)

The New Covenant provides a way to live before God. It provides a way to be forgiven. That is good news. There is no good news without Israel's New Covenant.

## 11. Salvation is from the Jews.

"You people of Shomron do not know what you bow down to. We bow down to what we know, for salvation is from the Jews." (Jn.4:22) What did Yeshua mean?

Paul explained: "The people of Israel—theirs is the legal right as sons, the glory, the covenants, the giving of the Law, the service, and the promises, whose are the fathers, and from whom is the Messiah as concerning the flesh, who is over all God blessed forever. Amen." (Rom. 9:4-5)

In all His glory, God, the God of Israel, has given Himself to Israel. He has made Israel His son. He has given Israel His promises and His covenants, atonement and the forgiveness of sin; and in the New Covenant, a new heart and God's Spirit. He has given Israel Yeshua the Messiah, the King of the Jews. He has given Israel His Kingdom, its just, holy, and eternal governmental foundation and structure, and its capital. He has given Israel His written and His living Word. He has given Israel both righteousness through faith and also the fathers of the community of faith. He has called Israel to enlighten the nations, and has made Israel the context for the redemption of a community of nations.

> THERE IS NO SALVATION FOR ANYONE WITHOUT THE JEWS, NOT JUST IN THE PAST, BUT ALSO IN THE PRESENT. GOD HAS GIVEN TO THE JEWS, AND ONLY TO THE JEWS, EVERYTHING THAT PERTAINS TO SALVATION.

It is Israel's olive tree, root and trunk, and only Israel's olive tree, that has been cultivated by God, and that is the channel through which His life flows. "The Gentiles have been made partakers of their spiritual things ..." (Rom. 15:27a) The mystery of the good news "is that the Gentiles are fellow-heirs, and fellow-members of the body, and fellow-partakers of his promise in Messiah Yeshua through the good news." (Eph. 3:6)

There is no salvation for anyone without the Jews, not just in the past, but also in the present. God has given to the Jews, and only to the Jews, everything that pertains to salvation. Gentiles can be grafted in to share those things, but they cannot take them away. The good news is "the power of God unto salvation," a salvation that is from the Jews.

## 12. God does not show favoritism.

In the only other verses where the phrase "the Jew first" appears, we are told that God has an order in judgment. The order in judgment follows from the relationship that God has established with Israel. The verses appear shortly after Rom. 1:16.

"God will give to each person according to what he has done. To those who by persistence in doing good seek glory, honor and what is eternal, He will give everlasting life. But for those who are self-seeking and who reject the truth and follow evil, there will be wrath and anger.

"There will be trouble and distress for every human being who does evil: for the Jew first, and also for the Gentile; but glory, honor and peace for everyone who does good: for the Jew first, and also for the Gentile. For God does not show favoritism." (Rom. 2:6-11)

Paul explains that the reason that both judgment and honor are to the Jew first is that "God does not show favoritism." As the LORD said to Israel, "You only have I known of all the families of the earth; therefore I will punish you for all your sins." (Amos 3:2) It is not identical treatment, it is equitable treatment. Much is required from the one to whom much is given. (Luke 12:48) Inasmuch as the good news is to the Jew first, judgment is also. Inasmuch as judgment is not complete, God's order has not changed.

By its nature, the good news is to the Jew first. In the Bible, there is no good news outside of a Jewish context. In that context, it is the announcement of the coming Messianic Kingdom.

## FOOTNOTE

1. Liddell and Scott, *Greek-English Lexicon*, Clarendon Press, Oxford, 1999, p.322

CHAPTER FOURTEEN

# A Tale of Two Bumblebees

*God Never Established Any Religion*

When my daughter was growing up, she had a friend whose father was a Baptist pastor. Their church did not want the children to be involved in Halloween with its emphasis on witches, demons, and other evils. So they sponsored an alternative "Harvest Party" with wholesome costumes and activities.

One Halloween, my daughter was over at her friend's house in the afternoon, making cookies for the Harvest Party. My daughter and her friend were dressed as clowns. They wore colorful, billowy costumes and cheerful face paint.

The friend's older sister and mother were dressed as bumblebees. They wore large, padded, cocoon-shaped costumes that were horizontally ringed with bright, wide bands of alternating yellow and black. Bobbing wire antennae on their heads and appropriate makeup on their faces completed the costumes.

At six thirty, they were all in their costumes, ready to go to the Harvest Party. The doorbell rang and the mother waddled to the door, antennae bobbing, and opened it. A young child, dressed as a pirate, gave the traditional greeting of "Trick or Treat!"

"I'm sorry, we don't celebrate Halloween," the bumblebee replied, and closed the door.

Within the bumblebee's own belief system, her statement made sense. However, we can legitimately wonder what passed through the mind of the young pirate. *'This woman answers the door. She's wearing a Halloween costume on Halloween, but she says that she doesn't celebrate Halloween.'* I suspect that the theological subtlety escaped him. I suspect

WITHIN THE BUMBLEBEE'S OWN BELIEF SYSTEM, HER STATEMENT MADE SENSE. HOWEVER, WE CAN LEGITIMATELY WONDER WHAT PASSED THROUGH THE MIND OF THE YOUNG PIRATE.

that the pronouncement of the bumblebee was beyond the comprehension of the young pirate.

The bumblebee could not see the obvious conflict between what she said and how she appeared to others. She was, in fact, quite oblivious to how she appeared to others.

# CHRISTIANITY

It was the best of religions; it was the worst of religions. It brought life, love, and compassion to a dark and cruel world. It also brought torture, repression, ignorance, slavery, and death to an innocent world. It burned with Light and Truth. It also burned the Bible and those who believed it.

Those who adhered to it built universities, hospitals, and orphanages. They also justified poverty, exploitation, war, and conquest. They brought food to the hungry, medicine to the sick, work to the destitute, and hope to the hopeless. They filled the earth with contempt for man, contempt for God's creation, and contempt for God.

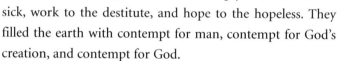

WHAT IS THIS THING CALLED "CHRISTIANITY"? THE BIBLE DOES NOT TELL US. THE BIBLE TALKS ABOUT SOMETHING ELSE.

What is this thing called "Christianity"? The Bible does not tell us. The Bible talks about something else.

Part of Israel's calling is to bring light to the nations so that they can be set free from the heavy darkness that enslaves them. Part of Israel's calling is to provide an expansive commonwealth so that those Gentiles who have been set free can be brought into a cultivated, nurturing context.

Through the centuries, many of those Gentiles who have been set free and brought in have recognized their debt to Israel, and have been eternally grateful. As Tolstoy said, "The Jew is that sacred being who has brought down from heaven the everlasting fire, and has illumined with it the entire world. He is the religious source, spring, and fountain out of which all the rest of the peoples have drawn their beliefs and their religions."[1] Many Gentiles have paid with their lives to protect, or even to identify with, this unique people.

On the other hand, others have devoted their lives to the destruction of this unique people. In the last 1700 years, different groups of Gentiles who claimed to follow "Christ" have formed their own religious systems with only contempt for the Jews. Even though Messiah is primarily the King of the Jews, these groups of Gentiles have often been characterized by nothing so much as their zeal to appropriate for themselves what belongs to the Jews, and to separate themselves as far as possible from the Jews. Insofar as they have succeeded in reaching their goal, they have only succeeded in removing themselves far from the God of Israel, the God of the Hebrews, the God of all the earth.

The different faiths of these opposite kinds of Gentiles—those who love and those who hate—have been called by the same name, "Christianity". With a content that varies from the divine to the demonic, a billion people today call this their religion. It is strange that such opposites travel under the same banner. It is hard for a little pirate to figure out.

Does anyone notice a contradiction here? Or perhaps the possibility that someone is oblivious to what others perceive quite clearly? There are at least two different kinds of something called "Christianity," and many different kinds of people who call themselves "Christians".

Regardless of which group we have in mind when we use these words, these are not God's categories. The Scriptures do not teach Christianity. Christianity is never mentioned in the Bible, not even once. This is not a question of vocabulary, but one of substance. The Scriptures do not sanction or establish any religious system at all, much less one that is separate from Israel or hostile to Israel.

God is the God of Israel. Messiah is the King of the Jews. Israel is the *ekklesia* of God. The covenants and the promises belong to the Jewish people. So does the right to be God's children. The Scriptures, Genesis to Revelation, are Jewish. So are the apostles, the good news, and the kingdom. What did Christianity add?

In speaking of the teaching of Copernicus, which the Church had banned, Pascal said, "It is not the decree of Rome which will prove that the earth remains at rest; and, if we had constant observations to prove that it does turn, not all the people in the world could stop it from turning, nor could they stop themselves from turning with it."[2] Some things are not subject to our desires, or limited by our knowledge. Men decree otherwise, but Jerusalem is still God's center in the earth.

In the second century, Ignatius of Antioch wrote some letters which strongly advocated the authority of an institutional Church. Ignatius may not be the author of all that is attributed to him. A hundred years ago, in his multivolume *History of the Christian Church*, Philip Schaff commented on the institutional episcopacy which first appeared in the Epistles of Ignatius. Then Schaff adds, "He is also the first who uses the term 'catholic church,' as if episcopacy and catholicity sprung up simultaneously. The whole story of Ignatius is more legendary than real, and his writings are subject to grave suspicion of fraudulent interpolation. We have three different versions of the Ignatian Epistles, but only one of them can be genuine; either the smaller Greek version, or the lately discovered Syriac."[3]

For the sake of simplicity, when I speak of Ignatius, I mean the figure we know through the letters that bear his name, even though the actual, historical man may well have been quite different. The literary Ignatius was anti-Jewish. There are inevitable theological consequences to that, since Yeshua is Jewish, the Scriptures are Jewish, and the God who gave the Scriptures describes Himself as the God of Israel. Since Ignatius distanced himself from the Jews, he drew his teaching from what was not Jewish, the Greek and Roman world with which he was familiar.

He was steeped in the Greek and Roman tradition of exalting religious officials, and he had a Gentile conception of authority. "Ignatius is exceedingly anxious in each community to strengthen respect for the bishop and presbyters. He ascribes the fullest kind of divine author- ity to their organization, and recognizes as valid no church, institution, or worship without their sanction."[4] He wrote, "It is evident that we should look upon the bishop as we do upon the Lord himself."[5]

"Let all of you follow the bishop, as Jesus Christ [follows] the Father…Without the bishop it is not lawful either to baptize or to celebrate a love-feast…. He that honors the bishop, shall be honored by God; he that does anything without the knowledge of the bishop serves the devil."[6]

All of this stands in contrast to what Yeshua told his followers: "Don't be like the Gentiles who lord it over one another." (Luke 22:25-26) It stands in contrast to the God-established role of the prophet to challenge priest, king, and people. It supports a system that denigrates indi- vidual responsibility and freedom.

Ignatius used the word *christianism*, to represent "the religion of Christ". "Therefore let us become his disciples and learn to live according to Christianism. For one who is called by any name other than this is not of God."[7] The word *christianism* is not in the Bible, nor in the writ- ings of the apostles or their disciples. But Ignatius anathematized anyone not called by this invented name.

In the last few centuries of our era, there has been some scholastic controversy over the dif- ference between the religion which "Christ" had, i.e. the way he lived, and the religion centered on worshipping "Christ," a religion which has developed throughout the following centuries. There is a very big difference—almost an unbridgeable gap—between the two.

What was the "religion" of Yeshua? Or, more correctly, how did Yeshua live? He lived a life in accordance with the holiness of God. As a Jew, he kept the commandments, laws, and statutes which God had given to the Jews in establishing His covenant with Israel at Sinai. These included all the commandments which God had already placed within all men.

Had Yeshua come into the world as a Gentile, he still would have lived a holy, righteous life, loving his neighbor as himself, and loving God with all his being. He would have lived accord- ing to the commandments of God in their universal form. But had Yeshua come into the world as a Gentile, he would not have been the Messiah. He would not have been the Savior.

Because of the way he lived, Yeshua could say to those who challenged him, "Can any of you prove me guilty of sin?..." (Jn. 8:46) Had he transgressed the covenant which God had made with Israel at Sinai, it would have been an easy matter to prove him guilty of sin. It would have been an easy matter to show that he was not the Messiah and could not atone for anyone else's sins, since he would have had sins of his own.

In his inward and outward faithfulness, Yeshua lived the life that God wanted of all Israel. And in doing that, he demonstrated the life that God wanted of all the children of Adam. There are particulars in the Scriptures that apply to Jews but not to Gentiles, to men but not to women, to Levites and Kohanim but not to all Israel. The text and context of the Scriptures indicate which requirements are particular and which are universal.

To those who follow Yeshua, the Messianic Writings say that, "Worship that God our Father accepts as pure and faultless is this: to look after orphans and widows in their distress and to keep oneself from being polluted by the world." (Ja. 1:27) That is what God calls worship, i.e. service to Him; a worship to which God continually called Israel. (e.g. Dt. 14:28-29; Ps. 68:5)

What about the religion centered on worshipping "Christ" which has developed throughout history? In general, this kind of worship is different from Biblical worship. This traditional worship is made complete in words, whether praise, creeds, or liturgy. In contrast, Biblical worship encompasses not only "the fruit of the lips," but also the overarching concept of *avodah*, meaning work—i.e. working for God.

Even the Greek word *leitourgia*, which is often translated as "liturgy," simply meant "a work that is done in public." It did not at all mean the repeated use of a particular religious text. Such use could be a form of *leitourgia*, but it is not at all what the word meant in normal Greek usage, nor in its specific appearances in the Messianic Writings. (e.g. Rom. 13:6; 15:27; 2Cor. 9:12; Phil. 2:30)

Here are some examples of how the word appears in the Septuagint. In all cases, it is used to translate the Hebrew *avodah*.

Num. 4:24,27 "This is the service/*leitourgia* of the Gershonite clans as they work and carry burdens... All their service/*leitourgia*, whether carrying or doing other work, is to be done under the direction of Aaron and his sons. You shall assign to them as their responsibility all they are to carry."

2Chr. 35:16 "So at that time the entire work/*leitourgia* of the LORD was carried out for the celebration of the Passover and the offering of burnt offerings on the altar of the LORD, as King Josiah had ordered."

Here's an example of how Paul used the word. Phil. 2:17 "Yes, and if I am poured out upon the sacrifice and *leitourgia* of your faith, I rejoice, and share in rejoicing with you all." The High

Church meaning assigned to leitourgia is not what it means in the Scriptures.

Likewise, the Greek *proskuneo*, which is often translated as "worship," comes out the same. It means to bow down to, to accept the authority of another in one's life; in this case, the Lord.

# CHRISTIANITY IS NOT JEWISH

Leaving aside the terminology, there is still much to be said about the substance of "Christianity." Years ago, Edith Schaeffer graciously wrote a book entitled, *Christianity is Jewish*. Her point was simply that faith in Jesus is Jewish, because that is the only Biblical context for such faith. Her point remains true today, because the Bible has not changed. If there were a Christianity that was nothing more than life-defining commitment to the God of Israel as confirmed by the Messiah of the Scriptures, then, perhaps, it could be said that Christianity is Jewish, albeit with a name that is strangely formed from a truncated English transliteration of an invented Jewish Greek marker for a Hebrew Biblical concept. It is a strangely formed name that hides rather than illuminates God's way.

Nevertheless, even if such a Christianity were to exist, the problem is that—after seventeen centuries of an imperial religion bearing the same name, after countless Christian attempts to annihilate the Jewish people and any connection with them, and after almost unceasing Catholic, Protestant, Orthodox, and Evangelical theological denunciation of the Jewish people and what God has given to them—such an understanding of "Christianity" is not possible. History and language will not allow it.

There is a systemic reason for both the history and the language produced. History shows us that different systems produce different results. Yeshua told his followers, "By their fruit you will recognize them. Do people pick grapes from thornbushes, or figs from thistles? Likewise every good tree bears good fruit, but a bad tree bears bad fruit. A good tree cannot bear bad fruit, and a bad tree cannot bear good fruit." (Mt. 7:16-18)

Christianity is not in the Bible—not the word, and not the concept. There is, however, a lot about Christianity in seventeen hundred years of history. Some of it is attractive. Most of it, however, forms an all but impenetrable barrier to Jews, Muslims, Hindus, Buddhists, and others.

Is that all Christianity has ever been? No, of course not. Christianity means many different things. Some of the greatest humanitarians and humanitarian actions have come out of Christianity. Some of the greatest servants of God and Man, and some of the greatest servants to Israel, did what they did because of what their Christianity taught them. They produced some of the most beautiful events in mankind's rather ugly history. God produced in them works of great beauty and love.

But it was God working in them, not Christianity. Christianity never contained God. It was never His habitation. It was never His creation. It did not add anything, at least not anything positive, to what God had already given to the world through the Jewish people. It did not provide a new savior or a new way to treat people. It did not provide new hope or new life. It did not provide new scriptures. All it did was provide a new name, a name which proclaimed separation from the Jewish people.

In other words, the magnificent actions of these exceptional great men and women—and they were exceptions—were the fruit of their adherence to the God who made all things, a God who stubbornly remains the God of Israel. Their actions were the fruit of their adherence to the Jewish Scriptures, i.e. Genesis to Revelation. "Whoever lives by the truth comes into the light, so that it may be seen plainly that what he has done has been done through God." (Jn. 3:21) Despite the mistaken manmade title, it was God who worked through them.

The title of Edith Schaeffer's book is not true. Christianity is **NOT** Jewish. Christianity is primarily a religious system birthed in the fourth century, one that has defined itself in opposition to the Jewish people for seventeen hundred years. All Jewishness has been removed from the major Church creeds. God's primary, and ongoing, commitment to the Jewish people has been removed from the Church creeds and theologies. They do not mention that the New Covenant is made with the Jewish people and that Gentiles must be grafted into Israel's olive tree. They do not acknowledge that Gentiles must be brought into the commonwealth of Israel or remain forever "foreigners to the covenants of the promise, without hope and without God in the world." (Eph. 2:12b)

As a group, the Anabaptists, to their credit, did not share in the general contempt and violence of Christianity towards the Jews. The Anabaptists themselves suffered enough contempt and violence from the same Christianity. From Augustine to Calvin, "Anabaptist" was the term of derision which Christianity had for those who believed in immersion as a Biblical step of faith and identification with Messiah, rather than as an initiation into a state society. And yet, the Anabaptists also dispossessed and disinherited the Jews, as did the rest. Like the rest, they became, in effect, branches cutting themselves off from the root and tree which support them. They viewed themselves as adherents of a new, separate religion, heirs of the promise without the Jews.

The Scriptures do not give a name other than "life" to living as God says we should. There are occasional references to "the Way," i.e. "the Way of the Lord," or "the Way of God." (cf. Acts 9:2, 18:25-26, 19:9,23) These are simple references to walking with God. The Scriptures do not establish a religion; they explain what it is to live in obedience to, and in harmony with, one's Creator and Redeemer.

*'Isn't this just a question of semantics, a quibbling over words? Aren't we still just talking about 'faith in Christ', no matter what we call it?'*

We are talking about what "Christ" is, and who "Christ" is. We are talking about what "faith" is, and why. We are talking about non-Jews being grafted into Israel's olive tree in order to live, and being adopted as children of Abraham. We are talking about which world provides the content for understanding the Biblical text and, therefore, Biblical faith. We are talking about Who is coming back, and why. When we seek to know these things in their Biblical context, we find something that is quite different from the 'faith in Christ' of Christianity.

Israel is going to turn to the Lord and be restored, but Israel is not going to come to Christianity. The nations will repent and come to the Lord, but they will not come to Christianity. You can call yourself and the faith by which you live your life anything that you want to, but consider how you appear to others. Consider a history that is, for most of the people of the world, confusing at best, and demonic at worst.

Humpty Dumpty said, "When I use a word, it means exactly what I want it to mean. Nothing more, nothing less." Humpty Dumpty, however, had problems, serious problems.

What if a word, one which God hasn't chosen to use, doesn't signify to other people what you want it to? What if a word which God hasn't chosen to use signifies the opposite of what you want it to? Would you be willing to set aside that word, even if you liked it? Come on Humpty, think about it..

## FOOTNOTES

1. *The Pentateuch and Haftorahs*, ed. by J. H. Hertz, Soncino Press, London, 1958, p. 45

2. Blaise Pascal, cited in Kesten, *Copernicus and His World*, p. 316

3. Philip Schaff, *History of the Christian Church, Vol. II*, Charles Scribner's Sons, NY, 1883, p.145

4. Ad. Ephesians c.6, quoted in Schaff, op. cit., p.147

5. Ad Smyrna c.8 –9, Schaff, pp.147-148

6. Ad magnesians, 10:1, *Ignatius of Antioch*, William Schoedel, Fortress Press, Phila., 1985, p. 126

7. *The Apostolic Fathers, Vol. I*, trans. by Kirsopp Lake, The MacMillan Co., NY, 1914, p. 167

# PART TWO

# Rebuilding the Highway

# REBUILDING THE HIGHWAY

I have a Jewish friend who was born in Poland. When she was ten years old, she was taken from her family and put into her first of several Nazi camps. When she came out five years later, everyone in her family, except for one sister, had been killed. After the war, she came to live in the United States.

A few years ago, I took her back to Poland for her first visit since then. We went to her hometown, to the property that had belonged to her family. (Some wonderful Polish friends took us everywhere.) We knocked on the door of the house. Someone else was living there. The woman became very nervous when she found out who Rose was, because, under Polish law, Rose could legally reclaim the house, the land, and all that had belonged to her family.

Rose was not interested in doing that. She just wanted to see what had been her home. It was familiar, but strange. It was no longer her home.

Not far away was the "new" synagogue. The Jewish community had finished building it in 1939, months before the Germans came. As we stood in the balcony, Rose had fond memories of sitting there with her grandmother. She recalled watching the service take place down below.

All that was left were the brick walls—no windows, no doors, no furniture, no ark, no Torah, no Jews. Nothing except the trash that people dropped as they took a shortcut through the building to get to the street on the other side. As we stood there, a man walked through the sanctuary and spat holy spit on the dirty Jewish floor.

We went to the Jewish cemetery, where her father had been buried. Before the war began, he had been attacked by Polish anti-semites, and consequently died of a heart attack. The Jewish cemetery was small, bordered by a large Christian cemetery. Rose kept searching, unsuccessfully, for her father's grave.

She stopped, looked around, and tried to figure out why she couldn't find it. It had been sixty years since she last visited his grave. Then she realized what had happened. Two-thirds of the Jewish cemetery was gone. It had been swallowed up by the larger Christian cemetery. Her father's grave had been in the area that had been taken over. Two-thirds of the Jews buried in the Jewish cemetery had been dispossessed and kicked out. As for Rose's father, even his grave had been taken from him, so that a Christian could be buried in it.

The years that followed the war were very difficult in Poland. The war had brought great destruction, and people were very poor. The Soviets oppressed and exploited everyone. People survived however they could. They took the houses, farms, and businesses that had belonged to their Jewish neighbors. After all, the Jews were no longer there. The Jews no longer needed what had belonged to them.

In finding inexpensive ways to build, some of the Polish people of Rose's hometown put the Jewish tombstones to new uses, as paving stones or as foundation stones. After all, the Jewish graves were no longer there. And, if they had been there, there were no Jews to come visit them.

ONCE, THERE WAS A HIGHWAY THAT GOD BUILT. IT WAS A HIGHWAY THAT LED FROM EVERY CORNER OF THE EARTH TO JERUSALEM. IT WAS FOR THE REDEMPTION OF ISRAEL AND THE SALVATION OF THE NATIONS.

I cannot express what Rose felt when she realized all this. I cannot express what I feel when I see how "the Church" has dispossessed the Jewish people of everything that is rightfully theirs. I cannot express what I feel when the Church calls "holy" what is unclean and abominable, and spits on what is holy. I can, however, do something about it.

In Isaiah 62, the LORD speaks of the steps necessary for the redemption of Israel. I want to speak a little bit about one part of one verse, verse 10: "Prepare the way for the people. Build up, build up the highway!"

Once, there was a highway that God built. It was a highway that led, from every corner of the earth, to Jerusalem. It was for the redemption of Israel and the salvation of the nations. God is rebuilding that highway. In the Messianic Age, all the nations will travel on it. All the Jews will rejoice in it. I am working on rebuilding one section of it.

People ask me, "What is the relevance of what you are saying? What are the practical implications?" But I am working on rebuilding a highway that no one thinks they need. It is a highway in the wilderness, and no one is travelling on it. No one is interested in it. For many centuries, the road has been declared "Closed!" and "Dangerous!" Everyone has been warned, "Trespassers will be prosecuted!"

People have built countless detours that go off in countless, different directions. Some of the detours wind around and up and down, and finally arrive, more or less, in a place that is not totally removed from the original destination. Some of the detours go to dead ends. And the detours have detours, and those detours have detours, too; and usually people get lost. They never get where they are going. They don't even know where they are going, but they have canonized the detours.

Epicycles on epicycles on deferents on eccentrics—all to preserve a system that is not right. It has never been right. It has always been wrong. These detours have been built over Jewish graves, paved with Jewish tombstones. But the historical and theo- logical voices cry, "Why not? The Jews are gone. We have needs, too."

Yes, you have needs, too. But God has made provision for you. God has made a way for you. You don't need to take as your own what belongs to someone else.

Besides, the Jews are not gone. The Jews are back. These were our lands. These were our houses. These were our graves. These were the things that God gave to us. We do not intend to dispossess you as you dispossessed us—you may humbly share equally in the inheritance—but we do intend to take up our identity and our call- ing. That you cannot have. If you understood what these things really are, you would not be rushing to claim them for yourself.

The calling of Israel is for your benefit. Don't impede it.

CHAPTER FIFTEEN

# God Who?

February 13, 2003, Jozsef Szajer, a member of the Hungarian parliament, said that together with more than 20 European parliamentary members, he would propose that the European Union constitution incorporate Christian values and a reference to God. Archbishop Istvan Seregely, the Chairman of the Catholic Bishops Council, pointed out that Christianity is the predominant religion in all the European states.[1]

The proposal was simple and logical. The European states have shared a common religion for many, many centuries. The god whom they worship as the supreme authority should be mentioned in the constitution which governs the lesser, human authorities who serve in his name.

Some European parliamentary members spoke against the proposal, presumably because they have a different god. For some, their god, i.e. their highest authority, is human reason or power. For others, the one they obey more than any other is their own physical appetites.

People say that there are three major monotheistic religions in the world—Judaism, Christianity, and Islam. Presumably there are other minor monotheistic religions, with a sole god who is not so well known. Many individuals, though they may not call their highest authority a god, bow down to only one power. The fact that each bows down to only one god does not mean that they all bow to the same god.

If we speak in bland generalities, we may be able to create the very thin illusion that all are serving the same god. The real test comes, however, when we examine the details and seek to establish the specific identity of a particular god. We can find the details in the lives of those who serve a particular god, as well as in the literature and history attributed to that god.

Who is the god of Europe? Or, perhaps more to the point, who is the god of the current political leaders of Europe? Whom do they serve? Whatever the true answer is, that is the god whose definition of good and evil, right and wrong will become the law of the European Union. Whoever makes the law that must be obeyed, that is the one who is the Sovereign, the highest authority, the god.

"God" is a generic term. The peoples of this world have many gods. The Bible speaks of "gods of silver or gods of gold" (Ex. 20:23), and "gods of wood and stone" (Dt. 4:28). The Bible also speaks of "the gods of Egypt" (Ex. 12:12), "the gods of the Amorites" (Josh. 24:15), "the gods of Aram, the gods of Sidon, the gods of Moab, the gods of the Ammonites and the gods of the Philistines" (Judg. 10:6). And it speaks of "the gods of Hamath and Arpad... the gods of Sepharvaim, Hena and Ivvah" (2Kgs. 18:34), "the gods of Edom" (2Chr. 25:20), and the gods of the Athenians (Acts 17:16-23).

Because each god has his or her own character, they make different claims about the nature of reality; and they make different demands of those who serve them. The Psalmist makes a simple observation about all these different gods. "Those who make them will be like them, and so will all who trust in them." (Ps. 115:8; 135:18) People become like the god they serve.

So when we talk about serving god, it is important to specify which god we mean. This is not a religious question. It is a question of authority, values, and goals. The answer determines the nature of the world that is being created.

How does the god revealed in the Bible identify Himself? Who is He? How does He distinguish Himself from all the other gods to whom people bow down? Only after we know the specific identity of this particular god can we answer the question, "What does God require?" That is the question that those who seek to serve Him must ask.

In the first chapter of the Bible, God is introduced as the Creator and Sustainer of all. Each of the thirty-one references to "God" in this opening chapter is generic. It is in the second chapter, that the Creator and Sustainer of all begins to be identified specifically.

## THE "SACRED NAME"

"This is the origin of the heavens and the earth when they were created, when the LORD/יהוה God made the earth and the heavens." (Gen. 2:4) In this second chapter, there are eleven uses of the Tetragrammaton, the four-letter name of God, יהוה. Through the Scriptures, according to my search engine, this Name appears in full form in about six thousand verses, sometimes more than once in a verse. It also appears thousands of times more in shortened form, the first two or three letters, in words like "hallelu-**yah**," and names like **Yeho**-shua (Joshua), Yesha-**yahu** (Isaiah), **Yo**-hanan (John), etc., etc.. Sometimes the four letter name is joined to another word to give a descriptive name.

Sometimes the shortened form of the first two letters, or maybe it's the first letter and the last letter, is given as the Name of God. For example, Ps. 68:5 (68:4 in Christian English translations) says: "Sing to God, sing praise to His Name. Extol Him who rides on the clouds—His

Name is yah/הי—and rejoice before Him." And Ps. 122:4 says: "That is where the tribes go up, the tribes of yah/הי, to praise the Name of the LORD/יהוה according to the statute given to Israel."

It is clear in many Biblical passages that this Name was pronounced. Early in human history, "men began to call on the Name of the LORD." (Gen. 4:26b) Abraham "built an altar to the LORD and called on the Name of the LORD." (Gen. 12:8b; 13:4; 21:33; 26:25; et al.)

The people of Israel were commanded, "You shall not use the Name of the LORD your God in vain, for the LORD will not hold anyone guiltless who uses His Name in vain." ("Ex. 20:7; Lev. 24:16; Dt. 5:11) This tells us two things: 1) the people of Israel knew the Name of the Lord; and 2) they were permitted to use the Name of the Lord, just not falsely or vainly.

> IT IS CLEAR IN MANY
> BIBLICAL PASSAGES THAT
> THIS NAME WAS
> PRONOUNCED. EARLY IN
> HUMAN HISTORY, "MEN
> BEGAN TO CALL ON THE
> NAME OF THE LORD."

Sometime after this, a man rebelled against this commandment. "The son of the woman of Israel blasphemed the Name with a curse; so they brought him to Moses." (Lev. 24:11) He said the Name in blasphemy, which he could not have done had he not known the Name.

On another occasion, Moses said, "I will proclaim the Name of the LORD. Oh, praise the greatness of our God!" (Dt. 32:3) Many centuries later, those who ascended to Jerusalem in pilgrimage sang, "From the rising of the sun to its going down, the Name of the LORD is to be praised." (Ps. 113:3)

Elijah challenged the prophets of Baal on Mount Carmel. "Then you call on the name of your god, and I will call on the Name of the LORD. The god who answers by fire—He is God." (1Kgs. 18:24) And this is how Elijah the prophet prayed: "O LORD, God of Abraham, Isaac and Israel, let it be known today that You are God in Israel and that I am Your servant and have done all these things at Your command." (1Kgs. 18:36)

The Talmud says that, in those days, men were to greet one another in the Name of the LORD. "It was also laid down that greeting should be given in the Name, in the same way as it says, 'And behold Boaz came from Bethlehem and said to the reapers, The LORD be with you; and they answered him, *The LORD bless you*'; and it also says, *The LORD is with you, you mighty man of valor*."[2]

In "The Wisdom of Sirach," written about 180 B.C.E., men are admonished, "Do not accustom your mouth to an oath; and do not form the habit of uttering the Name of the Holy One. For just as a servant who is constantly being questioned does not lack the marks of a blow, so the man who constantly swears and utters the Name cannot be absolved from sin."[3]

The Name of God identifies Him. Quite naturally, there is an interest today, as there has been at other times, in how this Name is pronounced. There is a "Sacred Name" movement which attaches great importance to the correct pronunciation of this Name.

The "Sacred Name" movement would seem to take its name from the translation of a passage in Josephus that describes the garments of the High Priest. "A mitre also of fine linen encompassed his head, which was tied by a blue riband, about which there was another golden crown, in which was engraven the sacred name: it consists of four vowels."[4] Josephus wrote in Greek, so it would seem that he was expressing the way to transliterate the sound in Greek letters, i.e. four Greek vowels.[5]

Other Greek sources actually tell us the pronunciation of the Name. Unfortunately, they tell us different pronunciations. Not only that, Greek transliterations of Hebrew words are often not even close to the original sounds. The Greek language does not have the same sounds as the Hebrew language, so an accurate transliteration is often not possible.

If we then take a Greek transliteration and transliterate it into English, we may find ourselves far removed from the original Hebrew. In the late nineteenth century, Alfred Edersheim commented on the word *Essenes*, which is the English transliteration of the Greek transliteration of some Hebrew word. He suggested that it comes from a Hebrew word that means "those outside". He noted "The eighteen or nineteen proposed explanations of a term, which must undoubtedly be of Hebrew etymology... their name Essenes (Εσσηνοι, Εσσαιοι) seems the Greek equivalent for Chitsonim (חיצונים)."[6] The Essenes, then, would be people outside the (Pharisaic) community; and their writings would be "outside (or *external*) writings," which is a known rabbinic designation.

Edersheim may well be right, but it can be very difficult to transliterate backwards into the original language. Notice that: 1. There were eighteen or nineteen different scholarly determinations of what the original Hebrew was; 2. "Essenes" is the English adaptation and transliteration of two different Greek transliterations, *essenoi* and *essaioi*; and 3. There is a great difference between *Essenes*, the English adaptation and transliteration of the Greek transliteration, and *Chitsonim*, the English transliteration of the possible original Hebrew word. Pronouncing the English, Essenes, or the Greek, *essenoi*, would not, in this case, bring us close to the original Hebrew pronunciation.

Since the "Sacred Name" appears in the Scriptures thousands of times, its correct pronunciation is not a trivial thing. In the "Sacred Name" movement, however, there are those with certainty as to how the Name is pronounced, but they do not agree with each other. By my count, with limited research into the materials of the movement, claims are made for nineteen different pronunciations of the Name, all in English transliteration.[7] And that does not tell us what to do with the different pronunciations of the two letter Name and the three letter Name of God.

Transliteration does not always give us the right pronunciation. Even when it does, it gives us sound without meaning, at least without the original etymological meaning. In the case of the Tetragrammaton, such transliteration tends to attribute power to the sound of the Name rather than to the One who bears the Name.

Transliteration creates a word that has no natural meaning in the secondary language. The transliteration only has meaning for those who know the word in its original language, or who have some sense of what it signifies. But the Tetragrammaton is a word that does have meaning. It signifies something, though it may be difficult for us to express exactly what that meaning is.

That difficulty itself may be part of the meaning. If we eliminate the difficulty, we may, in fact, be oversimplifying, and thereby missing some essential part of the meaning. We may be presuming a little too much.

## WHAT DOES "THE NAME" MEAN?

In rabbinic tradition, the Name is never pronounced, lest it be pronounced in an unworthy manner. Therefore, when the Name is read in Hebrew, it is replaced by *Adonai*, meaning "Lord".[8] The Scriptures give some support to this aspect of the meaning of the Name. There are about three hundred places in the Scriptures where the Tetragrammaton directly follows the Hebrew word *adonai*. The terms are not equivalent, but there is obviously a close relationship between them. (There are more than three thousand places where the generic word for "God" is still used.)

The Septuagint translators decided not to transliterate the Name. Instead, they tried to give a sense of its meaning. They used *kurios*, which is the Greek for "lord". Many English translations follow the usage of the Septuagint, but put "LORD" in capital letters to distinguish it.

On Mount Sinai, the LORD came down to Moses and proclaimed the Name of the LORD. "The LORD, the LORD, the compassionate and gracious God, slow to anger, abounding in love and faithfulness, maintaining lovingkindness to thousands, and forgiving wickedness, rebellion and sin. Yet He does not leave the guilty as innocent, visiting the iniquity of the fathers to the children and to the children's children to the third and fourth generation." (Ex. 34:6b-7)

All of this is the "Name" of the LORD. Yet it is significant that immediately after this unparalleled revelation of God and His nature, Moses calls the LORD "*adonai*," which is rendered as "*kurios*" in the Septuagint. "O Lord/*adonai*, if I have found favor in Your eyes, then let the Lord/*adonai* go with us." (Ex. 34:9a) Moses had just heard the Name of the LORD from the mouth of the LORD; and he did not see any problem with calling Him "lord".

The four-letter Name has meaning that is related to the Lordship of God, and also to His eternal existence. In Beersheva, Abraham "... called upon the Name of **the LORD, the Eternal God.**" (Gen. 21:33) In the wilderness, Moses asked the One in the burning bush, "Suppose I go to the descendants of Israel and say to them, 'The God of your fathers has sent me to you,' and they ask me, 'What is His Name?' Then what shall I tell them?"

"God said to Moses, 'I WILL BE WHAT I WILL BE. This is what you are to say to the descendants of Israel: 'I WILL BE/אהיה has sent me to you.'" (Ex. 3:13-14) So God's Name is I WILL BE WHAT I WILL BE (*ehyeh asher ehyeh*), and it also is I WILL BE (*ehyeh*). The implication is that God will always be for Israel what He is. "Name" here refers to God's character.

The Letter of Baruch, probably written in the first century B.C.E., uses the Greek *ho aionios*, i.e. "the Eternal," for the Tetragrammaton. (Bar. 4:10,14,20,22,24,35; 5:2) Other places, like Baruch 4:8 and Susannah 42 speak of "the Eternal God". Moses Mendelssohn used the German for "Eternal Being". John Calvin used the French for "the Eternal".[9]

"Name" is often used in the Scriptures to refer to character. Yeshua used it that way in his prayer. "I manifested Your Name to those whom You gave me out of the world.... I have made Your Name known to them, and will make it known in order that the love You have for me may be in them and that I myself may be in them." (John 17:6,26) To make the Name of the Father known, Yeshua did not teach on the Tetragrammaton; he revealed the character of God.

There are places in the Messianic Writings which quote verses from Tanakh that contain the Tetragrammaton. Neither the authors, nor the Author, chose to transliterate the Name. Instead, they give some sense of its meaning. They use *kurios*, i.e. lord. For example, "a voice of one calling in the desert, 'Prepare the way for the LORD/*kuriou*...'" (Mark 1:3, quoting Is. 40:3, which uses the Tetragrammaton) So the authors, and the Author, apparently found kurios to be an adequate way to give the sense of the Tetragrammaton.

The Name was not considered to be magical; that is, pronouncing the Name correctly did not cause supernatural things to happen. The Name was used to identify the one true God. If the pronunciation of the Name had been considered critical, or even necessary, then the apostles, or certainly Yeshua himself, would have provided that pronunciation. If the use of it had been considered critical, then their use of it would be recorded. It is not.

It is clear that "name" in the Bible is much more than a particular sound or label for someone. God said to Jacob, "Your name is Jacob, but you will no longer be called Jacob; your name will be Israel." (Gen. 35:10) A few verses later, we read that "Jacob set up a stone pillar at the place where God had talked with him... Jacob called the place where God had talked with him Bethel." (Gen. 35:14,15) After this, the name Jacob appears more than 200 times. God Himself used it when He said to Moses, "I am the God of your father, the God of Abraham, the God of Isaac and the God of Jacob." (Ex. 3:6)

Jacob's fame comes to him under the name of Israel, the name of the people God chose as His own, But Jacob's name did not cease to be Jacob. So "name" here must mean something other than the sound of certain syllables. "Name" is often used in the Bible to indicate one's reputation or accomplishments.

Jacob said of Manasseh and Ephraim, his grandsons, "the Angel who has delivered me from all harm may he bless these boys. May they be called by my name and the names of my fathers Abraham and Isaac, and may they increase greatly upon the earth." (Gen. 48:16) How were Manasseh and Ephraim "called by the names" of Abraham, Isaac, and Jacob? These names were not the sounds used to call them, but the identity by which they were known.

Mt.1:23 quotes Is. 7:14: "'The virgin will be with child and will give birth to a son, and they will call him Immanuel'—which means, 'God with us.'" This is immediately after Gabriel has just told Joseph that Miriam, "will give birth to a son, and you are to give him the name Yeshua, because he will save his people from their sins." (Mt. 1:21)

Nowhere in Matthew, or anywhere else in the Messianic Writings, is Yeshua called "Immanuel" by anyone. Matthew makes no attempt to explain this discrepancy, because it was not a discrepancy for him. Immanuel, i.e. God with us, is who Yeshua is. That IS his name, not in the sense of label, but in the sense of identity. That is the core of who he is.

In the Messianic prophecy of Is. 9:5/6E, we find the same thing. "For to us a child is born, to us a son is given, and the government will be on his shoulders. And his name will be called Wonderful Counselor, Mighty God, Everlasting Father, Prince of Peace."[10] He is not called by those names as labels or sounds. He is called by those names as his identity. The Rabbis give Messiah many additional names, all of which relate to his character or role. (cf. Sanh. 98b)

Here is how he is described in Rev. 19:16 for his return to earth: "On his robe and on his thigh he has this name written: King of Kings and Lord of Lords." This "name" tells us who he is and what he is coming to do. It is similar to some of the old Westerns, when the marshal would order those inside the barricaded cabin, "Open up in the name of the law." What is the "name" of the law? The "name" of the law is not a label or sound, but the authority and enforcement power which the law carries.

Benaiah, son of Jehoiada, was one of David's mighty warriors, but not one of the top three. The Scriptures tell us that, "He had a name equal to the three mighty men." (2Sam. 23:22b) It means that he had an equivalent reputation. "The Ammonites brought tribute to Uzziah, and his name spread as far as the border of Egypt, because he had become very powerful." (2Chr. 26:8)

In the plain of Shinar, all the children of Adam said, "Come, let us build ourselves a city, with a tower that reaches to the heavens, so that we may make a name for ourselves and not be scattered over the face of the whole earth." (Gen. 11:4) They meant that their accomplishment would give them a reputation.

DANIEL PRAYED, "YOUR CITY AND YOUR PEOPLE BEAR YOUR NAME." WHAT NAME OF GOD IS BORNE BY JERUSALEM AND ISRAEL?

Speaking of towers, "The Name of the LORD is a strong tower; the righteous run to it and are safe." (Prov. 18:10) This is an image of the protection found by those who make the LORD their refuge. It does not describe the Name as a label or sound, but as a characteristic.

Imagery like this is very common in the Scriptures. "For the LORD your God is a consuming fire..." (Dt. 4:24) "For the LORD God is a sun and a shield..." (Ps. 84:12H) Such imagery describes the nature of God.

On Mount Sinai, the LORD came down to Moses and said, "You shall not bow down to any other god, for the LORD, whose name is Jealous, is a jealous God." (Ex. 34:14) What does it mean that His Name is "Jealous"? It means that His nature is such that He demands Israel's sole affection and obedience.

After the Babylonian captivity, the returned remnant prayed: "You sent miraculous signs and wonders against Pharaoh, against all his officials and all the people of his land, for You knew how arrogantly the Egyptians treated them. You made a name for Yourself, which remains to this day." (Neh. 9:10) What name did God make for Himself? He brought judgment on the gods of the Egyptians and delivered Israel, His people. As Moses and Aaron told all Israel, "In the evening you will know that it was the LORD who brought you out of Egypt." (Ex. 16:6) God made Himself known as the God of Israel, the Deliverer of Israel.

Daniel prayed, "Your city and Your people bear Your Name." (Dan. 9:19) What name of God is borne by Jerusalem and Israel? The Tetragrammaton does not appear in the Hebrew words for Jerusalem and Israel. But He IS the God of Israel. He IS "the LORD who has chosen Jerusalem." (cf. Zech. 3:2) That is the way in which Jerusalem and Israel bear His Name. "... our Father, our Redeemer from of old is Your name." (Is. 63:16) His Name is taken from the identifying association which He has established.

# THE GOD OF ABRAHAM, ISAAC, AND JACOB

*'Okay, first you say that the Name of God is very important; and then you say that we don't need to know it; and that "Name" doesn't mean name anyway. What are you trying to say?'*

That's not exactly what I said, or at least that is not exactly what I meant. In the Scriptures, "name" means more than just a sound. Sometimes it means "reputation" or "character". Sometimes it means "accomplishment" or "authority". Sometimes it refers to a relationship that has been established. But the "Name" identifies and distinguishes which god we are talking about.

We have some friends who had their eighth child not long ago. For more than a month, they did not give him a name. It wasn't that they couldn't think of any, it's just that they hadn't had enough uninterrupted time to sit down, talk about it, and choose one name from their top three choices. That's what happens when you have eight children. They knew who the baby was, but they hadn't assigned a verbal label to him.

It was a problem, but the baby did have a last name and a permanent address, as well as some identifying physical characteristics. That's more than enough for the mass marketing companies. And since he wasn't yet going to school, applying for a job, or spending any time online, it didn't cause any major trauma or inconvenience. At some point in his life, of course, it would be helpful for him to have a first name as well as a last name.

But even when he has a first name, people won't always use it. Some of his friends will call him by his last name, and others will give him an embarrassing nickname. Some of the older children at school will know him as "John and Chris' little brother;" and the parents of those children will say, "That's Matt and Kim's youngest." When he becomes a teenager, the people who have assumed the heavy responsibility of keeping everyone else in the neighborhood informed may say disapprovingly, "That wild Jones boy is going out with the Smith girl."

All of this involves identity by association. These are different ways of identifying a particular individual. Everyone knows who is being talked about.

In the same way, we can easily know which god is spoken of in the Bible. He identifies Himself by the relationships which He has established. One of the most amazing things about the God of the Bible is how He, the infinite Creator of all, identifies Himself with particular, finite individuals.

Noa<u>h</u> said, "Blessed be the LORD, the God of Shem!..." (Gen. 9:26) He spoke of the God of Shem, but not of the god of Ham or the god of Japhet.

God promised Abraham, "I will establish My covenant as an everlasting covenant between Me and you and your descendants after you for the generations to come, to be your God and the God of your descendants after you." (Gen. 17:7) God was saying to Abraham, 'I am yours, and you are Mine.'

Abraham sent his servant to get a wife for Isaac. And the servant prayed, "O LORD, God of my master Abraham, give me success today, and show kindness to my master Abraham." (Gen. 24:12; cf. vv.27,42,48) The servant was asking a particular god for help.

After the death of Abraham, God appeared to Isaac. "The LORD appeared to him and said, 'I am the God of your father Abraham. Do not be afraid, for I am with you. I will bless you and will increase the number of your descendants for the sake of My servant Abraham.'" (Gen. 26:24) Who is God? He says that He is the God of Abraham.

When Jacob fled from his brother Esau and slept in the wilderness, God appeared to him in a dream and said: "I am the LORD, the God of your father Abraham and the God of Isaac. I will give you and your descendants the land on which you are lying." (Gen. 28:13) God identified Himself by the Tetragrammaton, and by His relationship with Abraham and Isaac.

As Jacob returned to face Esau, he prayed, "God of my father Abraham, God of my father Isaac, O LORD, who said to me, 'Go back to your country and your relatives, and I will make you prosper'…" (Gen. 32:9) After that, God blessed Jacob by giving him the name of "Israel," meaning "a prince with God". (cf. Gen. 32:28) The LORD already was the God of Abraham and the God of Isaac. He became the God of Jacob.

From the burning bush, God told Moses, "Say to the descendants of Israel, 'The LORD, the God of your fathers —the God of Abraham, the God of Isaac and the God of Jacob—has sent me to you.' This is My Name forever, the Name by which I am to be remembered from generation to generation." (Ex. 3:15) As long as forever lasts, this is how God wants to be known.

The world was filled with people, but God identified Himself with only one, Abraham, and not the rest. Then He added Isaac, and became the God of two. Then He added Jacob and became the God of three people. That may not sound very impressive, but that is the way the God of the Bible identifies Himself. That is what He said His Name is forever.

Elijah challenged the priests of Baal on Mount Carmel. "You call on the name of your god, and I will call on the Name of the LORD. The god who answers by fire—He is God." (1Kgs. 18:24b)

Elijah prayed, "O LORD, God of Abraham, Isaac and Israel, let it be known today that you are God in Israel and that I am Your servant and have done all these things at Your command." (1Kgs. 18:36) The LORD is the God of Abraham, Isaac, and Jacob. He is the God who answers by fire.

Yeshua challenged those who doubted the reality of the resurrection of the dead. He said that the proof of the resurrection lies in God continuing to be "the God of Abraham, and the

God of Isaac, and the God of Jacob." (cf. Mt. 22:32; Mark 12:26; Luke 20:37) Even after their death, that is how the LORD God identifies Himself, and He does not change.

How could the God of three people stand against the gods of the multitudes of Hittites or Egyptians. These peoples were so numerous that they had many gods. A god with three people? Laughable. Even if you add in their descendants, who were nothing but slaves in Egypt, this god didn't amount to much. At least that's what Pharaoh thought.

Moses and Aaron told Pharaoh, "This is what the LORD, the God of Israel, says: 'Let My people go, so that they may hold a festival to Me in the desert.'

"Pharaoh said, 'Who is the LORD, that I should obey Him and let Israel go? I do not know the LORD and I will not let Israel go.'" (Ex. 5:1-2)

Moses and Aaron responded that, "The God of the Hebrews has met with us. Now let us take a three-day journey into the desert to offer sacrifices to the LORD our God, or He may strike us with plagues or with the sword." (Ex. 5:3; cf. Ex. 3:18; 7:16; 8:10,26,27; 9:1,13, 10:3,25,26)

Pharaoh was not impressed. *The god of the Hebrews? He must be very weak and insignificant if all He has are these slaves. The god of Israel? Never heard of him.*

This, however, was the God who destroyed Pharaoh and his land. This was the God who destroyed Egypt for the simple reason that He IS the God of the Hebrews. (cf. Ex. 6:2-7) Pharaoh was introduced to the God of Abraham, Isaac, and Jacob, also known as the God of Israel, a.k.a. the God of the Hebrews, a.k.a. the Creator and Judge of all the earth. He was introduced to the God of Israel through the Ten Plagues.

Pharaoh spoke to Moses of "the LORD your God", because the LORD was not the god of Pharaoh. (cf. Ex. 8:28; 10:8,16,17) Pharaoh's officials told him to let the descendants of Israel go, because "the LORD their God" had destroyed Egypt. (Ex. 10:7) The God of Israel is Israel's God, not the god of Egypt or the god of any other particular people.

"Hear, O Israel: The LORD our God, the LORD is one.... For the LORD your God is God of gods and Lord of lords, the great God, mighty and awesome, who shows no partiality and accepts no bribes." (Dt. 6:4; 10:17)

Hezekiah prayed: "O LORD, God of Israel, enthroned between the cherubim, you alone are God over all the kingdoms of the earth. You have made heaven and earth.... It is true, O LORD, that the Assyrian kings have laid waste these nations and their lands. They have thrown their gods into the fire and destroyed them, for they were not gods but only wood and stone, fashioned by men's hands. Now, O LORD our God, deliver us from his hand, so that all kingdoms on earth may know that You alone, O LORD, are God." (2 Kings 19:15,17-19).

The LORD made a name for Himself in bringing Israel out of Egypt. He refers to this name in the Ten Commandments. "I am the LORD your God, who brought you out of Egypt, out of the land of slavery. You shall have no other gods before Me." (Ex. 20:2-3; cf. Dt. 5:6-7)

He proclaims it throughout the Torah. For example: "Use honest scales and honest weights, an honest ephah and an honest hin. I am the LORD your God, who brought you out of Egypt.... I am the LORD your God, who brought you out of Egypt to give you the land of Canaan and to be your God." (Lev. 19:36; 25:38)

He proclaims it in the Writings and in the Prophets. "I am the LORD your God, who brought you up out of Egypt. Open your mouth wide and I will fill it." (Ps. 81:10) "I am the LORD your God, who brought you out of Egypt. You shall acknowledge no God but Me, no Savior except Me." (Hos. 13:4)

Who is God? The LORD. Who is the LORD? He is the God of Abraham, Isaac, and Jacob, the God of Israel. David sang of the God who anointed him king of Israel: "For who is God besides the LORD? And who is the Rock except our God?" (Ps. 18:31) Moses blessed Israel: "May the LORD, the God of your fathers, increase you a thousand times and bless you as He has promised!" (Dt. 1:11; cf. Dt. 4:1, 6:3, 12:1; 26:7)

It is this same God, who raised Yeshua from the dead. As his ambassadors told the Council: "The God of our fathers raised Yeshua from the dead." (Acts 5:30a) As Peter told a crowd in the Temple: "The God of Abraham, Isaac and Jacob, the God of our fathers, has glorified His servant Yeshua." (Acts 3:13a)

As Ananias told Paul after praying for him to receive his sight: "The God of our fathers has chosen you to know His will and to see the Righteous One and to hear words from his mouth." (Acts 22:14)

As Paul proclaimed in Antioch, "Men of Israel and you Gentiles who worship God, listen to me! The God of the people of Israel chose our fathers..." (Acts 13:16-17)

As Paul said in his defense before Felix the governor, "I admit that I worship the God of our fathers as a follower of the Way, which they call a sect. I believe everything that agrees with the Law and that is written in the Prophets." (Acts 24:14)

This is the God of Yeshua the Messiah. This is the God that Miriam, the mother of Yeshua, praised. "He has helped His servant Israel, remembering to be merciful to Abraham and his descendants forever, even as He said to our fathers." (Luke 1:54-55)

This is the God whom Zechariah, the father of Yohanan, praised. "Praise be to the Lord, the God of Israel, because He has come and has redeemed His people." (Luke 1:68) So did the people who saw Yeshua's power. "The people were amazed when they saw the mute speaking, the crippled made well, the lame walking and the blind seeing. And they praised the God of Israel." (Mt. 15:31)

*'But this is not the primary way that He is identified in the New Testament.'*

I'm sorry, I don't know what a "New Testament" is. I suffer from a severe case of ONTRDD, commonly known as "Old and New Testament Recognition Deficiency Disorder". I am  absolutely unable to connect these terms to the Scriptures in any way.

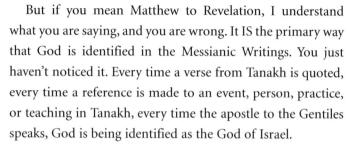

INDEED, MORE THAN ANY OTHER DESIGNATION, HUNDREDS OF TIMES, THE LORD REFERS TO HIMSELF AS "THE GOD OF ISRAEL."

But if you mean Matthew to Revelation, I understand what you are saying, and you are wrong. It IS the primary way that God is identified in the Messianic Writings. You just haven't noticed it. Every time a verse from Tanakh is quoted, every time a reference is made to an event, person, practice, or teaching in Tanakh, every time the apostle to the Gentiles speaks, God is being identified as the God of Israel.

Every time Messiah is mentioned, God is being identified as the God of Israel. That is one of the problems with reading a translation that speaks of "Christ" five hundred times instead of "Messiah". You don't recognize what is actually being said: 'This is the Anointed One of the God of Israel.  This is the King of the Jews.'

This is not to deny that the LORD is "the God of the spirits of all mankind". (cf. Num. 27:16; Jer. 32:27) It is simply to affirm that the Creator, Sustainer, and Judge of all has identified Himself in His Word and has made Himself known in the world in a particular, irrevocable way.

Indeed, more than any other designation, hundreds of times, the LORD refers to Himself as "the God of Israel." He also calls Himself, "Shepherd of Israel," "Rock of Israel," "Father to Israel," "Stone of Israel," "King of Israel," "Mighty One of Israel," "Holy One of Israel," "God in Israel," "God over Israel," "God to Israel," "God for Israel," etc., etc.. He also tells the world that He is the "God of Jacob," "Holy One of Jacob," "Mighty One of Jacob," "Portion of Jacob," et alia, et cetera. This is the way that God wants to be known. This is how He will make Himself known at the end of this age.

Yes, Balaam spoke of "the LORD my God." (cf. Num. 22:18) Yes, Hagar spoke of "the God who sees me," (cf. Gen. 16:13) And yes, God is not the God of Jews only (cf. Rom. 3:29), because He "accepts men from every nation who fear Him and do what is right." (Acts 10:35)

He accepted Rahab, who had heard of what He did in Egypt and what He did to the two kings of the Amorites who fought against Israel. And she said, "When we heard of it, our hearts melted and everyone's courage failed because of you, for the LORD your God is God in heaven above and on the earth below." (Josh. 2:11) Had she not recognized that the LORD God is Israel's God, she would not have escaped the destruction that came upon the rest of her people.

And yes, God called Cyrus "His anointed." (cf. Is. 45:1) In authorizing the rebuilding of the Temple, Cyrus recognized God as the God of heaven, and he recognized Him as more. "Anyone of His people among you—may His God be with him, and let him go up to Jerusalem in Judah and build the Temple of the LORD, the God of Israel, the God who is in Jerusalem." (Ezra 1:3)

People from every nation need to recognize God for who He is, for who He says He is. As the LORD says to Jerusalem, "Your Maker is your husband—the LORD Almighty is His Name. The Holy One of Israel is your Redeemer. He is called the God of all the earth." (Is. 54:5)

It may seem to some that I have belabored the point, but I plead innocence. God is the one who belabors the point. Surely He has the right to identify Himself however He chooses. Naaman finally humbled himself and recognized the God of Israel as the one true God. (cf. 2Kgs. 5:15)

Ruth knew it much earlier. And what Boaz said to her, in recognizing her decision to choose the people and the God of Israel, should be the hope of people from every nation. "May the LORD repay you for what you have done. May you be richly rewarded by the LORD, the God of Israel, under whose wings you have come to take refuge." (Ruth 2:12)

This does not mean that God cares only for Israel. He created Israel because He cares for all peoples. It is a big world, for us anyway, but the way is narrow. He is the Creator, Redeemer, and Judge of all, but He identifies Himself as the God of Israel.

For example, King Ahab of the northern kingdom of Israel married Jezebel, the daughter of the king of the Sidonians. They were an evil pair, and they led the people into great evil. Elijah the prophet pronounced a drought on the land as judgment.

To preserve the life of Elijah, the God of Israel told him to go to a town in Sidon. In that town, God supernaturally provided for Elijah through a poor widow, who had faith in Him. (cf. 1K. 17:9-24) The daughter of the king of Sidon was one of the most evil women in history; a poor widow in Sidon was one of the most faithful. The king of Israel provoked God to anger and judgment; a prophet of Israel served God in humility.

The God of Israel looks on the heart, not the passport; but His identity is not negotiable. He is not a generic god. He is not the same as the gods and idols of the nations. "The Portion of Jacob is not like these, for he is the Maker of all things, and Israel is the tribe of His inheritance. The LORD of hosts is His name." (Jer. 10:16)

If the constitution of the European Union were to refer to the God of Israel as the God whom the member states choose to serve, that would be significant indeed. That would be wonderful. That, however, is not likely. June 15, 2004, the European Union rejected the requests of some member nations to recognize God or Christianity in its new constitution. These nations, or at least their leaders, are serving their own gods.

The God of the Bible remains the God of Israel. That, unfortunately, will be the undoing of the European Union. That, unfortunately, will be the undoing of every earthly empire.

The baby's name, by the way, is Eric.


## FOOTNOTES

1. *RFE/RL NEWSLINE, Vol. 7*, No. 30, Part II, 14 February 2003

2. Berachoth IX.1, citing Ruth 2:4 and Judg. 6:12. Compare Luke 1:28.

3. Sir. 23:9-11, *Apocrypha*, Edgar J. Goodspeed translation, Vintage Books, NY, 1959. Note the similar admonition of Yeshua in Mt. 5:34 -37.

4. Josephus, *The Wars of the Jews*, Book V, Chapter V, Section 7

5. Centuries later, the individual Hebrew letters found in the Tetragrammaton were sometimes used to signify vowel sounds. That would not be the case in the Tetragrammaton, not only because it comes from a much earlier time when the letters were not used in that way, but also because of the order in which the letters appear. For example, the yod at the beginning cannot be assigned a vowel sound. In English, we would call these Hebrew letters consonants.

6. Alfred Edersheim, *The Life and Times of Jesus the Messiah, Vol.I*, Anson D.F. Randolph and Co., NY, 1886, p.332

7. IaHUeH, IAOUE, Iabe, Iae, Iao, IEUE, Yahweh, Yahwah, Yehowah, Yahveh, Yehovah, Yehwah, Yehwih, Iehouah, Iehovah, IOHOUAH, IOHOUA, IHOUAH, IEHOUA

   All of these are, of course, either English transliterations of Greek transliterations of the Hebrew, or English transliterations of the Hebrew. There are different systems of transliteration, and one must know the system in order to produce the correct pronunciation. In addition, the pronunciation of these transliterations by those who are neither native Hebrew speakers, nor native Greek speakers, will insure a variety of pronunciations.

   The addition of the traditional "Jehovah" would bring us to twenty, just surpassing the "eighteen or nineteen" etymologies that Edersheim found to be claimed for Essenes.

8. Some replace it by haShem, i.e. "the Name". Either way, in contemporary reading of the Hebrew text, the Name is never pronounced.

9. cf. *Scripture and Translation*, Martin Buber and Franz Rosenzweig, trans. by Lawrence Rosenwald with Everett Fox, Indiana U. Press, Bloomington, 1994. Rosenzweig remarks that "Calvin uses this austere, sublime, genuinely 'numinous' term to render the Old Testament name of God in the French edition he prepared in 1564 of his commentary on the Hexateuch... In 1588 Calvin's *L'Eternel* takes over the Geneva Bible altogether." pp.100-101

10. Sanh. 94a also refers Is. 9:6 to Messiah, but suggests that Hezekiah is the Messiah.

    Phil. 2:9 should be seen both in the light of the names given here, as well as Immanuel. "Therefore God exalted him to the highest place and gave him the name that is above every name." To which of Yeshua's many names is Paul referring? He is referring to Yeshua's identity, character, and accomplishments.

# CHAPTER SIXTEEN

# Hey Mate, What's a Messiah?

J'll be in Australia next month, speaking to some congregations about Messiah and his kingdom. They and I will make allowances for our differences in accent and language. One of the congregations is Russian speaking. I will have to explain at each place what I mean when I say, "Messiah". I will have to define the word in terms of the Scriptures. But I don't think the task will be that difficult.

However, if Yeshua had come to Australia two thousand years ago and announced that he was the Messiah, the natives would have replied, "That's nice, mate. What's a Messiah?" The same would have been true of any other people, except the Jews. Every other people might have had their own images of a savior or a world ruler, but they would not have known what Messiah is.

Every so often, a self-proclaimed "Christ" appears in Korea, or Kiev, or Kalifornia. The unfortunate gullible ones believe him, or her, because they do not connect "Christ" to the prophetic scriptures. They do not know or care about the God-given prophetic specifics that identify where and when Messiah is born, who his people are, how he will live, how he will die, etc., etc..

Many theologies, and the unfortunate gullible ones who believe them, do not connect "Christ" with the prophetic identifiers in the Hebrew Scriptures. Consequently, they make "Christ" whatever they want him to be, even if it is the opposite of what the prophets say that Messiah is. They do not comprehend that "the evidence for Yeshua is the spirit of prophecy." (Rev. 19:10c)

In Tanakh, God specifically described the person and work of Messiah, so that Israel could recognize him when he appeared. Israel was given the responsibility of then proclaiming him and his kingdom to the nations. The primary prophetic identification of Messiah is as a descendant of David, who will rule Israel from David's throne. This is not all that the prophets tell us about Messiah, but it is the primary way that they identify him.

The prophetic scriptures give the information that enables us to identify Messiah. The

Messianic Writings present the information necessary for us to determine whether or not Yeshua is the one described in Tanakh. For example, we can see this pattern of prophetic description and fulfillment in three familiar Messianic prophecies, each of which is cited in the Messianic Writings.

Isaiah voiced the Messianic hope of Israel. "For a child will be born to us, a son will be given to us; and the government will rest on his shoulders. And his name will be called Wonderful

EVERY SO OFTEN A SELF-PROCLAIMED "CHRIST" APPEARS IN KOREA, OR KIEV, OR KALIFORNIA. THE GULLIBLE ONES BELIEVE BECAUSE THEY DO NOT CONNECT "CHRIST" TO THE PROPHETIC SCRIPTURES.

Counselor, Mighty God, Eternal Father, Prince of Peace. There is no end to the increase of his government or of peace, on the throne of David and over his kingdom, to establish it and to sustain it with justice and righteousness from then on and forevermore. The zeal of the LORD of hosts will accomplish this." (Is.9:6-7; cf. Lk.1:27,30-33)

It is "to us," i.e. to Israel, that a child will be born and a son will be given. The LORD of hosts will give this son to His people to rule from David's throne, the throne of the King of Israel. That means that Messiah will be descended from David, having the legitimate right of royal inheritance. He will establish, sustain, and reign over David's kingdom, i.e. the land and the people of Israel.

In the Messianic Writings, we read that God sent the angel Gabriel to Miriam. "And the angel said to her, 'Do not be afraid, Miriam, for you have found favor with God. And behold, you will conceive in your womb, and bear a son, and you shall name him Yeshua. He will be great, and will be called the Son of the Most High; and the LORD God will give him the throne of his father David. And he will reign over the house of Jacob forever; and his kingdom will have no end.'" (Lk.1:30-33)

The parallel between Gabriel's proclamation and Isaiah 9:6-7 is evident. Yeshua comes to receive the throne of his father David, and to reign over the house of Jacob, i.e. the Jewish people, forever. His kingdom will have no end.

The second example is a prophecy of Jeremiah. "'Behold, the days are coming,' declares the Lord, 'when I shall raise up for David a righteous Branch. He will reign as king and act wisely and do justice and righteousness in the land. In his days Judah will be saved, and Israel will dwell securely. This is his name by which he will be called, *The LORD our righteousness.*'" (Jer.23:5,6)

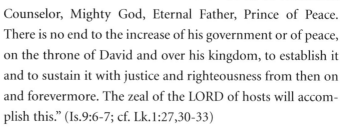

Jeremiah was prophesying just before the Babylonians destroyed Jerusalem and put an end to the Davidic kingdom. The LORD was promising to yet raise up a Branch, i.e. a descendent, of David, the root of the royal dynasty, to be king. "In his days, Judah will be saved, and Israel will dwell securely;" so this descendant of David will rule, as David did, over a united kingdom

Because Messiah, this Son of David will do justice and righteousness in the land of Israel, there will be salvation and security for the Jewish people. His life will signify that the LORD, and He alone, is our righteousness. The Scriptures affirm that Messiah will do this, but without indicating when it would be.

In the Messianic Writings, Zechariah, the father of Yohanan the forerunner of the Lord, prophesied: "Blessed be the LORD God of Israel, for He has visited us and accomplished redemption for His people, and has raised up a horn of salvation for us in the house of David His servant, as He spoke by the mouth of His holy prophets from of old, salvation from our enemies, and from the hand of all who hate us; to show mercy toward our fathers, and to remember His holy covenant, the oath which He swore to Abraham our father, to grant us that we being delivered from the hand of our enemies might serve Him without fear in holiness and righteousness before Him all our days.'" (Lk.1:67-75)

What the Holy Spirit said through Zechariah parallels the message through Jeremiah. Messiah is the king descended from David who will bring salvation, security, and righteousness to Israel. The message preceding the birth of Yohanan was that God was about to begin to do what He had promised to David and to Abraham, and had confirmed through Jeremiah.

At that time, God "raised up a horn of salvation for us [the Jews] in the house of David." But at that time, God did not give us "salvation from the hand of all who hate us," nor were we "delivered from the hand of our enemies," The Holy Spirit affirmed that Yeshua would do this, but did not tell us when it would be.

The third example is Micah 5:2. "But as for you, Bethlehem Ephratah, too little to be among the clans of Judah, from you one will go forth for Me to be ruler in Israel. His goings forth are from long ago, from the days of eternity." Bethlehem is the home town of King David, from the tribe of Judah. God was promising to send one of David's descendants to be His ruler in Israel. This descendant, however, would be unique, in that he has existed and gone forth for God from "the days of eternity."

The fulfillment of this prophecy, at least the initial part of it, is presented to us in Mt.2:1-6. The Gentile magi came to Jerusalem looking for the Messiah, but they did not know his name. They asked, in accordance with all that they did know about him, "Where is the one who has been born King of the Jews? For we have seen his star in the east, and have come to bow down to him." (Mt.2:2)

They came to bow down to the King of the Jews. This was not a religious act. It was a political act. All over the world, everyone knew what it meant to bow down to a king. They came to acknowledge and submit to his sovereignty. They came to the King of the Jews to commit themselves to loyalty and service.

Their question and their purpose made Herod very nervous. "And gathering together all the chief priests and scribes of the people, he began to inquire of them where the Messiah was to be born. And they said to him, 'In Bethlehem of Judea, for so it has been written by the prophet: *And you Bethlehem, land of Judah, are by no means least among the leaders of Judah. For out of you shall come forth a ruler, who will shepherd My people Israel.*'" (Mt.2:4-6)

YESHUA DID NOT NEED TO COME INTO THIS WORLD TO REIGN IN HEAVEN. HE WAS ALREADY REIGNING IN HEAVEN...YESHUA WAS BORN AS THE SON OF DAVID SO THAT HE CAN RULE FROM DAVID'S THRONE IN JERUSALEM.

Herod's inquiry as to where the Messiah was to be born showed that he understood who this King of the Jews was. Messiah is born King of the Jews, not appointed by Rome. The chief priests and scribes responded by quoting Micah 5:2. Yeshua is the shepherd of Israel, who comes forth from Bethlehem to be a ruler over Israel.

If we were to examine every Messianic prophecy in Tanakh, we would find the same. Ruling on David's throne in Jerusalem over all Israel is not just something that Messiah does. It is who he is. Yeshua has not yet done that.

"You are a king, then!" said Pilate. Yeshua answered, "You are right in saying I am a king. In fact, for this reason I was born, and for this I came into the world..." (John 18:37)

Yeshua did not need to come into this world to reign in heaven. He was reigning in heaven before he came into this world. Taking human form is irrelevant to rule in heaven. Yeshua was born into the royal line of Israel so that, as the Son of David, he can rule from David's throne in Jerusalem. The Scriptures emphatically declare that Messiah will do this. The one who is the Messiah will do all that the Scriptures say Messiah will do.

The purpose of the genealogies is to demonstrate that Yeshua is descended from David. The virgin birth of Yeshua is presented as the fulfillment of God's promise in Isaiah 7:13-14, which is made to the royal house of David. (Mt. 1:23) [As for the appropriateness of translating *alma* as "virgin," I suggest a booklet I have written, "God, the Rabbis, and the Virgin Birth".]

Any theology that presents a Christ who is not called to be king of the Jews is presenting a false Messiah. Such a Christ could be a worker of miracles. He could be the founder of a large world religion. But he could not be the Messiah of Israel. He would simply be another imposter.

The purpose of the gospels is to demonstrate that Yeshua is the Messiah of Israel, the one who will rule on David's throne. Because if he were not the Messiah, then he could not be the Redeemer and the Savior described in the Scriptures. If he were not the Messiah, then he could not atone for sin, and could not bring the new covenant. A theology that, in effect, denies that Yeshua is the prophesied King of Israel is a theology that denies that Yeshua is the Messiah.

It is the prophetic scriptures which identify who Messiah is. That is why Philip told Nathaniel, "We have found the one Moses wrote about in the Law, and about whom the prophets also wrote—Yeshua of Nazareth, the son of Joseph." (Jn. 1:45) More than anything else, more than everything else put together, Moses and the prophets wrote that Messiah is the one who will establish God's kingdom in Israel. The purpose of "as it is written," and "that it might be fulfilled" is to demonstrate that Yeshua did or will do everything that was prophesied of Messiah the King.

On numerous occasions, the gospels record that Yeshua openly responded to people's recognition of him as "the Son of David," i.e. Messiah the King. For example, Bartimaeus, a blind beggar, "began to cry out and say, 'Yeshua, Son of David, have mercy on me!'... and Yeshua said to him, 'Go your way, your faith has saved you.'" (Mk.10:47-52) It was Bartimaeus' expression of faith in the Son of David which brought him his sight.

A Canaanite woman came to him, crying out, "Lord, Son of David, have mercy on me! My daughter is suffering terribly from demon-possession." (cf. Mt. 15:22-28) Because she recognized him as Messiah, and because she recognized that Messiah was sent to the Jewish people, Yeshua healed her daughter.

Matthew says that the entry of Yeshua into Jerusalem on a donkey was in fulfillment of the prophecy in Zechariah: "Say to the daughter of Zion, 'Behold your king is coming to you gentle, and mounted on a donkey even on a colt, the foal of a beast of burden.'" (Mt.21:4,5) "And the multitudes going before Him, and those who followed after were crying out, 'Hosanna to the Son of David!'" (Mt.21:9) "Blessed is he who comes in the name of the LORD. Blessed is the coming kingdom of our father David. Hosanna in the highest!'" (Mk.11:9-10)

The multitudes rejoiced in receiving Messiah, David's Son. They knew that the kingdom of David would come with him. Their understanding was correct, but they did not know that he was not establishing his kingdom at that time.

Yeshua did not rebuke them or refuse to receive their worship. "And some of the Pharisees in the multitude said to Him, 'Teacher, rebuke Your disciples.' And he answered and said, "I tell you, if these become silent, the stones will cry out!" (Lk.19:39-40) Yeshua was saying that all

Creation would recognize him as the Son of David, the Messiah, the King of Israel, the Redeemer for all people.

When Yeshua was arrested and brought before Pilate, "Pilate asked him, saying, 'Are you the King of the Jews?' He answered him and said, 'It is as you say.'" (Lk.23:3) Pilate went out and asked the mob, "Shall I release for you the King of the Jews?" (Jn.18:39)

"Then Pilate therefore took Yeshua, and scourged him. And the soldiers wove a crown of thorns and put it on his head, and arrayed him in a purple robe; and they began to come up to him, and say, 'Hail, King of the Jews!' and to give him blows in the face." (Jn.19:1-3) The mockery of the Roman soldiers showed how they despised the Jews and their king. It was political. There was nothing religious about it. The Caesar of Rome ruled the earth, not the King of the Jews.

Pilate brought out a scourged, bleeding man, "And he said to the Jewish leaders, 'Behold your King!' They therefore cried out, 'Away with him, away with him, crucify Him!' Pilate said to them, 'Shall I crucify your King?' The chief priests answered, 'We have no king but Caesar.'" (Jn.19:14-15)

Like other criminals, Yeshua was crucified with his name and his crime on his stake, so that everyone could be warned by who he was and what he had done. It was written in Hebrew, in Latin, and in Greek. All four of the gospels record it: "Yeshua King of the Jews." (Mt.27:37; Mk.15:26; Lk.23:38; Jn.19:19)

Throughout the gospels, Yeshua is identified by the Messianic prophecies and titles that designate the King of the Jews. That designation is inseparable from the good news itself. It is the King of the Jews who is given to atone for the sins of the world.

The message the followers of Yeshua are called to proclaim is that of "Messiah crucified." (1Co.1:23) He is the one identified on the stake as "Yeshua, King of the Jews." His identification in death was the same as the proclamation at his birth. It is the core identity of the gospel message. It is "Yeshua, King of the Jews" whom the Messianic Writings proclaim as the Lamb of God who died to atone for the sins of the world. There is no good news without the King of the Jews. As Paul remarks, in the only verse in the Bible which says "the good news is...," "I am not ashamed of the good news of Messiah..." (Rom. 1:16)

Luke records that, following the resurrection, Yeshua appeared to two of the disciples, "And beginning from Moses and from all the prophets, he explained to them the things concerning himself in all the Scriptures." (Lk.24:27) He later appeared to the apostles and those with them, and "said to them, 'These are my words which I spoke to you while I was still with you, that all things which are written about me in the Law of Moses and the Prophets, and the Psalms must be fulfilled.' Then he opened their minds to understand the Scriptures." (Lk.24:44)

Yeshua spoke to them about "all" the Messianic prophecies in Tanakh. That is how he wanted them to know him. He spoke to them about the kingdom
of God. (Acts 1:3) He taught them that all the Messianic
prophecies speak about him, who he is, what he has done,
and what he will do.

On that basis, therefore, just before he ascended into heav-
en, they asked him a question, the one question which, given
the nature of all the Messianic prophecies, was the most logical and pressing. "Lord, is it at this time that you are restoring the kingdom to Israel?" That is to say, 'We now know that
you are the King of the Jews. You have shown us the prophecies that connect the outpouring of the Holy Spirit with the
restoration of Israel. And you have told us that we will soon
receive the Holy Spirit. So are you now going to establish your
Messianic kingdom upon the throne of David?'

THROUGHOUT THE
GOSPELS, YESHUA IS
IDENTIFIED BY THE
MESSIANIC PROPHECIES
AND TITLES THAT
DESIGNATE THE KING OF
THE JEWS. THAT
DESIGNATION IS
INSEPARABLE FROM THE
GOOD NEWS ITSELF.

"He responded, 'It is not for you to know the times or the
seasons which the Father has fixed by His own authority.' "
(Acts 1:6,7) In other words, 'God the Father has unalterably
fixed the date for the restoration of David's kingdom to

Israel. Since I am the prophesied Son of David, I will sit on David's throne, and rule over his
kingdom. But you do not need to know when that will take place. You will first proclaim
throughout the whole earth the coming of my kingdom.' Even as Yeshua had told them earlier, "But of that day and hour no one knows, not even the angels of heaven, nor the Son, but the
Father only." (Mt.24:36)

In the book of Revelation, the last book of the Bible, Messiah is still presented the same way.
John weeps greatly as he beholds in heaven that no one - no one in heaven, on earth, or under
the earth - is found worthy to open the scroll (of redemption). "And one of the elders said to
me, 'Stop weeping. the Lion that is from the tribe of Judah, the root of David, has overcome so
as to open the scroll and its seven seals.'" (Rev.5:5) The Lion of Judah, i.e. the King of the Jews,
is the only one who is worthy, the only one who has overcome. Only the Messianic King of the
Jews can open this scroll and bring redemption.

When John looked to see the Lion of Judah, he saw "a lamb standing as if slain." That is a
strange kind of lion. But the Lion of Judah overcame by being slain as a sacrificial lamb. That
is why the inscription on his stake said, "Yeshua, King of the Jews." As the Lamb of God, the
Lion of Judah overcame.

In the last chapter of the last book of the Bible, Yeshua gave his last recorded message to the communities of those who believed in him. He identified himself as the returning Son of David. "I, Yeshua, have sent my messenger to testify to you these things for the congregations. I am the root and the offspring of David, the bright and morning star." (Rev.22:16) He identified himself as the root and offspring of David, King of Israel, because that is how he returns to the earth.

Zechariah the prophet describes the day of that return as one on which all nations will be gathered against Jerusalem for battle. "Then the LORD will go forth and fight against those nations, as when He fights on a day of battle. And in that day, His feet will stand on the Mount of Olives, which is in front of Jerusalem on the east." (Zech.14:3,4) That is the place from which Yeshua ascended, after telling the disciples that the Father had fixed the day for the restoration of the kingdom to Israel. The prophetic message is that Yeshua will return to earth to destroy the enemies of Israel—who are at that point identical with the enemies of God—take up the throne of David in Jerusalem, and rule over all the earth.

IN CONTRAST TO THE BIBLICAL TEACHING, NOT ONE MAJOR CREED OF THE CHURCH EVEN IDENTIFIES "CHRIST" IN ANY WAY AS A JEW, MUCH LESS AS KING OF THE JEWS.

The Messianic Writings claim that Yeshua is the Messiah, the King of the Jews. They do this in echoing the prophets, announcing his birth, defining his ministry, and proclaiming his death, resurrection, and return. The Messiah of the Scriptures is primarily Israel's King, Israel's Redeemer, Israel's Savior.

It is in that role as the Son of David that he brings salvation to the Gentiles. The disciples called a council in Jerusalem to determine whether or not Gentiles had to become Jews in order to be disciples of Messiah. After much discussion, Jacob presented a conclusion.

"Shimon has reported how God first visited the Gentiles to take out from them a people for His name. This agrees with the words of the prophets. As it is written, 'After these things I will return. I will again build the tent of David, which has fallen. I will again build its ruins. I will set it up, that the rest of men may seek after the LORD; all the Gentiles who are called by My name, says the LORD, who does all these things.'" (Acts 15:14-17, citing Amos 9:11, 12)

The house of David is the royal house of Israel. It had staggered and fallen as a ruined tent. As the Son of David, Yeshua comes to restore the royal house of Israel so that salvation can come to the Gentiles. After all, God called Israel and her king to be a light to the nations.

In contrast to the Biblical teaching—and it is worth mentioning again—not one major creed of the Church even identifies "Christ" in any way as a Jew, much less as King of the Jews. Not as Messiah, not as the Son of David, not as the Lion of Judah. Instead of restoring the kingdom of David, the "Christ" of the creeds declares that the kingdom will never again exist. God's Messiah is Jewish. That is core identity. If that is removed, there is no Messiah, nor Redeemer. If that is removed, there is no atonement, no new covenant relationship with God.

Could someone truly believe in Yeshua and not know that he is Messiah? Perhaps, but what would they believe he is? If they do not know that he is the Messiah, then they cannot believe in "Messiah crucified". They cannot believe in "the good news of Messiah". "They cannot believe in "the good news of the kingdom".

Could someone have saving faith, but be ignorant of almost all the content of what saves them? Perhaps, but who can say? It is one thing to be ignorant; it is another to reject what is true. For the disciples, the Scriptures were their creed.

The designation and calling of Messiah as the King of the Jews cannot be separated from the good news itself, at least not from the good news presented in the Bible. It is the identification of the one who gave his life to atone for the sins of the world. It is the identification of the one who will return to rule the world.

Most of Christianity, from its establishment in the fourth century until today, denies that Jesus IS the King of the Jews, which is to say that most of Christianity denies that Jesus is the Messiah. There is no such thing in the Bible as a Messiah who is not the Son of David, the one who will restore David's kingdom and rule from his throne. The "Christ" of most of Christianity is not the Messiah.

Paul criticized the believers in Corinth, "because if someone comes to you and proclaims a Yeshua other than the Yeshua we proclaimed, or if you receive a different spirit from the one you received, or different good news from what you accepted, you put up with it easily enough." (2Cor. 11:4)

At a very early time, there were those who proclaimed a Yeshua different from the one in the Bible. There were those who proclaimed a good news different from the one in the Bible. There were those who came with a different spirit than the Holy Spirit.

The Messiah of the Scriptures regathers the Jewish people, and restores them to a living covenant relationship with the God of Israel. The "Christ" of the historical Church condemns the Jewish people to destruction and continual wandering as pariahs. The "Christ" of the historical Church cuts the Jewish people off from God, and annuls God's covenants with them.

The Messiah of the Scriptures establishes God's Law and righteousness in the earth. The Christ of the traditional Church annuls God's Law, and reduces righteousness to the affirma-

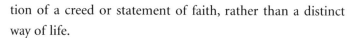

MESSIAH HAS BECOME A SERVANT OF THE JEWS ON BEHALF OF GOD'S TRUTH, TO CONFIRM THE PROMISES MADE TO THE PATRIARCHS, AND FOR THE GENTILES TO GLORIFY GOD FOR HIS MERCY.

—ROMANS 15: 8-9

tion of a creed or statement of faith, rather than a distinct way of life.

*'But didn't Christ do something new?'*

Of course he did. He did a thousand new things, but God had promised these things through the prophets. Yeshua atoned for the sins of Israel and the sins of the world. He brought the New Covenant, placing the Law of God in our hearts and minds, and bringing the promise of the Holy Spirit and the knowledge of God.

Yeshua demonstrated what it means for the Word of God to become flesh in this world. As the Holy Spirit said through Isaiah the prophet, "He brings princes to naught and reduces the rulers of this world to nothing." (Is. 40:23) He defeated death, and set all who trust in him free from sin and the fear of death.

But none of this means that Yeshua came to cast off Israel. None of this means that Yeshua is not what God said the Messiah would be. All of it means that God is faithful. "Messiah has become a servant of the Jews on behalf of God's truth, to confirm the promises made to the patriarchs and for the Gentiles to glorify God for His mercy." (Rom. 15:8-9)

Abraham is the father of all who believe in Yeshua. (cf. Rom. 4:11-12) Abraham is the heir of the world. (cf. Rom. 4:13) Yeshua came to fulfill, not to abolish. (cf. Mt. 5:17-19) That's why God begins his story, "The book of the origin of Yeshua the Messiah, the Son of David, the son of Abraham."

Yeshua came into this world that he might be the Son of Adam, and thereby be qualified to redeem the children of Adam. God revealed His plan to do that through the Son of David, of the tribe of Judah, of the children of Israel. Yeshua will be what he came to be. He will do what he came to do. And that is good news for Australians, Zimbabweans, and every other people.

CHAPTER SEVENTEEN

# The Promise Keeper

We all know that misunderstandings happen. They are a normal part of human life. Sometimes I am amazed that any communication at all can take place between different human beings.

Some people say one thing, but have no intention of doing it. That is not misunderstanding; it is misrepresentation. It is very frustrating to try to relate to such people. It's impossible to work with them. They are always denying that they said what they said, or that they meant what they meant. It doesn't matter if you have in writing, in their own handwriting, exactly what they did say. Their new claim, or denial, is not connected to what they said.

You cannot trust or believe anything such people say, because, to them, their words do not convey their meaning. Their meaning can only be found in what they say they intended or implied. The meaning only exists in their own head. Definitions, grammar, and logic are irrelevant to such people. There is no appeal of their executive fiat, because they themselves are the ultimate authority.

> IN THIS BOOK, I AM CONSCIOUSLY APPROACHING THE SCRIPTURES IN TERMS OF THEIR PLAIN, STRAIGHTFORWARD MEANING IN CONTEXT.

God is not like that, though many theologies teach that He is. God stands by everything He has said. What He promises, He will do. He is faithful and true.

Yes, there are different levels of meaning in what God says. Yes, sometimes He speaks in metaphors, parables, and allegories. He uses symbolism, and sometimes even speaks in mysteries. But He never declares that He didn't say what He said, nor does He ever claim that what He has said has no meaning at all. His words are to be understood in terms of what the words signify.

In this book, I am consciously approaching the Scriptures in terms of their plain, straightforward meaning in context. There are other levels of meaning and application, but these other levels can exist only because there is a primary meaning. The words have meanings that can be applied to other levels. The existence of other levels of meaning does not cancel the primary meaning; it depends upon it. That is why I am focusing on the straightforward meaning in context.

There are different aspects of context. There is the historical context, which tells us what issues are being addressed, who is addressing them, and what the particular words meant at that time. There is the immediate textual context, its style, and the verses which form a connected unit. There is also the context of that particular Biblical book, as well as that of the Scriptures as a whole. If the context indicates an allegory or mystery, then that is the plain meaning of the text.

When one person, or a group of people, detects his, her, or their own arbitrary symbolic meaning in a text that clearly says something else, there is a problem. In a later chapter, I do discuss a few parables to show that the traditional interpretation of them cannot be connected to the actual words. In another chapter, I focus on one aspect of the mystical approach of one theology. In a later volume, I will look at the major Christian theologies and their systems of interpretation.

So why am I talking about this now, if I write about it later? I am talking about this now because last month I was sitting with four theologians in a Chinese restaurant. The restaurant was well lit, and the background noise was minimal. We could see and hear each other quite well, but we could not understand each other at all. We were in different worlds, even though we had the same waitress.

Afterwards, one of the theologians explained to me, "It was like one of those black and white pictures that has two images. If you focus one way, it's a duck. If you focus another way, it's a rabbit. It is impossible to see both images at the same time. You can only see one or the other."

So, he said, they were saying, "Duck." And I was saying, "Rabbit." Back and forth, "Duck!" "Rabbit!" "Duck!!" "Rabbit!!" "Duck!!!" "Rabbit!!!" These are not words that one should be yelling in a Chinese restaurant.

I appreciate his illustration, but I do not believe that our disagreement was over two equally valid perceptions. I believe it was a difference in reality. To highlight that, I said that it is absolutely impossible to assign meaning to the words of the New Covenant to make it agree with their theology. "Your theology can only survive if the words have no meaning at all." They were very offended, and told me that I shouldn't say it was impossible. Because I always try to be accommodating—that's just the kind of person I am—I said, "Okay, it's not impossible. It's just that you can't do it."

They were still offended, but none of them offered to try to give any meaning to the words of the New Covenant. The words of the text are too clear. That is why every Christian theology bypasses the text of the New Covenant.

> " 'Behold, days are coming,' declares the LORD, 'when I will cut a new covenant with the house of Israel and with the house of Judah, not like the covenant which I cut with their fathers in the day I took them by the hand to bring them out of the land of Egypt, My covenant which they broke, although I was a husband to them,' declares the LORD.
>
> " 'But this is the covenant which I will cut with the house of Israel after those days,' declares the LORD, 'I will put My law within them, and on their heart I will write it. And I will be their God, and they will be My people. And they will no longer teach, each man his neighbor, and a man his brother, saying, "Know the LORD," for they will all know Me, from the least of them to the greatest of them,' declares the LORD, 'for I will forgive their iniquity, and I will remember their sin no more.'
>
> "Thus says the LORD, who gives the sun to lighten the day, and the fixed order of the moon and the stars to lighten the night, who stirs up the sea so that its waves roar; the LORD of Hosts is His name: 'If this fixed order departs from before Me,' declares the LORD, 'then the offspring of Israel also shall cease from being a nation before Me for ever.' Thus says the LORD, 'If the heavens above can be measured, and the foundations of the earth searched out below, then I will also cast off all the offspring of Israel for all that they have done,' declares the LORD." (Jer.31:31-37)

God is committed to what He has promised. This is the only new covenant in the Bible. It is the only one to which the LORD God of Israel is committed. He is not committed to what He has not promised.

Eight times in this brief passage of seven verses, the text is confirmed as the direct, explicit word of the LORD. That is a way of saying that every word is important, and every word will be fulfilled. The words have meaning.

God gave the promise of the New Covenant during some very dark days in the history of the Jewish people. Destruction, captivity, and exile had already overtaken those living in the northern kingdom of Israel. The same judgment had now come to the door of those living in the southern kingdom of Judah.

The unfaithfulness of the people of Israel had brought judgment from the God of Israel. In their own land, they had chosen to follow the idolatrous ways of the Gentiles. So God had removed them from their own land to make them live among the Gentiles. God had warned His people before they even entered the land that He would punish them in this way if they were unfaithful to the Law He gave them. (cf. Lev. 26 & Dt. 28)

Through the destruction of Jerusalem and the Temple, and through the exile among the Gentiles, God was bringing the ultimate judgment which He had decreed upon the Jewish people as a whole for breaking the Covenant of the Law. As Daniel prayed in exile: "Indeed all Israel has transgressed Your law and turned aside, not obeying Your voice. So the curse has been poured out on us, along with the oath which is written in the law of Moses the servant of God, for we have sinned against Him.

"Thus He has confirmed His words which He had spoken against us and against our rulers who ruled us, to bring on us great calamity; for under the whole heaven there has not been done anything like what was done to Jerusalem. As it is written in the law of Moses, all this calamity has come upon us..." (Dan. 9:11-13)

Though he himself was faithful, Daniel was included in the exile that was imposed for Israel's infidelity. Though he himself was faithful, Daniel included himself in the "all Israel [that] has transgressed Your law and turned aside, not obeying Your voice." Part of Daniel's faithfulness consisted of his affirmation of God's faithfulness to His choice of Israel. Had Daniel denied that, he himself would have been unfaithful. Part of Daniel's faithfulness consisted of his own unshakeable identification with the unfaithful people of Israel.

While that calamity, that ultimate judgment, was falling upon the whole house of Israel, God promised that He would yet establish a new covenant. This new covenant would bring the Jewish people into right relationship with Him.

God promised the New Covenant to a people who had been unfaithful. He promised it to the same old Israel which broke the covenant He cut with their fathers at Sinai. There is no "new Israel" mentioned here or anywhere else in the Bible. It is because all Israel has been unfaithful to God, and because God is still faithful to Israel, that He promised the New Covenant.

Since God insists that He will fulfill this promise, its terms are very important. To begin with, the New Covenant is cut by God with "the house of Israel" and the "house of Judah." It is "cut," because it is a blood covenant, established with the death of the sacrifice. This covenant between God and the Jewish people is sealed in the blood of Messiah, who is that sacrifice.

The promise of the New Covenant is given in the midst of judgment on both those "houses." The New Covenant is God's promise of restoration, in the midst of judgment. Earlier in the same context, God said: "'For behold, days are coming,' declares the LORD, 'when I will restore the fortunes of My people Israel and Judah.' The LORD says, 'I will also bring them back to the land that I gave to their fathers, and they shall possess it.'" (Jer.30:3)

Here is more of the context of the promise of the New Covenant. "'I am with you and will save you,' declares the LORD. 'Though I completely destroy all the nations among which I scatter you, I will not completely destroy you. I will discipline you, but only with justice; I will not let you go entirely unpunished.'" (Jer. 30:11)

"This is what the LORD says: 'The people who survive the sword will find favor in the desert; I will come to give rest to Israel…. I will build you up again and you will be rebuilt, O Virgin Israel. Again you will take up your tambourines and go out to dance with the joyful. Again you will plant vineyards on the hills of Samaria; the farmers will plant them and enjoy their fruit.'" (Jer. 31:2 ,4-5)

"I will surely gather them from all the lands where I banish them in My furious anger and great wrath; I will bring them back to this place and let them live in safety. They will be My people, and I will be their God. I will give them singleness of heart and action, so that they will always fear Me for their own good and the good of their children after them. I will make an everlasting covenant with them: I will never stop doing good to them, and I will inspire them to fear Me, so that they will never turn away from Me. I will rejoice in doing them good and will assuredly plant them in this land with all My heart and soul." (Jer. 32:37-41)

"This is what the LORD says: 'If I have not established My covenant with day and night and the fixed laws of heaven and earth, then I will reject the descendants of Jacob and David My servant and will not choose one of his sons to rule over the descendants of Abraham, Isaac and Jacob. For I will restore their fortunes and have compassion on them.'" (Jer. 33:25-26)

God's promise to be faithful to the descendants of Jacob is tied to His promise to David to raise up the Messianic King. Messiah will be the King of the descendants of Abraham, Isaac, and Jacob. There is no other context for Messiah. The promise to David to raise up his Son is as secure as God's promise to Abraham, Isaac, and Jacob to be faithful to their children. No more, no less.

God cut a covenant "with their fathers in the day I took them by the hand to bring them out of the land of Egypt." The people God brought out of Egypt are the "fathers" of those with whom He makes the New Covenant. The people with whom God makes the New Covenant are the descendants of those He brought out of Egypt. They are the physical descendants of Israel, the Jewish people.

To what is God referring when He says, "the covenant which I cut"? Beyond all doubt, beyond all dispute, He is referring to the Covenant of the Law which He cut with all Israel at Sinai. That generation of Jewish people, the ancestors of the Jewish people in Jeremiah's day, did not keep the Covenant of the Law. Subsequent generations also did not keep the Covenant of the Law. (Sour.) That is why God speaks of "My covenant which they broke."

God, however, was not unfaithful to Israel. He says, "I was a husband to them." God did not forsake His people. He promised to make the New Covenant with the same people whose fathers broke the Old Covenant. The LORD told Jeremiah, "...the house of Israel and the house of Judah have broken My covenant which I cut with their fathers." (Jer.11:10) That tells us who broke the covenant God cut with them when He brought them out of Egypt. It is explicitly that same people with whom God will make the New Covenant.

This is not a quiz show, but sometimes it is necessary to ask some dumb questions. What people did God bring out of Egypt, make a covenant with, and then witness their breaking that covenant? Whether or not you are going to make it to the next round, there is only one possible correct answer. [Hint: not "duck" and not "rabbit".] The correct answer is, "the Jewish people". That is the people, the only people, with whom the New Covenant is cut.

God promised this people a future restoration: "At that time they shall call Jerusalem 'The Throne of the Lord,' and all the Gentiles will be gathered to it, to Jerusalem, for the name of the Lord. Nor shall they walk anymore after the stubbornness of their evil heart. In those days the house of Judah will walk with the house of Israel, and they will come together from the land of the north to the land that I gave to your fathers as an inheritance." (Jer.3:17,18)

The New Covenant is a declaration of God's faithfulness despite Israel's unfaithfulness. It is a declaration of God's faithfulness overriding Israel's unfaithfulness. (If God's mercy could not override Israel's unfaithfulness, what hope would the Gentiles have?) The same people who used to walk "after the stubbornness of their evil heart" will no longer do so. The New Covenant will bring restoration—restoration to the land and to the LORD. It will create a holy people for a holy God.

"'I will put My law within them, and on their heart I will write it. And I will be their God, and they shall be My people. And they shall no longer teach, each man his neighbor, saying, "Know the LORD," for they shall all know Me, from the least of them to the greatest of them,' declares the LORD, 'for I will forgive their iniquity, and I will remember their sin no more.'"

It is a covenant that is for the benefit and well-being of individual Jews, but the covenant itself is not cut with individuals. It is a corporate covenant. It is cut with the house of Israel and the house of Judah, the same people who are physically descended from those who broke the covenant cut at Sinai.

He declares that His faithfulness to Israel is as sure as the "statutes" of Creation and the covenant that He cut with Noah. First, He identifies Himself as the Creator and Controller of all things. "Thus says the LORD, who gives the sun for light by day, and the statutes of the moon and the stars for light by night, who stirs up the sea so that its waves roar."

Then He declares that His faithfulness to Israel is as sure as the "statutes" of Creation and the covenant that He cut with Noah. "While the earth remains, seedtime and harvest, and cold and heat, and summer and winter, and day and night shall not cease." (Gen.8:22) It is even surer than that. Those who want to see God "cast off all the offspring of Israel for all that they have done" must measure the heavens above and search out the foundations of the earth beneath. Not an easy task, to be sure.

There is no shortage of theologians to proclaim that God has cast off all the offspring of Israel, but these theologians have never bothered to first measure the heavens, and then search out the foundations of the earth. Before believing their claims, we must ask these theologians, and some of them are now dead, to first do what God requires—measure the heavens and search out the foundations of the earth. Until then, we can believe in God's eternal faithfulness to Israel: "the offspring of Israel" will not "cease from being a nation before Me forever."

> HE DECLARES THAT HIS FAITHFULNESS TO ISRAEL IS AS SURE AS THE "STATUTES" OF CREATION AND THE COVENANT THAT HE CUT WITH NOAH.

The LORD follows this declaration with specific promises concerning physical Jerusalem. (cf. verses 38-40) Through the fulfillment of the New Covenant, God will restore the Jewish people to the land of Israel and to Himself. The promise is as sure as God Himself.

That is because, as we have already seen, the God of the Bible describes Himself as the God of Israel. That is the way He wants to be known. That is why those who know Him can say, "The LORD of all powers is with us; the God of Jacob is our stronghold." (Ps.46:7,11) That is why He Himself says to Zion, "Your husband is your Maker, whose Name is the LORD of all powers. Your Redeemer is the Holy One of Israel, who is called the God of all the earth." (Is. 54:5)

God's identity and integrity are bound up in His relationship with Israel. As King David prayed: "And what one nation on the earth is like Your people Israel, whom God went to redeem for Himself as a people and to make a name for Himself, and to do a great thing for You and awesome things for Your land, before Your people whom You have redeemed for Yourself from Egypt, from nations and their gods? For You have established for Yourself Your people Israel as Your own people forever, and You, O LORD, have become their God." (2Sam.7:23,24)

Think how bad it would look on God's résumé if He quit being the God of Israel, especially after only fifteen hundred years or so on the job. Think of how the other gods would make fun of Him. "Hey guys, there's the God of Israel! Oh no, that's not right. I forgot. He used to be the God of Israel, but He quit. He wasn't strong enough or smart enough to do the job. Such a small people, but they were too much for Him. Hey Loser, what are You doing for work now?" (Some of those other gods can be very nasty.)

The text in Jeremiah 31 makes it very clear that a new covenant is promised to the Jewish people. The text also makes it clear that nothing will prevent God from establishing this new covenant which He has promised to the Jewish people. The words themselves cannot be understood in any other way.

Unfortunately, virtually every great Christian theologian ignores the words, i.e. the text, of the New Covenant. That is because the words of the text cannot be made to fit with any Christian theology. These theologies are based on the assumption that the New Covenant is made with the Church. It is impossible to conclude that on the basis of the text. That is why the theologians ignore the text. There is absolutely no covenant anywhere in the Bible that is made with the Church.

The New Covenant is important. It brings forgiveness of sin and iniquity. It brings the knowledge of God. It brings God's Law into the heart and mind. It brings salvation. In what other covenant in the Scriptures will you place your hope?

The text in Jeremiah indicates beyond question that the New Covenant is cut between God and the Jewish people, the same people whose fathers broke the covenant God cut with them when He brought them out of Egypt. This text is quoted, from the Septuagint, in Hebrews 8:8-12. There it reads the same.

Did God bring the Church out of Egypt sometime before the days of Jeremiah? No, but let's pretend that He did. Did God make a covenant with the Church after He brought the Church out of Egypt? No, but let's pretend that He did. Did the Church break that covenant?

No matter how lively an imagination one has, and no matter how one distorts the text by trying to allegorize it, it is still impossible to make the words refer to the Church. It cannot be done. That is why the all the great theologians ignore the text completely. They know it cannot be done.

The New Covenant between God and Israel is established with the blood of Yeshua. "In the same way, after supper he took the cup, saying, 'This cup is the new covenant in my blood, which is poured out for you.'" (Luke 22:20) Paul reminds believers that, "In the same way, after supper he took the cup, saying, 'This cup is the New Covenant in my blood. Do this, whenever you drink it, in remembrance of me.'" (1Cor. 11:25) What Christians call "communion," or "the Lord's supper," or "eucharist" is supposed to be a reaffirmation of God's New Covenant with the people He brought out of Egypt.

Paul continues: "For whenever you eat this bread and drink this cup, you proclaim the Lord's death until he comes." (1Cor. 11:26) The King of the Jews died for the sins of the world. Proclaim that in your communion. He offers everyone the opportunity to find atonement in his death, "until he comes." When he comes, he comes as the Son of David, bringing deliverance for Israel, and judgment for her enemies. When he comes, he restores the throne of David in Jerusalem, and rules from it. Proclaim that in your Lord's supper.

Yeshua instituted the New Covenant with his Jewish ambassadors. After the resurrection, he then commanded them to fulfill their calling as Jews by being a light to the nations. (cf. Mt.28:19-20; Acts 13:47) The New Covenant is the means by which God's promises to Abraham, Isaac, and Jacob—to be a people set apart for Him, to be His dwelling place upon the earth, and to bring the nations back to Him—are to be fulfilled. Individual Jews who do not enter into the New Covenant do not receive its benefits.

During this present time, while still only a remnant of Israel believes, individual Gentiles who repent and believe can be brought into the commonwealth of Israel. Then they can share in the rights and responsibilities of the New Covenant. They are welcome. They are invited. They can, and should, remain Gentiles. That is what God created them to be.

They can share in the benefits of the New Covenant, but they cannot take it for their own. It is not cut with them, but with the house of Israel and the house of Judah, i.e. the whole house of Israel. Gentiles must be grafted into it. When Yeshua returns, this same New Covenant will be confirmed with all Israel.

An individual or group that is truly separate from God's covenants with Israel is, in Paul's words, "without hope and without God." Israel, the physical descendants of the people God brought out of Egypt, is the only context in which the New Covenant can be found.

CHAPTER EIGHTEEN

# Zion & Sons Building Co.

My wife and I, with the help of our children and some friends, built our house ourselves. After we selected and cleared the house site, we dug down to lay a foundation. Two to three feet down, we hit bedrock, everywhere. That became our foundation.

We had no choice. We had picked that site, and we had no desire to try to dynamite down through bedrock. Besides, we could never build a firmer foundation, a foundation which could not be shaken. We could not move the bedrock, so we built upon it. The bedrock determined how we built.

In a similar way, there is a foundation for Yeshua's *kahal/ekklesia*, a foundation which both determines and indicates what is being built. Yeshua asked his disciples, "'Who do you say that I am?' Shimon Kefa answered, 'You are the Messiah, the Son of the living God.'

"Yeshua responded to him, "Blessed are you, Shimon Bar Yonah, for flesh and blood has not revealed this to you, but my Father who is in heaven. I also tell you that you are Kefa, and on this rock I will build my congregation, and the gates of Sheol will not prevail against it." (Mt. 16:16-18)

Catholics and Protestants argue about the meaning of what Yeshua said. The Roman Catholic Church says that Jesus was declaring Peter to be the foundation of the Church. It claims that it itself is the Church/*ekklesia* that was built upon Peter.

Many Protestant Churches respond that Jesus was declaring Peter's declaration of faith in him to be the foundation of the Church. They claim to be that Church/ekklesia that was built upon Peter's declaration of faith. I say, the Catholics and the Protestants are both wrong; let's look at the text.

Yeshua approved Kefa's response as being from the Father in heaven. What exactly did Kefa say? He did not say "Christ," since he was not speaking English. And he did not say christos, since he was not speaking Greek. He said, "You are the Mashiakh, the Son of the living God." Kefa recognized Yeshua as the Messiah. That is what Yeshua affirmed as being the correct way to identify him; that is what Yeshua affirmed as being the way the Father identified him.

In their Anchor Bible commentary, W. F. Albright and C.S. Mann maintain that "The transliteration of the Gr. Christos by Christ in various English versions is inexcusable... In its original context the question posed by Jesus and answered by Peter as spokesman demanded commitment to Jesus as Messiah."[1]

Why does Kefa connect "Messiah" and "Son of the living God"? What is the connection? John records the same connection. "Then Nathaniel declared, 'Rabbi, you are the Son of God; you are the King of Israel.'" (John 1:49) Why does Nathaniel connect "Son of God" and "King of Israel"?

THERE ARE NO DENOMINATIONAL ACTIONS THAT SEEK THE RESTORATION OF THE DAVIDIC KINGDOM AS THEIR FIRST PRIORITY.

Both Peter and Nathaniel were thinking of the second Psalm. They quote from it in Acts 4:25-26. John quotes from or refers to it in Rev. 2:27; 12:5, and 19:15. Paul quotes from it in Acts 13:33. It is also quoted in Hebrews 1:5 and 5:5.

It is a vitally important scripture for understanding who Messiah is and what he comes to do. In this psalm, the Father declares that Messiah, Zion's King, is His Son.

"The kings of the earth take their stand and the rulers gather together against the LORD and against his Messiah [*m'shikho/christou*]."

"'I have installed My King on Zion, My holy hill.'"

"'I will proclaim the decree of the LORD: He said to me, You are my Son; today I have become your Father.'" (Ps. 2:2,6-7)

God had already declared that Israel is His Son. (e.g. Ex. 4:22) Because of that, Israel's King stands in a special relationship to the God of Israel. Before Solomon was born, God promised to raise up one of David's sons to be king after him. "I will be his Father, and he will be My son. When he does wrong, I will punish him with the rod of men, with floggings inflicted by men." (2Sam. 7:14; cf. Ps. 89:20-38/19-37E)

This is how Yeshua's Father in heaven revealed his identity; Yeshua is the Messiah, the King of Israel, the Son of God. Unfortunately, neither the Roman Catholic Church nor the Protestant Churches affirm the basic Messianic identification of Yeshua. Unfortunately, neither the Roman Catholic Church nor the Protestant Churches affirm the basic Messianic identification of Yeshua.

'*That's not true. They all claim that he is the Christ.*'

Yes, they all claim that he is the "Christ," but they do not identify their Christ as the Messiah. The "Christ" of the Church is defined quite differently from the Biblical, Jewish Messiah. Both history and doctrine bear that out. There are no Church creeds or statements of faith that affirm Yeshua as the Messiah, as the Son of David, or as the King of the Jews. There are no denominational actions that seek the restoration of the Davidic kingdom as their first priority. So on a very basic level, every Christian denomination is disqualified from being what Yeshua is building. Joining together for organizational purposes can have its benefits, but it is important to remember that, "Unless the LORD builds the house, its builders labor in vain." (Ps. 127:1a)

So let's now look at the Roman Catholic claim. If the Roman Catholic Church were built upon Peter, then several things would be evident in the nature of the Roman Catholic Church.

THE PETER OF THE ROMAN CATHOLIC CHURCH IS A CHRISTIAN WHO HAS LEFT THE JEWISH PEOPLE FAR BEHIND, TRAMPLED IN THE DUST OF REJECTION.

First, since the Peter of the Bible is a Jew, an ekklesia built upon him would at least honor, and not despise, that identity. It is not simply that Peter was a Jew, he IS a Jew, since all live before God. The attitude of the Roman Catholic Church, from its beginning, towards the Jews cannot be called one of honor. Though there are notable exceptions, the predominant attitude has been one of contempt.

Second, Peter was called by the King of the Jews to be one of his ambassadors to the Jews. He was not called to dispossess Israel. He was called to entreat Israel to receive its rightful inheritance. So an *ekklesia* built upon Peter would strive to fulfill this calling, rather than to eradicate it.

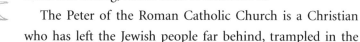

The Peter of the Roman Catholic Church is a Christian who has left the Jewish people far behind, trampled in the dust of rejection. The history of the Roman Catholic Church bears more than ample witness to this. The Kefa of the Bible is a Jew whose God-given, consuming goal in life was the redemption of Israel.

Third, Yeshua did not even name him "Peter". That is only the English transliteration of the Greek translation of what Yeshua actually did call him. As John tells us, "And he [Andrew] brought him [Shimon] to Yeshua. Yeshua looked at him and said, 'You are Shimon son of John. You will be called Kefa' (which, when translated, is *Petros*)." (Jn. 1:42)

Yeshua did not speak to Peter in Greek, but in Hebrew. He called him Kefa, not Peter. So the whole wordplay in the Greek text of Mt. 16:18—"You are *petros*, and upon this *petra* I will build my *ekklesia*"—does not even come from Yeshua. Nor does it come from Matthew's original text, since, as far as we know, Matthew wrote in Hebrew. The wordplay comes from whoever translated Matthew's writings into Greek. It is not what Yeshua said.

Fourth, Yeshua said to Kefa, following the resurrection, "feed my sheep." (Jn. 21:15, 16,17)

If there had been any need to explain whom his sheep were, Yeshua had already done that in saying, in the hearing of Kefa, to the Canaanite woman: "I was sent only to the lost sheep of the house of Israel." (Mt. 15:24) Yeshua was sent to the Jewish people. He did not go to any new, reconstituted Israel. Nor did he go to any Gentiles who were "really" the ten lost tribes in disguise. For Yeshua, "the house of Israel" was simply the Jewish people. He identified them as his sheep.

Yeshua came to fulfill what God promised through Ezekiel. "Son of Adam, prophesy against the shepherds of Israel. Prophesy and say to them: 'This is what the Lord, the Everpresent LORD says: Woe to the shepherds of Israel who only feed themselves! Should not shepherds feed the flock?... You have not strengthened the weak or healed the sick or bound up the injured. You have not brought back the strays or searched for the lost. You have ruled them harshly and brutally.... I will place over them one shepherd, My servant David, and he will tend them. He will tend them and be their shepherd." (Ezek. 34:2,4,23)

In telling Kefa to "feed my sheep," Yeshua was calling him to be part of the fulfillment of what God had promised to Israel through Jeremiah. "Woe to the shepherds who are destroying and scattering the sheep of My pasture! ...I will place shepherds over them who will feed them, and they will no longer be afraid or terrified, nor will any be missing.... The days are coming when I will raise up to David a righteous Branch, a King who will reign wisely and do what is just and right in the land [of Israel]." (Jer. 23:1,4,5)

It was to a disobedient Israel that God promised, "Then I will give you shepherds after My own heart, who will lead you with knowledge and understanding." (Jer. 3:15) Kefa was called to be one of those many shepherds. The Roman Catholic Church has never sought to feed the lost sheep of the house of Israel.

Fifth, Peter was not the head of the community of believers. In Jerusalem, he had to give account for eating with Cornelius. He was not the head of the community of believers in Antioch, because Paul rebuked him there for withdrawing from table fellowship with Gentiles. Nor was Peter the head of the community of believers anywhere else, including Rome.

Paul proclaimed Yeshua and the kingdom of God to the Jewish community in Rome. Many believed. Paul tells us that he did not build on anyone else's foundation, and he did not build on any foundation other than Messiah. The *ekklesia* in Rome, which Paul helped to found, was built upon the foundation of Yeshua the Messiah. It was not built upon Peter. Paul taught that there is no other foundation than Messiah. If the Roman Catholic Church had been built upon Peter, then it would have been built on the wrong foundation.

Let's look at the Scriptural identity of the foundation stone on which Yeshua's *ekklesia* is to be built. In the Biblical Hebrew context, what Yeshua was saying is actually quite clear. Neither

**"SEE I LAY IN ZION AS A FOUNDATION, A TESTED STONE, A PRECIOUS CORNERSTONE FOR A SURE FOUNDATION..." PETER IDENTIFIES THIS FOUNDATION STONE AS YESHUA.**

the Catholic claim nor the claim of the Protestant Churches agrees with the Scriptures.

After the resurrection, Peter told the rulers and elders of the people that Yeshua is "the stone you builders rejected, which has become the head of the corner." (Acts 4:11) Peter was quoting Psalm 118:22-23, as Yeshua had done earlier. (cf. Mt. 21:42; Mk. 12:10, Lk. 20:17) Yeshua and Peter both claimed that the stone the builders rejected is Yeshua.

In his first letter, Peter again refers to Ps. 118:22-23. "For in Scripture it says: 'See, I lay a stone in Zion, a chosen and precious cornerstone, and the one who trusts in him will never be put to shame. Now to you who believe, this stone is precious. But to those who do not believe, 'The stone the builders rejected has become the head of the corner.'" (1Pet. 2:6-7)

In this passage, Peter is also quoting from Isaiah 28:16. "So this is what the LORD God says: 'See, I lay a stone in Zion as a foundation, a tested stone, a precious cornerstone for a sure foundation. The one who trusts will never be dismayed.'" The cornerstone is declared to be the foundation stone.

To lay the foundation stone in place, God says, "I will make justice the measuring line and righteousness the plumb line..." (Is. 28:17) This stone will be the foundation on which God's just and righteous rule will be built. As we read in Ps. 89:14, "Righteousness and justice are the foundation of Your throne; love and faithfulness go before You."

Peter identifies this foundation stone as Yeshua. In identifying Yeshua as this stone, Peter was explicitly claiming that Yeshua is the Messiah, because Messiah is God's foundation stone. Peter never referred to himself as the foundation stone. To do so would have been to claim that he, Peter, was the Messiah.

Paul also was not confused about the identity of the foundation stone. He wrote to Gentiles, i.e. non-Jews, who had been "without citizenship in the commonwealth of Israel" before they trusted in Yeshua. (cf. Eph. 2:12) Because they had adhered to Messiah, the Son of David, he told them, "Consequently, you are no longer foreigners and aliens, but fellow citizens with those who are set apart and members of God's household, built on the apostles' and prophets' foundation—the chief cornerstone, Yeshua the Messiah himself. In him the whole building is joined together and rises to become a holy temple in the Lord." (Eph. 2:19-21)

As Paul says in 1Cor. 3:10-11, "By the grace God has given me, I laid a foundation as an expert builder, and someone else is building on it. But each one should be careful how he builds. For no one can lay any foundation other than the one already laid, which is Yeshua the Messiah." The only foundation stone that Paul knew about was Messiah. Peter was not the foundation that Paul laid. Nor was Paul himself. Nor was Peter's confession of faith. Yeshua is the foundation, the only foundation.

Additionally, every foundation must be laid somewhere. When we, as a family, began to build our house, we found that the location of the foundation stone determined how we would build. As we have seen, Peter quoted Is. 28:16, which says that God has laid His foundation in Zion, the city of David. (cf. 1Kgs. 8:1)

Everything that God is going to build will be built upon that foundation. You can dynamite bedrock, but you cannot move it. No one can remove God's foundation from Zion.

God has not laid His foundation stone in any other city. He has not laid His foundation stone in Rome, or Constantinople (the second Rome), or Moscow (the third Rome), or in any other subsequent Romes. These are not the foundation of what God is building. The only foundation stone God has laid is the one that He laid in Zion—the Jewish city, Jerusalem, the capital of the coming kingdom of God. "I have set My King on Zion, My holy hill." (Ps. 2:6) From where else would anyone expect the King of the Jews to reign?

Even in the time of the new heavens and the new earth, it is the new Jerusalem that comes down out of heaven from God. Jerusalem will still be the holy city, the city of God. There is no new Rome, or new Constantinople, or new Moscow, or new any other city that comes down out of heaven from God. The new Jerusalem comes down out of the new heavens to the new earth.

Whatever the Lord intends to build will be built upon the foundation that He has laid in Zion. The cornerstone comes from Judah. (cf. Zech. 10:4) Judah is the tribe from which David and all of God's anointed kings after him come. If Peter is the foundation of an *ekklesia* in Rome, then that *ekklesia* is one without Messiah, without covenants, without promises, without a kingdom or a hope. Where is the Chuch of any kind that is built upon a foundation in Zion? Jesus did not say, "I will build my Church," since he was not speaking English. And he did not say, "I will build my *ekklesia*," since he was not speaking Greek. He said, "I will build my *kahal*," referring to what the God of Israel had already promised.

In Mt. 16:16-18, Yeshua was talking about building what God had promised to Abraham. Yeshua is THE son of Abraham, the one who comes to fulfill what God promised to Abraham. Yeshua and his apostles are very careful to explicitly proclaim this. (e.g. Jn. 5:46-47; Acts 3:22-26, 26:5)

If Yeshua had been talking about building in some location other than Zion, then he would not be building what God had promised to Israel; he would be building something other than what God had promised. Yet Yeshua and his ambassadors are very careful to explicitly declare that he came to fulfill what God promised Israel through the prophets. (e.g. Mt. 5:17; Rom. 15:8)

The *kahal/ekklesia* of God in Matthew through Revelation is the same as the *kahal/ekklesia* of God in Genesis through Malachi. As we have seen, this is the commonwealth of Israel that God promised to make from Jacob, as a means of bringing the rebellious Gentiles back to Himself. (cf. Gen. 28:3; 35:11; 48:4)

Can we find a Church that is built upon Messiah, the King of the Jews? Or can we find one that weeps, as Yeshua did, for the welfare of Jerusalem and her children? The unfortunate, but undeniable answer is evident in creeds, theology, and statements of faith. The unfortunate, but undeniable answer is evident in past history and present policy. The answer is, "No, there is no such Church."

Can we find individual "Christians" or local "churches" whose heart is towards Israel? Yes, we can. But that does not make them separate from what God is building in Israel. To the contrary, it shows them to be a part of the commonwealth of Israel.

In the council at Jerusalem, it was determined that Gentiles who believed in Yeshua did not need to be circumcised. Why not? Because they were part of what God had promised Israel centuries before. "'In that day I will restore David's fallen tent. I will repair its broken places, restore its ruins, and build it as it used to be, so that they may possess the remnant of Edom and all the Gentiles who bear My Name,' declares the LORD, who will do these things.'" (Amos 9:11-12; cf. Acts 15:16-17)

God had promised that, in the Messiah, Israel's royal house, the house of David, would be raised up and would rule over "the Gentiles who bear My Name". That means these Gentiles would still be Gentiles, i.e. physically uncircumcised and not proselytes. But they would bear the Name of the God of Israel, the One who establishes David's kingdom.

The apostles understood the gathering in of the Gentiles to be the fulfillment of what God had promised to their fathers, to Israel, and to Israel's royal house. They rejoiced to see the gathering in of the Gentiles, even though at first they did not understand it. For them, Israel was, and remained, the only context that God had promised for the salvation of all peoples, and the only context that God needed. There is only one foundation; and it has been laid in only one place.

## FOOTNOTE

1. *The Anchor Bible, Matthew, Translation and Notes* by W.F. Albright and C.S. Mann, Doubleday & Co., Inc., Garden City, NY, 1971, P.194

CHAPTER NINETEEN

# The Commonwealth of Israel

"UNDER THE PSEUDONYM CHRISTOPHER NORTH, WRITER JOHN WILSON COMPOSED A
SERIES OF ARTICLES FOR A LONG-RUNNING COLUMN CALLED 'NOCTES AMBROSIANAE'
(1822-35) FOR BLACKWOOD'S MAGAZINE. THE COLUMN PROVIDED SOCIAL COMMEN-
TARY IN THE FORM OF DISCUSSIONS AT AN EDINBURGH PUB, AMBROSE'S TAVERN. IN ONE
PARTICULAR ARTICLE, WILSON AS NORTH WRITES, 'HIS MAJESTY'S DOMINIONS, ON
WHICH THE SUN NEVER SETS.' CHANGED TO THE MORE USER-FRIENDLY, 'THE SUN NEVER
SETS ON THE BRITISH EMPIRE," THE PHRASE HAS ENDURED AS THE MOST POPULAR TO
DESCRIBE THE EXTENT OF BRITAIN'S COLONIAL LAND HOLDINGS DURING THE AGE OF
IMPERIALISM UNTIL ITS FALL FOLLOWING THE SECOND WORLD WAR.... HOWEVER, AT ITS
HEIGHT IN THE 1930S, THE BRITISH EMPIRE SPANNED NEARLY A THIRD OF THE WORLD'S
LAND INCLUDING PROPERTIES IN ASIA, LATIN AMERICA, THE MIDDLE EAST, AUSTRALIA
AND AFRICA." [1]

The British Empire no longer circles the globe. The Empire was changed into a
commonwealth, starting with Canada in 1867. Empires rise and fall. So do
commonwealths. So do all human governments. So will all human governments.

In an empire, one nation rules all the others. In a commonwealth, each nation is self-
governing. In an empire, differences pose a threat to unity. In a commonwealth, differences are
a source of enrichment. In an empire, full legal rights belong only to an elite. In a commonwealth, full legal rights are the heritage of all.

In the British Commonwealth of Nations, every citizen was entitled to a British education,
a British passport, and British justice. A Kikuyu in Kenya and a Quebecois in Canada had as
much claim to British citizenship as any lord in London. They were fellow-citizens, fellow-
partakers, fellow-members, and fellow-heirs.

Nevertheless, Great Britain was the mother country, and no one could deny the special place
of her land and her people. To deny that would have been to destroy any basis for laying claim

to the benefits of belonging. To deny the particular place of the British people in the Commonwealth would have been an absurd display of arrogant ingratitude and ignorance.[2]

God has planned a commonwealth that will cover the earth. It begins in Jerusalem, the capital of Israel.

"Arise, shine, for your light has come, and the glory of the LORD is risen upon you. For, behold, darkness will cover the earth and thick darkness over the peoples. But upon you the LORD will arise and His glory will be seen upon you. Nations will come to your light, and kings to the brightness of your rising. Lift up your eyes and look about you: All assemble and come to you; your sons come from afar, and your daughters are carried on the arm.... Your sun will never set again, and your moon will wane no more; the LORD will be your everlasting light, and your days of sorrow will end." (Is. 60:1-4,20)

"The heavens declare the glory of God. The firmament proclaims the work of His hands." (Ps. 19:1) All of Creation speaks of, and points to God. From the earliest times, people could have known God, "since what may be known about God is plain to them, because God has made it plain to them. For since the creation of the world God's invisible qualities—His eternal power and divine nature—have been clearly seen, being understood from what has been made, so that men are without excuse." (Rom. 1:19-20)

People could know God, and they could know what God required of them, long before God created Israel, long before Yeshua lived on the earth, long before there was a Bible. People could know God, but each successive revelation provided a greater means of knowing Him.

GOD HAS PLANNED A COMMONWEALTH THAT WILL COVER THE EARTH. IT BEGINS IN JERUSALEM, THE CAPITAL OF ISRAEL.

In His grace, God has a greater purpose than just being known by separate individuals. All individuals are connected, because Adam is the father of all. The rebellion at the Tower of Babel brought a judgment of division, the beginning of the nations, but God had planned a way to put an end to the rebellion and bring Mankind together again. (e.g. Rev. 7:9) God intends to have all the earth bound together in a commonwealth of service to Him and to one another. All these varied descendants of Adam, recreated in the image and likeness of God, will live life in Spirit and in Truth.

From the beginning, with this in mind, God had already purposed and planned that there would be an Israel, that Yeshua would live on the earth, and that there would be a Bible. He planned the end from the beginning. He planned a redeemed people, headed by their King, their Redeemer.

God created Adam, but Adam turned away. Adam lost much of what God had given him, but God did not intend to lose Adam. Nor did He intend to abandon His purpose for Man.

Cain went his own way, but God told Cain, "If you do what is good, won't your countenance be lifted up? However, if you do not do what is good, sin is crouching at the door; it desires to have you, but you must rule over it." (Gen. 4:7) Cain chose not to do what was good. Instead, he chose to kill his brother Abel, who had been made in the image of God.

Abel, Enokh, and Noah were men who knew and believed God. Because they believed God, they knew what He wanted of them, and they chose to be obedient. Their contemporaries chose not to be obedient. "For although they knew God, they neither glorified Him as God nor gave thanks to Him, but their thinking became futile and their foolish hearts were darkened." (Rom. 1:21) They knew what was right and what was wrong, and they chose what was wrong. God destroyed all of Noah's generation (except for the eight in the ark), because they chose to do what they knew to be wrong.

When Noah came out of the ark, God repeated to him the commandment He had given to Adam: "And God blessed Noah and his sons and said to them, 'Be fruitful and multiply, and fill the earth.'" (Gen.9:1; cf. Gen.1:28) God was signifying that His original purpose for Man and the earth was still in effect, and that it would now be fulfilled through Noah and his descendants. In that generation, all the other descendants of Adam had been destroyed in the flood.

The descendants of Noah also chose what they knew to be wrong. Their rebellion led to the Tower of Babel. God did not destroy them all at Babel, as He had done in the flood, but He created great barriers of division to frustrate their evil unity. However, in God's eternal, unchanging plan, He had purposed to create a multitude of nations, a variety of cultures and languages. God furthered His own purposes in bringing judgment at Babel. From that time on, the descendants of Noah continued to shun the Truth and turn away from God.

Knowing that they would incline to evil, God had also purposed from the beginning to create a distinct people, to bring that multitude of nations/Gentiles back to Himself. Through this distinct people, He would reveal His nature in greater measure to all the other peoples, make His entry into the world, and prepare His rule upon the earth. Through them also, He would record His eternal plan in inspired writing. This people was created to bear witness to God in many ways.

When God called Abram, He declared to him that, "all the families of the earth will be blessed in you." (Gen.12:3) When He changed Abram's name to Abraham, and made him the father of what would become the Jewish people, He told him that he would also become "the father of a multitude of Gentiles [goyim]." (Gen.17:5)

Jacob was promised the same thing. When he was leaving home to find a wife, Isaac blessed him, saying, "May God Almighty bless you and make you fruitful and increase your numbers until you become a community of peoples." (Gen. 28:3) God would make Jacob into a particular, holy people, but He would also make Jacob a community of many peoples. The particular, holy people was to be the means of gathering the community of many peoples, the means of restoring the world to Divine order.

When Jacob returned with his wives and children, God said to him, "I am God Almighty. Be fruitful and multiply. A nation and a company of nations [kahal goyim] shall come from you, and kings shall come forth from you. And the land which I gave to Abraham and Isaac, I will give it to you, And I will give the land to your descendants after you.'" (Gen.35:11-12) God promised to make Jacob both a nation and a company of nations.

It is interesting that God repeated to Jacob the commandment and blessing—"Be fruitful and multiply"—which had initially been given to Adam. (Gen.1:28) The word translated as "land"—"I will give the land/*aretz* to your descendants after you"—is the same word used in God's original commandment to Adam—"fill the earth/*aretz*". But now God uses it to refer to the specific land set apart for this distinct people. God's purpose for the earth/*aretz* was now related to the people of Israel filling their land/*aretz*, and fulfilling their purpose in it.

GOD'S PURPOSE FOR THE EARTH/*ARETZ* WAS NOW RELATED TO THE PEOPLE OF ISRAEL FILLING THEIR LAND/*ARETZ*, AND FULFILLING THEIR PURPOSE IN IT.

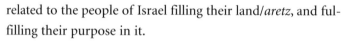

In repeating these things to Jacob, God was signifying that His original plan for the earth was still in effect, and that Jacob and the people that would come from him were the means of bringing it to fulfillment. For that purpose, God established a covenant relationship with Israel—with Israel only of all the peoples of the earth. "You only have I known of all the families of the earth..." (Amos 3:2) Israel was to be God's key for unlocking the nations, setting them free, and bringing them back to Himself.

God was not abandoning all the other families of the earth to futility and destruction. He was simply affirming the means He had chosen for their redemption—Noa̱h, Abraham, Isaac, Jacob. The earth was still for Man, and God had chosen Abraham to be the "heir of the world." (cf. Rom. 4:13) God was expressing His intent to restore the earth to its original purpose.

Even as God had walked in the Garden with Adam and Eve, so He promised Israel, "I will walk among you and be your God, and you will be My people." (Lev. 26:12) God promised Israel, "You will live in the land I gave your fathers. You will be My people, and I will be your

God." (Ezek. 36:28) Part of the fulfillment of God's promise and purpose is for Israel to live in the land God gave to their fathers.

As we have seen, throughout the Scriptures, God identifies Himself as the God of Israel. He chooses to identify Himself this way more than by any other particular title, perhaps more than all the others put together. The nations, the Gentiles, abandoned the one true God, and chose their own gods. The one true God then bound Himself to Israel.

God gave to Israel sonship, His glorious presence, His covenants—including the New Covenant in Messiah—His Word, His written instruction and law, His holy Temple, and His great promises. He irrevocably identified Himself as the God of Israel. Whatever God is in relationship to Israel—Creator, Father, Shepherd, Judge, Savior, Friend, Redeemer, Portion, etc.— He is. Whatever He is not in relationship to Israel, He is not.

As God said to Zion, "The Holy One of Israel is your Redeemer. He will be called the God of all the earth." (Is. 54:5b) All the earth will come to acknowledge Him.

He proclaims Himself the King of Israel, the ultimate, legitimate ruler of this people. He designated a particular land as their possession throughout eternity. He designated a capital, a royal city, and promised that He would rule from there over all the earth. He gave them His royal law, that they might prosper and live in the land. In short, He established a rule of government for the people in the land.

Israel is His established context for the redemption of a *kahal* of *goyim*, i.e. a company of nations. "Behold, I will make you fruitful and will increase your numbers. I will give you to be a *kahal* of peoples, and I will give this land to your descendants after you as an everlasting possession." (Gen. 48:4) The people of Israel will grow, they will inherit their own land, but they will also be God's commonwealth for all peoples.

Gentiles are naturally "separate from Messiah, aliens to the commonwealth [politeia] of Israel, and foreigners to the covenants of promise, having no hope and without God in the world." (Eph.2:12) Paul said that it is "my brethren, my kinsmen according to the flesh, who are descendants of Israel, to whom belongs the right as sons and the glory and the covenants and the giving of the Law and the service and the promises, whose are the fathers, and from whom is the Messiah according to the flesh, who is over all, God blessed forever. Amen." (Rom.9:3-5) These are the things that pertain to salvation and redemption.

By nature, Gentiles belong to another domain and dominion. By nature, they are foreigners, without the rights and responsibilities of citizenship in Israel. They are not naturally *bnay eer*, i.e. sons of the city. Their natural allegiance is to a city other than Jerusalem. But, contrary to nature, God is able and willing to graft individual Gentiles who trust Him into Israel's olive tree.

When the fullness of the Gentiles comes in, a major part of God's work of redemption and restoration will have taken place. John saw the final remnant of Israel sealed for God. "After this I looked and there before me was a great multitude that no one could count, from every nation, tribe, people and language, standing before the throne and in front of the Lamb." (Rev. 7:9a)

By pledging eternal allegiance to Israel's rightful king, Gentiles gain citizenship in the commonwealth of Israel. Israel's rightful king is the Lord of all the earth. By pledging eternal allegiance to him, Gentiles find their place in the Messianic Kingdom of God, which will fill all the earth.

Being descendants of Adam, most Jews did not trust/believe/obey God. They owed Him allegiance, but they did not give it to Him. Nevertheless, God always kept at least a remnant in Israel faithful to Himself. Paul and Kefa, Matthew and Mark, Silas, Barnabas, Apollos, and tens of thousands of others were part of the faithful remnant in their day.

Even today, most Jews have not entered into their own calling and purpose. Nevertheless, God's gifts to them and calling of them remain irrevocable. (cf. Rom.11:29) And in the consummation of God's purpose in this age, all Israel at the end of this age will be saved. As Paul reminded the repentant Gentiles, "After all, if you were cut out of an olive tree that is wild by nature, and contrary to nature were grafted into a cultivated olive tree, how much more readily will these, the natural branches, be grafted into their own olive tree!' (Rom. 11:24)

Gentiles who recognize the sovereignty of Messiah, the King of the Jews, are brought into the commonwealth of Israel alongside the faithful Jewish remnant. The King of the Jews reigns over them, too. "So then, you [Gentiles] are no longer strangers and foreigners, but you are fellow-citizens [sumpolitai] with those set apart [i.e. the Jewish believers], and are built upon the apostles' and prophets' foundation; Yeshua the Messiah being the cornerstone." (cf. Eph.2:19-20)

Believing Gentiles retain their identity as Gentiles, because that is the good thing that God created them to be. They retain their identity as Gentiles so that Abraham might be "the father of a multitude of Gentiles," and so that Jacob might enclose "a company of Gentiles." But they receive their life through Israel's olive tree (cf. Rom.11:17-24), so that they might be part of the commonwealth of Israel that God is establishing in the earth.

The Messianic King of Israel is the King of all who reign as kings, and Lord of all who reign as lords. (cf. 1 Tim. 6:15) But the rulers of the earth do not acknowledge Messiah as their Lord and King. They do not exercise their rule in submission to him. They are in defiant rebellion. That will change, because there is no authority except that which is from God. Messiah will rule over all the earth, a rule characterized by justice, peace, and joy in the Holy Spirit. He will raise up leaders in his own likeness and image.

God entrusted the message of redemption to the Jewish people, and brought it to the

Gentiles through them. The commonwealth of Israel remains the context of redemption for all peoples. As Yeshua said quite simply, "Salvation is from the Jews." Gentiles who have not been grafted into Israel's olive tree, and brought into the commonwealth of Israel, are still aliens from the covenants of promise, without hope, and without God.

It is, of course, possible for an individual to be ignorant of what God has done in his or her life. The ignorance would not change the reality, but it would cause confusion. It would hinder a person from properly responding to the grace of God.

For Gentiles who believe, no matter what they call themselves, the situation is similar to that faced by Naaman, the leprous commander of the Syrian army. He wanted to be healed, and that necessitated going to the prophet in Israel. (cf. 2Kgs. 5:8) He was willing to do that, but he was unwilling to humble himself and acknowledge that only the waters of Israel could cleanse him. "Naaman was furious and went away and said, '...Are not Abanah and Pharpar, the rivers of Damascus, better than all the waters of Israel? Could I not wash in them and be clean?' So he turned and went away in a rage." (2Kings 5:10–12)

Naaman's servants encouraged him to humble himself and be obedient. He did that, and he was healed. Then he proclaimed, "Now I know that there is no God in all the world except in Israel.... Please let me, your servant, be given as much earth as a pair of mules can carry, for your servant will never again make burnt offerings and sacrifices to any other god but the LORD." (2Kgs. 5:15-17) Naaman intended to make an altar in Syria from the soil of Israel so that he might sacrifice to the LORD, the God of Israel. Perhaps he didn't need the soil, but he had come to understand that only the God of Israel is God.

CONTRARY TO NATURE, GENTILES WHO BELIEVE/OBEY ARE GRAFTED INTO ISRAEL'S OLIVE TREE, THE TREE WHICH GOD HAS CULTIVATED FOR THOUSANDS OF YEARS.

It is not a question of which people is the best. None of them are. It is not a question of which people is the greatest. God chooses that which is least. It is simply a question of determining how God has designed the world, and how He brings redemption to it. As a Syrian, Naaman chose to serve the LORD God of Israel, rather than the gods of Syria.

Gentiles who believe/obey have become "fellow-partakers [with the faithful Jewish remnant] of the promise in Yeshua the Messiah." What exactly did God promise to Israel? The promise includes the Spirit of holiness (Acts 1:4), Israel's Savior and redeemer (Acts 13:23), the forgiveness of sin (Acts 13:32-39), the resurrection to life (Acts 26:6-8), and the legal right as sons in God's family (2Co.6:17-7:1). It includes knowing God and walking with Him. All of these things are available in God's New Covenant with Israel. All of these are available to Gentiles who enter into Israel's community of nations, i.e. the promised *kahal goyim*. None of these are available outside the commonwealth of Israel.

Contrary to nature, Gentiles who believe/obey are grafted into Israel's olive tree, the tree which God has cultivated for thousands of years. There, along with believing Israel, they receive their life from God. They receive their rights and their responsibilities.

Though the world is still filled with many who long to be the last great emperor, the sun has set on the great human empires. "But for you who fear My Name, the Sun of righteousness will arise with healing in its wings. And you will go out and leap like calves released from the stall" (Mal. 3:20/4:2E)

FOOTNOTES

1. Nicole Roth, http://athena.english.vt.edu/~jmooney/3044annotationsp-z/sunneversets.html
2. These two paragraphs are modified from "The Commonwealth of Israel," in my book, *The Church and the Jews: The Biblical Relationship.*

CHAPTER TWENTY

# Time for New Leadership

The eternal relationship between God and the Jewish people rests upon His nature. Because He is who He is, He is faithful. Because He does not change, His relationship with the descendants of Jacob stays intact. (cf. Mal. 3:6)

Let's look at two more scriptural passages which are very important in the traditional teaching that God has rejected and replaced the Jewish people. In both cases, the ancient tradition ignores and contradicts the actual text. Nothing in either text suggests what the tradition confidently asserts.

## THE PARABLE OF THE VINEYARD

In Matthew 21, Yeshua has a succession of confrontations with the ruling theopolitical officials. He throws out those who are buying and selling in the Temple. He overturns the tables of the moneychangers. He silences the chief priests and the elders of the people when they challenge his authority. He directs a parable to them about a father and his two sons, concluding, "Truly I say to you that the tax-gatherers and harlots will get into the kingdom of God before you." (v.31) He directly challenges the chief priests and elders, saying that they are serving themselves rather than ruling for God.

He then tells the parable of a landowner who rented out his vineyard to men who repaid him by beating and killing his servants and his son. Then he concludes the parable. "Yeshua said to them, 'Did you never read in the Scriptures, *The stone which the builders rejected, this became the chief cornerstone; this came about from the LORD and it is marvelous in our eyes?*

" 'Therefore I tell you that the kingdom of God will be taken away from you and given to a people who will produce its fruit.... 'And when the chief priests and the Pharisees heard his parables, they understood that he was speaking about them." (vv.42-45, citing Ps. 118:22)

The chief priests and the Pharisees understood that Yeshua was speaking about them. That is to say that the chief priests and Pharisees understood correctly that Yeshua was speaking about them. Yeshua said that the kingdom would be taken away from the chief priests and the Pharisees.

At that time, the chief priests and Pharisees were the rulers in Israel. They claimed both the authority of God and the authority of Rome. They were the builders who had rejected Messiah, the chief cornerstone. Therefore, Yeshua said, they would no longer be keepers of the LORD's vineyard, which is Israel (cf. Is.5:7). They would no longer rule over Israel, the kingdom of God (e.g. Ex. 19:6).

Before he was to die, King David gave Solomon, and the people, final instructions from the LORD. "Of all my sons —and the LORD has given me many —He has chosen my son Solomon to sit on the throne of the kingdom of the LORD, over Israel." (1Chr. 28:5) In sitting **on the throne of Israel, Solomon would sit on** "on the throne of the kingdom of the LORD," "So **Solomon sat on the throne of the LORD as king in place of his father David.**" (1Chr. 29:23a)

THE ANCIENT TRADITION CLAIMS THAT YESHUA SAID THE KINGDOM WOULD BE TAKEN AWAY FROM ISRAEL. THAT SEVERELY DISTORTS THE TEXT.

Mark and Luke record the same confrontation between Yeshua and the theopolitical rulers in the same way. "Then they looked for a way to arrest him because they knew he had spoken the parable against them. But they were afraid of the crowd; so they left him and went away." (Mark 12:12) "The teachers of the law and the chief priests wanted to arrest him immediately, because they knew he had spoken this parable against them. But they were afraid of the people." (Luke 20:19)

The ancient tradition claims that Yeshua said the kingdom would be taken away from Israel. That severely distorts the text. The people of Israel welcomed Yeshua and his teaching; so much so that the rulers, who were concerned only for their own power, were afraid to act against him. They wanted to arrest Yeshua, because he was exposing them for what they were, but they feared what the people would do if they did.

Josephus speaks of the number of Pharisees as 6000 men.[1] They may have outnumbered the Sadducees, but they were still a small minority in Israel. They were a much smaller group than those Jews who eagerly followed Yeshua. And some of the Pharisees, like Nicodemus, chose to follow Yeshua. Shortly after the resurrection, those Pharisees who did not believe in Yeshua were a much smaller group than all the Jews who did. And even some of those Pharisees who did not believe, like Saul of Tarsus, later came to faith in him. (cf. Acts 15:5)

Even among the Sadducees, there were those who chose to believe in him. "So the word of

God spread. The number of disciples in Jerusalem increased rapidly, and a large number of priests became obedient to the faith." (Acts 6:7)

But the theopolitical rulers as a whole were judged for the evil of their exploitation of the sheep of God's pasture. God had promised this judgment before. He had brought this judgment before. God had appointed rulers in Israel who had then turned away from Him. At specific times, God replaced those rulers. For example, he rejected Saul, and chose David.

He told Ezekiel, "Son of man, prophesy against the shepherds of Israel; prophesy and say to them: 'This is what the Sovereign LORD says: *Woe to the shepherds of Israel who only take care of themselves! Should not shepherds take care of the flock? You eat the curds, clothe yourselves with the wool and slaughter the choice animals, but you do not take care of the flock.... I am against the shepherds and will hold them accountable for My flock. I will remove them from tending the flock so that the shepherds can no longer feed themselves. I will rescue My flock from their mouths, and it will no longer be food for them.*'" (Ezek. 34:2-3,10)

God is the Shepherd of Israel. Israel is His flock. He appointed human shepherds to care for His flock. God promised to remove those human shepherds who exploit His flock.

He told Zechariah, "My anger burns against the shepherds, and I will punish the leaders; for the LORD Almighty will care for His flock, the house of Judah, and make them like a proud horse in battle. From Judah will come the cornerstone, from him the tent peg, from him the battle bow, from him every ruler." ( Zech. 10:3-4)

God entrusted His flock, the house of Judah, to shepherds, to leaders. Some of them served themselves rather than the flock. For what they did, they deserved punishment. God Himself promised to bring forth from Judah the cornerstone and the new leaders.

And in the context of a Messianic promise, God told Jeremiah, "Therefore this is what the LORD, the God of Israel, says to the shepherds who tend **My people**: 'Because you have scattered **My flock** and driven them away and have not bestowed care on them, I will bestow punishment on you for the evil you have done.... I Myself will gather the remnant of **My flock** out of all the countries where I have driven them and will bring them back to their pasture, where they will be fruitful and increase in number. I will place shepherds over them who will tend them, and they will no longer be afraid or terrified, nor will any be missing,' declares the LORD.

"'The days are coming,' declares the LORD, 'when I will raise up to David a righteous Branch, a King who will reign wisely and do what is just and right in the land. In his days Judah will be saved and Israel will live in safety. This is the name by which he will be called: *The LORD Our Righteousness.*'" (Jer. 23:2-6)

Israel had shepherds, but they were self-seeking. So God Himself promised to regather His flock, and bring it back to its pasture, the land of Israel. He promised to punish the evil shepherds and replace them with ones who would serve His flock, the same old flock that was being neglected. He doesn't speak of replacing the people, because He says that Israel is "My people," "My flock". He speaks of replacing the leaders.

Yeshua rebuked the corrupt leaders of Israel. He had compassion on the people of Israel, because they were as sheep without a shepherd. He wept for Jerusalem, and he appointed new Jewish leaders to care for the same people that God had brought out of Egypt. He told the twelve, "Truly I say to you, that you who have followed Me, in the time of restoration when the Son of Man will sit on His glorious throne, you also shall sit upon twelve thrones, judging the twelve tribes of Israel." (Mt.19:16-28; cf. Lk.22:28)

> HE DOESN'T SPEAK OF REPLACING THE PEOPLE, BECAUSE HE SAYS THAT ISRAEL IS "MY PEOPLE," "MY FLOCK." HE SPEAKS OF REPLACING THE LEADERS.

God took the kingdom away from the rulers of Israel who were abusing His people, and gave it to rulers who would serve them. God did not cast off His people; He removed and replaced their leaders.

As Peter wrote to the elders of the communities in Diaspora, "Be shepherds of God's flock that is under your care, serving as overseers—not because you must, but because you are willing, as God wants you to be; not greedy for money, but eager to serve; not lording it over those entrusted to you, but being examples to the flock." (1Pet. 5:2-3)

The parable of the landowner appears in Matthew, Mark, and Luke. In each account, Yeshua very clearly tells the chief priests and Pharisees that "the kingdom of God will be taken away from you." The kingdom cannot be left in the hands of those who reject the King. It must be put in the hands of those who are committed, with their lives, to serving the King.

Yeshua said nothing about replacing Israel with a different people. Nor did he say anything about replacing the old Israel with a new Israel. There is no "new Israel" mentioned in the Bible. The phrase does not appear. There is no "spiritual Israel" mentioned in the Bible. Nor is there a "reconstituted" Israel. Israel remains Israel. Within Israel, there is the faithful remnant, which has both physical descent from Abraham, Isaac, and Jacob, and also their faith.

In this parable, the text affirms that 1) Israel is God's kingdom; 2) the people of Israel welcomed Yeshua; and 3) authority over Israel is to be taken away from the chief priests and Pharisees, and given to those who will enable the Lord's vineyard to bring forth fruit. His vineyard will fill the earth with fruit.

Yeshua said to his disciples, "In the time of restoration, when the Son of Adam will sit on the throne of his glory, I tell you truly that you who have followed me, you also will sit on twelve thrones, judging the twelve tribes of Israel." (Mt. 19:28) Messiah will rule over all the earth, with his servants. He entrusts rule over Israel to his servants from Israel. Jews will rule over Israel, God's flock, God's people.

Instead of recognizing what is explicit in the parable, commentator after commentator, theologian after theologian blindly follows the tradition that claims the parable contains a rejection of Israel. That is what their tradition maintains, but there is nothing in the text to support it. They are unable to distinguish between their tradition and the reality of the text.

The astronomers and mathematicians who were contemporaries of Copernicus were not incompetent. They were highly skilled. But their allegiance belonged to the tradition more than it did to the facts.

There are many such cases where the ancient Christian tradition produces an "interpretation" in defiance of the text, and always in an anti-Jewish way. Let's look at one more that may be the most popular. The "interpretation" fits the tradition, but it does not fit the text in any way.

## THE PARABLE OF THE WINESKINS

"They said to him, 'John's disciples often fast and pray, and so do the disciples of the Pharisees, but yours go on eating and drinking.'

"Yeshua answered, 'Can you make the guests of the bridegroom fast while he is with them? But the time will come when the bridegroom will be taken from them; in those days they will fast.'

"He told them this parable: 'No one tears a patch from a new garment and sews it on an old one. If he does, he will have torn the new garment, and the patch from the new will not match the old. And no one pours new wine into old wineskins. If he does, the new wine will burst the skins, the wine will run out and the wineskins will be ruined. No, new wine must be poured into new wineskins. And no one after drinking old wine wants the new, for he says, 'The old is better.' " (Lk. 5:33-39; Mt. 9:14-17, cf. Mk. 2:18-22)

Many commentators claim that Yeshua was saying that the Law and God's relationship with Israel had passed away. Such claims are totally unrelated to and inconsistent with the text. Let's look at some of the commentators, then we'll look at the text.

Adam Clarke said: " 'The new wine will burst the bottles'—Both parables illustrate the incompatibility of the old and the new; of the life under the law (of Moses) and that under grace, (the Gospel;)... 'The old is better'—As Jesus had just shown how unsuitable and injurious it would be to bind up the essence and the life of the new theocracy with the forms and institutions of the old, so now he once more, by means of a parable, makes it intelligible how natural it is that the disciples of John and of the Pharisees should not be able to consent to the giving up of the old forms and institutions that had become dear to them, and to the exchanging of them for the new life in accordance with its fundamental principles."[2]

Clarke's commentary is typical. By his interpretation, Yeshua equated the fasting of the disciples of John and that of the disciples of the Pharisees with life under the law of Moses. But fasting does not represent the Law, and Yeshua said that, "The time will come when the bridegroom will be taken from them; then they [i.e. his disciples] will fast." By Clarke's interpretation, that would mean that after the death of Yeshua, his disciples will then embrace "life under the law of Moses" and "the old forms and institutions."

As for the incompatibility of Moses and the Gospel, Yeshua didn't know anything about it. To the contrary, he said, "If you believed Moses, you would believe me, for he wrote about me. But since you do not believe what he wrote, how are you going to believe what I say?" (John 5:47) In other words, someone who rejects Moses is in no position to believe Yeshua. Yeshua was saying that the problem with those sectarian Jews was not their allegiance to Moses, but quite the opposite, that they did not believe Moses.

Neither Paul nor any of the other "apostles" knew anything about the incompatibility of the Law and the Gospel. As Paul told Felix, "I believe everything that agrees with the Law and that is written in the Prophets." (Acts 24:14) Paul wrote about the inability of the Law of Moses to bring salvation, but that is something quite different. Refraining from murder will not save me, but it is in no way incompatible with "the Gospel". Loving my mother will not save me, but it's still a good idea.

We have adequate evidence that all the Jewish followers of Yeshua sought to live in accordance with the Law. For example, as Jacob told Paul in Jerusalem, "You see, brother, how many tens of thousands of Jews have believed, and all of them are zealous for the law." (Acts 21:20)

In the second century, Irenaeus recorded that "Thus did the Apostles, whom the Lord made witnesses of every action and of every doctrine...scrupulously act according to the dispensation of the Mosaic law."[3] He also condemns those who claimed that the Law of Moses is opposed to the gospel. "For all those who are of a perverse mind, having been set against the Mosaic legislation judging it to be dissimilar and contrary to the doctrine of the gospel, have not applied themselves to investigate the causes of the differences of each covenant."[4]

In the parable, Yeshua says that everyone knows that old wine is better than new wine. Clarke rejects this simple statement of fact, and argues instead that new wine is actually better than old wine. Clarke seems to be the one who is "not be able to consent to the giving up of the *old* forms and institutions that had become dear to [him]."

And what is the nature of the "the *new* life in accordance with its fundamental principles"? Yeshua summed it up in the great commandments of the law of Moses: Love the Lord your God with all your heart, soul, strength, and mind (Dt.6:5); and, love your neighbor as yourself. (Lev. 19:18) The fundamental principles of the new life are the same as the fundamental principles of human life ever since Mankind was created in the image and likeness of God.

A. T. Robertson said: "It is the philosophy of the obscurantist, that is here pictured by Christ. 'The prejudiced person will not even try the new, or admit that it has any merits. He knows that the old is pleasant, and suits him; and that is enough; he is not going to change' (Plummer). This is Christ's picture of the reactionary Pharisees."[5]

Yeshua relates a simple fact: given the choice between new wine and old wine, people will choose the old wine, because it is better. "No one after drinking old wine wants the new, for he says, 'The old is better.'" This is not a prejudice, it is a truth that people know from experience. The text says nothing about prejudice and refusing to try the new wine. Old wine is better, and people know it.[6]

Yeshua was asked was about fasting. There is nothing "reactionary" about fasting. God commends it. (e.g. Is. 58) Yeshua takes it for granted that those who seek righteousness will fast— "when you fast..." (Mt. 6:16-18) Robertson does not tie his interpretation to the text, he simply rejects the simple statement of fact, and asserts the opposite.

Yeshua was asked why his disciples didn't fast like the disciples of John and the disciples of the Pharisees. Andrew had been a disciple of John; Nicodemus and Paul had been disciples of the Pharisees. There is no philosophy being pictured here; it is a discussion of fasting.

Robertson doesn't want to call a disciple of John, like Andrew, an "obscurantist," a "prejudiced person," and a "reactionary". So he ignores the fact that the question is asked about them, too. It is only his own prejudice that leads him to attack the Pharisees. His own prejudice leads him to proclaim something unrelated to and contrary to the text.

E. Earle Ellis said: "The two parables illustrate the dichotomy between Christianity and traditional Judaism. To mix the 'new' with the 'old' will ruin both. Each has its place, but the new is more than the old revised. In the context of the pre-resurrection mission the issue was fasting. Luke's readers doubtless applied the Saviour's words to other issues (cf. Gal. 5:2ff)."[7]

Yeshua says nothing about Christianity. He says nothing about traditional Judaism. Neither one of them existed at the time. Nor did he say anything about the new being more than the old revised. He did say that the old is better than the new. These comments of Ellis do not relate to the text; they all come from his commitment to the ancient tradition.

It is true that, in the text, the issue is fasting; and it is probable that some of Luke's readers have "applied the Saviour's words to other issues." Ellis certainly did. But that does not tell us what Yeshua was talking about. If, following Ellis, fasting is equated with traditional Judaism, and not fasting is equated with Christianity, then Yeshua said that after his death, his disciples would turn to traditional Judaism.

Ellis does not bother to try to connect his interpretation to the actual statements in the parables. In fact, his interpretation is not connected to the actual statements in the parables. The failure of the commentators to deal with the text keeps them from noticing how contrary to the text their traditional interpretations of the two parables are. This is not interpretation.

According to these and similar commentaries, Yeshua ignored the question about fasting that he was asked. But we know that he didn't ignore the question, since the text tells us that "Yeshua answered, 'Can you make the guests of the bridegroom fast while he is with them? But the time will come when the bridegroom will be taken from them; in those days they will fast.'" Then he told them the two parables to illustrate his point.

IF FASTING IS EQUATED WITH TRADITIONAL JUDAISM IN THE PARABLE OF THE WINESKINS...THEN YESHUA SAID THAT AFTER HIS DEATH, HIS DISCIPLES WOULD TURN TO TRADITIONAL JUDAISM.

The commentators never connect the parables with the point Yeshua made. This is true not only of English commentators. It is the practice throughout Christendom, and throughout the centuries.

For example, "the *Slovo o zakone i o blagodeti* (*Discourse on Law and Grace*), attributed to the monk Ilarion of Kiev, dates back to the 'Golden Age' of Rus' culture. Internal evidence suggests that it was written ca. 1047-50. According to Simon Franklin, this sermon 'is *the* masterpiece of eleventh-century Kievan writing…, a superb demonstration of stylistic virtuosity, a cogent and forceful specimen of theological and historical exegesis, a major monument of Kievan culture and thought.'"[8]

It may well be all that, but it just isn't accurate. Here is Ilarion's rendition of the parable of the wineskins: "[Men] do not pour new wine, the teaching of Grace, into old skins, those having become antiquated in Jewry, otherwise the skins will burst and the wine will spill out."[9]

Ilarion inserts his own commentary into the quotation. By inserting it, Ilarion was advancing the standard Christian interpretation of this parable, namely: the old wine is the Law, and the old wineskins are the Jews and their religion; the new wine is Grace, and the new wineskins are the new Christian peoples and their religion.

This interpretation, like the others, makes no sense. To begin with, God's grace is not something that begins in the first century of this era. "Noa<u>h</u> found grace in the eyes of the Lord." (Gen. 6:8)

And, to repeat, the parable was told in response to a question about fasting. Fasting is just as much a part of the New Covenant as it is of the Old. It has nothing to do with whether one is Jewish or not.

Moreover, the version in Luke ends with the statement that "no one, after drinking old [wine] wishes for new; for he says, 'The old is better.' If we accept Ilarion's standard Christian exegesis, then, this phrase indicates that no one, after experiencing the Law, wishes for Grace; for the Law, like aged wine, is better.[10] If that were the case, then none of Yeshua's disciples, who were all Jewish and experienced in the Law, would have wished for Grace. And again, Ilarion's interpretation means that if Yeshua's disciples had somehow accepted God's grace, then after Yeshua is taken away from them, they will turn to the things that have "become antiquated in Jewry."

Commentator after commentator already knows that God has rejected the Jews and replaced them with the Christians. Everybody knows that. So it doesn't really matter what the text actually says. The text is only allowed to reaffirm what everybody already knows. The tradition demands that the text be interpreted to reaffirm what everybody knows.

How then should we understand the parables? In context, of course. Forget the tradition, and read the text for what it says.

Yeshua has been asked a particular question: 'John's disciples and the disciples of the Pharisees are fasting, why aren't yours?' He responds to that question by saying that it is not appropriate for his disciples to fast now, but it will be appropriate for them to fast after he is taken from them. To illustrate his answer, he tells two, or actually three, parables.

The first is about the bridegroom and the "sons of the huppah," i.e. "the friends of the bridegroom who prepared for him the bridal-chamber and attended on him at the wedding."[11] Yeshua compares himself to the bridegroom, and his disciples to the sons of the huppah. The time of the wedding and the preparation for it is a joyful time for them. Because of the Biblical importance of marriage, they were not required to observe some other aspects of the Law. The Talmud says, "A bridegroom and the best man, and all the wedding guests are free from the obligation of Sukkah all the seven days."[12]

Fasting is not appropriate for them then. To understand Yeshua's answer, we need to know when fasting is appropriate, and, therefore, what the purpose of fasting is.

David fasted to entreat God that his newborn son might recover and not die. (cf. 2Sam. 12:23) Jehoshaphat fasted because an enemy army was coming against him. (cf. 2Chr.20:3) Ezra fasted for protection. (cf. Ez.8:21) Daniel fasted for the restoration of Jerusalem. (cf. Dan.9:3) The king and inhabitants of Nineveh fasted to be saved from the judgment decreed against them. (cf. Jon.3:5) And the Lord commanded all Judah, "Even now, return to Me with all your heart, with fasting and weeping and mourning." (Joel 2:12)

Perhaps the best description of the purpose of fasting is given by God in Isaiah 58. "Is not this the kind of fasting I have chosen: to loose the chains of injustice and untie the cords of the yoke, to set the oppressed free and break every yoke? Is it not to share your food with the hungry and to provide the poor wanderer with shelter—when you see the naked, to clothe him, and not to turn away from your own flesh and blood?" (Is. 58:6-7)

These are always good things to do. At the end of this age, Yeshua will judge the nations on whether or not they did these things to the Jewish people. (cf. Mt. 25:31-46) These are things that Yeshua came to do. He himself fasted forty days and forty nights before he began his work. (cf. Mt. 4:2)

Nevertheless, it was not appropriate for his disciples to be fasting at that time, because the Liberator, the Provider, was present with them. Ultimately, the purpose of fasting is to bring near the presence and power of the kingdom of God. But that presence and power was right there with them, because he, as both the King and the Bridegroom, was there with them. They were witnessing, before their own eyes, the fulfillment of the purpose of fasting as presented in Is. 58.

They were witnessing the fulfillment of why Yeshua came, as prophetically presented in Isaiah 61:1-3. "The Spirit of the Lord God is on me, because the Lord has anointed me to preach good news to the poor. He has sent me to bind up the brokenhearted, to proclaim freedom for the captives and release from darkness for the prisoners, to proclaim the year of the Lord's favor and the day of vengeance of our God, to comfort all who mourn, and provide for those who grieve in Zion—to bestow on them a crown of beauty instead of ashes, the oil of gladness instead of mourning, and a garment of praise instead of a spirit of despair. They will be called oaks of righteousness, a planting of the Lord for the display of His splendor." (cf. Lk.4:16-21)

That is why, "When John heard in prison what Messiah was doing, he sent his disciples to ask him, 'Are you the one who was to come, or should we expect someone else?'

"Yeshua replied, 'Go back and report to John what you hear and see: The blind receive sight, the lame walk, those who have leprosy are cured, the deaf hear, the dead are raised, and the good news is proclaimed to the poor.'" (Mt. 11:2-5)

Consequently, fasting while Yeshua was with them would have been redundant, and would have indicated doubt in what was taking place. When Yeshua was taken from them—i.e. after the crucifixion, resurrection, and ascension—then they would fast. Then it would be appropriate in seeking the Kingdom of God.

Yeshua was not opposed to fasting. He taught, "When you fast, do not... But when you fast,... and your Father, who sees what is done in secret, will reward you." (Mt. 6:16-18) Yeshua said that the Father in heaven will reward those who humbly fast for appropriate purposes.

After Yeshua was taken from them, his disciples did fast. "While they were worshiping the Lord and fasting, the Holy Spirit said, 'Set apart for me Barnabas and Saul for the work to which I have called them.'" (Acts 13:2) "Paul and Barnabas appointed elders for them in each congregation and, with prayer and fasting, committed them to the Lord, in whom they had put their trust." (Acts 14:23)

The response of Yeshua to the question he was asked was not at all related to traditional Church condemnations of the Law of Moses and the people of Israel. Yeshua's response addressed the question, focusing on when it was appropriate to fast, and when it was not. The disciples were with the bridegroom, and it was appropriate for them to rejoice in that and in the liberation which he brought.

The first parable that Yeshua told to illustrate his point about fasting concerned an old garment that is torn. At that time, one did not throw out a garment simply because it needed to be patched. One patched it. Yeshua does not suggest that old garments should be thrown out when they tear.

He explained that it makes no sense to tear up a new garment to patch an old one. That would simply ruin both garments. It is appropriate to patch an old garment with material that has been shrunk and prepared. In the translations of Matthew and Mark, there is not even a mention of two garments that could, in some way, be compared. The issue is simply how to patch an old garment, an illustration of what is appropriate and what is not.[13]

Then Yeshua tells the parable of the wineskins. There is joy in the time of harvest, because there would be no provision for the coming year without that harvest. But much of the harvest, including the fruit of the vine, has to be prepared before it is consumed. The grapes are put in a vat and crushed to provide the juice to make wine. It takes time to make aged wine. There is a turbulent, lengthy process that must take place within the vessel that stores the wine. One rejoices in the new wine, but lets as much as possible of it remain in its containers until it becomes old wine.

The process of new wine aging puts pressure on the vessel in which it is contained. In the parable, the wine is contained in wineskins. As Job said, "inside I am like bottled-up wine, like new wineskins ready to burst." (Job 32:19) New wineskins are more flexible and can expand with the pressure. New wine is put into wineskins so that it can age.

Everybody knows, except for a few theologians, that aged wine is better tasting and more desirable than new wine, and that people will spend more to obtain it. New wine, which requires less time to produce, is poorer tasting and cheaper. New wine does not, in the Scriptures, represent God's grace or God's spirit. In fact, "Harlotry, wine, and new wine enslave the heart." (Hos. 4:11)

> EVERYBODY KNOWS THAT
> AGED WINE IS BETTER
> TASTING AND MORE
> DESIRABLE THAN NEW
> WINE, AND THAT PEOPLE
> WILL SPEND MORE TO
> OBTAIN IT.

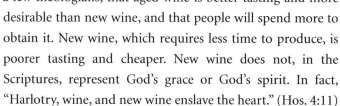

Every translator must make particular decisions in light of what he or she believes the text as a whole, and even the Scriptures as a whole, have to say. That is unavoidable. But sometimes translators impose their theology, or that of the ancient tradition, upon the text. That is avoidable. It distorts the text, and should be avoided.

For example, the NASV gives Lk. 5:39b as: "the old is good enough." In this case, "enough" is in italics to indicate that it is not found in the original text, but implied by it. But "enough" is not implied by the text. Its inclusion is only implied by the anti-Judaic tradition. It distorts, rather than completes, the plain sense of the text. It implies that new wine is better than old, which is the opposite of reality.

On Shavuot following the resurrection, when the Holy Spirit was poured out upon the Jewish disciples, they began to praise God in other tongues. They were mocked by some of the bystanders because of their unusual behavior: "They have had too much new wine." (Acts 2:13b) In other words, 'They're drunk on bad, cheap wine.' This is the mockery of ignorant bystanders. It is not God equating the Holy Spirit and new wine.

Yeshua was asked why his disciples weren't fasting. He answered the question he was asked. He illustrated his answer with parables. He explained that it was inappropriate for his disciples to fast at that time, but they would fast after he was taken from them. To everything there is a time and a season.

Whether in translation or interpretation, there is no textual reason to turn the parables into something that is unrelated to both the question and the rest of Yeshua's answer. The anti-Judaic interpretation ignores the data of the text, because the data does not fit the theological tradition. The tradition is invoked in order to nullify the text and create the illusion of a different, new context for redemption.

FOOTNOTES

1. Josephus, *Antiquities of the Jews*, 17, 2.4

2. *The New Testament, with Commentary* by Adam Clarke, Vol.5, Eaton & Mains, NY, 1884, p.241, citing John Peter Lange and Heinrich August Wilhelm Meyer

3. Irenaeus, "Against Heresies," *Ante-Nicene Christian Library, Vol.5/1*, trans. by A. Roberts and J. Donaldson, T & T Clark, Edinburgh, 1867, pp.313-314

4. ibid., p. 309

5. Archibald T. Robertson, *The Gospel According to Luke, Vol.2*, Broadman Press, Nashville, 1930, p.79

6. The Talmud places "old wine" among those things "which are beneficial for the whole body. Pes.42b

7. E. Earle Ellis, *The New Century Bible Commentary*, The Gospel of Luke, Wm. B. Eerdmans Pub. Co., Grand Rapids, 1996, p. 107

8. Simon Franklin, *Sermons and Rhetoric of Kievan Rus'*, (Cambridge: Harvard University Press, 1991), xxxi.

9. Aleksandr M. Moldovan, *"Slovo o zakone i blagodati"* Ilariona (Kiev: Naukova Dumka, 1984), 88; cf. Franklin, 13.

10. This section on Ilarion is taken from the paper, "A Preliminary Study of the Biblical Misquotes in Ilarion's Slovo", by Isaiah Gruber, 1998

11. Sukkah 25b, Soncino n.31, citing V. Mann, J., HUCA I, p. 335

12. Sukkah 25b

13. In Luke's translation, there are two garments, or materials, one old and one new, but there is no comparison between them. It is interesting that Luke uses the word imatiou to translate the word that Yeshua used for both the old garment, or material, and the new. We find this same word in the translation of the parable in Matthew 9:16. It then appears in Mt. 9:20-21: "Just then a woman who had been subject to bleeding for twelve years came up behind him and touched the *tzitzit* of his garment/*imatiou*. She said to herself, 'If I only touch his garment/*imatiou*, I will be healed.'" (cf. Mark 5:27-28; Luke 8:44) The word also appears in Mt. 14:36: People "begged him to let the sick just touch the *tzitzit* of his garment/*imatiou*, and all who touched him were healed." (cf. Mark 6:56)

    The *tzitzit* are the fringes commanded in the Law of Moses. (Num. 15:38-39; Dt. 22:12; cf. Zech. 8:23) The purpose of the *tzitzit* is to remind the people of Israel, throughout their generations, of the commandments of the Lord. By touching the *tzitzit* of Yeshua, people were healed. This is not, to say the least, supporting evidence for the Christian interpretation that sets the Law and the Gospel, Moses and Yeshua, in opposition to each other. It was because Yeshua lived according to the Law of Moses that he could bring such healing.

CHAPTER TWENTY-ONE

# A Choice Property

Some people think that God is not concerned with real estate. They are greatly mistaken. God made Adam from the earth and for the earth. Even as God is concerned with the descendants of Adam, so He is concerned with the earth that He made for their habitation.

God created real estate, i.e. the earth, and said that it was "very good". Its current tenants have not taken good care of it, but God intends to make it very good again. At the end of this age, there will be judgment on those who have defiled the earth. As the twenty-four elders say: "... The time has come for judging the dead, …and for destroying those who destroy the earth." (Rev. 11:18)

The land of Israel is a special place. God has chosen it for Himself. He calls it "My land". For God, it is the center of the earth. (cf. Ezek. 38:1-12) He is very concerned about what happens to it.

It may not the best location for some endeavors, but it was, and is, the perfect location for what God had planned for Abraham and his descendants. God made the land. He chose it for Abraham, Isaac, Jacob, and their descendants. The land of Israel is an integral, central part of God's calling of Abraham, an integral part of God's purpose for Abraham. In His first words to Abram, God presented the land to him as both his focus and his goal.

Perhaps Abraham had a nice place in Ur of the Chaldees, conveniently located. Perhaps his business was doing well, and he planned to retire early at the age of 110 or at least by 120. But God told him that it was time to relocate.

"Leave your country, your people and your father's household and go to the land I will show you. I will make you into a great nation and I will bless you; I will make your name great, and you will be a blessing. I will bless those who bless you, and whoever curses you I will curse; and all peoples on earth will be blessed in you." (Gen. 12:1-3)

The first part of Abram's faith and obedience was to leave the physical, geographical location where he was and go to the land that God had chosen for him and his descendants. It was only by going to the land that Abram would receive the promises of God.

The land is an indispensable part of God's purpose in calling Abraham. "I am the LORD, who brought you out of Ur of the Chaldeans to give you this land to take possession of it." (Gen. 15:7) God had something very concrete, very geographic, in mind in calling Abraham out of Ur. The purpose of calling Abraham out was to give him the land. What God had in mind for Abraham could not have been accomplished in Ur. The calling of Abraham cannot be separated from the land to which he was called.

In the Messianic Age, the earth will again be a beautiful place, especially Zion. Zion will then be an extremely desirable location, because Yeshua will be reigning over all the earth from there. "They will neither harm nor destroy throughout all My holy mountain, for the earth will be full of the knowledge of the LORD as the waters cover the sea." (Is. 11:9) Jerusalem will be the capital of the Kingdom of God. The land of Israel remains central to Biblical faith.

## 1. The land of Israel is an integral part of God's promise to Abraham and his descendants.

"The LORD appeared to Abram and said, 'To your offspring I will give this land.'" (Gen. 12:7a) God connected the possession of the land with the descendants He would give to Abraham. The children of Abraham are supposed to inhabit the land that God promised.

God often repeated the promise of the land to Abraham. "The LORD said to Abram after Lot had parted from him, 'Lift up your eyes from where you are and look north and south, east and west. All the land that you see I will give to you and your offspring forever. I will make your offspring like the dust of the earth, so that if anyone could count the dust, then your offspring could be counted. Go, walk through the length and breadth of the land, for I am giving it to you.'" (Gen. 13:14-17)

So when Abraham sent his servant out of the land to get a wife for Isaac, he was specific in his instructions. "The LORD, the God of heaven, who brought me out of my father's household and my native land and who spoke to me and promised me on oath, saying, 'To your offspring I will give this land'— He will send His angel before you so that you can get a wife for my son from there. If the woman is unwilling to come back with you, then you will be released from this oath of mine. Only do not take my son back there." (Gen. 24:7-8) If Rebekah had been unwilling to come to the land God promised to Abraham and his descendants, then she would not have become Isaac's wife.

"By faith Abraham, when called to go to a place he would later receive as his inheritance, obeyed and went, even though he did not know where he was going. By faith he made his home in the promised land like a stranger in a foreign country; he lived in tents, as did Isaac and Jacob, who were heirs with him of the same promise." (Hebr. 11:8-9)

Abraham himself did not then receive the land as his inheritance. Nor did Isaac and Jacob. They still have not yet personally received it. Some of their descendants have in part, but they themselves have not. But they will, because God, the God of Israel, is faithful. They will receive it in the Messianic Kingdom and in the ages to follow. "He gave him no inheritance here, not even a foot of ground. But God promised him that he and his descendants after him would possess the land, even though at that time Abraham had no child." (Acts 7:5)

### 2. The land of Israel is an integral part of the faith of Abraham.

In addition to the land being the initial focus for Abraham's faith, and in addition to his going to the land being the initial demonstration of Abraham's faith, the land itself is the specific reward for Abraham's faith.

"He took him outside and said, 'Look up at the heavens and count the stars —if indeed you can count them.' Then He said to him, 'So shall your offspring be.' Abram believed the LORD, and He credited it to him as righteousness. He also said to him, 'I am the LORD, who brought you out of Ur of the Chaldeans to give you this land to take possession of it.'" (Gen. 15:5-7) I brought you out to give you this land.

When he had no descendants, Abram believed the promise of the LORD that his descendants would be numerous, and that his descendants would possess the land. This is the faith which the LORD counted as righteousness for Abraham.

"On that day the LORD made a covenant with Abram and said, "To your descendants I give this land, from the river of Egypt to the great river, the Euphrates—the land of the Kenites, Kenizzites, Kadmonites, Hittites, Perizzites, Rephaites, Amorites, Canaanites, Girgashites and Jebusites." (Gen. 15:18-21)

God made this covenant with Abraham to give all the land to Abraham's descendants. God freely obligated Himself to do this, without requiring anything in return from Abraham or his descendants. The faith of Abraham cannot be separated from the land that was the object and reward of his faith.

### 3. The land of Israel is an integral part of God's covenant with Abraham.

In addition to the above unconditional covenant, God also included the land of Canaan as part of the covenant of circumcision, by which He made Abraham the father of the Jewish people, and also the father of many nations.

"As for Me, this is My covenant with you: You have become the father of many nations. No longer will you be called Abram; your name has become Abraham, for I have made you a father of many nations. I will make you very fruitful. I will make nations of you, and kings will come from you. I will establish My covenant as an everlasting covenant between Me and you and your descendants after you for the generations to come, to be your God and the God of your descendants after you. The whole land of Canaan, where you are now a foreigner, I will give as an everlasting possession to you and your descendants after you; and I will be their God." (Gen. 17:4-8)

God's covenant with Abraham is everlasting. So is the inheritance of the land of Canaan to Abraham's descendants. The land is given in spite of Israel's disobedience.

As Moses reminded Israel just before the people entered the land, "It is not because of your righteousness or your integrity that you are going in to take possession of their land; but on account of the wickedness of these nations, the LORD your God will drive them out before you, to accomplish what He swore to your fathers, to Abraham, Isaac and Jacob. Understand, then, that it is not because of your righteousness that the LORD your God is giving you this good land to possess, for you are a stiff-necked people. Remember this and never forget how you provoked the LORD your God to anger in the desert. From the day you left Egypt until you arrived here, you have been rebellious against the LORD." (Dt. 9:5-7)

GOD'S COVENANT WITH ABRAHAM IS EVERLASTING. SO IS THE INHERITANCE OF THE LAND OF CANAAN TO ABRAHAM'S DESCENDANTS. THE LAND IS GIVEN IN SPITE OF ISRAEL'S DISOBEDIENCE.

The eternal promise of the land is not dependent upon Israel's obedience. Israel's disobedience has consequences, one of which can be removal from the land, but it does not, it cannot, alter God's covenant with Abraham. God gave the land to Abraham, and thereby to Israel, to Abraham's physical descendants through Isaac and Jacob. He gave the land in the same covenant in which He promised to make Abraham the means of blessing to all the earth.

God's covenant with Abraham to make him the father of Israel and to make him the father of many nations cannot be separated from the land, which was part of the same everlasting promise.

## 4. The land of Israel is an integral part of God's judgment of the nations for how they treat Abraham and his descendants.

God promised Abraham, "I will bless those who bless you, and whoever curses you I will curse; and all peoples on earth will be blessed in you." (Gen. 12:1-3) The promise was repeated to

Jacob (Gen. 27:29), and to all Israel. (Num. 24:9) It is a promise to the physical descendants of Abraham, Isaac, and Jacob.

Pharaoh's Egypt tried to destroy the people of Israel. So God appeared to Moses and introduced Himself according to His promise of the land of Canaan to the fathers of Israel. "I am the God of your father, the God of Abraham, the God of Isaac and the God of Jacob.... So I have come down to rescue them from the hand of the Egyptians and to bring them up out of that land into a good and spacious land, a land flowing with milk and honey—the home of the Canaanites, Hittites, Amorites, Perizzites, Hivites and Jebusites....

"Go, assemble the elders of Israel and say to them, 'The LORD, the God of your fathers — the God of Abraham, Isaac and Jacob—appeared to me and said: I have watched over you and have seen what has been done to you in Egypt. And I have promised to bring you up out of your misery in Egypt into the land of the Canaanites, Hittites, Amorites, Perizzites, Hivites and Jebusites—a land flowing with milk and honey.'" (Ex. 3:6a, 8, 16-17)

God identifies Himself as "the God of Abraham, Isaac and Jacob," an identification which includes the promise of the land. He brings judgment on Pharaoh and Egypt because they afflicted the people of Israel and sought to keep Israel from inheriting the land. Redemption for Israel includes being brought into the land and possessing it.

> HE BRINGS JUDGMENT ON PHARAOH AND EGYPT BECAUSE THEY AFFLICTED THE PEOPLE OF ISRAEL AND SOUGHT TO KEEP ISRAEL FROM INHERITING THE LAND.

"I appeared to Abraham, to Isaac and to Jacob... I also established My covenant with them to give them the land of Canaan, where they lived as foreigners.... I am the LORD, and I will bring you out from under the yoke of the Egyptians. I will free you from being slaves to them, and I will redeem you with an outstretched arm and with mighty acts of judgment.... And I will bring you to the land I swore with uplifted hand to give to Abraham, to Isaac and to Jacob. I will give it to you as a possession. I am the LORD.'" (Ex. 6:3a, 4, 6, 8)

By an oath and by a covenant, God gave the land of Canaan to the physical descendants of Abraham, Isaac, and Jacob. Pharaoh would not let them go to their land. He wanted to keep them in bondage.

Pharaoh said, "Who is the LORD, that I should obey him and let Israel go? I do not know the LORD and I will not let Israel go." (Ex. 5:2) So the LORD enrolled Pharaoh in a continuing education program. That gave him the opportunity to learn enough to change his mind. But it was too late to save Pharaoh and Egypt from destruction.

Many centuries later, the LORD promised to judge the people of Edom and the people of every nation for their violence done to the children of Israel in the land. "Because of the violence against your brother Jacob, you will be covered with shame; you will be destroyed forever.... The day of the LORD is near for all nations. As you have done, it will be done to you; your deeds will return upon your own head." (Obad. 10,15) Those nations tried to destroy Israel; in return, they will be destroyed.

This is how it will be at the end of this age. All the nations will unite to try to keep the people of Israel from possessing the land of Israel. God will destroy all those nations who seek to do this.

"In those days and at that time, when I restore the fortunes of Judah and Jerusalem, I will gather all nations and bring them down to the Valley of Jehoshaphat. There I will enter into judgment against them concerning **My inheritance, My people Israel**, for they scattered **My people** among the nations and divided up **My land**." (Joel 3:1-2) That applies equally to those who divide the land for "political" reasons and those who divide the land for "religious" reasons.

God says that Israel is "My land". He has given it to the people of Israel. He will destroy every nation that fights against that. That will be the end of this age, an age in which the nations defy God.

"Then the LORD will go out and fight against those nations, as he fights in the day of battle. On that day His feet will stand on the Mount of Olives, east of Jerusalem... This is the plague with which the LORD will strike all the nations that fought against Jerusalem...

"Then the survivors from all the nations that have attacked Jerusalem will go up year after year to bow down to the King, the LORD of Hosts, and to celebrate the Feast of Sukkot/Tabernacles. If any of the peoples of the earth do not go up to Jerusalem to worship the King, the LORD Almighty, they will have no rain." (Zech. 14:3-4, 12, 16-17)

This age will end with the battle for Jerusalem. Does it belong to Israel? or can the nations do with it whatever they choose? The God of the Bible says that Israel is His people and His inheritance. Woe to those who think otherwise. Woe to those who think they can divide God's land. They will find themselves in the same continuing education program that God provided for Pharaoh.

"When the Most High gave the Gentiles their inheritance, when He separated the sons of Adam, He set up boundaries for the peoples according to the number of the sons of Israel. For the LORD's portion is His people, Jacob His allotted inheritance." (Dt. 32:8-9) Jacob is the portion, people, and inheritance of the LORD. The inheritance and boundaries of all the nations are set according to God's measure, Jacob. To deny the LORD His inheritance in Israel is to reject His sovereignty over all the earth.

As God's ambassador to the Gentiles, Paul tells them of how God had prophetically spoken of bringing His mercy to the Gentiles through Messiah. He quotes a few passages in Tanakh to establish this. For example, "Again, it says, 'Rejoice, O Gentiles, with His people.'" (Rom. 15:10)

Had they searched the Scriptures to gain understanding of God's intention, this is what they would have found: "Rejoice, O Gentiles, with His people, for He will avenge the blood of His servants; He will take vengeance on His enemies and make atonement for His land and people." (Dt. 32:43) Those Gentiles who have truly been grafted into Israel's olive tree will rejoice in that.

In the Messianic Age, all nations will come to Israel's capital, and bow down to Israel's King. If they refuse, they will be destroyed by drought. God's judgments on the nations, according to His promise to bless those who bless Abraham and curse those who curse him, cannot be separated from the land that God promised to Abraham.

### 5. The land of Israel is an integral part of the promise of the outpouring of the Spirit.

If we examine the prophetic scriptures in their context, we find that the promised outpouring of the Spirit is inextricably connected with the restoration of Israel and the reign of Messiah. "We cannot doubt that the Rabbinic Judaism of the first century would have regarded the Messianic Age or the Age to Come as the Era of the Spirit." It is the Spirit of God that enables the descendants of Abraham to walk in righteousness and thereby possess the land.

Yeshua explained these scriptures about the outpouring of the Spirit to his followers. It is worthwhile to take the time to look at a number of these passages, with only a minimal amount of comment—seven from Isaiah and four more from Ezekiel, Joel, and Zechariah. This will be enough to get an adequate understanding of what Yeshua taught his disciples about the outpouring of the Spirit.

1. "In that day the Branch of the LORD will be beautiful and glorious, and the fruit of the land will be the pride and glory of the survivors in Israel. Those who are left in Zion, who remain in Jerusalem, will be called holy, all who are recorded among the living in Jerusalem; when the Lord will have washed away the filth of the women of Zion; and will have cleansed the bloodstains from Jerusalem by a Spirit of justice and a Spirit of fire." (Is. 4:2-4)

   The Spirit of justice and fire is poured out to cleanse Jerusalem and the survivors in Israel, to make them holy. The Branch of the Lord, i.e. the Messiah, will make the land beautiful, glorious, and fruitful. As John, who immersed in water, said of Messiah, "He will immerse you in the Spirit of holiness and fire." (Mt. 3:11c)

2. "A shoot will come up from the stump of Jesse; from his roots a Branch will bear fruit.

The Spirit of the LORD will rest on him—the Spirit of wisdom and of understanding, the Spirit of counsel and of power, the Spirit of knowledge and of the fear of the LORD.... with righteousness he will judge the needy, with justice he will give decisions for the poor of the earth. He will strike the earth with the rod of his mouth; with the breath of his lips he will slay the wicked.... In that day the Root of Jesse will stand as a banner for the peoples; the nations will rally to him, and his place of rest will be glorious.... He will raise a banner for the nations and gather the exiles of Israel; he will assemble the scattered people of Judah from the four corners of the earth." (Is. 11:1-2,4,10,12)

The Spirit of the Lord will rest upon Messiah, the Branch, who is descended from Jesse, father of David. He will establish justice in the earth, and gather in the dispersed of Judah. He will destroy the wicked, but there will be those of the nations, i.e. the Gentiles, who come to him.

THE OUTPOURING OF THE SPIRIT WILL BRING JUSTICE, RIGHTEOUSNESS, FRUITFULNESS, AND SECURITY TO THE LAND AND PEOPLE OF ISRAEL. IN THAT DAY THERE WILL BE A RIGHTEOUS KING.

3. "Behold, a king will reign in righteousness and rulers will rule with justice.... The fortress will be abandoned, the noisy city deserted; citadel and watchtower will become a perpetual wasteland, the delight of donkeys, a pasture for flocks, until the Spirit is poured upon us from on high, and the desert becomes a fertile field, and the fertile field seems like a forest. Justice will dwell in the desert and righteousness live in the fertile field. The fruit of righteousness will be peace; the effect of righteousness will be quietness and confidence forever. My people will live in peaceful dwelling places, in secure homes, in undisturbed places of rest." (Is. 32:1, 14a,15-18)

The outpouring of the Spirit will bring justice, righteousness, fruitfulness, and security to the land and people of Israel. In that day, there will be a righteous king.

4. "Here is My servant, whom I uphold, My chosen one in whom I delight; I will put My Spirit on him and he will bring justice to the nations.... He will not falter or be discouraged till he establishes justice on earth. In his law the islands will put their hope." (Is. 42:1,4)

God puts His Spirit upon His chosen servant. His chosen servant will then bring justice to the nations and establish God's justice throughout the earth. Even the islands of the sea will submit to his law.

5. "For I will pour water on the thirsty land, and streams on the dry ground; I will pour out My Spirit on your offspring, and My blessing on your descendants. They will spring up

like grass in a meadow, like poplar trees by flowing streams. One will say, 'I belong to the LORD'; another will call himself by the name of Jacob; still another will write on his hand, 'The LORD's,' and will take the name Israel.

"This is what the LORD says—Israel's King and Redeemer, the LORD Almighty: I am the first and I am the last; apart from Me there is no God." (Is. 44:3-6)

God will pour out His Spirit on the people of Israel, who will turn to Him. The Lord will redeem Israel, and be her king.

6. "From the west, men will fear the name of the LORD, and from the rising of the sun, they will revere His glory. For He will come like a pent-up flood that the Spirit of the LORD drives along.

"'The Redeemer will come to Zion, to those in Jacob who repent of their sins,' declares the LORD. 'As for Me, this is My covenant with them,' says the LORD. 'My Spirit, who is on you, and My words that I have put in your mouth will not depart from your mouth, or from the mouths of your children, or from the mouths of your children's children from this time on and forever,' says the LORD." (Is. 59:19-21)

The Redeemer comes to Zion, and establishes His covenant with generations of the descendants of Jacob. That covenant entails His Spirit being put upon them and His word being put within them. All over the earth, from the east to the west, men will fear the Lord and submit to Him.

7. "The Spirit of the Sovereign LORD is on me, because the LORD has anointed me to proclaim good news to the poor. He has sent me to bind up the brokenhearted, to proclaim freedom for the captives and release from darkness for the prisoners, to proclaim the year of the LORD's favor and the day of vengeance of our God, to comfort all who mourn, and provide for those who grieve in Zion... They will rebuild the ancient ruins and restore the places long devastated. They will renew the ruined cities that have been devastated for generations." (Is. 61:1-4)

Messiah is anointed with the Spirit of the LORD to restore and redeem Zion and her children, and to bring vengeance on her enemies. Those redeemed in Zion will rebuild the cities and places which their enemies destroyed.

8. "I will give you a new heart and put a new spirit in you; I will remove from you your heart of stone and give you a heart of flesh. And I will put My Spirit in you and move you to follow My decrees and be careful to keep My laws. You will live in the land I gave your forefathers; you will be My people, and I will be your God." (Ezek. 36:26-28, cf. Ezek. 11:19-20)

God's Spirit will cause the people of Israel to follow His decrees and keep His laws.

That will enable them to live in the land of Israel in close relationship with God.

9. "'Then you, My people, will know that I am the LORD, when I open your graves and bring you up from them. I will put My Spirit in you and you will live, and I will settle you in your own land. Then you will know that I the LORD have spoken, and I have done it,' declares the LORD." (Ezek. 37:13-14)

God promises the restoration, even the resurrection of Israel. It is His Spirit that will give the people of Israel life and enable them to live in the land of Israel

10. "Then the LORD will be jealous for His land and take pity on His people.... Then you will know that I am in Israel, that I am the LORD your God, and that there is no other; never again will My people be shamed. And afterward, I will pour out My Spirit on all flesh—your sons and daughters will prophesy, your old men will dream dreams, your young men will see visions. Even on My servants, both men and women, I will pour out My Spirit in those days. In those days and at that time, when I restore the fortunes of Judah and Jerusalem, I will gather all nations and bring them down to the Valley of Jehoshaphat. There I will enter into judgment against them concerning My inheritance, My people Israel, for they scattered My people among the nations and divided up My land." (Joel 2:18, 27-29; 3:1-2)

God will restore the people and land of Israel, and live in their midst. He will pour out His Spirit on the sons and daughters of Israel, her old and young, men and women alike. He will fight against all the nations that sought to prevent the restoration of Israel.

11. "On that day I will set out to destroy all the nations that attack Jerusalem. And I will pour out on the house of David and the inhabitants of Jerusalem a spirit of grace and supplication. They will look on Me, the one they have pierced, and they will mourn for him as one mourns for an only child, and grieve bitterly for him as one grieves for a firstborn son....

"'On that day a fountain will be opened to the house of David and the inhabitants of Jerusalem, to cleanse them from sin and impurity. On that day, I will banish the names of the idols from the land, and they will be remembered no more,' declares the LORD Almighty. 'I will remove both the prophets and the spirit of impurity from the land.'" (Zech. 12:9-10; 13:1-2)

God will pour out His Spirit, causing Jerusalem and her children to turn to Him in mourning and repentance. He will cleanse the people and the land of impurity, so that they can live there in purity.

These are the major Scriptures concerning the outpouring of the Spirit. It is these that Yeshua, after his resurrection, explained to the disciples. The people of Israel are God's people, and the land of Israel is God's land. The outpouring of the Holy Spirit cannot be separated from the restoration of the land of Israel, which God promised to Abraham and his physical descendants through Isaac and Jacob, the people of Israel.

### Neither the Law nor the New Covenant cancel God's promise to Abraham.

Part of the original promise to Abraham and his descendants concerning the land of Canaan was that it would be theirs "for an everlasting possession." (Gen.17:8) "What I mean is this: The law, introduced 430 years later, does not set aside the covenant previously established by God and thus do away with the promise." (Gal. 3:17) The promise of the land precedes the covenant of the Law, and is not cancelled by Israel's disobedience to the Law.

When the descendants of Israel were disobedient, they would be driven off the land, but it would still be their everlasting possession. Sometimes, as with Abraham himself, possessions are not in the hands of their owner, who must await a future redemption.

"By faith [Abraham] lived as an alien in the land of promise, as in a foreign land, dwelling in tents with Isaac and Jacob, fellow heirs of the same promise." (Heb.11:9) It was their land, but it wasn't yet in their possession. "But on Mount Zion there will be those who escape, and it will be holy. And the house of Jacob will possess their possessions." (Obad.17)

"Thus says the Lord concerning all My wicked neighbors who strike at the inheritance with which I have endowed My people Israel, 'Behold I am about to uproot them from their land and will uproot the house of Judah from among them.'" (Jer.12:14) The land is given to the descendants of Abraham, Isaac, and Jacob forever. Those of the house of Judah who are planted among the nations will be uprooted and brought back to Israel.

The promise of the land is not cancelled by the New Covenant, which was introduced about 2000 years later. After giving the text of the New Covenant, God promises that Jerusalem will be rebuilt. "'The days are coming,' declares the LORD, 'when this city will be rebuilt for me from the Tower of Hananel to the Corner Gate.... The city will never again be uprooted or demolished.'" (Jer. 31:38-40)

It is to this land that Yeshua returns to restore the Davidic kingdom. In that day, as God promised Israel, "A little while, and the wicked will be no more. Though you look upon their place, they will be no more. But the humble will inherit the land and enjoy great peace." (Ps. 37:10-11; cf. Mt. 5:5)

### It is Biblically and historically incorrect to speak of the land of Israel as "Palestine."

Yeshua was born in "Bethlehem of Judea". (cf. Mt. 2:1, 5, 6) Bethlehem is in the land which God gave to the tribe of Judah. It is in the land of the Jews. It is the hometown of the King of the Jews.

There are seven places in the Bible where the Hebrew word "p'leshet" is used; Ex.15:14, Ps.60:8, Ps.87:4, Ps.108:9, Is.14:29 & 31, and Joel 3:4. Some translate it as "Palestine," others translate it as "Philistia." Regardless of which English word is used, the reference is to the land of the Philistines, not to the land of Israel. Basically, these references speak of God's judgments on the Philistines.

"Palestine" is not a Biblical synonym for the land of Israel. In the Bible, it is simply a designation for a small coastal strip in Canaan, from south of Jaffa to south of Gaza. (cf. Jer 47:1-7; Ezek.25:15-17; Am.1:6-8; Zeph.2:4-7)

Biblically, the land was called Canaan, the land of the Canaanites. God destroyed the Canaanites because of their iniquity, and gave the land to Israel, the people He created, for an inheritance forever. Then God calls the land "the land of Israel." Though it is the common usage of many, God never calls the land of Israel "Palestine." Never.

Historically, the name "Palestine" was applied by the Romans to Judea after they had crushed the Bar Kokhba Rebellion. It was intended as a punishment signifying that the Jews would never again live there. The use of the name "Palestine" was continued by the Holy Roman Empire, the Ottoman Empire, and the British Empire. But God never adopted that usage.

Scholars universally speak of "first century Palestine" etc. They are in error. Printed Bibles have maps of "Palestine in the time of the Maccabees" and "Palestine in the Time of Christ." All of this makes no sense. There was no "Palestine" in the time of the Maccabees or in the time of Christ. "Palestine" did not come into existence as a designation for the land of Israel until the second century. It is like publishing a map entitled "The British Empire in the time of Christ," or "The Soviet Union in the time of the Maccabees." These empires did not exist at those times.

Such designations show, whether intentionally or not, an anti-Biblical, anti-Judaic bias. The geographical annihilation of Israel is an evasion of historical reality, and a denial of clear Biblical teaching.

It is interesting that a Christian Bible with a map of Israel is a rare thing. They contain maps of "Canaan" and maps of "The Holy Land," but they do not have maps of "Israel." They have maps of "The divided kingdoms of Judea and Israel," but no maps of "Israel." They have maps of the "Land of the Twelve Tribes," and maps of "The Empire of David," and "The Empire of Solomon," but they do not have maps of "Israel."

Having the "old Israel" raised from the dead makes those who think of themselves as a "new Israel" very uneasy about the position they have carved out for themselves. That is why they are eager to embrace "Palestine" and to reject Israel. The call for an end to "the Israeli occupation of Palestine" would be far less appealing if it used God's designation for the land. After all, how many people can you stir up about ending "the Israeli occupation of Israel"?

Most of the Bible speaks about the land of Israel. A theology that cannot admit the past, present, and future existence of Israel is not a Biblical theology. It is an anti-Biblical theology.

There are some people who claim that they believe the Scriptures, but are completely unable to figure out if the State of Israel has any connection to the land of Israel and the promises of God. The greatest demonstration of God's power in the last nineteen hundred years, and they can't figure it out. Well, they still have a little time left.

"With cunning they conspire against Your people; they plot against those You cherish. 'Come,' they say, 'let us destroy them as a nation, that the name of Israel be remembered no more.'" (Ps. 83:4) But God has said to the descendants of Israel, "I am the LORD your God, who brought you out of Egypt to give you the land of Canaan and to be your God." (Lev. 25:38)

## MORE TORAH ABOUT THE LAND

Gen. 26:3-4 God said to Isaac, "Stay in this land for a while, and I will be with you and will bless you. For to you and your descendants I will give all these lands and will confirm the oath I swore to your father Abraham. I will make your descendants as numerous as the stars in the sky and will give them all these lands, and through your offspring all nations on earth will be blessed."

Gen. 28:4 Isaac said to Jacob, "May He give you and your descendants the blessing given to Abraham, so that you may take possession of the land where you now live as an alien, the land God gave to Abraham."

Gen. 28:13-15 God said to Jacob, "I am the LORD, the God of your father Abraham and the God of Isaac. I will give you and your descendants the land on which you are lying. Your descendants will be like the dust of the earth, and you will spread out to the west and to the east, to the north and to the south. All peoples on earth will be blessed through you and your offspring. I am with you and will watch over you wherever you go, and I will bring you back to this land. I will not leave you until I have done what I have promised you."

Gen. 35:11-12 God said to Jacob, "I am God Almighty; be fruitful and increase in number. A nation and a community of nations will come from you, and kings will come from your body. The land I gave to Abraham and Isaac I also give to you, and I will give this land to your descendants after you."

Gen. 50:24 Joseph said to his brothers, "I am about to die. But God will surely come to your aid and take you up out of this land to the land he promised on oath to Abraham, Isaac and Jacob."

Ex. 32:13 Moses said to God, "Remember your servants Abraham, Isaac and Israel, to whom You swore by Your own self: 'I will make your descendants as numerous as the stars in the sky and I will give your descendants all this land I promised them, and it will be their inheritance forever.'"

Ex. 33:1 The LORD said to Moses, "Leave this place, you and the people you brought up out of Egypt, and go up to the land I promised on oath to Abraham, Isaac and Jacob, saying, 'I will give it to your descendants.'"

Lev. 25:38 I am the LORD your God, who brought you out of Egypt to give you the land of Canaan and to be your God.

Lev. 26:42 God said to Israel, "I will remember My covenant with Jacob and My covenant with Isaac and My covenant with Abraham, and I will remember the land."

Num. 13:32; 14:37 [About the ten spies:] "And they spread among the children of Israel a bad report about the land they had explored. They said, 'The land we explored devours those living in it. All the people we saw there are of great size.... These men responsible for spreading the bad report about the land were struck down and died of a plague before the LORD."

Dt. 1:8 The LORD said to Israel, "See, I have given you this land. Go in and take possession of the land that the LORD swore He would give to your fathers—to Abraham, Isaac and Jacob—and to their descendants after them."

Dt. 30:4-5 "Even if you have been banished to the most distant land under the heavens, from there the LORD your God will gather you and bring you back. He will bring you to the land that belonged to your fathers, and you will take possession of it. He will make you more prosperous and numerous than your fathers."

Dt. 34:1-4 "Then Moses climbed Mount Nebo from the plains of Moab to the top of Pisgah, across from Jericho. There the LORD showed him the whole land —from Gilead to Dan, all of Naphtali, the territory of Ephraim and Manasseh, all the land of Judah as far as the western sea, the Negev and the whole region from the Valley of Jericho, the City of Palms, as far as Zoar. Then the LORD said to him, 'This is the land I promised on oath to Abraham, Isaac and Jacob when I said, I will give it to your descendants. I have let you see it with your eyes, but you will not cross over into it.'"

Ps. 105:8-11 "He remembers His covenant forever, the word He commanded, for a thousand generations, the covenant He made with Abraham, the oath He swore to Isaac. He confirmed it to Jacob as a decree, to Israel as an everlasting covenant: 'To you I will give the land of Canaan as the portion you will inherit.'"

Jer. 23:7-8 "So then, the days are coming," declares the LORD, "when people will no longer say, 'As surely as the LORD lives, who brought the descendants of Israel up out of Egypt,' but they will say, 'As surely as the LORD lives, who brought the descendants of Israel up out of the land of the north and out of all the countries where He had banished them.' Then they will live in their own land."

Hebr. 6:17-18 "Because God wanted to make the unchanging nature of His purpose very clear to the heirs of what was promised, He confirmed it with an oath. God did this so that, by two unchangeable things in which it is impossible for God to lie, we who have fled to take hold of the hope offered to us may be greatly encouraged."

## FOOTNOTES

1. W.D. Davies, *Paul and Rabbinic Judaism: Some Rabbinic Elements in Pauline Theology*, London, SPCK, 1948, p.216

2. The claim that the Hebrew for "forever" or "everlasting" really means "to the end of the age" is partly true, and partly false. In some cases it does mean that, but that is not all that it means. The English word "always" provides a helpful parallel. It means "every time," but it also means "as long as," and "forever."

   There are actually several different Hebrew expressions used to signify "forever." Most of them use the word "*olam*" by itself or with a prefix or suffix. Examples are "*me-olam*" [from *olam*], "*le-olam*" [to *olam*], and "*olamim*" [the plural of *olam*]. Looking at the use of such words in context is very helpful in understanding the meaning that they are given in the Bible.

   "*Olam*" is used quite often. Here are some examples of how it is used in terms of the children of Israel and the land. God promised Abraham, "And I will give to you and to your descendants after you, the land of your sojournings, all the land of Canaan, for an everlasting possession; and I will be their God." (Gen.17:8) "Then Jacob said to Joseph, 'God Almighty appeared to me at Luz in the land of Canaan and blessed me, and He said to me, "Behold, I will make you fruitful and numerous, and I will make you a company of peoples, and will give this land to your descendants after you for an everlasting possession."'" (Gen.48:3,4)

   "He has remembered His covenant forever, the word which He commanded to a thousand generations, the covenant which He made with Abraham, and His oath to Isaac. Then He confirmed it to Jacob for a statute, to Israel as an everlasting covenant, saying, 'To you I will give the land of Canaan as the portion of your inheritance.'" (Ps.105:8-11)

   The word is used to describe God's relationship with Israel. For example, "The Lord appeared to him from afar, saying, 'I have loved you with an everlasting love; Therefore I have drawn you with lovingkindness.'" (Jer.31:3) "And I will make an everlasting covenant with them that I will not turn away from them, to do them good; and I will put the fear of Me in their hearts so that they will not turn away from Me." (Jer.32:40)

   It is also used to describe the length of time that God is God (Gen.21:33), that He is King (Jer.10:10) and that His reign endures (Ps.66:7); how enduring are His arms (Dt.33:27), His righteousness (Ps.119:142), His salvation (Is.45:17), His lovingkindness (Is.54:8), His light (Is.60:19,20); and how long the righteous will live and the wicked will be abhorred (Dan.12:2).

   "*Me-olam*" is used to describe when the personification of wisdom was established. "The Lord possessed me at the beginning of His way, before His works of old. From everlasting I was established, from the beginning, from the earliest times of the earth." (Prov.8:23)

When David sought to build a house for the LORD, the LORD, in return, promised to build David a house. (2Sam.7) The phrase "ad olam" appears several times in this chapter. The Lord told David, "When your days are complete and you lie down with your fathers, I will raise up your descendant after you who will come forth from you, and I will establish his kingdom. He shall build a house for My name, and I will establish the throne of his kingdom forever. I will be a father to him and he will be a son to Me... And your house and your kingdom shall endure before Me forever; your throne shall be established forever." (vv.12-14,16) This section is generally understood to be speaking immediately of Solomon, but also to be speaking prophetically of Yeshua, the greater Son of David. It is explicitly applied to Yeshua in Hebrews 1:5.

The same phrase, "*ad olam*," is also used in Psalm 9:7: "But the Lord abides forever; He has established His throne for judgment." In these cases, "*ad olam*" is used to signify how long the throne of the Son of David will be established; how long Israel is established as the people of the Lord; and how long the name of the Lord is to be magnified, and how long the Lord will abide or sit as king.

"*Le-olam*" is used often in the Bible. Moses used it, for example, in interceding with God when Israel built the golden calf. "Remember Abraham, Isaac, and Israel, Thy servants to whom Thou didst swear by Thyself, and didst say to them, 'I will multiply your descendants as the stars of the heavens, and all this land of which I have spoken I will give to your descendants, and they shall inherit it forever.' So the Lord changed His mind about the harm which He said He would do to His people." (Ex.32:13)

It is also the word that is used to describe how long the mercy of the Lord endureth (1Ch.16:34), the truth of the Lord lasts (Ps.117:2), His word stands firm, His righteous judgments abide (Ps.119:89,160), His counsel stands (Ps.33:11), and His name lasts (Ps.135:13); how long the Lord will reign (Ps.146:10), His glory (Ps.104:31) and the Lord Himself shall endure (Ps.9:7).

It is also used to explain how long Yeshua is a priest according to the order of Melchizedek. (Ps.110:4) In Hebrews 7:3, Melchizedek is described as "...having neither beginning of days nor end of life, but made like the Son of God, he abides a priest perpetually." The same Greek phrase that is translated in this verse as "perpetually"[*eis to dienekes*], also appears in Hebrews 10:12-14, referring to Psalm 110: "But He [Yeshua], having offered one sacrifice for sins for all time, sat down at the right hand of God, waiting from that time onward until His enemies be made a footstool for His feet. For by one offering He has perfected for all time those who are sanctified."

Forever, le-olam, the land of Israel belongs to the people whom God did not destroy in the wilderness. Forever, le-olam/eis to dienekes, Jesus is a priest according to the order of Melchizedek. Forever, eis to dienekes, the sacrifice of Jesus atones for sins. Forever *eis to dienekes*, those who are sanctified are perfected by that sacrifice.

It is incorrect to say that these words and phrases only mean "to the end of the age." That is not the way that the Lord uses them in the Bible.

[This note, and the section on "Palestine," is taken and modified from my book, *The Church and the Jews: The Biblical Relationship.*]

CHAPTER TWENTY-TWO

# Coming Soon To a Location Near You

efore there was an Israel, God had a purpose for Adam and his descendants. God delegated His authority over the earth to Adam. When God created Man, He said, "Let us make man in Our image, according to Our likeness, and let them rule over the fish of the sea and the birds of the air, over the livestock, over all the earth, and over all the creatures that move along the ground." (Gen. 1:26) Man, in the image and likeness of God, was created to rule on the earth in service to God.

Man was not, however, left on his own to exercise that rule. God walked with Man in the Garden of Eden, and communicated to him. God ruled over them, male and female, instructing them as to what they should and should not do. From the very beginning, God was Lord and King over all the earth.

The almost immediate rebellion of Man against God did not change God's identity, His plans, or His purpose. God is King, and He will rule. It did, however, change life on earth.

Adam abused his authority, and polluted himself, the earth, and his relationship with every other creature and with his Creator. The children of Adam, as a whole, chose not to serve or associate with God. They filled God's earth with violence, cruelty, self-indulgence, oppression, and exploitation.

To make it difficult for the children of Adam to be united in evil, God divided them by different languages. Still, the individual nations refused to acknowledge His authority. In a world of abundance, they created deprivation.

So God created and set apart a particular people, Israel, in which, and by which, to establish His government and His likeness upon the earth. He defined Himself as the covenant-keeping God of that particular people. He entrusted oversight of His kingdom to the leaders of Israel, especially the kings and the priests.

But even before Israel requested a human king, the LORD made it clear that He would again establish His rule upon the earth. As Hannah prophesied, "those who oppose the LORD will be shattered. He will thunder against them from heaven. The LORD will judge the ends of the earth. He will give strength to His king and exalt the horn of His anointed." (1Sam. 2:10) The word translated as "His anointed" is *m'shikho*, i.e. King Messiah.

The same word, *m'shikho*, appears in Psalm 2, in the description of the final rebellion of this age against God. "The kings of the earth take their stand and the rulers gather together against the LORD and against His Anointed One. 'Let us break their chains,' they say, 'and throw off their fetters.'

"The One enthroned in heaven laughs; the LORD scoffs at them. Then He rebukes them in His anger and terrifies them in His wrath, saying, 'I have installed My King on Zion, My holy hill.'" (Ps. 2:2-6)

The rulers of this planet think that being created in the image and likeness of God is a form of bondage. They think that the commandments to love God and love their neighbor are like chains around their desires. They think they will find freedom by rebelling against the rule of God and His Anointed One.

God mocks their destructive arrogance. His anger and His wrath will force them to recognize the One they despise. God's King will rule over all the earth, even as Adam was created to do. Messiah will rule from a particular place on the earth, Zion.

**On the planet Earth, this one small speck in the universe, there is an ongoing rebellion against the rule of heaven. God has promised to put an end to that rebellion and to re-establish His rule here. Messiah, His King, will do that.**

The Scriptures are filled with praise to God for being the righteous and rightful ruler of the earth. For example, "How awesome is the LORD Most High, the great King over all the earth!" (Ps. 47:2) But the praise is often specific, because God has picked a land, a city, and a people in which to center His kingdom upon the earth. "Beautiful on high, the joy of all the earth, is Mount Zion on the sides of the north, the city of the Great King." (Ps. 48:2) Messiah, the King of the Jews, will rule in Israel, in Jerusalem, his city.

God created and called Israel for this purpose. "You will be for Me a kingdom of priests and a holy nation." (Ex. 19:6a) Israel would be God's kingdom upon the earth. Israel would serve as God's priests upon the earth, for all the nations. That is why God chose Jerusalem as the place for His earthly Temple.

As King David prayed, after he had gathered an abundance for the building of the Temple, "Yours, O LORD, is the greatness and the power and the glory and the majesty and the splendor, for everything in heaven and earth is Yours. Yours, O LORD, is the kingdom. You are exalted as head over all." (1Chr. 29:11)

From the beginning to the end of Tanakh, God makes it clear that He desires and intends for all mankind to live under His beneficent rule. Even Cyrus, king of Persia, recognized and sought to submit to the rule of heaven. "The LORD, the God of heaven, has given me all the kingdoms of the earth and He has appointed me to build a temple for Him at Jerusalem in Judah." (Ezra 1:2)

Nebuchadnezzar was compelled to learn that even the kingdom of Babylon must bow before the God of Israel. "The command to leave the stump of the tree with its roots means that your kingdom will be restored to you when you acknowledge that Heaven rules." (Dan. 4:23H/4:26) Earthly kingdoms are to be ruled by the heavenly King. Earthly rulers will be forced to acknowledge and submit to His dominion on the earth.

To "acknowledge that Heaven rules" means to acknowledge that God rules. "Heaven," the place of God's throne, is used to represent God Himself. In the books of the Maccabees, "Heaven" is used this way.

"So now **let us cry to Heaven, if perhaps He** will accept us and remember His covenant with our fathers and crush these forces before us today." (1Macc. 4:10)

"And they returned singing and **blessing Heaven, because He** is good and His mercy endures forever." (1Macc. 4:24)

"And all the people fell on their faces and **blessed Heaven, who had prospered them.**" (1Macc. 4:55) "Heaven" is used as a euphemism for God. The desire for Heaven's rule on earth is a desire for God's rule on earth.

God showed Daniel four mighty kingdoms of men, kingdoms that would be made subservient to the kingdom of God. "In the time of those kings, the God of heaven will set up a kingdom that will never be destroyed, nor will it be left to another people. It will crush all those kingdoms and bring them to an end, but it itself will endure forever." (Dan. 2:44)

**Though the kingdoms of men will pass away, God will set up a kingdom upon the earth that will endure forever. In time, it will crush and subdue all other kingdoms upon the earth. This kingdom will be entrusted to those who belong to Him, but it will be His kingdom.**

"Then the sovereignty, power and greatness of the kingdoms under the whole heaven will be handed over to those set apart, the people of the Most High. His kingdom will be an everlasting kingdom, and all rulers will bow down and obey Him.'" (Dan. 7:27)

There is one consistent message throughout the Scriptures: "The LORD will be king over the whole earth. On that day the LORD will be one, and His Name will be one.... If any of the peoples of the earth do not go up to Jerusalem to bow down to the King, the LORD Almighty, they will have no rain." (Zech. 14:9,17)

In Rabbinic writings, the "Kingdom of Heaven" and the "Kingdom of God" indicate the ruling authority of God over the earth.[1] Consequently, the traditional liturgy is saturated with prayers for the establishment of God's kingdom upon the earth. For example, Kaddish contains the request: "May He reign in His kingdom in your lifetime and in your days, and in the life of all the house of Israel, swiftly and soon. And let us say, Amen." In the Amidah, we say, "And You alone O LORD will reign over all Your works, on Mount Zion, the dwelling place of Your glory, and in Jerusalem, Your holy city, as it is written in Your holy writings: The LORD will reign forever, your God O Zion, from generation to generation. Halleluyah."

God purposed to spread His kingdom from Israel and fill the earth anew with holiness and wholesomeness. It is the establishment of the Kingdom of God upon the earth, and only the establishment of the Kingdom of God upon the earth, that brings that restoration. It is the solution to the tragedy of what Man has done to himself, his neighbor, and God's creation.

God created Israel as the essential component of His plan for restoration. Within Israel, He chose the tribe of Judah. From the tribe of Judah, He chose David, and promised him, "Your house and your kingdom will endure forever before Me; your throne will be established forever." (2Sam. 7:16)

The kingdom of the LORD was put in the hand of David and those of his sons who would have the right to rule. Even as God had entrusted His kingdom on earth to Adam, so He later entrusted it to David.

The Queen of Sheba said to Solomon, "Praise be to the LORD your God, who has delighted in you and **placed you on the throne of Israel**. Because of the LORD's eternal love for Israel, He has made you king, to maintain justice and righteousness." (1Kgs. 10:9) In Chronicles, her words are recorded slightly differently. "Praise be to the LORD your God, who has delighted in you and **placed you on His throne as king to rule for the LORD your God**. Because of the love of your God for Israel and His desire to uphold them forever, He has made you king over them, to maintain justice and righteousness." (2Chr. 9:8) The throne of Israel, the Davidic throne, is the throne of the LORD, God of Israel, upon the earth.

Abijah, son of Rehoboam, son of Solomon, son of David, spoke of God's kingdom, which had been entrusted to David and the kings who would be descended from him. He said to Jeroboam son of Nebat, who had rebelled against the house of David, "And now you plan to resist the **kingdom of the LORD in the hand of the sons of David**." (2Chr. 13:8a) Abijah said that to resist the kingdom of David was to resist the kingdom of the LORD. The LORD affirmed the words of Abijah by giving him a great victory, even though his army was surprised by an ambush and vastly outnumbered. (2Chr. 13:17-20) The kingdom of Israel, the Kingdom of God, was to be ruled by the rightful heir of the house of David.

It is in the context of this scripture-fueled desire and expectation that Yohanan, whose name means "the LORD is gracious," prepared the way of the Lord by proclaiming the nearness of the coming kingdom of God. [In English translations, he is called "John."] "Repent, for the kingdom of heaven is near." (Mt. 3:2) His announcement electrified the very air, because of what was known to be the entire thrust of Tanakh. It was a signal, a singular announcement that the beginning of the end had come for all the kingdoms of men, in their rebellion upon the earth.

From Matthew to Revelation, that same thrust and goal is presented and proclaimed. The goal and culmination of Biblical faith is the establishment of the kingdom of God, i.e. the personal rule of God upon the earth. The fact that it is coming is the reason that people must repent or face judgment.

Yeshua himself proclaimed this message. "From that time on Yeshua began to proclaim, 'Repent, for the kingdom of heaven is near.'" (Mt. 4:17) "Yeshua went throughout Galilee, teaching in their synagogues, preaching the good news of the kingdom, and healing every disease and sickness among the people." (Mt. 4:23)

The "good news" **IS** "the good news of the Kingdom." The rule of Heaven will be established upon the earth. Yeshua never announced a cancellation of God's plans to rule over the earth. Jerusalem remains the city of the Great King. (cf. Mt. 5:35)

The kingdom is the reward for the faithful. "Blessed are the poor in spirit, for theirs is the kingdom of heaven.... Blessed are those who are persecuted because of righteousness, for theirs is the kingdom of heaven." (Mt. 5:3,10)

Yeshua sent his disciples to proclaim the message of the kingdom. "As you go, proclaim this message: 'The kingdom of heaven has come near.'" (Mt. 10:7) "Heal the sick who are there and tell them, 'The kingdom of God has come near to you.'" (Luke 10:9)

That is the message that the world needed to hear then, and needs to hear now. That is the message that prepares the way of the Lord. That is the message Yeshua told his followers to proclaim. "And this good message of the kingdom will be proclaimed in the whole world as a testimony to all nations, and then the end will come." (Mt. 24:14)

**It is the good news of the kingdom—the declaration that the Lord will reign over all the earth—that must be proclaimed in all the earth. It is the good news of the kingdom that heralds the end of all other rule upon the earth. The issue is not the establishment of the reign of God in heaven; God already reigns in heaven. The issue is the establishment of the reign of God upon the earth.**

God's kingdom on earth is what Yeshua tells his disciples to seek first in and through their lives—"But seek first His kingdom and His justice"—and long for in their prayers: "Your kingdom come—Your will be done on earth as it is in heaven." The two latter phrases are equivalent. The disciples are not supposed to be praying, "Take us to Your kingdom," or "Take us to heaven." They are supposed to be praying, "Establish Your kingdom upon the earth." That is what they are supposed to be seeking. When His kingdom comes, the will of God will be done on earth as it is in heaven.

That is why the last prayer of the Bible is, "Come, Lord Yeshua." (Rev. 22:20) It is not an appeal for an escape from the earth. It is a declaration of commitment, a longing for the kingdom to be established upon the earth, a longing to be free.

Yeshua came to fulfill God's purposes and promises to Adam, to Abraham, Isaac and Jacob, to Israel, and to David. (e.g. Lk. 1:54-55,72-73; Rom. 15:8) Accordingly, he became a son of Adam in order to redeem both the children of Adam, and also the earth (*adamah*) that had been entrusted to his care. God demonstrated His intention to redeem the earth by taking upon Himself the form of the children of Adam. The earth was created to be a good place to live.

In the same way, God also demonstrated that He intends to redeem Israel. Yeshua became the Son of David, the King of Israel, to enable Israel to fulfill her role as a kingdom of priests, representing God to the peoples, and interceding for the peoples to God. "God's gifts and His call are irrevocable." (Rom. 11:29)

It is necessary because it is part of God's plan to instruct and liberate the nations. "Many peoples will come and say, 'Come, let us go up to the mountain of the LORD, to the house of the God of Jacob. He will teach us His ways, so that we may walk in His paths.' The law will go out from Zion, the word of the LORD from Jerusalem." (Is. 2:3) Yeshua became the Son of David to rule from Jerusalem and establish God's rule over all the earth.

As it was prophetically said of Messiah, "The LORD will extend your mighty scepter from Zion. You will rule in the midst of your enemies." (Ps. 110:2) Messiah rules from Jerusalem, and his kingdom increases until it covers all the earth.

"Of the increase of his government and peace there will be no end. He will reign on David's throne and over his kingdom, establishing and upholding it with justice and righteousness from that time on and forever. The zeal of the LORD Almighty will accomplish this.... In that day the Root of Jesse will stand as a banner for the peoples; the nations will come to him, and his place of rest will be glorious." (Is. 9:7; 11:10, cf. Luke 1:33)

God promised to entrust His authority to rule over the earth to Messiah, His faithful king in Israel, the rightful heir to David's throne. "All kings will bow down to him and all nations will serve him." (Ps. 72:11) That day will bring an end to all the personal and national tragedies that surround us.

The admonition to "Pray for the peace of Jerusalem" (Ps. 122:6) has applicability to the events of every day in history, but more than that, it is a call for the establishment of God's kingdom upon the earth. For it is the return of Messiah that brings peace and deliverance to Jerusalem, and God's kingdom upon the earth. (cf. Zech. 14)

Yeshua promised his ambassadors that they would inherit the kingdom of Heaven upon the earth. "You are those who have stood by me in my trials. And I confer on you a kingdom, just as my Father conferred one on me, so that you may eat and drink at my table in my kingdom and sit on thrones, judging the twelve tribes of Israel." (Luke 22:28-30, cf. Mt. 19:28) The kingdom of God is not about eating and drinking, but about justice, peace, and joy in the Holy Spirit. But people will eat and drink in that kingdom.

The twelve tribes of Israel will be upon the earth. So will Messiah's Jewish ambassadors. They will serve as administrators in the coming Kingdom of God. " 'Well done, my good servant!' his master replied. 'Because you have been trustworthy in a very small matter, take charge of ten cities.' " (Lk. 19:17)

When Yeshua rode into Jerusalem, the people greeted him, saying, "Blessed is the coming kingdom of our father David!" (Mark 11:10a)

"Some of the Pharisees in the crowd said to Jesus, "Teacher, rebuke your disciples!"

"I tell you," he replied, "if they keep quiet, the stones will cry out." (Luke 19:39-40)

The kingdom is coming, no matter who says otherwise. The kingdom will be proclaimed. The religious rulers may try to stop that proclamation, but they will not succeed. "We know that the whole creation has been groaning as in the pains of childbirth right up to the present time." (Rom. 8:22) If men will not proclaim the coming of the kingdom, then the rocks will.

*'But didn't Jesus say that the kingdom of God is within you?'*

No. Some English translations of the Greek translation of what he said put those words in his mouth, but that does not seem to be an accurate representation of what he said. The words can be translated that way, but it makes no sense in the context.

"Being asked by the Pharisees when God's kingdom would come, he answered them, 'God's kingdom does not come with careful observance; neither will they say, *Look, here!* or, *Look, there!* for behold, God's kingdom is in your midst.' He told the disciples, 'The days will come when you will desire to see one of the days of the Son of Adam, and you will not see it.'" (Lk. 17:20-22)

In the previous chapter, Luke tells us that some Pharisees had mocked Yeshua for teaching the importance of using one's wealth for the purposes of God. Yeshua responded, "You are those who justify yourselves in the sight of men, but God knows your hearts. For that which is exalted among men is an abomination in the sight of God." (Lk. 16:15)

God knew what was within them, in their hearts. It was not the kingdom of God. Yeshua said, "Out of the heart come evil thoughts, murder, adultery, sexual immorality, theft, false testimony, slander." (Mt. 15:19) He told them that their hearts were hardened, and far from God. (Mt. 19:8; 15:8)

He told them there was uncleanness within them. "Woe to you, teachers of the law and Pharisees, you hypocrites! You are like whitewashed tombs, which look beautiful on the outside but on the inside are full of dead men's bones and everything unclean." (Mt. 23:27) The kingdom of God was not within them.

THE KINGDOM IS THE GOAL, THE FOCUS, OF THE SCRIPTURES...THE KINGDOM IS WHAT YESHUA ASCENDS TO HEAVEN TO RECEIVE, AND WHAT HE RETURNS TO EARTH TO ESTABLISH.

They had asked him when God's kingdom would come, i.e. what would bring it. It is not likely that Yeshua told them that all they needed to do was look within themselves.

In the context, Yeshua was telling them that with all their careful observation, they have missed what is right in front of them. The king was standing in their midst, and they did not recognize him. How would they ever recognize the kingdom?

Then Yeshua turned to his disciples and told them that soon enough they would long for these days when he is right there in their midst. They will long for his return, because that is when his kingdom will come. (cf. Lk. 17:22-24)

Some Gentiles, who were afar off, will be brought near into the kingdom, and joined to the faithful Jewish remnant. "I say to you that many will come from the east and the west, and will take their places at the feast with Abraham, Isaac and Jacob in the kingdom of heaven." (Mt. 8:11)

King David had foreseen it long before: "All the ends of the earth will remember and turn to the LORD, and all the families of the Gentiles will bow down before Him, for the kingdom belongs to the LORD and He rules over the nations." (Ps. 22:27-28/28-29H) The kingdom is the goal, the focus of the Scriptures. The LORD will rule over all the nations of the earth.

The kingdom is what Yeshua ascends to heaven to receive, and what he returns to earth to establish. (cf. Luke 19:12) "Then the King will say to those on his right, 'Come, you who are blessed by my Father. Take your inheritance, the kingdom prepared for you since the creation of the world." (Mt. 25:34) Since the creation of the world, the kingdom has been prepared and waiting. "The holy ones of the Most High will receive the kingdom and will possess it forever—yes, for ever and ever." (Dan. 7:18)

The kingdom is what the unrighteous will not inherit. "Or do you not know that the unrighteous will not inherit the Kingdom of God? Do not be deceived. Neither the sexually immoral, nor idolaters, nor adulterers, nor male prostitutes, nor homosexuals, nor thieves, nor covetous, nor drunkards, nor slanderers, nor those who seize what is another's, will inherit the Kingdom of God." (1Cor. 6:9-10, cf. Gal. 5:19-21, Eph. 5:5)

After the resurrection, Yeshua gave the disciples the correct understanding of the prophetic scriptures about Messiah and the kingdom of God. "And beginning with Moses and all the Prophets, he explained to them what was said in all the Scriptures concerning himself." (Luke 24:27) "He said to them, 'This is what I told you while I was still with you: Everything must be fulfilled that is written about me in the Law of Moses, the Prophets and the Psalms.' Then he opened their minds so they could understand the Scriptures." (Luke 24:44-45)

Without doubt, Yeshua taught them things they did not know before; he gave them understanding they did not have before. But all that he gave them came out of the Scriptures. God had said through the prophets that the Son of David would restore the kingdom to Israel with justice and righteousness. (cf. Is. 9:6; Jer. 23:5; Mic. 5:2; et al.)

Gabriel had told Miriam the same. The Holy Spirit also reaffirmed it through Zechariah, Simeon, Anna, etc., etc..

After the resurrection, Yeshua did the same. "He appeared to them over a period of forty days and spoke about the kingdom of God." (Acts 1:3) Yeshua explained to the disciples the Scriptures about the Kingdom of God—the promise to David, the restoration of Israel, and the destruction of her enemies. Then he said, "Do not leave Jerusalem, but wait for the gift my Father promised, which you have heard me speak about. For John immersed in water, but in a few days you will be immersed in the Holy Spirit." (Acts 1:3b-5)

Yeshua had given the disciples correct understanding of the Messianic prophecies, the kingdom of God, and the outpouring of the Spirit, which is directly connected to the restoration of Israel and the reign of Messiah. They were to proclaim its nearness. Then he said that the Spirit would come upon them in a few days.

It seemed that Yeshua was announcing the imminent restoration of the kingdom of David, i.e. the establishment of his own kingdom, but the disciples were not sure. They knew that the Spirit had been poured out upon the 70 elders in the time of Moses. They knew that Yeshua had taught them that the Kingdom of God was not going to appear right away. (e.g. Lk. 19:11ff)

"So when they met together, they asked him, 'Lord, are you at this time going to restore the kingdom to Israel?' He said to them: 'It is not for you to know the times or dates the Father has set by his own authority. But you will receive power when the Ruakh haKodesh comes on you; and you will be my witnesses in Jerusalem, and in all Judea and Samaria, and to the ends of the earth.'" (Acts 1:6-8)

Their question was the natural logical fruit of what Yeshua had taught them from the Scriptures about the outpouring of the Spirit, the restoration of Israel, and the establishment of the Kingdom of God upon the earth. In response, Yeshua confirmed the restoration of the kingdom to Israel. He said that God the Father, by His own unchallengeable authority, has unalterably fixed the date of that restoration. It was simply not given to his disciples to know when that would be.

This is how Luke records it. "It is not for you to know the times or seasons the Father has secured/*etheto* by His own authority." (Acts 1:7) The same Greek word, *etheto*, is used to say that Peter was "put" in prison (Acts 12:4), to say that the Holy Spirit "appointed" overseers (Acts 20:28), to say that God "set" different members in the body (1Co. 12:18), and to say that He "established" certain specific forms of service in the community (1Co. 12:28). In other words, the kingdom will surely be restored to Israel. That is as securely established as God's authority is.

Yeshua had told his followers to make the establishment of the kingdom of God their highest priority. The return of Messiah and the establishment of his kingdom will free this world from its bondage, darkness, and death. But he told the disciples that they had much to do before that would take place. The Holy Spirit would empower them to go into all the world and proclaim the inevitable coming of the kingdom, as well as the judgment and transformation which it would bring.

The initial outpouring of the Spirit, which they were to await, was the beginning and guarantee of what was prophetically promised. (cf. 2Cor. 1:22, 5:5; Eph. 1:14) What God had promised through the prophets, what Yeshua had taught them about the restoration of the kingdom, was still yet to be fulfilled. The promises and restoration would only take place with his return. As Peter later explained, "He must remain in heaven until the time comes for God to restore everything, as He promised long ago through His holy prophets." (Acts 3:21)

The coming kingdom of God is the good news the apostles and disciples proclaimed after the resurrection. "When they believed Philip as he proclaimed the good news of the kingdom of God and the name of Yeshua the Messiah, they were immersed, both men and women." (Acts 8:12)

Paul and Barnabas traveled in the Diaspora, proclaiming the message of the kingdom to Gentiles as well as Jews. Many believed, and congregations were established. "Then they returned to Lystra, Iconium and Antioch, strengthening the disciples and encouraging them to remain true to the faith, saying, 'We must go through many hardships to enter the kingdom of God.' " (Acts 14:21b-22) The motivation for pressing on is that those who endure will enter the kingdom of God.

The coming kingdom was more than a part of what Paul proclaimed. It was the core. Without the kingdom, Yeshua is not a king. In Ephesus, "Paul entered the meetingplace and spoke boldly there for three months, arguing persuasively about the kingdom of God." (Acts 19:8)

After more travel in Macedonia, Greece, and other parts, Paul headed back to Jerusalem. As he took his leave of the elders of the congregation in Ephesus, he spoke of what had been and what would be. "Now I know that none of you among whom I have gone about proclaiming the kingdom will ever see me again. Therefore, I declare to you today that I am innocent of the blood of all men. For I have not hesitated to proclaim to you the whole will of God." (Acts 20:25-27) For the years of his service among them, Paul had proclaimed God's kingdom, thereby encompassing "the whole will of God." Because of that, he was "innocent of the blood of all men."

At the end of Acts, Paul proclaimed in Rome, as always, the coming kingdom of God. "From morning till evening he explained and declared to them the kingdom of God and persuaded them about Yeshua from the Law of Moses and from the Prophets." (Acts 28:23b)

In a sense, the last verse of Acts sums up the entirety of Paul's ministry. "Boldly and without hindrance he proclaimed the kingdom of God and taught about the Lord Yeshua the Messiah. (Acts 28:31)

Jacob spoke of the kingdom as the long promised inheritance of those who live the faith God has given. "Listen, my dear brothers: Has not God chosen those who are poor in the eyes of the world to be rich in faith and to inherit the kingdom He promised those who love Him?" (Ja. 2:5)

Peter encouraged believers to: "make every effort to add to your faith... and you will receive a rich welcome into the eternal kingdom of our Lord and Savior Yeshua the Messiah." (2Pet. 1:5,11) Some people think that because the kingdom is *eternal*, it must be in heaven. Heaven is no more eternal than the earth is. Both were created, and, as Kefa goes on to point out, both will be destroyed and replaced by a new heaven and a new earth. (cf. 2Kefa 3:10-13)

John spoke of himself as, "your brother and companion in the suffering and kingdom and patient endurance that are ours in Yeshua." (Rev. 1:9a) He went on to describe the visions God had given him to reveal the victory of Messiah. One of them concerns the redemption God brings through the blood of the Lamb.

"And they sang a new song: 'You are worthy to take the scroll and to open its seals, because you were slain, and with your blood you purchased men for God from every tribe and language and people and nation. You have made them to be a kingdom and priests to serve our God, and they will reign upon the earth." (Rev. 5:9-10) Those purchased for God by the blood of the Lamb will reign in the kingdom of God upon the earth.

It will take the judgments of God to make that happen. "The seventh angel sounded his trumpet, and there were loud voices in heaven, which said: 'The kingdom of the world has become the kingdom of our Lord and of His Messiah, and He will reign for ever and ever.'" (Rev. 11:15)

The rulers of this world will not voluntarily give up their power. There will be war upon the earth and war in heaven. At that time, Michael, the great prince who stands guard over the people of Israel (Dan. 12:1), will defeat the Dragon. "The great dragon was hurled down—that ancient serpent called the Accuser, or Adversary, who leads the whole world astray. He was hurled to the earth, and his angels with him. Then I heard a loud voice in heaven say: 'Now have come the salvation and the power and the kingdom of our God, and the authority of His Messiah. For the Accuser of our brothers, who accuses them before our God day and night, has been hurled down.'" (Rev. 12:9-10) When the Accuser of Israel [cf. Zech. 3] is cast down, then the salvation, power, and kingdom of our God will imminently transform the earth.

Yeshua returns to the earth, defeats the Adversary upon the earth, and establishes his Messianic kingdom, upon the earth. "I saw thrones on which were seated those who had been given authority to judge. And I saw the souls of those who had been beheaded because of their testimony for Yeshua and because of the word of God. They had not bowed down to the beast or his image and had not received his mark on their foreheads or their hands. They came to life and reigned with Messiah a thousand years." (Rev. 20:4) It will be the fulfillment of what was long promised.

After the Millennial kingdom, God will make all things new. There will be a new heaven, a new earth, and a new Jerusalem. "I saw the Holy City, the new Jerusalem, coming down out of heaven from God, prepared as a bride beautifully dressed for her husband. And I heard a loud voice from the throne saying, 'Now the dwelling of God is with men, and He will live with them. They will be His people, and God Himself will be with them and be their God.'" (Rev. 21:2-3)

The New Jerusalem is not synonymous with heaven. The new Jerusalem is prepared in heaven until the new Earth is created. Then it comes down out of heaven to the new Earth.

As He promised, God will dwell upon the earth in the midst of His people. "I did not see a temple in the city, because the LORD God Almighty and the Lamb are its temple. The city does not need the sun or the moon to shine on it, for the glory of God gives it light, and the Lamb is its lamp. The nations will walk in its light. The kings of the earth bring their glory and honor into it." (Rev. 21:22-23)

The kingdom of God upon the earth will endure forever and ever. "No longer will there be any curse. The throne of God and of the Lamb will be in the city, and His servants will serve him.... There will be no more night. They will not need the light of a lamp or the light of the sun, for the LORD God will give them light. And they will reign for ever and ever." (Rev. 22:3,5)

The apostles, their disciples, their disciples' disciples, and their disciples' disciples' disciples all accepted and taught the Biblical assurance of the coming kingdom of God upon the earth. When they said "kingdom," they meant the return of Yeshua to rule from the throne of David over all the earth.

"The overwhelming usage of 'kingdom' in the second-century Christian literature is eschatological."[2] When the believers of the first two centuries said "kingdom," they meant the return of Yeshua to rule from the throne of David over all the earth. Lack of faith in the physical Messianic kingdom indicated an unbeliever or heretic.

As Justin Martyr pointed out in the middle of the second century, "I, and all other entirely orthodox Christians, know that there will be a resurrection of the flesh, and also a thousand years in a Jerusalem built up and adorned and enlarged, as the prophets Ezekiel and Isaiah, and all the rest, acknowledge.... [Those] so-called Christians who yet do not acknowledge this... in reality are godless and impious heretics [who] dare to blaspheme the God of Abraham, and the God of Isaac, and the God of Jacob."[3]

Messiah is the Son of David. He restores David's kingdom. To believe in a "Christ" who does not restore the Davidic kingdom is to believe in a "Christ' is not the Messiah. It is an accusation that the god of Abraham, Isaac, and Jacob is not faithful.

"With Origen in the early third century there arose a thinker who was able to incorporate the 'Gnostic' dimension of the kingdom, the inward rule of God in the soul, into orthodox thought... Origen thus marks the turning point."[4] Origen's teaching was not, however, "orthodox thought," for Origen was a heretic, excommunicated twice. He replaced the kingdom of God with a Gnostic one.

There is no such thing in the Bible as a Messiah who does not rule and reign in Jerusalem over David's kingdom and over all the earth. A "Christ" who does not restore the Davidic kingdom is not the Messiah. Yeshua, on the other hand, "went throughout Galilee, teaching in their synagogues, proclaiming the good news of the kingdom, and healing every disease and sickness among the people." (Mt. 4:23)

The Kingdom of God is not part of the message, it IS the message. "Repent, i.e. turn to the LORD God of Israel, because the kingdom of God is coming."

Through the prophets, God promised the Messianic redemption of Israel. "In the last days, the mountain of the house of the LORD will be established as the chief of the mountains, and will be raised above the hills; and all the Gentiles will stream to it. And many peoples will come and say, 'Come, let us go up to the mountain of the LORD, to the house of the God of Jacob;

that He may teach us concerning His ways, and that we may walk in His paths. For the law will go forth from Zion, and the word of the LORD from Jerusalem.'

"He will judge between the nations and will settle disputes for many peoples. They will beat their swords into plowshares and their spears into pruning hooks. Nation will not take up sword against nation, nor will they train for war anymore." (Is.2:2-4; Mic.4:1-4)

This will be the fulfillment of what God had promised Israel throughout her history. "I will put My dwelling place among you, and I will not withdraw from you. I will walk among you and be your God, and you will be My people." (Lev. 26:11-12) "Son of man, this [Jerusalem] is the place of My throne and the place for the soles of My feet. This is where I will live among the children of Israel forever." (Eze. 43:7)

THERE WILL BE AN INTERLUDE IN HEAVEN, BUT YESHUA WILL BE REIGNING ON THE EARTH, IN JERUSALEM. THOSE WHOM HE HAS PURCHASED WITH HIS BLOOD WILL ALSO REIGN UPON THE EARTH.

The King, the Lord of hosts, will be ruling from Jerusalem. The Bible does not present Rome, Constantinople, Moscow, New York, the Hague, nor any other place as a replacement for Jerusalem. Not even heaven.

There will be an interlude in heaven, but Yeshua will be reigning on the earth, in Jerusalem. Those whom he has purchased with his blood will also reign upon the earth. "They will be priests of God and of Messiah and will reign with him for a thousand years." (Rev.20:4-6)

The ambassadors and elders met in Jerusalem to decide what to do with the Gentiles who were believing in Messiah. Jacob reminded them, "... how God first showed His concern by taking out from the Gentiles a people for His Name. The words of the prophets are in agreement with this, as it is written: 'After this I will return and rebuild I will raise up the tabernacle of David. Its ruins I will rebuild, and I will restore it, that the remnant of men may seek the LORD, and all the Gentiles who bear My Name, says the LORD, who does these things.'" (Acts 15:14-17)

The "tabernacle of David" is the "royal house of David." That is Israel's royal house. The prophetic promise is that God will again raise up an heir of David to rule, so that Gentiles who seek the LORD may find Him and be called by His Name. The King of Israel will rule in Israel, from Jerusalem, Israel's capital.

To the one who overcomes, Yeshua has promised to "give authority over the Gentiles; and he shall rule them with a rod of iron." (Rev.2:26-29) The Gentiles will be upon the earth. Those who rule over them will do so on the earth.

Peter had said to Yeshua, "Behold, we have left everything and followed You; what then will there be for us?" Jesus told them that in the age to come, they would "sit upon twelve thrones, judging the twelve tribes of Israel." (Mt.19:16-28; cf. Mt.12:27; Lk.22:24-30) The tribes of Israel will be upon the earth. Those who judge them—i.e. those who exercise a continuing administration for God, as in the ministry of Samuel and the other "judges"—will do so upon the earth.

"The kingdoms of the world become the kingdom of the one who is our Lord and Messiah himself, and he will reign for ever and ever." (Rev. 11:15) The ultimate purpose of God in creating Man and the earth is the establishment of the Kingdom of God. God governs the universe, and He intends to govern this planet as well. God intends to dwell and rule on the earth in the midst of His people.

This is not because God is addicted to power; it is because God loves those He has created. It is because God loves us so much that He made us in His own image and likeness. There is nothing greater that He can give to us.

"All the nations You have made will come and bow down before You, O Lord; they will bring glory to Your Name." (Ps. 86:9)

## FOOTNOTES

1. E.g. Ber. II.1
2. E. Ferguson, "The Terminology of Kingdom in the Second Century," in *Studia Patristica, Vol. XVII*, pp.670, edited by Elizabeth A. Livingstone, Pergamon Press, Oxford, 1982
3. Justin Martyr, *The Dialogue with Trypho*, translated by A. Lukyn Williams, S.P.C.K., London, 1930, p.169, Sec. 80.1-5
4. E. Ferguson, "The Terminology of Kingdom in the Second Century," op. cit., p.673

TWENTY-THREE

# An Irrevocable Calling

If the problem with the world were only the past and present leaders of the nations of the world, then there would be an easy solution. Get new leaders. Vote them in, or start the revolution. That would solve everything. Unfortunately, the leaders are just a symptom of a far deeper problem.

In creating Man, God gave him responsibility for more than himself. That is part of being created in the image and likeness of God. Man's decision to live for himself alone brought brokenness into the world.

Even the planet we inhabit has been enslaved. It was entrusted to Adam, but he chose to obey the wrong spirit. From the Tower of Babel on, the goyim/nations of the earth have chosen to live in rebellion against God.

As a means of bringing them back to Himself, God chose to establish a covenant relationship with Abraham. That relationship was dependent only upon God's own nature. God chose Isaac, Jacob, and the people of Israel as Abraham's heirs. They inherited the calling, the covenants, and the promises.

The world is broken. It needs to be fixed. In Hebrew, this necessity is called *tikkun olam*, the repairing, or restoration, of the world. This is the underlying reason for the creation and calling of Israel—God's desire and plan to set the world right again. Through Israel, God brought into the world the Scriptures, the Messiah, the covenants, etc..

As long as the world is broken, God's covenants and promises to Israel must remain. Israel is His means of bringing restoration and healing to the world. That is why, by oath and by covenant, God promised to Abraham, and his descendants through Isaac and Jacob, multifaceted gifts, calling, and purpose.

God's purpose in creation never depended upon the faithfulness of Adam. Likewise, His purpose in redemption does not depend upon the faithfulness of any man or people. The grace and power of the God of Israel are sufficient, despite the shortcomings of His people.

"Who is a God like you, who pardons sin and forgives the transgression of the remnant of his inheritance? You do not stay angry forever but delight to show mercy. You will again have compassion on us; You will tread our sins underfoot and hurl all our iniquities into the depths of the sea. You will be true to Jacob, and show mercy to Abraham, as you pledged on oath to our fathers in days long ago." (Mic. 7:18-20)

Yeshua paid the price of redemption, but this world is still waiting to be free. That transformation from death to life will come when the people of Israel return to the God of Israel. "The creation itself will be liberated from its bondage to decay and brought into the glorious freedom of the children of God." (Rom. 8:21)

That is why Paul actively sought to fulfill his calling as a Jew. So did tens of thousands of others. But even for those who were not fulfilling their calling from God, that calling still remained. Paul, as God's Jewish ambassador to the Gentiles/nations, tried to get Gentile believers to understand this.

"I am speaking to you Gentiles. Inasmuch then as I am the ambassador to the Gentiles, I make much of my ministry in the hope that I may somehow arouse my own people to envy and save some of them.... As far as the good news is concerned, they are enemies on your account; but as far as God's choice is concerned, they are loved on account of the patriarchs, because God's gifts and His call are irrevocable." (Rom. 11:13-14, 28-29)

God's gifts to the Jewish people and God's calling of the Jewish people are irrevocable. Literally, they are "not to be repented of". Individual Jews can spurn both the gifts and the calling, but God will not repent of creating Israel for this purpose. He has no need to. He knew what He was doing. And He still knows what He is doing. The gifts and the calling remain.

We will look briefly at why these gifts and calling are irrevocable. To some extent, this chapter is a reiteration, with a different focus, of things that have been covered in previous chapters. So I will try to make the points concisely, without the repetition of all the scriptural support given in those chapters.

## ISRAEL'S GIFTS AND CALLING ARE IRREVOCABLE BECAUSE:

### 1. God is the God of Israel.

The word "god" by itself simply means "a deity". It does not tell us which deity. In different cultures, different deities are indicated by the word. The Bible is very specific in designating the one true God.

The Creator of all chose to establish a relationship with Abraham, and become known as the God of Abraham (e.g. Gen. 24:12). He chose Abraham's son Isaac, and became the God of

Abraham and Isaac. (e.g. Gen. 28:13) He chose Isaac's son Jacob, and became known as the God of Abraham, Isaac, and Jacob. (e.g. Ex. 3:6)

He changed Jacob's name to Israel, chose his twelve sons, and became known as the God of Israel. The primary identification of God in His Word, hundreds of times, is the God of Israel. The God of Israel is the God of the Bible.

As He said to Israel, "You only have I known of all the families of the earth..." (Am. 3:2) As He promised forever, "I the LORD do not change. So you, O descendants of Jacob, are not destroyed." (Mal. 3:6)

In a time of adversity, God spoke to Israel about the time of restoration: "Be glad, O people of Zion, rejoice in the LORD your God,... Then you will know that I am in Israel, that I am the LORD your God, and that there is no other. Never again will My people be shamed." (Joel 2:27) God has made the physical descendants of Abraham, Isaac, and Jacob His people, His children. "This is what the LORD says: 'Israel is My firstborn son.'" (Ex. 4:22)

**EVERYTHING WE KNOW ABOUT GOD—SHEPHERD, SAVIOR, FATHER, KING, PORTION, ETC.—IS WHAT HE IS IN RELATIONSHIP TO ISRAEL.**

And so, God made Israel His representatives in the earth. Everything we know about God—Shepherd, Savior, Father, King, Portion, etc.—is what He is in relationship to Israel. "You are My witnesses that I am God." (Is. 43:12)

God promises to judge the nations for how they treat Israel, His representative. "I will bless those who bless you, and whoever curses you I will curse..." (Gen. 12:3; Gen. 27:29; Num. 24:9) Yeshua described the fulfillment of this promise of judgment at the end of this age. "When the Son of Man comes in his glory, and all the angels with him, he will sit on the throne of his glory. All the Gentiles will be gathered before him... I tell you the truth, whatever you did for one of the least of these brothers of mine, you did for me.'... " (Mt. 25:31-46)

Israel itself will be judged too, but "'I am with you and will save you,' declares the LORD. 'Though I completely destroy all the nations among which I scatter you, I will not completely destroy you. I will discipline you but only with justice. I will not let you go entirely unpunished.'" (Jer. 30:11)

God would have to reject His own identity, becoming an "unknown god," in order to sever His relationship with Israel. He would have to resign as the God of Israel, the one title more than all others by which He calls Himself in the Bible. But, since **God's** nature does not change, His **identity** cannot be revoked.

## 2. Messiah is the King of the Jews.

The identity of Messiah is expressed in the Scriptures with specific content. Throughout the Scriptures, all the way to the end, Messiah is the King of the Jews. That is the way he is described by the prophets, announced by the archangel, presented to Israel and the world, put to death, and identified in his return. In the Bible, there is no such thing as a Messiah who will not rule from David's throne.

If God's purpose for Israel has expired, then, of necessity, so must His purpose for Messiah, Israel's King. By identity, gifts, and calling Messiah is chosen within Israel and for Israel. If Israel is no longer chosen, then Messiah is no longer chosen. There would no longer be a Messiah.

Since Yeshua is the same yesterday, today, and forever, he will not forfeit his identity, the Davidic throne, or his people. His Father will not take back the kingdom He has given. Messiah's purpose remains only as long as Israel's purpose remains, and vice versa. **Messiah's identity** is irrevocable.

## 3. God promised by covenant and swore by Himself, without any conditions, to give Abraham, Isaac, Jacob, and their descendants the land of Canaan as an everlasting possession.

"All the land that you see I will give to you and your offspring forever." (Gen. 13:15) "As for Me, this is My covenant with you... The whole land of Canaan, where you are now an alien, I will give as an everlasting possession to you and your descendants after you; and I will be their God." (Gen. 17:8) There was nothing unknown to God when He said, "I will be their God."

The land is central in God's plan of redemption of the earth. The only condition on which it was given is that God be God, the Owner of heaven and earth. For God to revoke His eternal promise of the land of Israel to Abraham and the people of Israel, He would have to forsake His own identity and integrity, and abandon the earth to the forces of darkness. That He will not do. **The covenant and the oath** are irrevocable.

## 4. God has made Israel His kingdom upon the earth and Jerusalem its capital.

"'I have installed My King on Zion, My holy hill.'

"'I will proclaim the decree of the LORD: He said to me, You are My Son; today I have become your Father. Ask of Me, and I will make the nations your inheritance, the ends of the earth your possession.'" (Ps. 2:6-8)

God has enthroned His King on Zion, because Israel is His land. In the coming age, all nations will come up to Jerusalem to bow down to the King of Israel. "If any of the peoples of the earth do not go up to Jerusalem to bow down to the King, the LORD Almighty, they will have no rain." (Zech. 14:17) "For the law will go forth from Zion, and the word of the LORD from Jerusalem." (Is.2:3c; Mic.4:2c) God will make the world whole.

In the time of the new heavens and earth, God will dwell in Jerusalem forever and ever. "The city does not need the sun or the moon to shine on it, for the glory of God gives it light, and the Lamb is its lamp. The nations will walk by its light, and the kings of the earth will bring their splendor into it." (Rev. 21:23-24)

To revoke His decree, God would have to disown Yeshua as King, and abandon His intention to rule over all the earth from Jerusalem. "The throne of God and of the Lamb will be in the city, and His servants will serve Him." (Rev. 22:3b) **God's choice of Jerusalem** is irrevocable.

## 5. God called Abraham to make him, and Israel through him, the context of redemption for all peoples.

"I will make you into a great nation... and all peoples on earth will be blessed through you." (Gen. 12:2-3) He promised that, "A nation and a company of Gentiles/nations shall come from you, and kings shall come forth from you." (Gen.35:11b; cf. Eph. 2:11-19) Gentiles who submit to Yeshua are brought into the commonwealth of Israel.

"I have made you a father of many nations. I will make you very fruitful. I will make nations of you, and kings will come from you. I will establish My covenant as an everlasting covenant between Me and you and your descendants after you for the generations to come, to be your God and the God of your descendants after you." (Gen. 17:5b-7)

Yeshua summed it up: "Salvation is from the Jews." God has given the Jewish people all that pertains to salvation. He has given the Jewish people His promises and covenants, which bring atonement, forgiveness of sin, a new heart, and the Spirit of God. He has given Israel His King and His Kingdom, with its just government and its capital. He has given the Jewish people His written and His living Word;

GOD HAS CALLED ISRAEL TO ENLIGHTEN THE NATIONS, AND TO BE THE CONTEXT FOR THE REDEMPTION OF A COMMUNITY OF NATIONS.

righteousness through faith and the fathers of the community of faith. He has called Israel to enlighten the nations, and to be the context for the redemption of a community of nations.

Through Israel, God makes salvation available to the nations. If they are brought into Israel's commonwealth, then "The Gentiles have been made partakers of their spiritual things..." (Rom. 15:27a) So if God were to take back what He has given to Israel, there would be no salvation for anyone. God would have to change His identity in order to abandon His covenant with Abraham and His New Covenant with Israel. He would have to abandon His plan to redeem the children of Adam. The Gentiles would be left "without hope and without God." **God's calling of Abraham** is irrevocable.

### 6. God promised to make Israel the means of redemption for all peoples.

The Jewish people are God's instrument for bringing the nations back to Himself. They are His means for fixing this broken world. That is why God created and set Israel apart—"You will be for Me a kingdom of priests and a holy nation.' These are the words you are to speak to the children of Israel." (Ex. 19:6; 1Pet. 2:9 refers to this.1) As priests, the people of Israel are to teach the Gentiles to be holy. The people of Israel are God's witnesses to declare His Truth.

Israel was created and called by God to be a light to the Gentiles. As Shaul and Barnabas reminded the Jewish community in Pisidian Antioch, "For this is what the Lord has commanded us: 'I have made you a light for the Gentiles, that you may bring salvation to the ends of the earth.'" (Acts 13:47, quoting Is.49:6) If God withdrew the calling of Israel, it would leave the Gentiles in darkness.

"Therefore go and make disciples of all the Gentiles, immersing them in the name of the Father and of the Son and of the Holy Spirit, and teaching them to obey everything I have commanded you. And surely I am with you always, to the very end of the age." (Mt. 28:19-20) If God withdrew the calling of the Jewish people, it would leave the Gentiles untaught, in disobedience, and lost.

When all Israel turns to her God, the world will be set free from the darkness and death in which it now lies. "For if their rejection is the reconciliation of the world, what will their acceptance be but life from the dead?" (Rom. 11:15) If God's calling of Israel is revoked, then the world will remain under the rule of death. **God's redemptive purpose** is irrevocable.

### 7. The good news is to the Jew first.

That is its nature. Only a non-Biblical or anti-Biblical "good news" can be other than to the Jew first.

There is only one verb, "**is**," that applies to all the clauses in Rom. 1:16, and defines the nature of the good news. **If theology overrules grammar to change the verb to "was", so that the good news was to the Jew first, then Rom. 1:16 tells us that the good news was the power of God unto salvation. If theology overrules the text to change the verb to "was", so that the good news was to the Jew first, then the good news was also to the Greek.** If the good news is no longer to the Jew first, then it is no longer also to the Greek, and it is no longer the power of God unto salvation.

The good news itself is part of God's promise to Abraham. "... and all peoples on earth will be blessed through you." (Gen. 12:2-3) It was proclaimed to Abraham, and inherited by Isaac, Jacob, and all Israel. If the peoples of the earth are no longer to be blessed in Abraham, then they have no salvation. There is no alternative plan. **The good news** is eternal. (cf. Rev. 14:6) The good news is irrevocable.

### 8. God promised to make Israel, the people and the land, a place of habitation for Himself upon the earth.

"I will walk among you and be your God, and you will be My people." (Lev. 26:12) God promised Israel, "You will live in the land I gave your fathers; you will be My people, and I will be your God." (Ezek. 36:28)

The land of Israel is central in God's plans for the future of Man and the earth. "Son of Man, this [Jerusalem] is the place of My throne and the place for the soles of My feet. This is where I will live among the children of Israel forever.'" (Eze. 43:7) "And the name of the city from that time on will be: THE LORD IS THERE." (Ezek. 48:35b)

**God's promise** has not been cancelled. **God's intention** has not changed. It is irrevocable. He will redeem the earth and its inhabitants, and dwell in Jerusalem upon the earth.

### 9. What God requires of man is described and presented in His relationship with Israel.

God speaks to all peoples through the Written Word and the Living Word, both of which He brought into the world in Jewish form. The Jewish people "have been entrusted with the very words of God." (Rom. 3:2b) Those words of God overwhelmingly speak of His relationship with the people of Israel. That is His way of teaching the Gentiles.

"In the last days, the mountain of the house of the LORD will be established as chief among the mountains; it will be raised above the hills, and all nations will stream to it. Many peoples will come and say, 'Come, let us go up to the mountain of the LORD, to the house of the God of Jacob. He will teach us His ways, so that we may walk in His paths.' The law will go out from Zion, the word of the LORD from Jerusalem." (Is. 2:2-3)

Righteousness and justice are given specific content in God's relationship to the Jewish people. So is holiness. So is atonement. So is peace. So is love. So is every Biblical concept.

These are not empty concepts. They are not concepts that people may define however they choose. They are specific, and they are concrete. They are not universal concepts, in the sense that their true content can be found anywhere. They are defined in the Jewish Scriptures,

Genesis to Revelation, in God's relationship with Israel. They are made real in the life of Israel.

God called the Jewish people to be the keeper, illustrator, and teacher of His Word. To sever His relationship with Israel, God would have to withdraw His Word, and choose to leave the Gentiles in darkness. **His Word** is irrevocable.

*"But God could replace Israel with the Church. God could use the Church instead of Israel. The Church is Israel. The Church could..."*

I know this is hard to comprehend, but "the Church" is not in the Bible. The Biblical *ekklesia* is not something other than the commonwealth of Israel. The God of the Bible does not have a "Church". No replacement takes place. What is it about "irrevocable" that you don't understand?

As we read in Hebr. 2:12, quoting Ps. 22:22, Ps. 21:22 in LXX: "He says, 'I will declare Your Name to my brothers. In the presence of the *ekklesia* I will sing Your praises.'" The original word in Psalm 22 is *kahal*. *Ekklesia* is simply the Greek word chosen to represent the *kahal* of Israel.

> THERE ARE MANY WHO
> ACCUSE ISRAEL. THEY FILL
> THE POLITICAL AND
> RELIGIOUS WORLD. THEY
> CONSIDER ACCUSING
> ISRAEL TO BE THEIR
> SERVICE TO THEIR WORLD
> AND TO THEIR GOD.

It is not just semantics. **It is a profound reality; a reality that is secured by God's identity, Messiah's identity, God's covenant and oath, God's choice of Jerusalem, God's calling of Abraham, God's redemptive purpose, the good news, God's intention to dwell upon the earth, and God's Word.** That is why God's gifts and calling of the Jewish people are irrevocable.

The name of the prophet Zechariah means "the LORD remembers." That is the theme of the book of Zechariah, God's faithfulness to the Jewish people. "Then he showed me Joshua/Yeshua the high priest standing before the angel of the LORD, and Satan standing at his right side to accuse him. The LORD said to Satan, 'The LORD rebuke you, Satan! The LORD, who has chosen Jerusalem, rebuke you! Is not this man a burning stick snatched from the fire?'" (Zech. 3:1-2)

The Hebrew word *Satan* means "accuser". The Accuser stood next to Joshua/Yeshua, the High Priest, to accuse him (*l'sitno*). There are many who accuse Israel. They fill the political and religious world. They consider accusing Israel to be their service to their world and to their god. Unfortunately, sometimes it is. They need to switch gods.

Joshua/Yeshua, the High Priest, is representing the Jewish people before God. The High Priest intercedes for the Jewish people before God. In the Septuagint, Joshua's name is *Iesous*, i.e. "Jesus". Jesus intercedes for Israel; Satan accuses Israel. It shouldn't be hard to pick a side.

The LORD's response is simple. He does not say that the Jewish people are without sin. He does not even say that Israel has less sin than the Gentiles. He just says, 'I have chosen them.' He considers that to be a sufficient response. "The LORD rebuke you, accuser! The LORD, who has chosen Jerusalem, rebuke you!"

To deny God's gifts and calling to Israel is to envision a different god, not the one of the Bible. It is to deny that the God of the Bible is truly God.

## FOOTNOTE

1. Peter was appointed by Yeshua as an apostle to the Jews, not to the Gentiles. [cf. Gal. 2:7-8] That was his calling, and therein lay his authority. That is why 1Peter is addressed to Jews, i.e. "to those chosen who are living as strangers in the Diaspora in Pontus, Galatia, Cappadocia, Asia, and Bithynia."

# THE MOTH

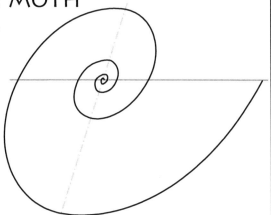

The plot below is a logarithmic spiral with angle of descent 17 degrees starting at 5 o'clock.

The distance the entity is from the source is r = 1 at initial time in this example.

In this example the moth will be at source after traveling the hypotenuse of the above triangle which will be 1.732303245*(Pie) radians which is almost 360 degrees.

(skewed +20 degrees)

The expediential function starts at -Pi/3 which is 5 o'clock in the complex plane.

Exp(i*x) with a weight that changes in magnitude as a function of the angle x is the equation for a spiral in the complex plane.

0.2886330678 is the weight that runs the cosine argument from 0 to Pi/2 as x goes from 0 to 1.732303245*Pi

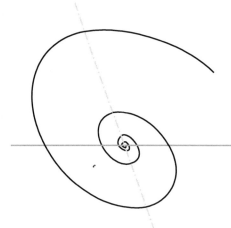

http://www-gap.dcs.st-and.ac.uk/~history/ Curves/Equiangular.html

(skewed -20 degrees)

Maple Code

```
>complexplot(cos(0.2886330678*x)*exp
(I*(x - Pi/3)), x = 0 .. 1.732303245*Pi);
```

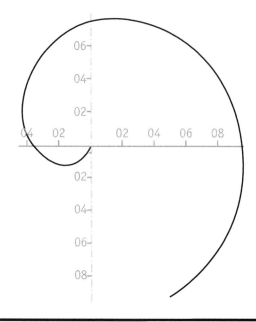

TWENTY-FOUR

# Compound Error

Moths and other insects have compound, multifaceted eyes. This enables them to see close objects very clearly, much more clearly than a human being does, but it gives them very poor distance vision. There may be 10,000 or 20,000 such facets in each eye. Each facet receives the light that comes from an external object and focuses it into an image. The image is coded and electrically transmitted by the nerves to the brain. The brain processes the information it receives from the thousands of eyes via the nerves. Vision takes place entirely inside the head.

The brain combines and reconciles the information in the multiple images, and determines where the actual object, a burning candle perhaps, is externally located. In the case of the moth, even though the received image may be accurate, there is a systematic error in determining the location of the actual external object. The brain of the moth determines that the object is, for example, 17 degrees to the right of where it actually is.

The moth sees the image clearly, but it sees it in the wrong place. The moth thinks that it is flying straight towards the light, but it is actually flying straight towards an image of the light that is misplaced 17 degrees to the right. The eyes and brain of the moth are continually making inflight corrections, and so the moth spirals in towards the light, always aiming 17 degrees off.

Somewhere in the moth's system of vision, there is a systematic misinterpretation of the data which **always** results in determining a false location for the actual object. Perhaps the systematic error is in the coding of the image before it is sent via the nerves; perhaps it is in the transmission of the encoded data by the nerves; perhaps it is in the processing of the data by the brain. In any case, somewhere the moth is systematically misinterpreting the data and **always** flying to the wrong place, even though it is flying towards the right object.

The larger the angle of displacement is, the wider and longer will be the spiral that the moth flies before it reaches the burning candle. As long as the angle of displacement is less than 90 degrees, the moth will eventually, if it lives long enough, spiral in and reach the candle. If the angle of displacement were 90 degrees—which is to say that the image projected by the moth's brain would be 90 degrees away from the actual object—then the spiral path would change into a circle. The moth could fly straight towards the image it sees, for its whole life, but it would never get any closer. All the inflight correction it does will only result in the moth circling the object continually at a constant distance.

If the angle of displacement is more than 90 degrees, the moth, in flying towards the image it sees, will actually get farther away from the object itself. It will spiral out instead of in. No matter how well-meaning the moth is, it will always fly hopelessly in the wrong direction, eventually losing sight of the image, its initial goal and destination.

We can say that the problem comes from the compound nature of the eyes, but actually it is a problem of interpretation. The eyes produce an accurate image of the object placed before them. They may produce 10,000 or 20,000 accurate images, each slightly different from the next. The problem is that the correct data is systematically misinterpreted. Because of that systematic misinterpretation, the candle, the source of the light, is never where the moth thinks that it is.

Now imagine that there is also a systematic error in how the image is received. An incorrect image is then produced and accurately transmitted, or an incorrect image is produced and then inaccurately transmitted. This incorrect data is then systematically misinterpreted. The moth flies in a systematically wrong direction towards a systematically incorrect image. Welcome to systematic theology.

## THE IMAGE AND THE LIGHT

*'So you're right, and everyone else is wrong? These great theologians were not stupid. They were not evil men.'*

It is amazing what the great theologians did with what they had. Most of them were not evil, though a case can certainly be made that some of them were. That, however, is beside the point. We are not now talking about their character or their intelligence, but about their teachings.

For every systematic theologian, there is a Biblical anomaly which cannot be reconciled within their system. 'The *planetoi*, my lord, the *planetoi*.' Nineteen hundred years in exile, and now the nation of Israel exists in the land of Israel again, contrary to all political, sociological, and theological wisdom. This is retrogression. It is, as the British might say, highly irregular. And it is very upsetting to the rest of the world.

But it is quite to be expected in the Scriptures. It is guaranteed in the Scriptures. Throughout the centuries, there have been those who believed the Scriptures and, therefore, expected the restoration of the people of Israel to the land of Israel.

It is better to believe what is true, though despised, than to believe what is traditional and accepted, but false. Copernicus simply chose to recognize the anomaly rather than to pretend that it did not exist. He had no use for all the mathematical devices that were invented to give the illusion that the anomaly did not exist.

Systematic theology creates a mental framework for classifying and filing information. When information comes which does not fit into this cognitive framework, there are three basic possibilities: 1. Alter the information to make it fit the system, i.e. distort it; 2. Alter the cognitive framework, i.e. move away from the system; or 3. Receive the information but refuse to alter the cognitive framework, thereby creating cognitive dissonance, i.e. internal mental conflict.

Twenty-five years ago, I was in a car with three young pastors, driving to a retreat. I was trying, unsuccessfully, to communicate to them how they were missing the centrality of Israel in understanding God's revelation and plan of redemption for all the earth. So I asked a question.

"What percentage of the Bible would you say is about God's relationship with Israel?"

"Ninety percent," Peter responded. He wasn't confident in that percentage, but he was being cooperative.

"Okay," I said. "Let's say it's 90 percent, or 85 percent, or 78.3 percent, or whatever it is, but it's a highly significant percentage of the Bible." They all agreed.

"Now when was the last time that you preached about Israel, not about Israel as an illustration for you to talk about yourselves, but actually about Israel?" They were silent. Of the three of them, none of them ever had. They were young, but not unique.

A few months ago, I was having lunch with a friend who is a pastor. He mentioned that he had been looking at a classic 600 page book of systematic theology.[1] In the index of the book, he found all the theological concepts the author considered important, and much more besides. But in the index, there was no listing for "Israel". There was one listing for "Jews," in which the well-respected theologian explained that God's promises to them should not be believed, since they were contrary to his entire theology. Israel and the Jews had no place in the author's system. He read the whole Bible, studied all about God, and could not see any importance to the Jewish people.

78.314 percent, or something like that, of the Bible is about God's relationship with the Jewish people, and this theologian was able to figure out everything about God, Christ, Church, salvation, and everything else that is theologically significant, without Israel or the Jews. He was able to figure out everything, but the problem is that he figured it out wrong. Not all wrong, but certainly wrong enough.

There is a reason for this blindness and neglect. There is a reason for this systematic error. Every Christian theology appropriates, in one way or another, what the God of Israel has given to the Jewish people. That is because the God of Israel has given to the Jewish people everything that pertains to salvation.

Paul said, "theirs is the right as sons, the glory, the covenants, the giving of the Law, the service, and the promises. Theirs are the fathers, and to them the Messiah is physically related, who is over all God blessed forever. Amen." (Rom. 9:3-5) Paul was writing about those in Israel who do not believe. God has given these things to Paul's unbelieving, physical, Jewish kinsmen. These things do not benefit those who reject them, but, nevertheless, God's gift is irrevocable. The theologians look at these things and see them in a systematically incorrect location. They see them in Christianity. But Christianity is not in the Bible.

Christian theology must appropriate these things, otherwise, it would have nothing to offer. Each theology has its own unique problems, but they all have some basic errors in common. These systematic errors create the illusion that what God has given to the Jewish people is located far away from them. These systematic errors maintain the system. They affect translation, interpretation, doctrine, and behavior. They create a distorted image, and locate that distorted image far from the actual object.

Here are four simple, basic, Biblical teachings that every systematic theology distorts, ignores, or denies. After doing that, the theologians then confidently fly off in the wrong direction.

1. **Messiah is the King of the Jews.** A "Christ" who does not rule from David's throne in Jerusalem, both in the Messianic age and in the time of the new heavens and earth, is not the Messiah.

2. **God has always kept a faithful remnant in Israel.** The descendants of Abraham, Isaac, and Jacob continue to be God's covenant people. God did not create another covenant people.

3. **The New Covenant is made between the God of Israel and the descendants of Abraham, Isaac, and Jacob.** This is the only covenant that brings salvation in Yeshua.

4. **Gentiles who recognize the King of the Jews as Lord are brought into the commonwealth of Israel.** God is faithful to His promise to Jacob to make Israel a kahal goyim.

We will look at the systematically errant flight of one theological community as an example. Covenant Theology will be the example, because one of those three young pastors from twenty-five years ago became a professor at a seminary that champions Covenant Theology. He's a kind and gentle man, with a gracious heart towards the Jewish people. I appreciate him, but I do not appreciate his theology.

Not long ago, after five hours of discussion, I said to him, "Al, I know you. What's in your heart is different from what is in your theology." He thought for awhile, took inventory, and said, "You're right." In his case, it's a wonderful thing that God looks on the heart.

I want to highlight some of the theological concepts which have been invented to mute the Biblical evidence. Theological conviction should never be an excuse for ignoring what is explicit in the Scriptures. Theological conviction should never be an excuse for ignoring the normal use of language in context, the normal meaning of words, or the principles of grammar.

There are some good things about Covenant Theology, as there are about other theologies. In Covenant Theology, there is a recognition of the importance of the Kingdom of God. There is a recognition of the necessity of the Law of God in human society. There is a recognition that "Israel" is the only context for redemption. (Unfortunately, this "Israel" is said to be unrelated to the Jewish people.)

There were also many good things about pre-Copernican astronomy. From the inside, it fit almost all the facts. It was observably true in everything that seemed to matter. It gave people assurance of their place in the universe. It was good enough for almost everyone. But there were some facts that didn't fit, insignificant ones. These insignificant facts meant that the whole system was wrong. These insignificant facts meant that almost everyone was completely comfortable with what was not true. The system provided them with a false assurance.

Covenant Theology systematically rejects what is explicit in the Scriptures, and embraces instead what the theologians presume is implied. The unique theological devices of Covenant Theology are all designed to dispossess the Jewish people of what God has given them, and to relocate these things in the Church.

## EPICYCLE NUMBER 1:
### There is a Covenant of Grace which encompasses all the other covenants.

This "Covenant of Grace" is not mentioned anywhere in the Scriptures. The Bible does not record who made this covenant, what its terms are, or what sacrifice established it. Nor does the Bible say what the purpose of this Covenant of Grace is. The Bible does not tell us if this covenant provides atonement or forgiveness, or if it requires faith, works, or anything. The Bible does not tell us anything about this Covenant of Grace, because the Bible does not mention it at all.

This invented "Covenant of Grace" is very misleading. It has nothing to do with the actual grace of God, a grace which is primarily demonstrated in the Scriptures in God's relationship with the descendants of Abraham, Isaac, and Jacob. It is, in fact, opposed to that grace. The purpose of this "Covenant of Grace," and all the theological devices associated with it, is to claim that God was not gracious to the Jewish people. However, if God's grace was not sufficient to keep the Jewish people, then it certainly will not be sufficient to keep anyone else.

This "Covenant of Grace" presents God as less gracious than He really is. It does not give us something better than what is in the Scriptures. It does not make God's mercy and forgiveness more available.

Nor does this "Covenant of Grace" encompass all the other covenants that actually are in the Bible. Paul noted that "the covenants" belong to the Jewish people. The "Covenant of Grace" is raised up in opposition to that.

God's covenant with Abraham was inherited by Isaac and Jacob. In accordance with it, God promised Jacob that "A nation and an assembly of nations will come from you ...'" (Gen. 35:11) The "Covenant of Grace" does not include this; it denies it.

The New Covenant is graciously made between the LORD and the people whose fathers broke the Covenant of the Law. It adequately provides atonement for sin. It adequately provides salvation, God's Spirit, and new life for any and every person who will humble himself, or herself, to enter into Israel's commonwealth. The "Covenant of Grace" does not encompass this; it rejects it.

The "Covenant of Grace" is not in the Scriptures, and it does not encompass the covenants that are. It is a denial of God's grace to the Jewish people. It is only a device to free its advocates from the responsibility of dealing with the actual Biblical text. It enables them to distance themselves from what they see as God's undesirable Jewish connections.

The "Covenant of Grace" is not about grace at all. It is only a theological device designed to get rid of the Jews. There is a psalm about those who devise their own covenant in order to inherit for themselves the possessions of Israel.

"O God, do not keep silent. Be not quiet, O God, be not still. See how Your enemies are astir, how Your foes rear their heads. With cunning they conspire against Your people; they plot against those You cherish.

'Come,' they say, 'let us destroy them as a nation, that the name of Israel be remembered no more.' With one mind they plot together; **they form a covenant against You.** ...

Make their nobles like Oreb and Zeeb, all their princes like Zebah and Zalmunna, who said, **'Let us inherit for ourselves the pastures of God.'**

Make them like tumbleweed, O my God, like chaff before the wind. As fire consumes the forest or a flame sets the mountains ablaze, so pursue them with Your tempest and terrify them with Your storm.

Cover their faces with shame so that men will seek Your Name, O LORD. May they ever be ashamed and dismayed; may they perish in disgrace. Let them know that You, whose Name is the LORD—that You alone are the Most High over all the earth." (Ps. 83:1-5,11-18/2-6,12-19H/82:/2-6,12-19LXX)

## FCCENTRIC NUMBER 1:

### The New Covenant is made between God the Father and God the Son.

Should anyone momentarily forget the "Covenant of Grace" and still think that the New Covenant is essential and unique in its importance, the theologians seek to make its very clear text meaningless and irrelevant. The very clear words of the text say that the New Covenant is between God and the Jewish people.

This means that God's purpose for the physical descendants of Abraham, Isaac, and Jacob has not changed. It means that He has not created an alternate "people of God". This has "implications" the theologians do not like. Israel is the only ship afloat.

*"Ahoy captain, people in the water. Multitudes of them."*

*"Poor devils, they're without hope and without God. We have to go in after them. Stay close together. These murky theological waters can be treacherous."*

Covenant theologians are aware of the difficulty that the Scriptures present to their theology. So they introduce a few intermediate devices. These devices are designed to get rid of the Jews altogether, to make sure there are no survivors. The Church takes over the mission and identity of the Jewish people.

The actual words and terms of the New Covenant present insurmountable obstacles to the theologians. To begin with, the text says that the New Covenant is made between the LORD and the house of Israel and house of Judah. In the Scriptures, "the house of Israel" or "the house of Judah" means the "the family of Israel" or "the people of Judah". The words have real meaning in the real world.

"House" designates more than one individual. It designates a family, an entire lineage. The text says that the New Covenant is made with a family, not with an individual.

In fact, all the plurals in the text of the New Covenant are irreconcilable with the eccentric notion that God the Father is making this new covenant with God the Son: "the covenant I made with **their fathers** ... I will put My law in **their minds** and write it on **their hearts**. I will be **their God**, and **they** will be **My people**.... And they will no longer teach **each man his neighbor**, or a **man his brother**, saying, Know the LORD, because **they** will all know Me, **from the least of them to the greatest**... For I will forgive **their iniquity** and will remember **their sins** no more."

How would Yeshua have come to be "the house of Israel," which broke away from acknowledging David's heirs as king? How would Yeshua have come to be "the house of Judah," which later plunged into its own idolatry? The New Covenant is to be made with a people who have been unfaithful.

Certainly, Yeshua, as High Priest, can represent and intercede for that people before God, but he cannot be that people. He cannot be a man and his neighbor, or a man and his brother. Did he break the Covenant of the Law? The New Covenant is promised to a people who broke the Old Covenant. Words have meaning, especially to God.

**THERE IS NO WAY TO FORCE SUCH AN INTERPRETATION UPON THE TEXT.**

If these words don't have the normal meanings they are given in the Scriptures and in ordinary language, then they still must have some meaning. And there must be some kind of rule by which we can know what these extraordinary meanings are and when they are to be applied. The theologians do not help us out here.

The text says, "**their** fathers". Is God the Son a plural being? If not, then he does not fit the text.

The text says "I will put My law in **their** minds and write it on **their** hearts." How many minds and hearts does God the Son have? Wouldn't God the Son already have had God's law in his heart and mind?

God says, "I will be **their** God," and "they will **all** know Me." Will God the Father be "**their** God" because God the Son has multiple personalities? How does "**all**" apply to God the Son? Wasn't God the Father already the God of God the Son? And didn't God the Son already know God the Father?

The textual reason that "**they** will **all** know Me" is because "I will forgive **their** iniquity and will remember **their** sins no more." Is God the Father forgiving the iniquity of God the Son? Is He promising to no longer remember the sins of God the Son?

There is no way to force such an interpretation upon the text. We understand that Isaiah prophesied that Messiah would make his soul a guilt offering to atone for the sins and iniquities of Israel. The purpose of the atonement is to enable all Israel to know the LORD.

In chapters 8 and 9 of Hebrews, the text of the New Covenant is quoted and discussed. Yeshua is called a mediator of the covenant, but there is no discussion of the covenant being between God the Father and God the Son. This would have been the ideal place to state and explain that. Instead, the covenant is presented as being between God and Israel, just as the first covenant, the one made at Sinai, was. How could the Holy Spirit have missed this opportunity to clarify the issue?

Was the covenant at Sinai also between God the Father and God the Son? If so, then it is unfortunate that Moses did not understand or record that. It is deplorable that none of the prophets understood it either. Nor did any Biblical author express it anywhere.

What shall we say about the LORD Himself thinking that the descendants of Abraham, Isaac, and Jacob were supposed to obey the terms of the covenant? and punishing them when they didn't? The majority of the Bible is written with the understanding that the Covenant at Sinai was made between God and the people of Israel.

If the covenant at Sinai was between God the Father and God the Son, what was wrong with it? Why did it have to be replaced? Did God the Son break that covenant?

If, however, the theological response is that the covenant at Sinai was not between God the Father and God the Son, then why is the covenant at Sinai even mentioned? What possible relationship could it have to a New Covenant between God the Father and God the Son? If God the Father and God the Son didn't make an old covenant with each other, then how could they make a new covenant with each other? According to the Biblical text, it is the existence of a previous covenant that makes this a "new" covenant. For the covenants, "new" and "old" are comparative terms. "By calling this covenant new, He has made the first one old." (Heb. 8:13a)

The covenant theologians do not answer these questions for us. They avoid the Biblical text. They remain in their systematic theology.

## EPICYCLE NUMBER 2:

### 'Jesus is Israel.'

If it somehow turns out that the New Covenant is between God and Israel, the theologians still have a way to avoid the dreaded Jewish connection. Israel is no longer Israel, "Jesus is Israel." What exactly do the words in this theological statement mean?

It is clear that the statement equates "Jesus" with "Israel". Let us suppose that this "Jesus" is the one who is described in the Scriptures, even though this "Jesus" is clearly not the prophesied Son of David. What then does "Israel" mean in this statement?

In the Scriptures, "Israel" is used to refer to Jacob, to his descendants, to a portion of his descendants (especially the faithful remnant), or to the leaders of his descendants. Does the statement mean that "Jesus" is Jacob, or Jacob's descendants, or a portion of his descendants, or the leaders of his descendants? No, the "Israel" of the theologians doesn't mean any of those things from the Scriptures. It means something else.

"Israel" is also used in the Scriptures to refer to the land, to the united kingdom, and to the northern kingdom. In the statement, "Jesus is Israel," does "Israel" mean the land, the united kingdom, or the northern kingdom? No, it doesn't mean any of these things from the

Scriptures. It means something else.

We cannot substitute "Jesus" for "Israel" in the more than 2300 verses in the Scriptures where the word, or a form of it, appears, because those verses won't make much sense if we do. That is not what the theologians have in mind. They have a meaning of their own.

They can't quite say "Israel" means "the people of God," because Jesus isn't a people. And they don't want to say that Jesus is the representative head of Israel, because they want to cut off that head and put it on another body. (And you thought that Dr. Frankenstein's Neighborhood Bible Club was ghoulish.)

Louis XIV said, "L'etat, c'est moi," i.e. "The state, I am the state." Is this, more or less, what the statement, "Jesus is Israel," means? Well, it's something like that, except the Sun King wasn't saying that he was the only person in France. He was just saying that he was the only person who counted, that France was embodied in him. The theologians are more autocratic than that.

In the statement, "Jesus is Israel," "Israel" doesn't have any specific meaning. It is a rather hazy abstraction. Nevertheless, I can help you understand, because of a brief encounter I had with some Western theologians who explained it to me.

*Now if you'll just hold your horses, son, I'll tell you what "Israel" means in that there statement "Jesus is Israel." "Israel" means "the good guys". Yep, that's right pardner, the good guys.*

*That don't sound right to you? Then you must be a stranger in these here theological parts. In this territory, when we says "Israel," that's what we mean, the good guys. Yep, that's what we mean.*

*And when we say "that's what we mean," then, by golly, that settles it. Don't matter none what those words mean where you come from, stranger, cause you ain't there now. You're here. And here, words mean what we say they mean. We don't need no dictionaries, and we ain't got much use for no grammar neither. You got a problem with that?*

*Put that gun down, mister. It won't do you no good to get riled up. We've got you surrounded, and we'll blow your fool head off before you can pull that trigger.*

*That's right, put it down, and listen up good. When we say, "Jesus is Israel," why that means that Jesus is the good guys, and them there Jews ain't. It means that all the good promises of God to them Jews are taken over by Jesus, and then he gives them to us. Them Jews can keep all them bad promises, those about judgment and stuff like that. You see, podner, Jesus kicks them Jews right out, and takes over. And then he deputizes us, and we get everything that was theirs. All the good stuff. And we run the place.*

*Now, cowboy, take a good look around you. You can see we've got the upper hand here. Use your head, boy. Do you want Jesus or do you want those infernal Jews? I suggest you do as we say, and throw in your lot with the winners. Right now, friend, you're on the wrong side.*

*How about you trading that mangy black skunk-stinking little hat o yourn for a brand new bound-for-glory big white one?*

As the sun sinks slowly in the West, and as the West sinks rapidly into darkness, we still have just enough light to see that the purpose of this ideological device is to get rid of the Jews. It is an ingenious ideological device by which Israel itself is made *judenrein,* i.e. free of Jews. In this theology, if Jesus is Israel, then all the Jews can be thrown out, and the promises to Israel can be fulfilled to Jesus. And since he doesn't need them, he can pass them on to the Church

This can only be done, however, with a Jesus who is not the King of the Jews. That is, this can only be done with a Jesus who is not the Messiah. The real Messiah is the King of the Jews, and he comes to bring his people back to their God, not to cut them off from their God. It is the King of the Jews, not the Destroyer of the Jews, who died on the tree to atone for sin.

Since the members of the faithful remnant of Israel are kept by God's grace, the theologians need a different conception of grace. Since the members of the faithful remnant, at least, are Israel, the theologians need a Jesus who annihilates even the faithful remnant. That is the only way that Jesus alone could become Israel. Covenant Theology denies the existence of the faithful remnant of Israel. To the contrary, however, God is faithful to His promises and gracious to His people, the Jewish people.

As one member of the Jewish remnant wrote to another: "If we are faithless, He remains faithful, because He cannot deny Himself." (2 Tim. 2:13) Paul said that he was part of that faithful remnant. "I ask then: Did God reject his people? By no means! I am a man of Israel myself, a descendant of Abraham, from the tribe of Benjamin." (Rom. 11:1) "Are they Hebrews? So am I. Are they men of Israel? So am I. Are they Abraham's descendants? So am I." (2Co. 11:22)

God has always kept some among the physical descendants of Abraham, Isaac, and Jacob faithful to Himself. The existence of the faithful remnant does not demonstrate Israel's faithfulness or worthiness, but it does demonstrates God's faithfulness and grace. The presence of the faithful remnant indicates the continuity of God's purpose in and through Israel.

By rejecting and dismissing the faithful remnant, the theologians are proclaiming that God has denied Himself. Paul says that God kept a remnant in Israel who believed, but the rest were hardened. Paul warns Gentile believers to remember the ongoing natural relationship that even Jews who have not yet believed still have with their God. "After all, if you were cut out of an olive tree that is wild by nature, and contrary to nature were grafted into a cultivated olive tree, how much more readily will these, the natural branches, be grafted into their own olive tree!" (Rom. 11:24) By God's design, it is "their own olive tree".

Every ·Christian theology requires some discontinuity, some break in God's relationship with the Jewish people. But God has no need to start over with a new Israel. He has maintained His relationship with the old one. "I the LORD do not change. So you, O descendants of Jacob, are not destroyed." (Mal. 3:6) The existence of the faithful remnant means that there is no discontinuity at all in God's relationship with the Jewish people.

God had established this relationship with Abraham, Isaac, Jacob, and the twelve tribes. The Covenant of the Law made at Sinai did not sever or interrupt this relationship. It was a means of continuing the relationship. The New Covenant does not sever or interrupt this relationship. It is a means of continuing the relationship. There is no discontinuity at all.

The existence of the faithful Jewish remnant is explicit and obvious in the Messianic Writings. After all, this faithful remnant is the source of the Messianic Writings. To recognize the reality and significance of the Jewish remnant is to recognize a continuity in God's relationship with and purpose for the Jewish people, a continuity that offers no possibility for inserting a new people of God. Most of the time that "Israel" appears in the Scriptures, it refers to an unfaithful people.

When did the "Jesus" of Covenant Theology become Israel? No one knows. No one knows for how long he became Israel. At some unknown time, he became Israel just long enough to get rid of all the Jews. After he did that, then he made the Church Israel. It happened so quickly that the Scriptures do not record where or when it happened.

In the Scriptures, it didn't happen with the incarnation, because Yeshua came to "reign over the house of Jacob". He was "born King of the Jews."

It did not happen in his years of ministry, because he "was sent only to the lost sheep of the house of Israel." It did not happen in his crucifixion and death, because he died as "King of the Jews". Isaiah, the Jewish prophet, declared to his people that "the punishment that was upon him brought us peace, and by his wounds we are healed."

It did not happen in his resurrection, because he affirmed to his Jewish apostles that the time of the restoration of the kingdom to Israel was fixed by the Father's authority. The 11 proclaimed that God exalted Yeshua in order to "give repentance and forgiveness of sins to Israel." (Acts 5:31) Paul proclaimed in Antioch: "God has brought to Israel the Savior Yeshua, as He promised." (Acts 13:23) God had told Ananias that Paul would carry His Name to "the people of Israel."

Shimon Kefa spoke to crowds in Jerusalem as "Men of Israel," saying, "Therefore let all Israel know…" (Acts 2:22,36; 3:12; 4:10) The believers prayed and spoke to the God of "the people of Israel". (Acts 4:27) They used words in a normal way.

Jesus will not become Israel with his return to the earth, because he brings reward to the Gentiles who have helped the least of his Jewish brethren; and he brings judgment on the

Gentiles who have ignored them. The Son of David, the King of the Jews, comes back to raise up Jerusalem and her children from the dust where Gentiles have trampled them. He gathers the Gentiles before him for judgment. "The King will reply, 'I tell you the truth, whatever you did to one of the least of these brothers of mine, you did to me." (Mt. 25:40,45) Because their Christ is not the Son of David, many of these theologians do not believe that he is coming back.

There is no place in the Bible where "Israel" becomes unconnected to the physical descendants of Abraham, Isaac, and Jacob. Of the more than 2300 verses in the Bible that mention "Israel," the approximately 1200 verses that mention "Yeshua," and the approximately 500 verses that mention "Messiah," there is not a single verse anywhere in the Bible that refers to Yeshua as Israel in place of the Jews. King of Israel, yes. Israel, no. Representative of Israel, yes. Israel, no. There is one section in Isaiah which may have an intentional double application to both Israel and her Messiah, who is her representative head. Later, we will look at that section separately.

No one in the Messianic Writings ever speaks of Yeshua as Israel in displacement of the Jews. Matthew doesn't. Mark doesn't. Luke doesn't. John doesn't. Paul doesn't. Peter doesn't. Jacob doesn't. Yeshua himself doesn't. God doesn't. They all use "Israel" to refer to, well, you know, Israel. "Israel" is never, as in not ever, used in the Messianic Writings to mean "Jesus".

There are two verses in the Messianic Writings where "Israel" refers to the faithful remnant. (Rom. 9:6; Gal. 6:16) Every other time, "Israel" refers to the Jewish people as a whole, or to the land of Israel.

As a final note, the theological assertion is actually quite degrading. At the time of the Golden Calf, God said that He would destroy the rest of Israel and make a new people from Moses. Moses rejected the offer, claiming that what God spoke of doing would cause the Egyptians to blaspheme Him, and would be contrary to His promises to Abraham, Isaac, and Jacob. (Ex. 32:10-14) Instead, Moses offered himself to be blotted out of God's book to atone for Israel. (Ex. 32:30-34)

For this, Moses deserves the highest praise. He showed the highest character and the greatest love. He was the humblest of men. Paul also was willing to be eternally cursed if that would bring salvation to "my brethren, my physical kinsmen, who are Israelis". These theologians do not feel the same way. They do not know God as Moses and Paul did, and they have convinced themselves that the Jewish people are not Israel.

According to Covenant Theology, Jesus accepted the offer that Moses turned down, apparently not caring that it would show God to be unfaithful and untrustworthy. According to Covenant Theology, Jesus decided, "I alone will be Israel." This is a distortion of the character of the one sent to be the Savior of Israel, and a distortion of the character and grace of the One who sent him.

Copernicus was not sympathetic to the mathematicians and astronomers who held their system together with invented devices. "But they are in exactly the same fix as someone taking from different places hands, feet, head, and the other limbs—shaped very beautifully but not with reference to one body and without correspondence to one another—so that such parts made up a monster rather than a man."[2]

## ECCENTRIC NUMBER 2:
### 'Jesus is the olive tree of Romans 11.'

Jesus is not even mentioned in Romans 11. That is because there is no need to mention him. The chapter is about Israel, both the faithful remnant and the unfaithful majority. The chapter is an exhortation to Gentile believers not to think that God has cast off Israel, whom Paul explicitly identifies as the physical descendants of the 12 sons of Israel. (cf. Rom. 11:1-5)

Paul writes about the faithful remnant in Israel. He quotes God's rebuke of Elijah for thinking that he was the only one left. Paul categorically rejects the claim that God has cast off Israel, by pointing to himself and his own physical lineage in the tribe of Benjamin. For Paul, that physical descent, united with the faith of Abraham, is proof of God's faithfulness to Israel.

In Romans 11, Paul presents the most explicit teaching in the Bible on the faithful remnant in Israel. He does not equate Jesus with Israel. Obviously, there could be no faithful remnant of Jesus himself.

Paul calls the physical descendants of the patriarchs "Israel," whether they believe or not. He says that for these physical descendants of the tribes of Israel, whether they are cut off or not, the olive tree is "their own olive tree." (v.24) He says that partial hardening has come to Israel. (v.25) He says that all Israel, as opposed to the current faithful remnant, will be saved. (v.26) None of this makes any sense at all if Jesus is Israel.

Nowhere in Scripture does anyone say that Jesus is the olive tree. But to all Israel, God said: "The LORD called you a thriving olive tree with fruit beautiful in form. ..." (Jer. 11:16) Of Israel, He said, "His young shoots will grow. His splendor will be like an olive tree, his fragrance like a cedar of Lebanon." (Hos. 14:6)

For Jews, whether they believe in Yeshua or not, Israel is "their own olive tree." Israel is an olive tree which God cultivated for thousands of years. Because there is no alternative tree, no alternative covenant, and no alternative people of God, Gentiles must enter into Israel's polity in order to enter into Israel's New Covenant with God. The covenant is not made with any other people. Nor is there any other covenant that will bring salvation.

That is why Paul writes about the grafting of the Gentiles as wild branches into Israel's cultivated olive tree. Gentiles who repent and believe in Messiah receive their life through an olive tree that is not naturally their own. The root is not theirs; the tree is not theirs.

Gentiles who enter into Israel's polity through the New Covenant become part of the community of nations which God promised to make from Jacob. (cf. Gen. 35:11) This is the greater *kahal/ekklesia* of Israel. It is the *kahal/ekklesia* of Messiah, who will rule from David's throne over both Israel and the nations.

Gentiles who enter into Israel's commonwealth through the New Covenant do not become Jews. They remain Gentiles, wild branches who have also received the amazing grace of the God of Israel. Otherwise there would be no fulfillment of these promises of God to Jacob and to Messiah. Nor would there be any fulfillment of God's promise to make Abraham the father of many nations.

### EPICYCLE NUMBER 3:
**'"This is My Beloved Son" must be understood in light of God saying, "Israel is My son, My firstborn. (Ex 4:21ff) This shows that God is calling Jesus "Israel" in replacement of the Jews.'**

There is a very strange logic here, the self-serving logic of replacement. If Yeshua is called anything that Israel is called, the theologians conclude that he replaces Israel; that is, when they perceive a positive benefit to being Israel. If they perceive a negative disadvantage to being Israel, then, in those cases, they determine that Jesus doesn't replace Israel.

This logic of replacement is only applied against Israel, and not against others. For example, angels are called the sons of God. By the logic of replacement, "This is my Beloved Son" would show that God is calling Jesus an angel, and thereby replacing all the angels with Jesus. Satan is among these angels who are called the sons of God. By the logic of replacement, "This is my Beloved Son" would show that God is calling Jesus "Satan," and thereby replacing Satan with Jesus.

Some of those who were destroyed in the time of Noah are called sons of God. (cf. Gen. 6:4) By the logic of replacement, "This is my Beloved Son" would show that God is calling Jesus those who rebelled before the flood. It would show that God is replacing them all with Jesus.

Paul says that all believers are called to be the sons and daughters of the LORD Almighty. (2 Cor. 6:18) By the logic of replacement, "This is my Beloved Son" would show that God is replacing all other believers with Jesus.

This is not logic; it is self-serving prejudice. The fact that both Jesus and Israel are called "My Son," does not in any way indicate that Jesus must be called "Israel". The same logic would indicate that Jesus must be called "the angels," "Satan," "all believers," etc..

Nor does the fact that both Jesus and Israel are called "My Son" indicate in any way that Jesus must replace Israel. If there is legitimate logic to it, then the same logic would indicate that Jesus must replace "the angels," "Satan," "all believers," etc..

There is no reason that these can't all be called God's son. Many people have more than one son or daughter. There is no reason why, if Messiah is the Son of God, that Israel and the angels and all believers can't also be called the same. There is no Biblical reason.

In Covenant Theology, the theologians have no problem with the angels being called the sons of God, because there is no advantage in replacing the angels with Yeshua. They have no problem with believers being called the sons and daughters of God, because there is no advantage in replacing the believers with Yeshua. But somehow, they find great advantage for themselves in replacing Israel with Yeshua.

God called Ezekiel "son of Man". When Yeshua called himself "the son of Man," did he mean that he replaced Ezekiel? In a vision, Daniel sees Messiah as a "son of Man". (cf. Dan.7:13) After this, Gabriel calls Daniel "son of man". (cf. Dan. 8:17) Did Gabriel mean that Daniel had replaced Messiah? No.

What is the theological advantage in replacing Israel? It is quite simple. Israel has been given everything that pertains to salvation and the kingdom of God. If Jesus is Israel in replacement of the Jews, then all the Jews are dispossessed from Israel. Since an Israel that is only one person is a little strange, all the Christians, or whichever segment of them the theologians favor, are then included.

The theologians create a false opposition between Jesus and the Jewish people; "they can't both be God's Son, can they?" They create a false opposition between Gentile believers and the Jewish people. By doing this, they deny the mystery of the gospel. "This mystery is that through the gospel the Gentiles are heirs together with Israel, members together of one body, and sharers together in the promise in Yeshua the Messiah." (Eph. 3:6)

So the covenant theologians say people must choose between Jesus and the Jewish people. Choosing Jesus is made to mean rejecting the Jews. That was the logic of the Inquisition. Ruth made a better choice: "Your people will be my people."

Biblically, the Messiah is the Savior of the Jews, restoring the Jewish people to God. The Christ of Covenant Theology cuts the Jewish people off from God. He does the opposite of what the Messiah does.

Theology like this is no mere academic exercise. Though the Holocaust was a unique event in history, it has its precursors and its repetition in the common theological practice of the total elimination of the Jewish people. The theological claim is the same as the Nazi command, "Raus, Juden raus," i.e. "Out, Jews out!"

**DEFERENT NUMBER 1:**

*"I am the true vine" (John 15:1) indicates that Jesus replaces "Israel".*

Yeshua claims to be the true vine. That is explicit. That is what he meant to communicate.

Did he also mean to communicate that he, being the true vine, replaces the Jews as "Israel"? He did not state that; nor did anyone else in the Bible. It is not explicit, but the covenant theologians claim that it is implied.

Let's look at the text in context. In John 15, Yeshua is speaking to the Jews he has chosen as his ambassadors. He tells them they are already clean (v.3); he tells them that they are his branches (v.5). He tells them that he has loved them as the Father has loved him (v.9). He says that he has told them these things so that his joy may be in them, and their joy may be full (v.11).

> Dear Theologians,
>
> Yeshua has chosen, appointed, and loved the Jews to whom he is speaking. He calls them to bear much fruit. They probably think this has something to do with God's promise in Isaiah 27:6: "In days to come Jacob will take root, Israel will bud and blossom and fill all the world with fruit."
>
> This is the same Yeshua who wept over Jerusalem. If he were announcing that God had rejected the Jews, how joyful would that make him? How joyful would it make his Jewish ambassadors?
>
> Please explain to these Jewish disciples of the King of the Jews how, in your theology, his choosing them really means that God is casting off the Jews.
>
> Yours truly,
> Bewildered

*'But Israel was supposed to be the true vine. The Jews failed to be that, so God replaces Israel with Jesus as the true vine, the true Israel.'*

There are 70 verses in the Scriptures where the word "vine" or "vines" appears. The vine is often used symbolically in metaphors and parables. For example, it is used that way in the dream of Pharaoh's chief cupbearer. (cf. Gen. 40:9-13)

Most of the time a vine is used in this way, it symbolizes something other than Israel. There are, however, four places where Israel is compared to a vine, one that did not produce fruit as it was supposed to—Jer. 2:21, Ezek.19:10, Hos. 10:1, and Ps. 80:8,14,16. There is a related passage in Isaiah 5, where the house of Israel is the vineyard of the LORD, which does not produce good fruit. (cf. Is. 5:7) So there are passages that picture Israel as an unfaithful, or untrue, vine.

By saying, "I am the true vine," Yeshua seems to be contrasting himself with this image of Israel. That would seem to be the point of the word "true". Yeshua is contrasting himself with Israel, not equating himself with Israel. In other words, if the vine that showed itself to be false is Israel, then the true vine is something that is not identical with Israel. *

Dt. 32:32 speaks of "the vine of Sodom," which bears poisonous, bitte fruit. It is a false vine. By Yeshua saying "I am the true vine," did he imply that he is the true Sodom? That would follow from the reasoning of Covenant Theology.

There are four appearances of the word "Israel" in the gospel of John. The forerunner of the Lord, said, "I myself did not know him, but the reason I came immersing in water was that he might be revealed to Israel." (Jn.1:31) For the one who came to prepare the way of the Lord, "Israel" meant the Jewish people.

Nathaniel called Yeshua "the King of Israel." (Jn.1:49) For Nathaniel, "Israel" meant the Jewish people. Yeshua affirmed Nathaniel's expression of faith.

The crowd that welcomed Yeshua as he rode into Jerusalem said, "Blessed is the King of Israel." (Jn.12:13) For them, "Israel" also meant the Jewish people.

Yeshua called Nicodemus a "teacher of Israel". (Jn.3:9) It does not seem likely that Yeshua was calling Nicodemus his own mentor. For Yeshua, "Israel" meant the Jewish people.

There is another verse in the gospel of John where a form of the word "Israel" appears. "When Jesus saw Nathaniel approaching, he said of him, "Here is a true/alethos man of Israel, in whom there is nothing false." (John 1:47)

We all overlook some things. I have read the Bible many times, but I am always discovering new verses in it. I suspect that someone comes along while I am sleeping and inserts these new verse that were never there before. I can't prove it, but I have no other explanation for how these new verses appear.

I wonder if John 1:47 is a new verse for the covenant theologians. Wouldn't this one verse alone cause them to abandon their theology? Yeshua did say, "I am the true/*alethine* vine," but he also said that Nathaniel was "a true/*alethos* man of Israel". Yeshua made both these statements, so there must not be any conflict between them. Yeshua does not say that he is true Israel, but he does say that Nathaniel is. God has always kept a faithful remnant in Israel.

## DEFERENT NUMBER 2:

*"In Is. 49:3, God prophetically says to Jesus, "You are My servant, Israel, in whom I will display My splendor." This shows that Jesus is Israel, and not the Jews.'*

In the Scriptures, there are a number of people whom the LORD, God of Israel, calls "My servant". Abraham, Moses, Caleb, and Zerubbabel are among them. God says the same about Job and Nebuchadnezzar, though they were not Jewish.

In the book of Isaiah, the LORD calls Isaiah, Eliakim son of Hilkiah, David, Israel, Jacob, and Messiah—each one of them—"My servant". There are several passages in chapters 41 through 53 that speak of the Servant of the LORD. Most of these passages speak of Jacob/Israel as the servant of the LORD. Some of them speak of Messiah as the servant of the LORD. There are a few passages that are somewhat ambiguous, seeming to speak alternately of both Israel and Messiah, who is the King of Israel, the one who leads Israel in righteousness.

Isaiah 49:3 seems clear enough, though it occurs in an ambiguous passage. "He said to me, 'You are My servant, Israel, in whom I will display My splendor.' But I said, 'I have labored to no purpose; I have spent my strength in vain and for nothing. Yet what is due me is in the LORD's hand, and my reward is with my God.'"

The verse does not seem to be speaking prophetically of Yeshua. "I have labored to no purpose; I have spent my strength in vain and for nothing." Yeshua did not say anything like that.

On the other hand, such things are often said about Israel. Moses warned Israel of the consequences of turning away from the Law of the LORD: "Your strength will be spent in vain..." (Lev. 26:20) Isaiah characterized the restoration that would come to Israel after that judgment: "They will not labor in vain..." (Is. 65:23)

In Is. 49:3, there is the promise: "You are My servant, Israel, in whom I will display **My splendor.**" In the book of Isaiah, both before and after this verse, God promised that He would do this to Israel. In an earlier passage, the LORD promises, "I am bringing My righteousness near, it is not far away; and My salvation will not be delayed. I will grant salvation to Zion, **My splendor** to Israel." (Is. 46:13)

In a later passage, "the LORD, your Savior, your Redeemer, the Mighty One of Jacob" promises Zion, "Then will all your people be righteous and they will possess the land forever. They are the shoot I have planted, the work of My hands, for **the display of My splendor.**" (Is. 60:21; cf. v.16)

Chapters 40 through 66 of Isaiah are often called "the book of consolation," because they speak about God's comfort to and restoration of a chastised Israel. Isaiah 49:3 is part of that promise of consolation. It is addressed to "My servant Israel," as are Isaiah 41:8-9, 43:10, 44:1-2,21, 45:4, and 48:20. The content in it appears elsewhere, and is applied to the Jewish people, but nowhere applied to Jesus.

Some of the surrounding verses seem to speak of Messiah. "And now the LORD says—He who formed me in the womb to be His servant to bring Jacob back to Him and gather Israel to Himself, for I am honored in the eyes of the LORD and my God has been my strength—He says: 'It is too small a thing for you to be My servant to restore the tribes of Jacob and bring back those of Israel I have kept. I will also make you a light for the Gentiles, that you may bring My salvation to the ends of the earth.'

"This is what the LORD says—the Redeemer and Holy One of Israel—to the one who was despised and abhorred by the nation, to the servant of rulers: Kings will see you and rise up, princes will see and bow down, because of the LORD, who is faithful, the Holy One of Israel, who has chosen you." (Is. 49:6-7)

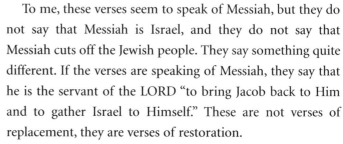

IT IS A PERVERSE THEOLOGICAL LOGIC THAT TURNS A PROMISE OF RESTORATION INTO AN ACT OF REJECTION.

To me, these verses seem to speak of Messiah, but they do not say that Messiah is Israel, and they do not say that Messiah cuts off the Jewish people. They say something quite different. If the verses are speaking of Messiah, they say that he is the servant of the LORD "to bring Jacob back to Him and to gather Israel to Himself." These are not verses of replacement, they are verses of restoration.

Jerusalem is also spoken of as despised by the nations. "The sons of your oppressors will come bowing before you; all who despise you will bow down at your feet and will call you the City of the LORD, Zion of the Holy One of Israel. Although you have been forsaken and hated, with no one traveling through, I will make you the everlasting pride and the joy of all generations" (Is. 60:14-15)

And God promises the Jewish people, "Instead of their shame My people will receive a double portion, and instead of disgrace they will rejoice in their inheritance; and so they will inherit a double portion in their land, and everlasting joy will be theirs." (Is. 61:7) The people are despised. Their city is despised. Their king is despised.

As one of the restored descendants of Jacob, Paul treats Is. 49:6 as referring to God's calling for the Jewish people. As part of the faithful remnant, he says, "For this is what the LORD has commanded **us**: 'I have made you a light for the Gentiles, that you may bring salvation to the ends of the earth.'" (Acts 13:47) Paul does not apply the verse to Messiah, he applies it to the remnant in Israel who are faithfully delivering the message of Messiah.

It is a perverse theological logic that turns a promise of restoration into an act of rejection. In the Bible, Messiah is the Savior and Redeemer of the Jewish people. Covenant Theology annuls and cancels God's promises and covenants to them.

## DEFERENT NUMBER 3:
### 'But didn't John the baptist say that God would cut down Israel's tree.'

No, he didn't. He said, "The ax is already at the root of the trees, and every tree that does not produce good fruit will be cut down and thrown into the fire." (Mt. 3:10) He spoke of many trees, because he was comparing every individual to a tree that must bear good fruit. Yeshua said the same thing. "Every tree that does not bear good fruit is cut down and thrown into the fire." (Mt. 7:19)

John said this to the Pharisees and Sadducees who had come out to him. (cf. Mt. 3:7) In calling them to an immersion which signified repentance, he said that some trees, i.e. some among them, would bear good fruit. Those trees would remain. Some trees, i.e. some among them, would not bear good fruit. They would be cut down.

Nothing in the text indicates that this is a general statement about all Israel being cut off from God. That is contrary to the meaning of the text.

## ECCENTRIC NUMBER 3:
### *"You seem to place more importance on the Old Testament than on the New. We believe that Jesus provides the last and authoritative word, and therefore the Old Testament must be interpreted by the New."*

Please be patient with me. As I mentioned earlier, I suffer from a very severe case, incurable and mildly contagious, of ONTRDD, commonly known as "Old and New Testament Recognition Deficiency Disorder". It's starting to act up now. I have learned to live with this disorder, but sometimes, in certain large meetings, I feel like I am suffocating.

I am totally unable to connect either term to anything in the Scriptures. Consequently, I am not placing "more importance on the Old Testament than on the New." I am not placing any importance on "the Old Testament" at all. I don't even believe that "the Old Testament" exists. How could I place any less importance on it than that?

It is true, however, that I feel the same way about "the New Testament". "Old Testament" and "New Testament" are not Biblical terms. They are theological terms. They are anti-Biblical terms.

As for the statement that "the Old Testament must be interpreted by the New," since neither one of them exists, this is a sure prescription for fantasy. Besides, what these theologians really mean is that, "the New Testament must be interpreted according to our theology, and the Old Testament must likewise be nullified."

To be blunt, they are claiming that the Word of God passes away, and that it passes away according to their dictates. They do not attempt to interpret the text of the New Covenant, whether in Jeremiah or in Hebrews. Nor do they interpret God's everlasting promises to Israel. They simply dismiss them, saying that these scriptures cannot be believed. In similar fashion, they ignore or dismiss the vast majority of Messianic prophecies, which speak of the restoration of Israel. This practice is many things, but it is not interpretation.

Concerning the Scriptures, the historical and Biblical reality is that God's people could only accept a later revelation if it agreed with the known, authentic, authorized earlier revelation of God, i.e. Tanakh. Tanakh was given 1500 to 500 years before the Messianic Writings. It prophesies and defines Messiah, the New Covenant, God's community, and the good news. The earlier document is the only basis for determining whether the later document should be accepted or rejected. The later document must agree with the known, authorized revelation of God in order to be accepted.

This particular "Eccentric" theological device indicates a belief that one part of the Bible is superior to another, and that the two parts are in conflict with each other. If there were a conflict between Tanakh and a later revelation, then it would be necessary to reject the later revelation, since Tanakh was already known to be God's Word.

The reason the theologians find the two parts of the Bible to be in conflict is that their theology rejects and displaces the Jewish people. Tanakh and the Messianic Writings form one consistent book. The conflict the theologians impose between the Messianic Writings and Tanakh is really just a conflict between their own theology and the Biblical text.

Additionally, this claim presents a rather low view of Yeshua. In a sense, it is a practical rejection of the incarnation. If the Word became flesh, then there is no difference between the first word and the last word. If Yeshua is the Word, then his authority in Tanakh is not less than his authority in the Messianic Writings. If he is the same yesterday, today, and forever, then the Messianic Writings do not contradict or annul Tanakh.

**ECCENTRIC NUMBER 4:** ...

**DEFERENT NUMBER 4:** ...

FOOTNOTES
1. Louis Berkhof, *Systematic Theology*, Wm. B. Eerdman's {Publishing Co., Grand Rapids, 1986
2. Nicholaus Copernicus, *On the Revolutions of the Heavenly Spheres*, trans. by C. G. Wallis, *Great Books of the Western World, Vol. 16*, Encyclopedia Britanniica, Chicago, 1952, p. 507

# RECOGNIZING ISRAEL'S CALLING AND IDENTITY

THE GOD OF ISRAEL IS THE ONE TRUE GOD.

THE SCRIPTURES, FROM GENESIS TO REVELATION, ARE JEWISH.

THE PEOPLE OF ISRAEL ARE THE PEOPLE OF GOD,
HIS CHILDREN, HIS WITNESSES.

THE LAND OF ISRAEL IS HIS LAND;
HER CAPITAL, JERUSALEM, IS HIS CITY.

ISRAEL'S KING IS GOD'S CHOSEN KING FOR ALL THE EARTH.

THE KING OF THE JEWS DIED TO ATONE
FOR THE SINS OF THE WORLD.

THE JEWISH PEOPLE ARE CALLED TO SERVE GOD
AND BE HIS PRIESTS FOR THE NATIONS.

THE NEW COVENANT IS MADE BETWEEN THE GOD OF ISRAEL
AND THE PEOPLE OF ISRAEL.

ISRAEL IS GOD'S KINGDOM, THE ONLY CONTEXT FOR REDEMPTION.

GENTILES WHO RECOGNIZE THE SOVEREIGNTY OF ISRAEL'S KING
ARE BROUGHT INTO ISRAEL'S COMMONWEALTH,
THROUGH ISRAEL'S NEW COVENANT.

THE LAW OF GOD'S KINGDOM HAS BEEN GIVEN TO ISRAEL.

THE GOOD NEWS IS THE MESSAGE OF THAT COMING KINGDOM.

GOD WILL DWELL ON THE EARTH IN JERUSALEM
IN THE MIDST OF THE JEWISH PEOPLE.

~

## "SALVATION IS FROM THE JEWS"

CHAPTER TWENTY-FIVE

# Bienvenidos Amigos

*Humble Positions Available, Equal Opportunity*

Copernicus was an astronomer. He did not discover anything, except what had always been true. He simply reinterpreted the data, free from the constraints of a universally accepted cosmology. Others had started from that accepted cosmology, and had consequently misinterpreted the same data. Copernicus did not bring his conclusions to the data; he reached his conclusions from the data. For many people, that is difficult to do.

The implications of what Copernicus taught were not all readily apparent. As they did become apparent, the experts in other fields initially rejected his astronomical teaching, because it did not fit with what they believed to be true in their own field. Each other science had its own knowledge, structure, tradition, and experts.

"For other sciences his suggestions simply raised new problems, and until these were solved the astronomer's concept of the universe was incompatible with that of other scientists. During the seventeenth century, the reconciliation of these other sciences with Copernican astronomy was an important cause of the general intellectual ferment now known as the scientific revolution."[1]

Some of what the experts in other fields believed and taught was not true. It had never been true, but everyone thought that it was. Fortunately, there were some people in those other fields who were willing to consider the possibility that the acknowledged truth was not true. Their willingness to think, to consider a view that fit the data but overthrew the established system, led to a revolution in learning and discovery.

You have almost finished reading this book. Maybe you suspected, before you started, that the Jews, the wandering *planetoi* of Christian theology, were the anomaly that could not be explained or contained within the accepted system. Maybe you already knew that God considered Jerusalem the center of His work in the earth. If so, I hope I have added to your understanding, and hope that you will begin to communicate to others the things you have learned.

Or maybe you are not convinced. In that case, let me try to encourage you from the Scriptures to come to a decision. There is a lot at stake.

Salvation is from the Jews. If you have shared in salvation, then you are indebted to the Jewish people. You should pay what you owe. Those who bless the Jewish people will be blessed; those who curse them will be cursed.

God entrusted His Kingdom to the Jewish people; and your highest priority should be to seek the establishment of His Kingdom upon the earth. Jerusalem should be more important to you than your greatest joy. The return of all Israel to the God of Israel will bring this world out of its present death into the life of the Messianic Age. That age will be characterized by justice, peace, joy, and the personal rule of Messiah over all the earth.

*'But how can the Jews be that important?'*

How can the planets be that important? The motion of the planets did not affect anyone's life in any way. [My apologies to the astrologers in our midst.] All it did was show that most people did not want to ask questions. Most people preferred the assurance of the experts—even if it was a false assurance—to the unsettling, disorienting search for truth.

We are coming to a very non-religious time of decision for all the earth. God is drawing the nations, one way or another, to Jerusalem, the center of His purposes in the earth. There are other centers of religion, of culture, of finance, of power, but God will not honor them. People will have to choose. In the next volume, we will examine the nations and those who rule them. In the meantime, here is a brief message from our Sponsor.

"I will gather all nations and bring them down to the Valley of Jehoshaphat. There I will enter into judgment against them concerning **My inheritance**, **My people Israel**, for they scattered **My people** among the nations and divided up **My land**. ... Multitudes, multitudes in the valley of decision! For the day of the LORD is near in the valley of decision. The sun and moon will be darkened, and the stars no longer shine. The LORD will roar from Zion and thunder from Jerusalem; the earth and the sky will tremble. But the LORD will be a refuge for **His people**, a stronghold for **the people of Israel**.

"Then you will know that I, the LORD your God, dwell in **Zion, My holy hill**. **Jerusalem** will be holy. Never again will foreigners invade her." (Joel 3:2,14-17)

Why is a geographically insignificant piece of land, inhabited by a numerically insignificant people, the center of such global conflict? Aren't there more important things for the world right now? Why is Israel the center of conflict between Heaven and a rebellious earth? Surely God has more important concerns, doesn't He?

Apparently not. God says the coming confrontation is about "My inheritance, My people, My land, and My holy hill—Israel, Zion, Jerusalem." He says He will judge all the nations for what they have done to this insignificant land and insignificant people. As He promised Israel, "I will bless those who bless you and curse those who curse you." It is much the same as Yeshua described the judgment of the Gentiles upon his return. "Inasmuch as you did it to the least of these my brothers, you did it to me."

Christianity and "the Church" have never been able to understand, explain, or appreciate the anomaly of the Jews. That is because Christianity and the Church are substitutes for Israel and the kingdom of God. They are substitutes for God's context of salvation, redemption, and the harvest of the earth. Much of Christianity has created a "Christ" who is not Jewish, and is not the Messiah.

God did not create Christianity. He did not create "the Church". Neither is even mentioned in the Bible. They will never be adequate for containing or explaining what God is doing in the earth. They will never be adequate for containing or explaining the one little anomaly that fills the pages of the Scriptures. God created Israel; and He created Israel with a view to re-establishing His kingdom upon the earth. This will not change, no matter what theological twists and turns men may take.

There is no Kingdom of God without Israel. That is why so much of Christianity has rejected the Kingdom of God. They do not want the God of Israel to rule on the earth. They do not want the God of Israel. Why do they despise "life from the dead" for the world?

As a little added incentive, you could consider Korah. "Korah (son of Izhar, the son of Kohath, the son of Levi) and Dathan and Abiram, sons of Eliab, and On son of Peleth (sons of Reuben) rose up against Moses with 250 men of the sons of Israel who were leaders of the community, respected men who had been called from the congregation. They gathered together against Moses and against Aaron, and said to them, 'You have gone too far! The whole community is holy, every one of them, and the LORD is in their midst. Why then do you set yourselves above the kahal of the LORD?'" (Num. 16:1-3)

God had made certain choices. He had chosen Abraham out of all the people on the face of the earth. He had chosen Isaac. He had chosen Jacob. He had created and chosen the people of Israel, in distinction from all the nations of the earth. (The Bible is the story of God's relationship with Israel and, through Israel, with all the earth.) Within Israel, God had chosen the tribe of Levi for special service; and within the tribe of Levi, God had chosen Aaron and his descendants for the priesthood.

These are God's choices, these are His callings. Dathan, Abiram, and On were chosen to be part of Israel, but they wanted more for themselves. Korah was chosen to serve the LORD as part of the tribe of Levi, but he thought he was more important than that. Together they thought they could overturn God's choice.

"Moses also said to Korah, 'Now listen, you sons of Levi! Is it a small thing for you that the God of Israel has separated you from the community of Israel to bring you near to Himself to do the work of the Tabernacle of the LORD and to stand before the community to serve them? He has brought you near and all your brothers, the sons of Levi, with you. But now you are trying to get the priesthood too. It is against the LORD that you and all your followers have banded together. Who is Aaron that you should grumble against him?'" (Num. 16:8-11)

All these men had been chosen by God, but it was not enough for them. In their eyes, the LORD had chosen others instead of them for greater honor. They saw God's choice of others as demeaning to themselves. They were wrong. They did not understand the meaning and purpose of God's choice.

Who was Aaron? Nobody special, just the one whom God had picked as His high priest. They wanted to dispossess and replace him. But their feelings and their actions—their rebellion—did not change the fact of God's unchanging choice.

Korah and his companions in rebellion are a metaphor. They were real people, but they represent all those who cannot accept the authority which God has established. Not content with being part of the people of God, they demand to be in charge.

They were not content with the grace of God in bringing them to Himself. Like Korah with Moses, they have felt slighted by God's choice of the Jews. They have thought they could overturn God's choice, and have sought to dispossess those whom He has chosen. In so doing, they have made choices which were neither wise nor godly. They have set up their own religious system, much like Jeroboam and his calves in Samaria. They have had a lot of popular support, but God has not been impressed.

Moses warned the assembly, "Move back from the tents of these wicked men! Do not touch anything belonging to them, or you will be swept away because of all their sins." (Num. 16:26)

God is going to judge the world for how it treats the people He created and chose as His own; and when God says, "My people," He means the Jewish people. No theology will provide an exemption from that judgment.

*'But if we abandon Christianity and the Church and go in the direction you suggest, what would we have?'*

Decide whether or not these things are true. If they are not true, then don't worry about it. If they are true, then you would not be abandoning anything in the Scriptures. You would not be abandoning any brothers or sisters in the faith. You would only be abandoning a system that obscures and replaces Biblical reality.

You would have the life of Messiah, and you would be part of the commonwealth of Israel. You would lose the Old Testament and the New Testament, but you would have the Jewish Scriptures, from Genesis to Revelation, instead.

You would have the one true God as your Father. You would have Messiah, His Son, and the ambassadors he sent into all the world. You would have the glory of God and the Holy Spirit, with the motivation and empowerment to serve God in righteousness. You would have Abraham, Isaac, Jacob, and the prophets. You would have the New Covenant, with the forgiveness and atonement it brings. You would have the Kingdom of God, and the responsibility to proclaim the good news of its coming.

Today, there is a faithful Jewish remnant that God has kept for Himself by His grace. Tomorrow, the final generation of Israel will welcome back Israel's rightful king. You would be fellow-citizens and fellow-heirs. You would be fellow-members of the body of Messiah, and fellow-partakers of the promises of God. Not you alone, but you along with the descendants of Abraham, Isaac, and Jacob.

*'But don't we have those things now, though the terminology may be different, in Christianity and the Church?'*

It is possible that you personally are partaking of those things now, but if you are, it is not through Christianity or the Church. God never gave any of these things to Christianity or the Church. So these things cannot be found there.

If you personally have these things, it is only because, by God's grace, you have been grafted into Israel's olive tree. All of these things are only provided by the God of Israel to the people of Israel. If you have been grafted into Israel's olive tree, then you have been made partakers, along with the faithful Jewish remnant, of everything God has given.

What would you be lacking? You would no longer have a religion, but you would have life instead. Does that make you feel nervous and insecure?

God offers a new cosmology. The time for the fragmentation of life into religious, political, and other compartments is over. In God's cosmology, all of life is unified. All of it is contained within His one overriding purpose for mankind and for the earth. God sees only one sphere, His Kingdom. Nothing, and no one, is exempt.

God offers a new physics with a different understanding of the laws that govern physical events. God Himself is the law, the Source of all that connects causes with their effects. One of those connections is that He will bless those who bless the Jewish people, and He will curse those who curse them. You will know people by their fruit, not by their labels.

God offers a new conception of space with a different understanding of how the geography of the earth is ordered. He has set Jerusalem in the center, with the nations around her. When the center is established, all the nations will find their place in God. When all Israel comes to the LORD, this world will be raised out of the death in which it now lies, into the life of an age characterized by justice, peace, and joy in the Holy Spirit. Every nation will enjoy that in the commonwealth ruled by the King of the Jews.

And God offers a new idea of man's relation to Himself, in accordance with what God's purpose for Man is. Loving God is no longer an abstraction, no longer just a feeling. It is a way of living.

Alyosha Karamazov understood it. "'Little heart of mine, my joy, believe me, every one is really responsible to all men for all men and for everything. I don't know how to explain it to you, but I feel it is so.' ...

"'But how can I possibly be responsible for all?' everyone would laugh in my face. 'Can I, for instance, be responsible for you?'"[2]

Cain knew the answer to that question, but he thought that he could bluff God by being belligerent. It did not work. It never works.

You may answer the question any way you like, but only one answer is correct. Man is called to desire, pray and work for, above all else, the establishment of the Kingdom of God and His justice upon the earth. When the good news of the kingdom has been proclaimed in all the earth, then the end of this violent, unclean age will come.

Neither the cosmology, the physics, the conception of space, nor the relationship are really new. If they seem new, it is only because they have been buried for so long by the accepted ancient tradition. It is only because the highway has been torn up, abandoned, and littered with trash and weighty obstacles. God's ways are actually much older than the religions and traditions of men, and much better, too.

The old religious cosmology seemed to work for a long time, but it was never right. All the experts agreed on it, and common sense affirmed it. So people just ignored the obvious errors, and assumed that new theological equations and devices could make everything all right. They were wrong, and the time for man-made cosmology is over.

*'But would we Gentiles then have to become Jews?'*

Not at all, quite the contrary. God promised to make Israel a commonwealth, a community of nations, *kahal goyim*. You would only have to become what God created you to be, the righteous in every nation. But you would have to humble yourself enough to agree with Yeshua that, "Salvation is from the Jews." God created Jews so that there could be Gentiles for Jesus.

That does not mean that Jews are better. The Bible never teaches that. The sins of Israel are recorded for all the world to see, for all the world to know how gracious and merciful God, the God of Israel, is. It just means that this is God's plan, through those who are despised and rejected of men, to bring redemption to all the earth.

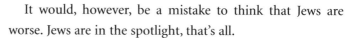
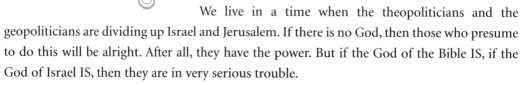

**GOD CREATED JEWS SO THAT THERE COULD BE GENTILES FOR JESUS.**

It would, however, be a mistake to think that Jews are worse. Jews are in the spotlight, that's all.

If you are a Gentile and you seek to become a Jew, or if you are a Jew and you seek to become a Gentile, then you are rejecting God's purpose for your life. There is nothing wrong with what God created you to be. His redemption enables you to find and live your life. There is a purpose for it.

We live in a time when the theopoliticians and the geopoliticians are dividing up Israel and Jerusalem. If there is no God, then those who presume to do this will be alright. After all, they have the power. But if the God of the Bible IS, if the God of Israel IS, then they are in very serious trouble.

Those who want power and wealth are free to pursue them. Those who want to control and exploit others are likewise free to choose the way that is right in their own eyes. Those who want to feed their lusts are free to seek their own desires. Those who think their own word is law and God's Word is irrelevant are free to try to conform the world to their own image.

Those who want to be part of a power elite, an institution, a religion, or a set of traditions are free to choose the one they like. Those who want the approval of men more than the approval of God are likewise free to pursue that goal. That is the beauty and the terror of the way that God has made us.

"Let the one who does wrong continue to do wrong. Let the one who is vile continue to be vile. Let the one who does right continue to do right. And let the one who is holy continue to be holy." (Rev. 22:11)

Do what you want to do, but choices have consequences. "Let us hear the end of the discussion of everything: Fear God and keep His commandments, because this is for every man. For God will bring every deed into judgment, with all that is hidden, whether it is good or evil." (Eccl. 12:13-14) In the midst of a generation that thinks God is dead and so are His laws, the LORD, the Everpresent God of Israel, will come to judge the earth.

The earth is the LORD's, but Israel is His land. Every mountain and hill is His, but Mt. Zion is His holy hill. Every city and its inhabitants belong to Him, but Jerusalem is holy in a way that no other city is. Jerusalem is His city, the capital of His coming kingdom.

The God of Israel has different plans for this earth than the theopoliticians and the geopoliticians do. "In the last days the mountain of the LORD's house will be established as chief among the mountains. It will be raised above the hills, and all the nations will stream to it. Many peoples will come and say, 'Come, let us go up to the mountain of the LORD, to the house of the God of Jacob. He will teach us His ways, so that we may walk in His paths.' The law will go out from Zion, the word of the LORD from Jerusalem." (Is. 2:2-3)

God has good plans for the earth. The nations, i.e. the Gentiles, will repent and come to bow down to the God of all the earth, the Holy One of Israel. They will return to the Creator of all, from whom they turned away before God had even brought Israel into existence. "However, the nation or kingdom that will not serve you will perish; it will be utterly ruined." (Is. 60:12)

Gentiles, like Jews, do not need a religious system or institution. They do not need a political solution. They need to come to God, surrender to Him, and receive His best. God did not give Israel a religion; He entrusted a kingdom to her and gave her life. Gentiles need to come into that kingdom. Every other kingdom is coming down.

How bizarre it is to think that one can embrace the King of the Jews while shunning his people. If a man comes to bow down to the King of the Jews, what will his attitude be towards the Jews? If a man seeks the God of Israel, what will his attitude be towards Israel?

Those who want this God, His Messiah, His people, His message, and His hope are also free to choose. Besides, why are you asking me these questions? Accept your freedom, and find out for yourself. That's your responsibility.

## THE CLEANSING OF THE OUTCAST

I was speaking at a large congregation in Ecuador. Since many people wanted to be "baptized," the pastor asked me to speak on "A Jewish view of baptism." Since "baptism" is the English transliteration of a Jewish Greek word for a Hebrew Biblical practice, I found the topic very appropriate.

I spoke on Leviticus 14, the law for the leper in the day of his cleansing. I focused on what had taken place to the leper in regard to the community of Israel. Before he was cleansed, he had to live alone, apart, outside the community. Everything he touched became unclean. He had to "wear torn clothes, let his hair be unkempt, cover the lower part of his face and cry out, 'Unclean! Unclean!'" (Lev. 13:45) Everyone would stay away, staring at him with either fear, pity, or contempt. He could not come near the Sanctuary of God.

When the one who was unclean was made clean, there were many symbolic acts which he and the priest who examined him performed. Among these, he was to be immersed, and then draw near to the LORD with sacrifices. Then he could join the community. He was set free from a living death, and given new life.

All of us sin. In many ways, those who sin without repentance and atonement are like lepers—separated from God, His life, and His community. When the Lord cleanses us, He brings us into the community of the living, the redeemed community of Israel. It is the same for everyone, whether Jewish or Gentile.

I admit that this was not a flattering comparison to make. But if you have read this far, you know that flattery is not one of my gifts.

At this congregation in Ecuador, each one who wanted to be immersed had been already cleansed by the King of the Jews. That should lead to humility and gratitude. Every one of them had been an unclean outcast, without hope and without God. "But now in Yeshua the Messiah, you who once were far away have been brought near through the blood of Messiah." (Eph. 2:13)

Gentiles who have become fellow-citizens in the commonwealth of Israel should glorify God for His mercy. (cf. Rom. 15:8-9, quoting 2Sam. 22:50/Ps.18:49) They should do so in fulfillment of what was prophesied. And the Jews who are redeemed should praise God for His grace in their lives and in the lives of the redeemed among the Gentiles. They should recognize this as the confirmation of God's promises to Abraham, Isaac, and Jacob.

Those of us who are Jews and have been cleansed ourselves are in no position to frown upon God's grace to those Gentiles who turn from their sins to the God of Israel. After all, the text says, "He has told you, Adam, what is good and what the LORD seeks from you—that you do justice, love mercy, and walk humbly with your God." (Mic. 6:8) He has told all Mankind, not just Jews. God hasn't changed, and His purpose for Man hasn't changed.

You don't need a religion to fulfill that purpose. You need life. You need to trust in the LORD with all your heart, and you need the power of His Spirit. As Shimon Kefa said about Cornelius and his household: "So if God gave them the same gift as He gave us, who believed in the Lord Yeshua the Messiah, who was I to think that I could oppose God?" (Acts 11:17)

We can freely say to such Gentiles, "Bienvenidos a la ciudadania de Israel." Welcome to the commonwealth of Israel.

Bienvenidos hermanos y hermanas.

Bienvenidos amigos.

FOOTNOTES

1.    Thomas S. Kuhn, *The Copernican Revolution: Planetary Astronomy in the Development of Western Thought*, Harvard U. Press, Cambridge, 1985, P.2

2.    Fyodor Dostoevsky, *The Brothers Karamazov*, ed. Manuel Komroff, Signet Books, NY, 1958, pp. 264, 276